The Ownership of
ENTERPRISE

Henry Hansmann

THE BELKNAP PRESS OF
HARVARD UNIVERSITY PRESS
Cambridge, Massachusetts
London, England

First Harvard University Press paperback edition, 2000

Library of Congress Cataloging-in-Publication Data

Hansmann, Henry.
    The ownership of enterprise / Henry Hansmann.
      p. cm.
    Includes bibliographical references and index.
    ISBN 0-674-64970-2 (cloth)
    ISBN 0-674-00171-0 (pbk.)
      1. Corporations—United States. 2. Business enterprises—United
States. 3. Nonprofit organizations—United States. 4. Private
companies—United States. 5. Employee ownership—United States.
6. Stock ownership—United States. 7. Mutualism—United States.
8. Corporation law—United States. I. Title.
HD2785.H32   1996
338.7´0973—dc20   96-25625

To Marina

Contents

Preface

When I was a graduate student at Yale studying both law and economics, I became interested in nonprofit organizations, which seemed to present interesting problems in both disciplines. As a consequence, my doctoral dissertation in economics, as well as my early professional articles in both law and economics, concentrated on nonprofits. That work led me in turn to reflect on mutual companies, which seemed in many ways similar to nonprofits, and to write about them as well. From mutuals it was natural to turn to consumer cooperatives, and then to producer cooperatives, and then to employee-owned firms, which are producer cooperatives of a special type. Finally, I ended up focusing on the role and structure of the most familiar form of producer cooperative, the investor-owned business corporation.

Thus, by a rather circuitous path, I came to the issues of standard corporate structure, governance, and finance that are the more customary focus of interdisciplinary work in law and economics. This indirect route turned out to be as instructive as it was interesting, however. One gains valuable perspective on questions of ownership by starting with those institutions in which ownership, in the customary sense, is most strongly and intentionally suppressed. This book, which builds on my earlier work, follows the reverse order in its presentation, beginning with business corporations and ending up with nonprofits and mutuals. Nevertheless, the influence of my original unconventional order of approach is evident from the start.

In studying any given organizational form, I have generally followed the simple practice of first examining the range of situations in which that form is found and then looking for theories that can explain the observed pattern. Although this might seem the obvious thing to do, a good deal of contemporary work in organizational theory has not proceeded that way. Rather, following a tradition now well established in economics, it has first developed a theory and then sought to impose the theory on the facts. (I confess to having done this myself sometimes in other areas—it can be fun, and occasionally fruitful.) Employee ownership is a strong case in point. There has evolved in recent decades a large literature that seeks to explain the economic virtues and vices of employee ownership without first bothering to ask where employee-owned firms are actually found and what their characteristics are. Once one looks at the answers to those simple questions, one is led quickly to conclusions that are at odds with much of the existing literature—as I seek to show in two of the chapters that follow.

My regard for analysis well grounded in observation is strongly reflected in this book. Although Part I is largely dedicated to presenting the analytic framework that underlies the book as a whole, subsequent chapters offer a substantial amount of factual detail about the industries and firms whose organization those chapters seek to explain. These facts are often interesting in themselves, quite beyond the support they provide for the theories and arguments I offer. I hope that readers will come away from this book with a sense that contemporary society contains a much more varied and complex set of institutions than we commonly realize, and that even many organizations whose names have long been familiar have structures that are rather surprising.

I owe thanks to many individuals and institutions for valuable assistance at various stages in the book's evolution. A John Simon Guggenheim Memorial Foundation fellowship provided the initial opportunity to work out the book's central ideas. The first chapters were drafted at the Rockefeller Foundation's gorgeous retreat in Bellagio. The Yale Law School and its superb deans, Guido Calabresi and Anthony Kronman, have continually provided generous support, as did the Harvard Law School and Dean Robert Clark during a year's visit there.

A number of people have helpfully offered comments on the book manuscript at various stages, including Bruce Ackerman, Douglas Allen, Fabrizio Barca, Paul Donahue, Richard Geddes, Jeffrey Gordon, John Hetherington, Reinier Kraakman, Dean Lueck, Michael Montias, Mark Ramseyer, Mark Roe, Roberta Romano, Susan Rose-Ackerman, Charles Sabel, Burton Weisbrod, and Oliver Williamson. I am indebted to them all. And I am likewise indebted to many other colleagues and students—far too many to mention by name—who helped me work through the issues explored in this book long before the final manuscript began to take shape.

Finally, I am immensely grateful to my wife Marina for her patience, faith, and encouragement in this and in all my projects.

Introduction

We tend to take it for granted that, in the absence of government intervention, large-scale enterprise will be organized in the form of investor-owned firms. Thus the term "capitalism," with its implication that the means of production are owned by investors of capital, remains the name commonly given to the system of economic organization found in Western Europe, North America, and Japan. Yet investor ownership is not a logically necessary concomitant of free markets and free enterprise. Rather, it is quite contingent, a form of organization that is often but not always dominant given current technologies.

Even in the United States, the world's great exemplar of corporate capitalism, non-investor-owned enterprise plays a prominent role in many important industries. Employee-owned firms have long been widespread in the service professions—such as law, accounting, investment banking, and medicine—and are now expanding in other industries as well. The recent employee buyout of United Air Lines is a conspicuous instance. Farmer-owned producer cooperatives dominate the markets for basic agricultural commodities. Consumer-owned utilities supply electric power to 10 percent of the population. Key firms such as MasterCard, Associated Press, and True Value Hardware are service and supply cooperatives owned by local businesses. Occupant-owned condominiums and cooperatives are rapidly displacing investor-owned rental housing. Mutual companies owned by their policyholders sell half of all life insurance and a quarter of all property and liability insurance. And nonprofit firms, which have no owners at all, account

1

for most nongovernmental hospitals, colleges, schools, and daycare centers, as well as a large share of the nation's nursing homes, health maintenance organizations, and health insurance companies.

The United States is not unusual in this regard. Non-investor-owned enterprise plays a similarly large role in other developed market economies. That role is continuing to expand, and is conspicuously larger in advanced economies than it is in less-developed economies.

In this book I explore the reasons for this diverse pattern of ownership. I seek to explain why different industries, and different national economies, exhibit different distributions of ownership forms. Toward this end, I try to offer a broader perspective on the character and functions of ownership in general, providing insight not only into forms of ownership that are frequently neglected but into investor ownership as well. I also seek to illuminate the roles that alternative forms of ownership can and should play in the future.

I draw my analytic tools principally from economics and particularly from recent work on the organization of the firm. More specifically, this book is largely in the tradition of the "new institutional economics," which is distinguished by its focus on transaction costs and information costs. Yet while I rely heavily on economic analysis, I also bring other perspectives to bear where appropriate, paying particular attention to the characteristics of different structures for decision making, to historical processes, and to the legal and regulatory systems within which firms are organized. I have tried to make the book accessible to noneconomists, and have confined technicalities and discussion of the literature to the notes wherever possible.

The primary focus of the book is on those firms—such as broadly held business corporations, partnerships, cooperatives, and mutual companies—in which ownership is shared among numerous persons. One reason for this emphasis is the dominance of these firms in contemporary economies. Another reason is that widely shared ownership gives rise to special problems that call for focused attention. To create a viable firm in which ownership is shared among persons who have diverse interests is difficult, and the problems involved—what might be termed the internal politics of the firm or, more abstractly, the costs of collective decision making—have a critical bearing on the patterns of ownership that we observe and the ways in which firms are structured internally. This fundamental issue has received far too little attention.

What Can Be Learned?

At the narrowest level, this book addresses a variety of questions about particular forms of ownership. Why, for example, is investor owner-ship the dominant, yet far from universal, form of ownership in all modern market economies? Why have employee-owned firms tradi-tionally been so common among service professionals and so rare in other services and in industry? Why has the latter pattern begun to change so rapidly in recent years, as investor-owned firms have dis-placed partnerships among service professionals while, at the same time, employee ownership has been spreading in the industrial sector? Why are consumer cooperatives so common—far more so than is generally realized—among wholesale and supply firms but so rare among retail firms? Why is it that, while farmer-owned and worker-owned firms are common, other forms of producer cooperatives are rare? Why has condominium housing, which was effectively nonexist-ent in the United States before 1960, spread so explosively through the nation's real estate markets in recent decades? Why did mutual com-panies play a more dominant role in insurance and banking in the nineteenth century than in the twentieth, and do they continue to serve an important function today? And why—to turn to a much smaller but nonetheless intriguing sector—are there not more investor-owned golf courses?

But one need not have a strong interest in alternative forms of ownership to find the comparative study of organizational types in-structive. The exercise has important lessons even for those whose interests are largely confined to investor-owned enterprise. Analysis of the role and performance of partnerships, cooperatives, mutuals, and nonprofits provides a useful means of measuring the managerial effi-ciency of conventional business corporations and deepens our under-standing of the ways in which, and the extent to which, product markets and capital markets—including the market for corporate control—serve to police that efficiency. To look at investor-owned firms in isolation, as the existing literature has largely done, is often misleading. We learn much more about them by comparing them with other forms of enterprise. Otherwise, as a statistician might put it, there are too few degrees of freedom, and too little variance, to assess the influence of key variables.

The study of alternative forms of ownership also offers insight into broader issues concerning social organization in general. For example, it provides perspective on the extent to which the vagaries of history determine the character of the organizational forms that appear in contemporary societies. More specifically, it permits us to appreciate the processes and the speed with which anachronistic organizational forms are replaced by more efficient ones. It also allows us to explore the ways in which legal structure—including organizational law, tax law, and regulatory law—governs organizational evolution. And it even helps us to see whether and to what degree organizational change drives, or is driven by, legal change.

Finally, since a firm that has numerous owners must employ some form of collective choice mechanism through which those owners can exercise control, all such firms necessarily have a strongly governmental, or political, character. Examining the forms and performance of these collective choice mechanisms allows us to acquire important knowledge about political institutions in general. In fact, because collectively owned firms are so numerous and so varied, and because they are subject to the forces of market selection, for many purposes they provide a better means of studying political institutions than do the governmental entities that are the usual focus of work in political science. By studying the structure of ownership in private firms we gain a strikingly strong perspective on the relative virtues of politics and markets in governing social activity—a question that has been at the center of Western political and economic debate for much of the past two centuries.

The perspective on these issues that this book offers might be useful even if it involved no more than a reaffirmation and extension of prevailing ideas. In fact, however, the evidence assembled here indicates that, in fundamental ways, the conventional wisdom about the forces guiding choice of organizational form is often misleading or mistaken. For example, the capital intensity of an industry and the degree of risk inherent in the industry both play a much smaller role than is commonly believed in determining whether firms in that industry are investor-owned. Similarly, the agency costs of delegated management—the "separation of ownership and control"—that are so much a focus of current literature on the economics of organization are at best of secondary importance in determining which organizational forms are viable; indeed, tight managerial discipline is a two-edged sword that can severely increase a firm's costs of contracting with nonowners. Employee ownership offers much stronger efficiencies than it is generally credited with, and would be far more widespread if it were not critically handicapped by the very thing that is often considered its greatest virtue, namely, the opportunity it affords for active worker participation in governance. Nonprofit firms commonly compete quite effectively with for-profit firms even in the absence of public or private subsidies. And governmental consumer protection regulation has often played a critical role in permitting investor-owned enterprise to vie with, and ultimately displace, cooperative, mutual, and nonprofit firms.

Social Science and Social Policy

This book is largely an exercise in positive, or descriptive, social science. As such, its principal purpose is to explore, as objectively as possible, the reasons for the patterns of enterprise ownership that we observe. Yet it has an important policy dimension as well.

There is considerable enthusiasm today for promoting forms of ownership other than the conventional investor-owned corporation. Much of this interest centers on labor-managed enterprise and reflects an unusual convergence of economic thought from opposite ends of the political spectrum. On the left, recent years have brought the final collapse of state socialism as a persuasive economic ideal throughout the world. In the resulting ideological void, "workplace democracy" has emerged as the principal institutional reform that commands widespread support among critics of capitalism. Worker control of enterprise, it is hoped, will succeed where state control has failed in equalizing power and wealth and in decreasing worker alienation and exploitation. Reformers on the right, in turn, have become increasingly discouraged with the efficiency of traditional forms of labor-management relations. As an alternative, many have turned to employee ownership, hoping that it will improve productivity and increase worker identification with the interests of capital.

This enthusiasm for worker-owned enterprise has begun to be translated into policy. Employee ownership is now promoted in the United States by large tax subsidies, by exceptional provisions in the pension laws, and by special corporation statutes for employee-owned firms. In Western Europe, worker codetermination is now mandated for all large enterprise in Germany and has been proposed for the European

Community as a whole. And in the formerly socialist countries of Eastern Europe there is widespread interest in worker ownership for newly privatized state enterprise. Yet the wisdom of all such policies remains subject to intense debate.

Issues of ownership are also central to important problems of policy in a variety of other areas. For example, does the rapid conversion of rental to condominium housing represent an improvement in welfare, or is it a costly inefficiency induced by rent control and tax subsidies? Is the domination of the agricultural markets by farm marketing cooperatives an efficient response to market imperfections and scale economies, or is it simply cartelization at the expense of consumers? Do nonprofit hospitals, health insurance companies, and health maintenance organizations serve a valuable function that the rapidly expanding investor-owned firms in those industries do not, or are they just inefficient anachronisms? Does the recent rapid growth in mutual liability insurance companies offer a promising remedy for the insurance crisis? Might the costly collapse of the savings and loan industry have been averted if stock firms had not been so freely permitted to displace mutual firms in that sector? Is consumer ownership of utilities a promising way to avoid the inefficiencies of both private monopoly and public rate regulation? Does collective ownership of a franchisor by its franchisees avert the problems of opportunism to which franchise contracting is otherwise prone?

More generally, the basic legal framework that governs different forms of enterprise ownership has developed ad hoc, without systematic thought as to the functions played by the various forms or to their interrelationships. The corporation statutes governing cooperative, nonprofit, and mutual companies are generally poorly structured and vary widely from one jurisdiction to another. Tax law, which has been designed principally with the conventional investor-owned firm in mind, creates systematic biases for and against other ownership forms. And alternative forms of ownership operate under special regulatory and antitrust regimes that have never been well rationalized.

In the past, it has been difficult to deal clearly with any of these issues because we have lacked a coherent understanding of the roles that are, can be, or ought to be played by the various forms of ownership involved. I hope to provide the basis for a more informed approach.

Ideology

Much of the existing literature on ownership, and particularly on worker-owned and consumer-owned enterprise, reflects some degree of ideological commitment. Authors frequently come to the subject with a passion either to advocate or to discredit a particular form of ownership. I try here, in contrast, to be relatively disinterested. Although nobody is unblinkered by ideology, I do not consciously bring to this project strong commitments either for or against any particular form of ownership in itself, whether investor-owned, worker-owned, consumer-owned, producer-owned, nonprofit, or governmental. Indeed, I believe the evidence indicates that a broad range of ownership types have useful roles to play in modern economies and that those roles vary with time and circumstance. The principal objective of this book is to analyze those roles.

Comparative Perspectives

The primary focus here is on institutions in the United States. I do, however, pay considerable attention to patterns of institutional development in other countries both to affirm and, where necessary, to qualify the generality of the conclusions offered. In fact, as subsequent chapters illustrate, the distribution of ownership types in the United States is strikingly similar to that found in other market economies, and where differences appear they are generally explicable in terms of the same considerations that explain the U.S. pattern. Consequently the book should have nearly as much value in understanding other economies as it does in understanding the United States.

Nonprofit and Governmental Enterprise

The principal focus of this book is on firms that are privately owned in one fashion or another. But the book's analytic framework is also helpful in understanding when it is efficient for a firm to have no owners at all—that is, to be organized as a nonprofit institution. Moreover, since nonprofit firms are the asymptotic extreme in the separation of ownership and control, their study throws important light on the characteristics of owned enterprise. Part IV devotes specific attention to nonprofit enterprise.

The role of public enterprise is an important issue that deserves much more thoughtful attention than it has received. That role is, I believe, usefully illuminated by the book's analytic framework. Nevertheless, I do not offer an extended discussion of public enterprise. Rather, I deal with it only where necessary to explore important questions about the role and structure of private enterprise, as in the case of the utilities examined in Chapter 9 and the exclusive residential communities discussed in Chapter 10.

Organization of the Book

The three chapters in Part I offer a general theory of enterprise ownership. Subsequent chapters then employ that theoretical framework to explore the role played by particular forms of ownership in particular industries. The chapters dealing with specific industries or organizational forms in Parts II–IV are mutually supporting and cumulative. One can learn much more about the strengths and weaknesses of different organizational forms by comparing them with one another, or by observing how the same form fares in different industries, than one can learn simply by observing a single form within a single industry. Thus one gains an important perspective on problems of governance and capital supply in worker-owned firms (Chapters 5 and 6) by studying farm supply cooperatives (Chapter 8) and housing cooperatives and condominiums (Chapter 11). The significance of the separation of ownership and control in investor-owned firms (Chapter 4) is similarly illuminated by comparing those firms with wholesale and supply cooperatives (Chapter 8) on the one hand and with nonprofit and mutual firms (Chapters 12–14) on the other.

For all the interest in organization theory today, the comparative study of organizations remains much neglected. I hope to prove that it has impressive things to teach us.

PART I

A Theory of Enterprise Ownership

1

An Analytic Framework

A firm's "owners," as the term is conventionally used and as it will be used here, are those persons who share two formal rights: the right to control the firm and the right to appropriate the firm's profits, or residual earnings (that is, the net earnings that remain with the firm after it has made all payments to which it is contractually committed, such as wages, interest payments, and prices for supplies). The reference to "formal" rights in this definition is important. Formal control, for instance, does not necessarily mean effective control. In firms that are incorporated—which comprise most of the institutions of interest to us here, including business corporations, cooperatives, nonprofits, and mutual companies—formal control generally involves only the right to elect the firm's board of directors and to vote directly on a small set of fundamental issues, such as merger or dissolution of the firm. Moreover, in large business corporations the shareholders, who hold formal control, are often too numerous and too dispersed to exercise even these limited voting rights very meaningfully, with the result that corporate managers have substantial autonomy. Hence it has long been common to speak of "the separation of ownership from control," reflecting the substantial autonomy of corporate managers.[1]

Nevertheless, I shall principally be concerned with exploring assignment of the *formal* legal or contractual rights to control and residual earnings. As we shall see in the chapters that follow, there are often strong reasons for giving the formal right of control to a particular class of persons even when those persons are not in a position to

11

exercise that right very effectively. For this reason, among others, the assignment of these formal rights—which is to say, the assignment of ownership—tends to follow strong and clear patterns.

In theory, the rights to control and to residual earnings could be separated and held by different classes of persons. In practice, however, they are generally held jointly. The obvious reason for this is that, if those with control had no claim on the firm's residual earnings, they would have little incentive to use their control to maximize those earnings, or perhaps even to pay out the earnings received. To be sure, this problem would not arise if all important decisions to be made by those with control could be appropriately constrained in advance by contractual arrangements between them and the holders of the rights to residual earnings. But the essence of what we term "control" is precisely the authority to determine those aspects of firm policy that, because of high transactions costs or imperfect foresight, cannot be specified ex ante in a contract but rather must be left to the discretion of those to whom the authority is granted.[2]

Not all firms have owners. In nonprofit firms, in particular, the persons who have control are barred from receiving residual earnings. As we shall see, however, the same factors that determine the most efficient assignment of ownership also determine when it is appropriate for a firm to have no owners at all.

The Structure of Ownership

In the discussion that follows, it will be helpful to have a term to comprise all persons who transact with a firm either as purchasers of the firm's products or as sellers to the firm of supplies, labor, or other factors of production. I shall refer to such persons—whether they are individuals or other firms—as the firm's "patrons."

Nearly all large firms that have owners are owned by persons who are also patrons. This is obvious in the case of consumer and producer cooperatives, which by definition are firms that are owned, respectively, by their customers and by their suppliers. It is also true of the standard business corporation, which is owned by persons who lend capital to the firm. In fact, the conventional investor-owned firm is nothing more than a special type of producer cooperative—a lenders' cooperative, or capital cooperative. Because we so commonly associate ownership with investment of capital, and because the comparison of investor-owned firms with cooperatives of other types will be at the core of the analysis that follows, it is worthwhile to elaborate briefly on this point.

Consider, first, the basic structure of a typical producer cooperative. For concreteness, we can take as a simple, stylized example a dairy farmers' cheese cooperative, in which a cheese factory is owned by the farmers who supply the factory with raw milk. (The example is not fanciful; farmer-owned cooperatives account for 45 percent of all natural cheese produced in the United States.)[3] The firm pays its owners—or "members," as they are usually termed in a cooperative—a predetermined price for their milk. This price is set low enough so that the cooperative is almost certain to have positive net earnings from the manufacture and sale of its cheese. Then, at the end of the year, the firm's net earnings are divided pro rata among the members according to the amount of milk they have sold to the cooperative during the year, and distributed as patronage dividends. All voting rights in the firm are also apportioned among its farmer-members, either according to the amount of milk each member sells to the firm or, more simply, on a one-member-one-vote basis. Some or all of the members may have capital invested in the firm. In principle, however, this is unnecessary; the firm might borrow all of the capital it needs. In any case, even where members invest in the firm, those investments generally take the form of debt or preferred stock that carries no voting rights and is limited to a stated maximum rate of dividends. Upon liquidation of the firm, any net asset value—which may derive from retained earnings or from increases in the value of assets held by the firm—is divided pro rata among the members, according to some measure of the relative value of their cumulative patronage.

In short, ownership rights are held by virtue of, and proportional to, one's sale of milk to the firm. Not all farmers who sell milk to the firm need be owners, however; the firm may purchase some portion of its milk from nonmembers, who are simply paid a fixed price (which may be different from the price paid members) and do not participate in net earnings or control.

The structure of a consumer cooperative is similar, except that net earnings and votes are apportioned according to the amounts that members purchase from the firm rather than the amounts they sell to it.

Now imagine a hypothetical "capital cooperative" with a form precisely analogous to that of the dairy cooperative. The members of the capital cooperative each lend the firm a given sum of money, which the firm uses to purchase the equipment and other assets it needs to operate (say, to manufacture widgets—or cheese). The firm pays the members a fixed interest rate on their loans, set low enough so that there is a reasonable likelihood that the firm will have net earnings after paying this interest and all other expenses. The firm's net earnings are then distributed pro rata among its members according to the amount they have lent, with the distributions taking place currently, as dividends, or upon liquidation. Similarly, voting rights are apportioned among members in proportion to the amount they have lent the firm. To supplement the capital that it obtains from its members, the firm may borrow money from lenders who are not members, but who simply receive a fixed rate of interest (which may be different from the fixed rate paid to members) without sharing in profits or control.

This hypothetical capital cooperative is, transparently, a producers' cooperative just as is the dairy cooperative. Yet this capital cooperative in fact has precisely the structure that underlies the typical business corporation. If this is not immediately obvious, it is perhaps just because, in a business corporation, the fixed interest rate paid on loans from the firm's lender-members—whom we conventionally term "shareholders" or "stockholders"—is typically set at zero for the sake of convenience, thus obscuring the fact that the members' contributions of capital are, in effect, loans.

To be sure, there are also various other ways in which capital cooperatives (that is, business corporations) are often structured a bit differently from other types of cooperatives. For example, in a business corporation the loans from members are usually not arranged annually or for other fixed periods, but rather are perpetual; members can withdraw their capital only upon dissolution of the firm, although an individual member may be free to sell his or her interest in the firm to another person before then. In other types of cooperatives, in contrast, members often remain free to vary the volume of their transactions with the firm over time, and even to terminate their patronage altogether. This distinction is not, however, fundamental. Investor-owned business corporations sometimes permit members to redeem their invested capital at specified intervals or even (as in the standard partnership) at will; open-ended mutual funds are a familiar example. Conversely, cooperatives often require that members make a long-term commitment to remain patrons. For example, electricity generation and transmission cooperatives commonly insist that their members, which are local electricity distribution cooperatives, enter into thirty-five-year requirements contracts.[4] Agricultural marketing and processing cooperatives, such as the cheese cooperative just described, often require that their members commit themselves to sell to the cooperative a given amount of their production each year for a period of several years.[5] And mutual life insurance companies, which are essentially consumer cooperatives owned by their policyholders, originally issued only nonredeemable policies that committed policyholders to make premium payments—that is, to continue to purchase a specified amount of insurance from the firm—for the rest of their lives.[6]

The allocation of voting rights is another area where business corporations often differ somewhat from other types of cooperatives. In business corporations, the general rule is one-share-one-vote; that is, votes are apportioned according to the amount of capital contributed to the firm. In many cooperatives, in contrast, the rule is one-member-one-vote, with no adjustment for the volume of patronage of the individual members. Again, however, the difference is neither universal nor fundamental. The charters of many eighteenth- and nineteenth-century American business corporations limited the number of votes an individual shareholder could exercise regardless of the number of shares he owned; only in the twentieth century did the practice of one-share-one-vote become nearly universal.[7] And, while the statutes governing cooperatives sometimes still impose a rule of one-member-one-vote, this is not universal and many cooperatives allocate votes proportionally to their members' volume of patronage. (We shall consider later why these different voting rules arose and survived.)

In sum, a business corporation is just a particular type of cooperative: a cooperative is a firm in which ownership is assigned to a group of the firm's patrons, and the persons who lend capital to a firm are just one among various classes of patrons with whom the firm deals.

Conversely, supplying capital to the firm is simply one of many transactional relationships to which ownership can be tied, and there is nothing very special about it. Ownership of a firm need not, and frequently does not, attach to investment of capital. Indeed, contrary to some popular perceptions and even to some more sophisticated organizational theory, ownership of the firm need have nothing to do with ownership of capital, whether physical or financial.[8]

To be sure, it might be argued that ownership is necessarily connected to capital in the sense that the owners of a firm, whether they are suppliers or customers or workers or whatever, are the persons who effectively own the firm's capital, such as its plant and equipment. For example, in our cheese cooperative, one might argue that the farmer-members own the firm's capital in the sense that they collectively have title to, and will profit or lose from fluctuations in the value of, the cheese factory's plant and equipment.

But this is not necessarily true. The firm could rent rather than own the land, buildings, and equipment it uses. It could in fact have title to no physical assets whatever yet still be a large and prosperous firm.[9] It could even have no net financial assets, distributing all profits to members as they are earned and maintaining a line of credit at a bank sufficient to ensure that it can pay bills in periods when expenses temporarily exceed receipts.[10] The members of the cooperative might *choose* to invest some of their personal funds in the firm, or to have the firm retain some of its profits for internal investment. Indeed, as subsequent chapters will discuss at greater length, there are good reasons why the owners of most types of firms, including producer and consumer cooperatives, choose to invest some financial capital in the firm they own. But it is not *necessary* that owners of a firm also be investors in the firm.

Even though the ordinary business corporation is, as I have just argued, essentially a lenders' cooperative, I shall continue to follow the usual convention here and generally use the term "cooperative" to refer only to patron-owned firms *other than* investor-owned firms.

The Structure of Organizational Law

From these observations we can gain a helpful perspective on the general structure of corporation law.

In the United States, basic corporation law is state law rather than federal law. The typical state has three general corporation statutes: a business corporation statute, a cooperative corporation statute, and a nonprofit corporation statute. Most of the organizations we shall be concerned with in this book are formed under one or another of these three types of statutes. (There are, however, a number of exceptions. For example, mutual banks, mutual insurance companies, and housing condominiums are often formed under special corporation statutes specifically designed for them. And the employee-owned firms that are common in the service professions are often formed as partnerships or professional corporations, which are also governed by separate statutes.)

A cooperative corporation statute typically accommodates all types of producer and consumer cooperatives, from retail grocery cooperatives on the one hand to farm processing and marketing cooperatives, such as our cheese factory, on the other. Once it is understood that investor-owned firms are in essence capital cooperatives, it follows that in principle investor-owned corporations could also be formed under cooperative corporation statutes rather than, as is customary, under the separate business corporation statutes.[11] There is no fundamental reason to have business corporation statutes at all; they are just specialized versions of the theoretically more general cooperative corporation statutes. It is appropriate to have separate business corporation statutes simply because it is convenient to have a form that is customized for the most common type of cooperative—the lenders' cooperative—and to signal to patrons more clearly the type of cooperative with which they are dealing.[12] For similar reasons, some agricultural states have separate corporation statutes for another particularly common type of producer cooperative, the agricultural marketing cooperative; some states have special statutes for worker cooperatives; and some states have separate statutes for consumer, as opposed to producer, cooperatives.

The partnership statutes, in contrast, are not as specialized as the corporation statutes. Each state has only one general partnership statute, and under that statute partnership shares can be given in return for any type of patronage—whether it involves the provision of inputs such as labor or capital or the purchase of the firm's products—or to persons who are not patrons at all.

Although cooperatives are sometimes loosely said to be "nonprofit," nonprofit corporations are conceptually quite distinct from cooperatives. The defining characteristic of a nonprofit organization is that the persons who control the organization—including its members, directors, and officers—are forbidden from receiving the organization's net earnings. This does not mean that a nonprofit organization is barred from earning profits; rather, it is the *distribution* of the profits to controlling persons that is forbidden. Thus by definition, a nonprofit organization cannot have owners. A well-drafted nonprofit corporation statute imposes this "nondistribution constraint" on any organization formed under the statute, and hence prohibits the formation, as a nonprofit corporation, of any form of cooperative and of any other form of owned enterprise.

What Must a Theory of Ownership Explain?

In principle, a firm could be owned by someone who is not a patron. Such a firm's capital needs would be met entirely by borrowing. Its other factors of production would likewise be purchased on the market, and its products would be sold on the market. The owner would then be a pure entrepreneur, of roughly the character described in Frank Knight's classic work,[13] simply controlling the firm and receiving its (positive or negative) residual earnings after all output was sold and inputs were paid for. Such firms are rare, however. Rather, ownership is commonly in the hands of one or another group of the firm's patrons—that is, in the hands of persons who have some other transactional relationship with the firm, either as suppliers or as customers.[14]

It follows that a general theory of enterprise ownership must explain at least two things: First, why is ownership generally given to the firm's patrons? Second, what factors determine the particular group of patrons—whether lenders of capital, suppliers of labor or other inputs, or purchasers of the firm's products or services—to whom ownership is given in any particular firm?

The remainder of this chapter sketches such a theory, and the two following chapters flesh out its details. Parts II–IV then offer illustration and further refinement of the theory through detailed application to particular industries and particular organizational types.

The Firm as a Nexus of Contracts

In developing a theory of ownership, it helps to view the firm—as economists increasingly do these days—as a nexus of contracts.[15] More precisely, a firm is in essence the common signatory of a group of contracts. Some of these contracts are with vendors of supplies or services that the firm uses as inputs, some are employment contracts with individuals who provide labor services to the firm, some are loan agreements with bondholders, banks, and other suppliers of capital, and some are contracts of sale entered into with purchasers of the firm's products. In small firms organized as sole proprietorships, the individual proprietor signs these contracts. In a corporation or a partnership, the party that signs the contracts is a legal entity. Indeed, one of the most important functions of organizational law is to permit the creation of a juridical person—a single legal entity—that can serve as the signatory to contracts.

A firm's contracts generally commit it to certain actions, such as making payments to vendors or delivering goods or services to customers. But contracts typically also leave the firm with some discretion. An employment contract, for example, generally gives the firm some freedom to choose the particular tasks to which the employee will be assigned; a loan contract commonly gives the firm some choice concerning the uses of the borrowed funds; and a contract of sale often affords the firm some latitude in the methods to be used to produce the goods or services promised to a given customer. The right to exercise this discretion is a vital component of control over the firm, and is by definition the prerogative of the firm's owners. The firm may itself also own assets outright, of course, in which case the exercise of discretion over the use of those assets is included among the control rights belonging to the owners of the firm. Again, however, outright ownership of assets is not an essential aspect of what we call a firm.[16]

Broadly speaking, each transaction that a firm enters into is embedded in one or the other of two relationships between the firm and the patron who is the other party to the transaction. In the first of these relationships, which I shall call "market contracting," the patron deals with the firm only through contract and is not an owner. In the second, which I shall simply call "ownership," the patron is also an owner of the firm.

By terming the first of these two relationships "market contracting" I do not mean to imply that there is necessarily a competitive market for the goods or services in question. The relationship between the firm and its patron may, for example, be one of bilateral monopoly, with only one potential trading partner on each side of the transaction. Rather, I use the expression "market contracting" here simply to emphasize that the patron in question can control the firm's behavior only by seeking enforcement of his contract with the firm, or by threatening to cease transacting with the firm in favor of whatever other alternatives the market offers him. Where the relationship is one of ownership, in contrast, the patron has the additional option of seeking to control the firm's behavior directly through the firm's mechanisms for internal governance. Moreover, by using the term "market contracting" I do not mean to suggest that the relationships in question are necessarily short-term, as on a spot market; rather, I shall use the term to encompass also long-term, highly interdependent contracting of the type sometimes referred to as "relational" contracting.[17]

Using this terminology, we would then say that, in an investor-owned firm, the transactions between the firm and the patrons who supply the firm with capital occur in the context of ownership, while transactions with workers, other suppliers, and customers all take the form of market contracting. An employee-owned firm, in contrast, obtains labor inputs from workers whose relationship is one of ownership, but obtains its capital and other supplies, and sells its products, through market contracting. And a consumer cooperative, in turn, obtains capital, labor, and all other inputs through market contracting while selling the goods or services it produces in transactions embedded in ownership.

To be sure, patrons occasionally have some but not all of the prerogatives of ownership, putting their relationship with the firm somewhere ambiguously between ownership and market contracting. The relationship between a firm and its employees under German codetermination, which will be examined in Chapters 5 and 6, is a conspicuous example. In general, however, the simple dichotomy between market contracting and ownership that I have described here will be adequate for our purposes.

An Overview of the Theory

If a firm were entirely owned by persons who were not among the firm's patrons, then all the firm's transactions involving inputs and outputs would take the form of market contracting. Although feasible in principle, in practice this is likely to be quite inefficient. Market contracting can be costly, especially in the presence of one or more of those conditions loosely termed "market failure"—for example, where there is an absence of effective competition, or where one of the parties is at a substantial informational disadvantage. We shall examine the costs of market contracting more closely in Chapter 2. For the present we need simply note that, where these costs are high, they can often be reduced by having the purchaser own the seller or vice versa. When both the purchaser and the seller are under common ownership, the incentive for one party to exploit the other by taking advantage of market imperfections is reduced or eliminated. Assigning ownership of a firm to one or another class of the firm's patrons can thus often reduce the costs of transacting with those patrons—costs that would otherwise be borne by the firm or its patrons. To assign ownership to someone who is not among the firm's patrons would waste the opportunity to use ownership to reduce these costs.

Pursuing this logic we can then ask, for any given firm: what is the lowest-cost assignment of ownership? By "lowest-cost assignment of ownership" I mean the assignment of ownership that minimizes the total costs of transactions between the firm and all of its patrons. (Alternatively, I mean the assignment of ownership that maximizes the total net benefits—benefits minus costs—of transactions between the firm and its patrons. Since a forgone benefit can be considered a cost, these definitions are equivalent.) The analysis just offered suggests that, all other things equal, costs will be minimized if ownership is assigned to the class of patrons for whom the problems of market contracting—that is, the costs of market imperfections—are most severe. For example, if the firm is a natural monopoly vis-à-vis its customers, but obtains its capital, labor, and other factors of production in reasonably competitive markets, then total costs are likely to be minimized by assigning ownership to the firm's customers. This presumably helps explain why, as discussed in Chapter 9, so many rural electric utilities are organized as consumer cooperatives.

If ownership were always perfectly effective, in the sense that it eliminated all costs of market contracting without imposing any new costs of its own, then there would be no more to a theory of ownership than this. In fact, however, ownership itself involves costs. Some of these costs are what might be called "governance" costs; they include the costs of making collective decisions among the owners, the costs of monitoring managers, and the costs of the poor decisions and excessive managerial discretion that result when collective decision making or managerial monitoring are imperfect. Another cost is the risk bearing associated with receipt of residual earnings. We shall explore these and other costs of ownership in detail in Chapter 3. For the moment we need simply note that, like the costs of market contracting, these costs can vary greatly from one class of patrons to another. Some patrons, for example, are in a much better position than others to govern the firm effectively. Similarly, some are better able than others to bear the risk associated with the right to residual earnings. Consequently, when deciding which class of patrons is to own the firm, the costs of ownership must be considered in addition to the costs of market contracting. For example, Chapter 9 offers evidence that the costs of consumer ownership in an electric utility are significantly higher in urban areas than in rural areas, and that this is an important reason why utility cooperatives are much less common in urban areas than in rural areas.

The least-cost assignment of ownership is therefore that which minimizes the sum of all of the costs of a firm's transactions. That is, it minimizes the sum of (1) the costs of market contracting for those classes of patrons that are not owners and (2) the costs of ownership for the class of patrons who own the firm.

Although this theory is simple in basic concept, it is important when applying the theory to realize that the costs of market contracting for any given class of patrons may depend on which of the other classes of patrons owns the firm.[18] This will become clearer in Chapter 3.

Survivorship

It is reasonable to expect that, over the long run, cost-minimizing forms of organization will come to dominate most industries. Two mechanisms press in this direction. The first is conscious design and imitation on the part of the entrepreneurs who organize firms: a firm's entrepreneurs, together with those persons who expect to be among the firm's patrons, have an incentive to adopt a cost-saving organizational form and share the resulting savings among themselves. The second is market selection: higher-cost forms of organization tend to be driven out of business by their lower-cost competitors. If we observe that a particular form of ownership is dominant in a given industry, this is a strong indication that the form is less costly than other forms of ownership would be in that industry.

In Parts II–IV we shall use this "survivorship test" as important evidence of the relative cost of different forms of ownership. There are, however, a number of reasons why this test might not be an entirely accurate measure of comparative organizational costs. Most obviously, public subsidies or regulation might give a special advantage to one form over another. Moreover, the diffusion of new forms through conscious imitation does not always happen quickly,[19] and for various reasons market selection can operate quite slowly as well.[20] In interpreting the pattern of ownership that appears in any given industry, we must be attentive to these considerations. In fact, we shall gain important insight into the processes of organizational evolution when we consider the temporal pattern of change in ownership forms in some of the industries examined in later chapters.

What Kinds of Costs?

Some might object that there are other values served by assignment of ownership besides cost minimization and that therefore the cost-minimizing form of ownership might not be the one that is most desirable from a social point of view, or even the one that is chosen by the parties involved. I use the term "cost" here, however, to include all interests and values that might be affected by transactions between a firm and its patrons. For example, among the costs of contracting for labor on the market might be a subjective sense of alienation or disempowerment that could be alleviated if the workers instead owned the firm. In fact, one of the fruits of this inquiry is a better understanding of the range of values, both subjective and objective, that are served by ownership, and of the relative significance of those values to persons who deal with the firm.

Thus I use the expression "cost-minimizing" here to mean "efficient" in the economist's very broad sense of that word—that is, to refer to a situation in which there is no alternative arrangement that could make any class of patrons better off, by their own subjective valuation, without making some other class worse off to a greater degree.[21]

In general, the only persons whose interests are importantly affected by the assignment of ownership in a firm are the firm's patrons. In the long run, moreover, all costs that patrons bear under any particular assignment of ownership—whether those costs are pecuniary or non-pecuniary—should be reflected in the contractual terms under which they will agree to transact with the firm. As a consequence the firms that survive in the market should not be those that simply minimize pecuniary costs, but those that are efficient in the broader sense.

To give the theory sketched here more substance, the next two chapters examine in greater detail the most important costs inherent in market contracting and ownership, respectively.

2

The Costs of Contracting

There are several types of market imperfections—most of which are familiar to students of economics—whose costs can potentially be reduced by assigning ownership to the affected patrons. We shall survey here, in very general terms, the most common of these problems in market contracting and discuss briefly their potential effect on the assignment of ownership. Since our principal object at this point is simply to develop an overview and a general catalog of the categories of costs involved, we shall not dwell here on details or refinements of theory or application.[1] Later chapters will offer more extensive illustrations and more elaborate analysis.[2]

Simple Market Power

Frequently, owing to economies of scale or other factors (such as cartelization or regulation) that limit competition, a firm has market power with respect to one or another group of its patrons. The affected patrons then have an incentive to own the firm and thereby avoid price exploitation. Firms often have a degree of monopoly power in dealing with their customers, and this is a common reason for organizing the firm as a consumer cooperative. Electric utility cooperatives are a conspicuous example. Monopsony—market power vis-à-vis the firm's suppliers rather than its customers—is sometimes also a motivation for patron ownership, as it clearly was in the early development of agricultural marketing and processing cooperatives.

More specifically, by owning a firm that has market power, customers can avoid two types of costs. The first is paying a monopoly price for the goods or services that the customers purchase from the firm. The second is underconsumption of the firm's goods or services owing to their excessively high price.

The first type of cost is likely to be by far the largest from the customers' point of view. But it is only a private cost to the customers—a matter of distribution between them and the owners of the firm—and not a social cost. If a monopolistic investor-owned firm is converted to customer ownership, any savings to its current customers from a reduction in the price they pay will be offset by an equal loss to the former owners. This type of cost consequently does not provide an incentive for customers to purchase a firm from existing investor-owners, since those owners will only be willing to sell the firm for a price that includes the present value of the future monopoly profits they will lose by virtue of the sale. This private cost can, however, provide a strong incentive for customers to establish a *new* firm on their own, or to use the threat of doing so to acquire the existing monopolist's plant at a reasonable price.

The second type of cost—the distortion in consumption resulting from a price above cost—is a true social cost. The prospect of its elimination may therefore provide an incentive even for an existing monopolist to sell his firm to his customers so he can share with them the resulting efficiency gains.

Ex Post Market Power ("Lock-In")

Problems of monopolistic exploitation can also arise after a person begins patronizing a firm even if, when the patronage began, the firm had a substantial number of competitors.[3] These problems arise where two circumstances are present. First, upon entering into the transactional relationship the patron must make substantial transaction-specific investments—that is, investments whose value cannot be fully recouped if the transactional relationship with the firm is broken. Second, the transactions are likely to extend over such a long period of time, and are sufficiently complex and unpredictable, that important aspects of future transactions cannot be reduced to contract in advance but rather must be dealt with over time according to experience. In such circumstances, the patron becomes locked in to a greater or lesser degree once she begins patronizing the firm: she loses the protective option of costless exit if the firm seeks to exploit her.

Labor contracting provides an example. At the time an individual first enters the labor force there are likely to be many firms with which she could obtain employment. As a consequence, she will be in a position to make those firms compete with one another for her services. After she has taken a job with a particular firm and worked with that firm for a number of years, however, her skills are likely to become specialized to that firm to some degree, and her flexibility for retraining may also diminish. She thus may be substantially more productive at her present firm than she would be elsewhere. Moreover, she may have made important personal investments in the community where her employer is located—investments that cannot be recouped if she leaves that community. Her spouse may be employed there, her children may be accustomed to the local school system, and her entire family may have developed strong personal ties with other members of the community. In short, with time it may become increasingly costly, both professionally and personally, for her to change employers. When this happens, her present employer is in a position to act opportunistically toward her in setting wages or other terms of employment, compensating her only well enough to prevent her from leaving and thereby, in effect, appropriating the value of the job-specific investments, both professional and personal, that she has made.

An individual who perceives the possibility of such an outcome when first seeking employment is likely to insist on higher initial wages to compensate her for the risk of subsequent exploitation, and she may refuse employment altogether with a firm that, though otherwise an attractive employer, cannot effectively bind itself not to act exploitatively in the future. Likewise, after accepting employment with a firm, she will have suboptimal incentives to make firm-specific investments, such as acquiring knowledge or skills that are valuable only to that firm or buying an expensive or idiosyncratic house that is just right for her family but might be difficult to resell if she should leave the firm and seek employment elsewhere.

This problem of "lock-in" can be mitigated by assigning ownership of the firm to the patrons who are potentially affected by it. This point is now familiar from studies of vertical integration, where lock-in has come to be recognized as an important incentive for merging two individual firms when one of the firms is an important customer or supplier of the other.[4] But the lock-in problem can also help explain why ownership of a firm is extended, not just to another individual enterprise with which the firm deals, but to a whole class of the firm's patrons—which is the situation of most interest to us here.[5] In particular, lock-in apparently provides an incentive not only for worker ownership but also for various forms of consumer ownership: a conspicuous example is the common practice, discussed in Chapter 8, of making franchisees the collective owners of their franchisor.

The Risks of Long-Term Contracting

There are various common situations in which a firm and its patrons have strong incentives to enter into a long-term contract. One of these is to avoid the possibility that transaction-specific investments will expose one or both parties to opportunistic behavior by the other. Another is to allocate specific risks between the parties. And yet another is to mitigate the problems of adverse selection that are endemic to insurance and related industries.[6]

Even where long-term contracts are relatively successful in dealing with these types of problems, the contracts themselves can generate substantial risk for a firm and its patrons. As conditions change during the term of the contract, the price(s) specified in the contract can produce a substantial windfall gain for one party and a corresponding loss for the other. A long-term contract can therefore become a pure gamble between the parties, inefficiently creating large risks for both where there is little or no underlying social risk (that is, where the parties taken together face no risk, but rather are engaged in a zero-sum transaction). For example, the vagaries of inflation have this effect on all long-term contracts whose price terms are written in nominal dollars—as contracts effectively had to be written before the development of reliable price indices, and as many contracts are still written. Making the patrons the owners of the firm eliminates much of this risk: what the patrons lose as patrons they gain as owners, and vice versa. As we shall see in Chapter 14, this has historically been, and may continue to be, an important reason for the success of mutual life insurance companies.

Asymmetric Information

Contracting can also be costly when the firm has better information than its patrons concerning matters that bear importantly on transactions between them or, conversely, when the patrons have better information than does the firm.

For example, a firm often knows more than its customers about the quality of the goods or services that it sells. This is especially common when the contracted-for goods or services are complex or difficult to inspect. The firm then has an incentive to deliver a lower-quality performance than it promises. Customers, in turn, have an incentive to distrust the firm, and may offer to pay only the value of the worst possible performance or decline to purchase at all.[7] The result is an inefficient transaction: although the customers are getting just what they are paying for, and the firm is getting paid no more than is necessary to cover the cost of the quality of performance it is providing, both the customer and the firm would prefer a higher-quality performance and a higher price. Firms can sometimes manage this problem by investing in a reputation for quality, but that strategy generally takes time and can often provide at best a partial palliative.

In these circumstances, customer ownership has the virtue that it reduces the firm's incentive to exploit its informational advantage. A simple example is provided by agricultural fertilizers and livestock feed. When commercial fertilizers and feed were first introduced on the market at the beginning of the twentieth century, farmers had difficulty determining their contents. As a consequence, the quality of the products offered on the market was low. The response of many farmers, as discussed in Chapter 9, was to form supply cooperatives to manufacture and distribute the feed and fertilizer they needed. Even more conspicuous examples can be found in the service industries, including savings banking and life insurance.

It is not just in dealing with customers, however, that the firm may have an informational advantage. The same problem can arise between the firm and its suppliers or employees. An investor-owned firm may skimp on efforts to assure its workers continuity of employment or to maintain a safe workplace, and the firm's workers, in anticipation of this, may invest less in firm-specific skills or insist upon higher wages than they would otherwise. Worker ownership may promise more efficient labor relationships in this respect.

The problem can also run the other way, with the patrons possessing information about their own level of performance that is unavailable to the firm. Managers of an apartment building may not be able to police the degree of care taken by tenants in maintaining their units, and insurance companies may not be able to monitor the safety precautions taken by their insureds. (Indeed, the insurance business is the original source of the term "moral hazard" that is now commonly employed to refer to the incentive to skimp on effort that asymmetric information creates.) Similarly, workers are likely to know more than their employer concerning the amount of effort they are devoting to their job. Patrons in these situations have an incentive to behave opportunistically, and firms can be expected to adjust their prices or wages to compensate. By reducing this incentive for opportunism, patron ownership has the potential to improve the terms on which patrons can deal with the firm. Where the class of patrons is numerous, however, the incentive for individual patrons to exploit their informational advantage at the expense of others may remain strong even with patron ownership—an issue we shall examine more carefully when considering mutual companies and worker-owned firms.

Strategic Bargaining

Asymmetric information can also result in costly strategic bargaining. A firm's management commonly has information about the firm's plans and prospects that is not available to its patrons, and a firm's patrons often have information about their own preferences and opportunities that is unavailable to management. If the patrons in question do not own the firm, they may have little incentive to reveal their private information to the firm, because that would give the firm an advantage it would otherwise lack in bargaining with them. Likewise, the firm's management will often have no incentive to share its private information with the patrons. Moreover, even where the firm would gain from disclosing information to its patrons, or vice versa, credible disclosure may be impossible.

In the presence of private information of this sort, substantial time and effort can be lost in contractual negotiations. The parties have an incentive to delay reaching an agreement in order to test the other side's true willingness to compromise and to signal their own resolve. The strikes and lockouts that often accompany labor contracting provide a familiar illustration.[8] Patron ownership can reduce or eliminate this strategic behavior, because it removes the incentive for either the firm's management or its patrons to hide information from each other or to take advantage of information that the other lacks.

Communication of Patron Preferences

When patrons cannot credibly communicate their preferences to management, inefficiencies may arise beyond the costs of strategic bargaining. In particular, management may have difficulty finding the least-cost combination of contractual terms that will satisfy the firm's patrons.

Consider a firm's efforts to choose an appropriate mix of wages, fringe benefits, and workplace amenities to offer its employees. What are the workers' preferences concerning tradeoffs between financial compensation and working conditions? What balance do they prefer between current and deferred compensation, or between job security and higher wages? What is their preferred tradeoff among job safety, workplace aesthetics, speed of production, and variety of work? If management lacks this information, it may fail to find the package that offers the greatest satisfaction to the employees per dollar spent by the firm. Yet if the workers do not own the firm, they have an incentive to misrepresent their preferences on such matters for the sake of enhancing their overall bargaining position. And management, knowing that the workers have an incentive to dissemble, has reason to disbelieve the workers, whether they are in fact speaking honestly or not. Consequently, workers may fail to communicate their true preferences even though both the firm and the workers would be better off if those preferences could be credibly communicated.

Patron ownership, by removing the conflict of interest between patrons and owners, reduces these obstacles to communication.

Compromising among Diverse Patron Preferences

Often a firm must deal on the same terms with all patrons in a given class even though individuals within that class have differing preferences. The firm may be constrained to offer the same working conditions to all of its employees or the same quality of goods or services to all of its customers. In these circumstances, market contracting can lead the firm to choose an inefficient compromise among its patrons' differing preferences. This problem occurs because a firm contracting in a market has an incentive to accommodate the preferences of the marginal patron. Yet efficiency generally calls for choosing conditions that suit the preferences of the average patron, and these preferences may be quite different from those of the marginal patron.[9]

Consider a firm's choice of the appropriate level of safety for its workers. The firm has an incentive to adjust safety to respond to the tradeoff between higher wages and enhanced workplace safety that satisfies the marginal workers—that is, those workers who are indifferent between remaining with the firm at the current wage and working conditions or seeking employment elsewhere. But the preferences of the marginal worker may not be those of the average worker. For instance, the marginal worker may be a young person who will happily take large risks in return for higher wages, while the average worker is an older person with family commitments who is much more risk averse. As a result, the level of workplace safety chosen by the firm may not be that which most efficiently meets the needs of the firm's workers as a whole.

Where the patrons in question own the firm, they are likely to make decisions collectively by voting in some fashion. And voting—particularly the conventional majority rule—tends to favor the preferences of the median member of the group rather than those of the marginal member. Although the preferences of the median patron may not be those of the average patron, they will often be closer to the average than are the preferences of the patron who is marginal in the market. Patron ownership can thus offer advantages in selecting an appropriate compromise when patron preferences diverge.

Alienation

Advocates of "noncapitalist" forms of ownership—such as worker-owned firms, consumer cooperatives, and nonprofits—frequently express, explicitly or implicitly, ideological opposition to capitalist (investor-owned) enterprise. The rhetoric is often vague, simply decrying the "alienation" or "exploitation" said to characterize capitalist firms. At bottom, this opposition to investor-owned enterprise frequently seems to be rooted in concerns about market failures of the types just surveyed—for example, concerns that investor-owned firms, in dealing with their customers or workers, will take advantage of market power, lock-in, or informational asymmetries. But sometimes opposition to capitalism also seems rooted in concerns about what we might term the "transactional atmosphere" of market exchange. A clear analysis of the problem is difficult to find. But perhaps part of what is involved is an objection to the subjective experience of market contracting itself.

Market contracting is, in an important sense, an adversarial process: purchasers try to obtain the best goods or services at the lowest price possible; sellers try to provide the lowest-cost goods or services at the highest price possible. Some individuals enjoy this contest, and most participants in market economies are acculturated to engaging in it with a fair degree of indifference, at least in conventional commercial contexts. Yet some individuals evidently find it unpleasant to obtain or provide goods or services through such adversarial relationships.

One source of this unpleasantness is presumably the vigilance required to protect oneself from exploitation when transacting on the market. This vigilance could appropriately be included among the costs of market failure described earlier, since without market failure vigilance would often be unnecessary. In addition, however, some individuals may have preferences concerning the types of relationships they have with other people, preferences that go beyond the quality or price of the goods and services ultimately received through those relationships or the vigilance those relationships require. They may dislike the experience of having an adversarial relationship when they would instinctively prefer to have relationships that are more cooperative, trusting, or altruistic. For such individuals, there may be considerable value in eliminating the most tangible adversarial link in the chain of commerce by owning the firm they patronize (say, by purchasing through a consumer cooperative or selling through a producer cooperative) or by patronizing a nonprofit firm.

In assessing the relative efficiency of alternative economic arrangements, received economic theory generally ignores such preferences concerning transactional processes, as opposed to preferences concerning transactional outcomes such as price and quality of performance. It does not necessarily follow, of course, that these preferences are unimportant. And, where they *are* important, market contracting brings the cost of running counter to them.

An alternative interpretation of alienation is that individuals gain important satisfaction from having a feeling of control over an enterprise they patronize, or from participating with other patrons in its governance—a satisfaction that may be lost when they deal with the firm only through market relationships. More will be said about this in the next chapter.

Who Bears the Costs?

When contracting with a given class of patrons is costly, the patrons involved will sometimes bear those costs. For example, customers are likely to bear most of the costs of a firm's monopoly in its product market. But in many cases some other class of patrons will end up bearing the costs of contracting. If a given firm hires labor in a competitive market, then the firm's workers generally will not bear any special costs that are involved in contracting with the firm. Rather, those costs are likely to be borne by the firm's owners, customers, or suppliers of other factors of production, depending on the nature of the other markets in which the firm contracts. Regardless of who bears the costs, however, there is an incentive to reduce those costs wherever possible by reorganizing the firm with a more efficient form of ownership.

Who Owns Whom?

We have been speaking of reducing the costs of market contracting by having the patrons own the firm. In principle, those costs could also be reduced by having the firm own its patrons. Where there is only one patron involved, there is often no important distinction between these two forms of vertical integration. But where—as in the cases of principal interest here—multiple patrons are involved, there commonly is a difference. Ownership of a single firm by multiple patrons does not create the same incentives as does ownership of the patrons by the firm.

If the problem is that patrons, having information inaccessible to the firm's management, can behave opportunistically toward the firm, then this problem is not completely solved by having the patrons own the firm. There remains an incentive for each patron to act opportunistically even as an owner, since he will bear only a small fraction of the cost of his behavior, while the rest falls on the other patron-owners. Consequently, where it is the patrons rather than the firm that have the informational advantage, it is potentially more efficient for the firm to own the patrons than for the patrons to own the firm.

In some situations, however, it is infeasible for the firm to own its patrons. In particular, when the patrons are individuals such as workers or consumers, legal prohibitions on personal servitude, as well as a variety of practical contracting problems, obviously bar this arrangement. If the firm and its patrons are to be connected by ownership, the patrons must own the firm.

For related reasons, ownership of the patrons by the firm can sometimes be impractical even where the patrons are not individuals but instead are other firms. Consider the common case—discussed at length in Chapter 8—of a wholesaler owned as a cooperative by the retail stores to which it sells. The problems of market failure to which this ownership arrangement responds (typically market power on the part of the wholesaler) might alternatively be solved by having the wholesaler own the retail stores. And, of course, fully integrated chain store operations of the latter type are common. But that arrangement can create diseconomies of scale, including loss of the strong incentives for efficient operation that exist when the individual retail stores are owned separately by their local managers. Having the stores collectively own their supplier, rather than vice versa, can be the superior arrangement. In short, the costs of ownership are often asymmetric between a firm and its patrons—a point that emerges even more clearly in the next chapter.

3

The Costs of Ownership

We have observed that ownership has two essential attributes: exercise of control and receipt of residual earnings. There are costs inherent in each of these attributes. Those costs fall conveniently into three broad categories: the costs of controlling managers, the costs of collective decision making, and the costs of risk bearing. The first two categories are associated with the exercise of control. The third is associated with the receipt of residual earnings. All of these costs can vary substantially in magnitude from one class of patrons to another.

We shall survey these three types of costs here in general terms. As with the costs of market contracting surveyed in the preceding chapter, subsequent chapters will offer deeper analysis and more copious and detailed illustrations.

Costs of Controlling Managers

In large firms, and especially in firms with a populous class of owners, the owners must generally delegate substantial authority to hired managers.[1] Thus, in widely held business corporations, as in large cooperatives, most decision-making authority is delegated to the firm's board of directors, who in turn delegate most operational decisions to the firm's senior officers. This delegation brings with it the costs commonly labeled "agency costs." For our purposes, these costs can conveniently be broken down into two types: the costs of monitoring the managers and the costs of the managerial opportunism that results from the failure to monitor managers with perfect effectiveness.[2]

Monitoring

If the patron-owners of a firm are to control its management effectively, they must incur the costs of (1) informing themselves about the operations of the firm, (2) communicating among themselves for the purpose of exchanging information and making decisions, and (3) bringing their decisions to bear on the firm's management. I shall refer to these costs collectively as "monitoring costs." These costs can vary substantially among different classes of patrons. Since patrons are likely to accumulate information about the firm simply as a by-product of transacting with it, the cost of monitoring for a given class of patrons will generally be inversely proportional to the importance, frequency, and duration of the patron's transactions with the firm.[3] The costs of monitoring will also depend on the ease of organizing the patrons for collective action, which may depend in turn on factors such as the patrons' physical proximity to one another and to the firm.

For example, tenants in an apartment building generally have relatively low monitoring costs. They deal repeatedly with the building's management, often for a number of years, in transactions that involve a significant fraction of their budget. They therefore have both the opportunity and the incentive to learn a great deal about how well the building is managed. Close proximity also permits easy organization for collective action. These are important factors in the viability of tenant ownership of apartment buildings through cooperatives and condominiums, as will be discussed further in Chapter 12.

Finally, the number of patrons among whom ownership is shared affects monitoring costs. If all patrons are to participate effectively in decision making, then a large class of owners requires substantial duplication of effort in becoming informed. Moreover, the monitoring efforts of any individual owner have the properties of a public good for the owners as a group: the benefits of that monitoring are enjoyed by all other owners as well, regardless of whether they have undertaken any monitoring of their own. Consequently, as the number of owners grows, each individual owner's share of the potential gains from effective monitoring decreases, thus reducing the individual's incentive to monitor.

It follows that, where the class of owners is large, it may be prohibitively costly to induce the owners to undertake anything beyond the most cursory monitoring. In itself, this argues for the smallest group of owners possible—preferably a single owner. The fact that, despite this, a large firm often has a very large class of owners therefore suggests that either or both of two things must be true. First, the costs of market contracting would be much higher under any alternative assignment of ownership. Second, the costs of managerial opportunism are modest even though the firm's owners cannot actively supervise the managers. We shall first explore the latter possibility. Then, at the end of the chapter, we shall return to the former.

Managerial Opportunism

To the extent that the owners of a firm fail to exercise effective control over its managers, the managers have an opportunity to malinger or engage in self-dealing transactions. Clearly this can sometimes be costly.[4] Yet the conduct of a firm's managers is conditioned by a variety of constraints and incentives beyond direct sanctions or rewards from the firm's owners. There are important limits to the costs of managerial opportunism even in firms whose nominal owners are in a poor position to do any active monitoring of the firm's management at all.

Consider first self-dealing. The transactions necessary for managers to divert to themselves a significant fraction of the residual earnings in a large firm are often difficult to conceal. Moreover, these transactions are in most cases explicitly proscribed by contract or by law, thus exposing the managers to a variety of moral, contractual, tort, and criminal sanctions that can be brought to bear without collective action on the part of the firm's owners. In particular, self-dealing managers expose themselves to shaming by fellow workers, friends, or family, to derivative suits initiated by individual shareholders or enterprising lawyers, and to civil or criminal prosecution by the state (including, conspicuously, the tax authorities).

To be sure, although legal, contractual, and moral constraints may generally suffice to keep managers from putting their hand in the till, they will not necessarily ensure that managers work hard and make effective decisions. Again, however, pride and moral suasion provide important motivation, particularly for the types of individuals who work their way to the top of a managerial hierarchy. The need for the firm to prosper if managers are to keep their jobs or, even better, to enhance them, also provides an important work incentive.[5] Moreover, it may be a mistake to exaggerate the degree of effort or ingenuity that is required of the senior managers in a typical business enterprise, and thus the potential gains from better monitoring of those managers by a firm's owners. In many firms, imitation of standard managerial practices may suffice for relatively successful performance.

In sum, the inability of a firm's nominal owners to exercise much direct control may result in only a modest amount of organizational slack, at least when compared with any realistic alternative.[6] Indeed, in the chapters that follow we shall encounter large groups of firms (including mutual life insurance companies and nonprofit hospitals) that have been successful over long periods of time in competitive environments without any effective exercise of control by owners whatever—often without even having any owners.

There is, however, one costly managerial perquisite—excessive retention of earnings—that is not easy to detect or proscribe, that is likely to bring approval rather than censure from friends and colleagues both inside and outside the firm, and that is generally encouraged rather than checked by managers' desires to retain or build their empire. Retentions benefit managers by creating a buffer against adversity and by increasing the size of the firm that the managers control. But retentions are costly to the firm's owners if the rate of return on the retentions is less than the return available on investments outside the firm or if, regardless of the rate of return the retentions bring, the funds retained can never be recovered by the current owners (as happens in some mutuals and cooperatives). This problem is most easily discerned in nonprofit[7] and mutual firms, but it is arguably the principal source of inefficiency in investor-owned firms as well.[8] And because excessive retention of earnings tends to enhance rather than decrease the survival value of a firm, those firms that are particularly subject to this tendency—as firms with diffuse ownership are—may actually be favored rather than pressured by the invisible hand of market selection.

Whatever the nature of the managerial opportunism involved, where the losses it brings are smaller than the costs of the monitoring that would be required to prevent it, it is of course efficient for the firm's owners to tolerate the opportunism. Agency costs, therefore, are the sum of the costs incurred in monitoring and the costs of managerial opportunism that result from the failure or inability to monitor with complete effectiveness.

Collective Decision Making

When many persons share ownership of a firm, there are likely to be differences of opinion concerning the firm's policies and programs. Sometimes those differences will merely reflect different judgments about the most effective means for achieving a shared goal. More serious differences arise, however, when the outcome of the decision will affect different owners differently. Broadly speaking, this could happen for either of two reasons.

First, the individuals involved may differ in the way in which they transact with the firm as patrons—that is, in the nature of the goods or services they sell to, or purchase from, the firm. To take a simple example, a decision to repair the elevators in a four-story cooperative apartment building will benefit the first-floor residents much less than those on the fourth floor. The residents, depending on where they live in the building, may therefore disagree on the desirability of paying costly overtime to get the repairs done quickly. Similarly, if a worker-owned firm must shut down one of its two plants, the workers at the two plants are likely to have very different preferences about which plant should be chosen.

Second, the owners may have differences in preferences that arise from their personal circumstances rather than from any differences in their transactions with the firm. A decision by a cooperative apartment building to accelerate repayment of the principal on the building's mortgage may affect members differently depending on their personal liquidity and tax status even if they occupy identical apartments and have identical leases. Or a decision by a worker-owned firm to shift to riskier lines of business, and thereby increase the chance that the firm will fail, is likely to be less attractive to older workers than it is to younger workers who, though doing the same job, are more easily retrainable and have fewer ties to the local community.

In order for a firm's owners to make decisions when their interests differ, they must employ some form of collective choice mechanism. The nearly universal approach is to adopt a voting scheme, with votes apportioned either by volume of patronage or on the basis of one-member-one-vote. When the interests of the individual owners are diverse, such mechanisms for collective choice engender costs. These costs, which for future reference we can label the "costs of collective decision making," are logically distinct from agency costs. They can be large even in firms, such as modest-sized partnerships, in which there are no hired managers and hence no significant agency costs. Conversely, the costs of collective decision making can be negligible in large corporations in which ownership is widely shared and hence agency costs are large, as long as the owners have highly homogeneous interests.

To make this distinction clear, we can define "agency costs" as the costs of monitoring and managerial opportunism that the firm would incur even if the interests of all owners were identical. The "costs of collective decision making" are then the additional costs that result from heterogeneity of interests among the owners. Unlike agency costs, the costs of collective decision making have been largely neglected in the literature on corporate control and the economics of organizational form.[9] Nevertheless these costs play a crucial role in determining the efficiency of alternative assignments of ownership.

The collective choice mechanisms employed within firms are essentially political mechanisms. Their costs are therefore characteristically the costs of political mechanisms in general. In recent decades, the "public choice" literature has begun to provide a more systematic understanding of these costs, which might be termed the costs of "political failure," analogous to the costs of "market failure" that affect market mechanisms. Although that literature still leaves us with a very partial understanding of these costs, some general characterizations are possible.

The costs associated with collective choice mechanisms are of two broad types. First, there are the costs resulting from inefficient decisions—that is, from decisions whose outcomes fail to maximize the aggregate welfare, or surplus, of the owners themselves as a group. Second, there are the costs of the decision-making process itself.

Costly Decisions

Inefficient decisions can arise in several ways. To begin with, as already noted, majority voting tends to select the outcome preferred by the median member of the group, while efficiency generally calls for the outcome preferred by the average member. Where the median and the average member have substantially different preferences, voting can produce seriously inefficient decisions.[10] Consider again the hypothetical four-story cooperative apartment building with a broken elevator. If the residents of the first two floors, who do not use the elevator, outnumber the residents of the top two floors who do, then the residents as a whole might vote not to pay overtime to hasten the repairs, even though the money thus saved is substantially less than the costs, both pecuniary and nonpecuniary, that the delay imposes on the residents of the upper floors.

Alternatively, control over the political process can fall into the hands of an unrepresentative minority who, intentionally or unintentionally, use that control to make decisions that inefficiently exploit the majority in favor of the minority. This is particularly likely to happen when, as is often the case, some patrons are better situated to participate effectively in collective decision making than others—perhaps because they have few other demands on their time, or have special managerial expertise, or have special access to information. For example, governance of a cooperative apartment building might be dominated by those residents of the building who are retired, even if they are in the minority, because they have more time to attend meetings. As a consequence, improvements that primarily benefit the retirees, such as elevator repairs, might be emphasized at the expense of those that do not, such as repairs to the children's playground, even if the reverse priorities would be more beneficial to the building's occupants as a whole.

Whether it is the majority that inefficiently exploits the minority or vice versa, the dominant group need not be particularly venal for the resulting costs to be substantial. It is sufficient that, as is natural, the decision makers' own interests simply have more salience for them than do the interests of others.

Costly Process

The costs of the collective choice process, in turn, may also have several sources. Even if individual owners always seek to exercise their right of control without opportunism and to reach the decisions that will be most efficient for the owners as a whole, they may need to invest considerable time and effort in obtaining knowledge about the firm and about other owners' preferences, and in attending the meetings and other activities necessary to reach and implement effective collective decisions. We also know from public choice theory that the possibility of a voting cycle[11] among alternatives increases as preferences among the electorate become more heterogeneous.[12] Such cycling may be costly if there are transaction costs involved in repeatedly altering the firm's policies. More important, the instability that underlies cycling can give extraordinary power to those in control of the voting agenda to obtain the outcomes they desire, no matter how inefficient those outcomes may be.[13] Finally, if owners seek to behave strategically, then further costs may result from efforts to hide or discover information or to make or break coalitions.

Methods exist for limiting these process costs. Delegation of authority to committees, for example, can reduce the costs of participation, inhibit cycling, and facilitate vote trading that will mitigate the median voter problem. But delegation can also produce seriously inefficient outcomes by empowering committee members to impose their own idiosyncratic preferences on the group as a whole.[14]

Resolving Conflicts

Even if the owners of a firm are heterogeneous in their interests, the costs of collective decision making may nevertheless be low if there is some simple and salient criterion for balancing those interests. Consider the division of the firm's net earnings among its owners. This is potentially controversial where the character or volume of the transactions between individual owners and the firm varies substantially. Important examples, which we shall examine closely in Chapter 6, involve employee-owned firms in which the employees differ in the types of work they do. The costs of reaching agreement on an allocation of earnings, and the possibility that the resulting allocation will create inefficient incentives, may be manageable if it is easy to account separately for the net benefits bestowed on the firm by transactions with individual owners and to apportion the firm's earnings according to that accounting. Alternatively, if the value of each individual owner's transactions with the firm is difficult to measure, a rule of equal division may serve as a focal point[15] on which agreement can easily be reached, thus minimizing the process costs of decision making though perhaps creating some inefficient incentives. Law firms often follow one or the other of these approaches: some use explicit multifactor productivity formulas to determine partners' shares; others follow a simple rule of equal division of earnings among all partners of a given age. Where such clear and conventional decision-making criteria are absent, however, workable agreement among the owners can take a long time to reach, and may in fact never be reached.[16]

Participation

In some cases, the process of collective decision making arguably yields benefits for the patrons involved and not just costs. In fact, advocates of worker ownership often suggest that participation in control of the firm through democratic processes is of value in itself, quite apart from the practical import of the substantive decisions that result,[17] and a similar argument is sometimes made on behalf of consumer cooperatives and other forms of noncapitalist enterprise.[18] Although the reasons for valuing participation in this way are seldom spelled out explicitly, at least three can be identified.

First, individuals might simply enjoy the experience of participating in collective decision making—attending meetings, debating alternatives, assuming offices—as a social activity that is satisfying in itself. That is, political activity may in effect be a consumption good. Second, as is sometimes argued in the context of worker ownership, individuals may gain psychological satisfaction from the feeling of being in control, and this feeling may be enhanced for a firm's patrons by permitting them to participate directly in the decision making of the firm.[19] Third, as has also been argued on behalf of worker ownership in particular, participation in collective decision making within the firm may be useful training for participation in the democratic political processes of the larger society, and might be valued for this reason not only by the individuals involved but also by the rest of society.[20]

But note that these benefits, real though they may be, still involve tradeoffs. To grant the franchise and the associated benefits of participation to one group of patrons typically requires denying them to all other groups of patrons. Advocates of alternative forms of ownership sometimes overlook this point. For example, it has been argued, on behalf of worker ownership, that it is inconsistent to have democracy at the level of the state and not at the level of the firm.[21] Yet in fact there is democracy in the typical investor-owned firm; it is just that the investors of capital do the voting rather than the workers. Converting to worker ownership means not only enfranchising the workers but also disenfranchising the firm's investors while continuing to deny the franchise to the firm's consumers. Consequently, the question generally is not whether there is voting in a firm, but rather who votes. If the benefits of participation as a good in itself are greater for one group of the firm's patrons than for another, then this becomes a further consideration in assigning ownership.

The value to individuals of participation as a good in itself is an empirical question that is illuminated by the analysis of existing ownership patterns in subsequent chapters. Interestingly, the evidence suggests strongly that for all classes of patrons—including, in particular, employees—the benefits of participation are generally insufficient to outweigh the costs of collective decision making.

Why Not Make Everybody an Owner?

In theory it would be possible to have all classes of patrons share in collective decision making, and thus not completely disenfranchise anyone. This is essentially the position taken by those who feel that every group affected by a business firm's decisions—its "stakeholders," such as workers, customers, suppliers, members of the local community, and environmental groups—should have representation on the firm's board of directors.[22] Moreover, one might think that this would also have the important advantage of reducing the costs of market contracting for all of the firm's patrons and not just for a single group of them.

But because the participants are likely to have radically diverging interests, making everybody an owner threatens to increase the costs of collective decision making enormously. Indeed, one of the strongest indications of the high costs of collective decision making is the nearly complete absence of large firms in which ownership is shared among two or more different types of patrons, such as customers and suppliers or investors and workers.

Risk Bearing

The preceding discussion has focused on the costs associated with the first element of ownership: the exercise of control. But there are also costs associated with the second element of ownership: the right to residual earnings. Most conspicuous among these is the cost of bearing important risks associated with the enterprise, since those risks are often reflected in the firm's residual earnings.[23] One class of a firm's patrons may be in a much better position than others to bear those risks—for example, through diversification. Assigning ownership to that class of patrons can then bring important economies.

This is a familiar explanation for the prevalence of investor-owned firms. It is not true, however, that lenders of capital are the only low-cost risk bearers. For example, customers can also be in a good position to bear the risks of enterprise, particularly where the goods or services involved are a small fraction of the customers' budget or where the customers are themselves firms that can pass the risk on to their own owners or customers. Moreover, the existing literature often imputes to a firm's noninvestor patrons, and to employees in particular, a greater degree of risk aversion than they actually seem to exhibit. Indeed, the evidence offered here suggests that the importance of risk bearing as an explanation of ownership is commonly overstated.

Entrepreneurship

So far we have been focusing on the costs of ownership for an established firm. But there are also costs associated with organizing a firm in the first place or with changing a firm's form of ownership. We can think of these costs as the costs of entrepreneurship.

If, initially, the prospective owners of a new firm had to assemble and organize themselves on their own before establishing the firm, then it would generally be impossible for any numerous and widely dispersed class of patrons to assume ownership. But in fact the organization of a firm is generally brokered. An entrepreneur first establishes the firm by herself and then sells it to the patrons who will ultimately own it. In the process, the entrepreneur organizes the patrons into a group.

For example, widely held business corporations are typically organized first as closely held firms. Subsequently, shares are sold off to members of the investing public in a stock offering brokered by an investment banking firm. Similarly, new condominium and cooperative housing is usually built by a single developer who initially owns the entire building and then sells the separate units to individuals who ultimately become, collectively, the owners of the building. And the numerous worker-owned plywood manufacturing cooperatives in the Pacific Northwest, discussed in Chapters 5 and 6, were in many cases established by individual promoters who would form a company and then find workers to buy it.

Established firms, moreover, can often change their form of ownership relatively easily. For instance, over the past century a number of investor-owned insurance companies have converted into mutual (policyholder-owned) companies and vice versa. Since the 1970s, large numbers of apartment buildings have converted from investor ownership (that is, rental) into cooperatives or condominiums. And more recently a number of investor-owned industrial firms have been sold to their workers. Because such transactions can be brokered, the costs of the transactions are often modest relative to the value of the firm. As a consequence, the costs of changing forms of ownership need not have an important bearing on the forms that ultimately survive. Two factors can, however, make the costs of changing a serious impediment.

First, important economies derive both from the presence of established brokers who specialize in ownership transactions and from the existence of standardized procedures for handling those transactions. Where such institutions have not yet developed, the costs of adopting or converting to a particular form of ownership may be high.

Second, when a firm's owners do not effectively control the incumbent managers, the managers may seek to preserve their autonomy or their jobs, by substantially raising the costs of changing the firm's form of ownership. The managers are particularly likely to be successful in this regard where, as in many cooperative and mutual firms, shares in ownership are not freely marketable.

Both of these factors produce inertia in the selection of organizational forms. This inertia is more pronounced for some forms of ownership than others. As we shall see, there are industries in which anachronistic forms of ownership have remained firmly embedded long after they have lost their original efficiency advantage over other forms.

Applying the Calculus

Although the particular categories of costs described here do not exhaust all the efficiency considerations relevant to ownership, they usefully organize those that appear most important. Ignored here are some other considerations, such as the "horizon problem," the problem of "perverse supply response," and the tendency of cooperatives to "degenerate" into investor-owned firms, that have sometimes been emphasized in the literature but that do not seem to play a fundamental role in determining patterns of ownership. These latter considerations will be discussed later in the context of particular industries that illustrate the issues involved.[24]

The chapters that follow show how tradeoffs among the various costs described here determine the structure of ownership in particular industries. In anticipation of those analyses, some general comments about these tradeoffs are in order.

As noted in Chapter 1, the efficient assignment of ownership minimizes the sum, over all the patrons of the firm, of the costs of market contracting and the costs of ownership. If the class of patrons for whom the costs of market contracting are highest is also the class for whom the costs of ownership are lowest, then those patrons are unambiguously the most efficient owners. This is often the case for small businesses.

Farms in the staple grain crops, such as wheat and corn, are obvious examples. It is not costly to borrow most of a farm's capital on the market, because the land, equipment, and crops can be pledged as security. Nor is it costly to sell the farm's products on the market, since they are simple, standardized, and easily evaluated by their purchasers (and since, to the extent that the purchasers have market power, this can be dealt with by farm-owned marketing cooperatives). Most farm inputs are also sufficiently simple and standardized to permit their purchase on the market with little cost, and farm-owned supply cooperatives provide a good solution where this is not the case. In contrast, hiring all of the labor for the farm on the market would generally lead to serious inefficiency owing to the difficulty of monitoring farm work—essentially a problem of asymmetric information—and this problem cannot be solved by having the farm own its workers. These costs of labor contracting can, however, largely be avoided by giving ownership of the farm to the family that provides most of the farm's labor. As for the costs of ownership, two of the three principal categories of those costs—the costs of monitoring managers and the costs of collective decision making—are obviously low for family farms. The chief cost of family ownership is risk bearing, and this can be mitigated by passing risk on to the market (via futures contracts), to insurers (via crop insurance), to the government (via price supports), and to creditors (via default).

Yet frequently—and especially in large-scale enterprise where the relevant classes of patrons are sizable—the efficient assignment of ownership is not so obvious. One reason is that, when the costs of market contracting are high for a given class of patrons, the costs of ownership are often high too, and for much the same reason: because it is costly for the patrons in question to become informed about how well the firm is serving them. Life insurance policyholders in the early nineteenth century provide an example we shall return to. Contracts alone were insufficient to assure the policyholders that their insurance company would ultimately pay off on their policy, yet the policyholders were too numerous and dispersed to exercise meaningful control over their insurance company if they owned it collectively.

Such patrons are often efficient owners, despite their high costs of ownership. Even if they cannot monitor the firm's management effectively, and thus cannot exercise much control over the firm beyond that available simply through market transactions with the firm, it does not follow that there is no substantial gain from having those patrons own the firm. To use Albert Hirschman's felicitous terminology,[25] it can be efficient to assign ownership to a given class of patrons even if, for those patrons, voice adds little to exit in controlling the firm. An important reason for this is that, by virtue of their ownership, the patrons are assured that there is no other group of owners to whom management is responsive. It is one thing to transact with a firm whose managers are nominally your agents but are not much subject to your control; it is another to transact with a firm whose managers are actively serving owners who have an interest clearly adverse to yours.[26]

In short, the costs of contracting for a class of patrons may be substantially reduced by making those patrons the owners even if they will only be very passive owners. Thus life insurance companies in the early nineteenth century were typically owned by their policyholders. Large U.S. industrial corporations in the twentieth century are arguably another example, as will shortly be discussed.

In the extreme, when both the costs of market contracting and the costs of ownership are exceptionally high for a given class of patrons, the efficient solution is sometimes to assign ownership to none of the firm's patrons but instead to form an unowned, or nonprofit, firm. Making owners of anyone other than those high-cost patrons would inefficiently threaten those patrons' interests. Yet making those patrons owners would result in no meaningful reduction in the agency costs of delegated management, while leading to useless administrative burdens (such as keeping track of and communicating with the nominal owners) and running the risk that the members of some subgroup will succeed in using their authority as owners to disadvantage fellow patron-owners who are less well positioned.

In any event, as we shall see in Chapters 13–15, the distinction between nonprofit firms and firms owned by patrons who are very poor monitors is often negligible. Indeed, the tenuous character of that distinction is an important theme even in the following chapter on investor ownership.

PART II

Producer-Owned Enterprise

4

Investor-Owned Firms

Many of the considerations that make investor ownership the dominant form of organization in large-scale enterprise are familiar. By reviewing these considerations here in terms of the analytic framework outlined in Chapters 1–3, however, we gain added insight into the advantages and limitations of investor ownership, and we establish as well a basis for comparing investor ownership with the other forms of ownership surveyed in later chapters. Indeed, all of the chapters that follow explore, implicitly or explicitly, the relative virtues of investor ownership, since each of those chapters takes investor ownership as its basic reference point and asks, in essence: why has a form of ownership other than investor ownership achieved a prominent role in the industries in question here? In this chapter we shall set up some basic terms for this comparison by offering a preliminary survey of the costs and benefits, for investors of capital, of ownership versus market contracting.

Costs of Market Contracting

As noted in Chapter 1, in theory a firm could borrow all of the capital it needs, with no capital being contributed by the owners of the firm—whether those owners are another class of the firm's patrons, such as its customers or workers, or whether they are third parties who do not otherwise transact with the firm. There are, however, serious costs involved in obtaining all of a firm's capital on the market in this fashion.

Market Power

The capital market today is so large relative to the size of any individual firm that no firm has market power as a borrower of capital. Consequently, avoidance of monopsonistic exploitation is obviously not among the reasons why lenders of capital assume ownership of the firms in which they invest. Rather, problems of asymmetric information and lock-in are the principal sources of the costs of obtaining capital through market contracting, and it is these problems that provide the strongest incentive for assigning ownership to investors.

Asymmetric Information

If a firm obtains most or all of its capital through debt financing, the firm's owners have both the incentive and, often, the opportunity to divert to themselves a substantial share of the sums borrowed. The most direct method is for the owners simply to pay themselves excessive dividends and salaries and to engage in other lucrative self-dealing transactions with the firm, diverting funds that the firm could have retained to ensure repayment of the loan. If, either as a result of this self-dealing or for exogenous reasons, the firm then becomes insolvent and cannot repay the loans, the owners will have profited at the lenders' expense. A more indirect means to the same end is for the owners to invest the firm's borrowed funds in highly speculative projects that will pay off handsomely if successful but that also have a substantial risk of serious failure. If the projects succeed, the owners will receive all of the return above the fixed payment due the lenders; if, alternatively, the projects fail and the firm is bankrupted, the loss will fall principally on the lenders.[1]

The owners' incentive to behave this way can be curbed by having them post security for the loan. This can be easily arranged if the loan proceeds are invested in physical assets that are highly fungible, since the lenders can then take a lien on those assets or simply own the assets themselves (so that the loan is in kind rather than in cash—that is, the firm rents the assets). But posting security is not a solution where, as is common, the borrowed money is invested in organization-specific assets. An alternative is for the firm's owners to pledge their personal assets as collateral.[2] This is, in fact, a common procedure in small firms. Where large-scale enterprise is involved, however, and the ownership class is numerous, this device is so cumbersome as to make it impracticable. Among other things, it would be difficult for lenders to keep track of the value of the numerous pledges of security, and it would be expensive to foreclose on a large class of small guarantors in case of default.[3] Corporations in general are thus characterized by limited liability, which is to say that the owners (whether investors of capital, consumers, workers, or whatever) are liable to the firm's creditors for no more than the amount of funds they have directly invested in the firm.[4]

Yet another mechanism for avoiding opportunism by the firm's owners is to put clauses in the debt contract—the loan agreement or bond indenture—that limit the firm's ability to make highly speculative investments or to make distributions to its owners. Such contractual restrictions are in fact common when a firm borrows a substantial fraction of its capital. But it is difficult to design enforceable clauses of this sort that provide adequate security to the lenders without depriving the firm of the flexibility that it needs to operate efficiently, and this difficulty increases severely as the firm's debt-equity ratio grows.[5]

Lock-In

These problems of asymmetric information are substantially magnified by lock-in. If lenders could withdraw their investments from the firm at will, this would provide them with substantial (though still highly imperfect) protection from opportunism on the part of the firm's owners. But where, as is common, firms must make investments in long-lived assets that are organization-specific, this approach is unworkable. Short-term borrowing would then bring not only the transaction costs of continuous refinancing but, more important, the threat of inefficient runs on the firm's assets by its creditors. For as soon as a few lenders came to suspect that the firm's future income stream might not be sufficient to repay its debts, they would have an incentive to withdraw their loans (or, equivalently, insist on a significantly higher interest rate). But this would further impair the security of the loans of any lender who did not withdraw at the same time. Hence there would be a strong incentive for all the firm's lenders to race to be among the first to withdraw their loans as soon as there appeared to be a possibility of default by the firm. In other words, the lenders would be caught up in a multiperson prisoner's dilemma.

The simplest solution to this problem is to make the duration of the loans received by the firm roughly coterminous with the life expectancy of the firm-specific assets they finance. But this locks in the lenders and substantially increases their exposure to opportunism on the part of the firm's owners.

As a consequence, the costs of opportunistic exploitation of lenders can often be significantly reduced only by having the lenders themselves (or at least those among them whose investments cannot be covered by liens against fungible assets) own the firm—or, put the other way, by having the owners of the firm supply a substantial portion of the capital required to purchase firm-specific assets.[6]

Inflexibility and Risk Creation

The threat of opportunistic behavior is not the only cost of obtaining most or all of a firm's investment capital on the market. Risk creation is another, and one that is less commonly remarked. We have already noted that, if a firm is to borrow the funds necessary to finance firm-specific assets, it must generally borrow long term. And in fact corporate bonds have traditionally had very long maturities—often twenty or thirty years. Yet a long-term fixed-interest bond involves a pure gamble between the borrower and the lender on future inflation rates, creating private risk substantially in excess of social risk. When the lenders own the firm, and are thus on both sides of the transaction, this excess private risk disappears.

Strategic Behavior

To avoid opportunism on the part of a firm's owners, debt financing is typically inflexible, requiring payment of interest and principal when due regardless of whether there is sufficient cash flow currently available. This means that when a heavily indebted firm cannot meet its interest payments, yet the firm is still worth preserving as a going concern, the existing debt must be renegotiated, either through bankruptcy proceedings or through a private workout. Both debtholders and the firm's owners have an incentive to behave strategically in those negotiations, which makes them costly.[7] Equity financing—making the lenders the owners—largely avoids these costs.

Costs of Ownership

We have seen that the costs of obtaining capital through market contracting can be substantial. When we turn to the costs of ownership for investors of capital, we get a more ambiguous picture.

Risk Bearing

An obvious advantage of investor ownership is that it generally leads to low costs of risk bearing. Lenders of capital are commonly in a better position to bear risk than other patrons for two reasons. First, they may be wealthier and thus less risk averse at the margin. Second, and more important, they are in a position to eliminate firm-specific risk through diversification of their investments. The divisibility of capital, of course, greatly facilitates such diversification. Other types of patrons—employees, in particular—often face much higher costs in spreading their transactions across a number of different firms in different industries.

Monitoring Managers

A familiar liability of investor-owned firms, however, is that investors are frequently in a poor position to discipline management. In the typical publicly traded U.S. business corporation, no individual shareholder possesses a block of stock sufficiently large to provide a meaningful degree of control. This is true not only for individual shareholders, but even for groups of shareholders that might wish to act collectively in influencing corporate activity. For example, the five largest shareholders in General Motors—themselves institutions that represent the interests of highly dispersed individuals—together hold less than 6 percent of the corporation's stock.[8] As a result, the managers of many large corporations have long been essentially self-appointing and self-policing, free of direct accountability to their company's owners.[9]

This dispersion of shareholdings in the United States is not merely a consequence of the unconstrained play of market forces. Rather, it is also the product of governmental regulation.[10] A century of accumulated state and federal legislation, populist in its original political impetus and, once enacted, defended by entrenched interests (particularly corporate managers), inhibits most institutions with adequate financial resources—such as banks, insurance companies, pension funds, or mutual funds—from accumulating a sufficiently large fraction of the stock of any single corporation to permit significant control, or from actively exercising the authority potentially afforded by whatever shares the institutions hold. At the same time, the federal securities laws have long made it difficult for groups of shareholders, including in particular institutional shareholders, to act in concert to assert control over a corporation's management.[11]

Would more concentrated shareholdings, and more activist institutional shareholders, be the norm if this regulation were removed? We cannot say for sure. Shareholdings are much more concentrated in most other advanced economies, including Germany and Japan, which might be taken as evidence that concentration is the more efficient pattern.[12] But, for reasons we shall come to shortly, the comparison may not be telling. We can only say that the prevailing dispersion of shareholdings in the United States is not necessarily evidence that such dispersion is the least-cost structure for investor ownership.

Whether or not the prevailing highly dispersed pattern of shareholdings is to some extent artificially induced, investor ownership has generally remained the dominant form of organization for large-scale enterprise. In most industries, the agency costs induced by fragmented shareholdings are evidently insufficient to render ownership by some other class of patrons—customers, workers, or suppliers—more efficient than investor ownership.

One possible reason for this is that there are mechanisms that keep the agency costs of dispersed shareholdings within reasonable bounds.[13] Important among these mechanisms is the hostile takeover. The threat of takeover by investors with the incentive, power, and knowledge to discipline management may serve as a surrogate for the direct exercise of oversight and control by a corporation's current shareholders in keeping corporate management in line.[14] There is in fact substantial evidence that, on average, the wave of takeovers in the 1980s brought significant efficiencies.[15] Among that evidence are the large premia that have been paid for target companies, commonly exceeding 30 percent of the acquired corporation's pre-takeover stock price.[16] The magnitude of those premia also suggest, of course, that a hostile takeover is a crude instrument, effective only when the potential efficiencies from concentrating control exceed such a premium. Still, a crude upper bound on agency costs is better than none.

Yet there are reasons to believe that, however effective they can sometimes be, hostile takeovers may not be a crucial factor in the long-run success of the widely held business corporation. First, in substantial part, the efficiency gains from the great takeover wave of the 1980s appear to have come in large part from one-time restructurings, and particularly from disassembling the conglomerates built up in the preceding decades.[17] Takeovers may be far less effective in controlling more ordinary forms of managerial slack. Second, and more important, the hostile takeover in its modern and most effective form—a tender offer seeking to purchase a majority of a firm's publicly held stock—is a relatively recent innovation. The hostile tender offer first appeared in 1956 and remained little used until the 1960s. In the 1950s and earlier the proxy fight—which is to say, direct voting by a corporation's existing dispersed shareholders—was the principal mechanism available for a hostile change of control. Yet business corporations with widely dispersed shareholdings have been commonplace in the United States for more than a century.[18]

It is also important to recognize that whatever the agency costs of dispersed shareholdings, concentrated shareholdings also have their costs. To begin with, while highly dispersed shareholdings run the risk of management entrenchment, the same can be true of concentrated shareholdings. Germany may be an example. A substantial fraction of the stock of German industrial firms is commonly held by a small group of banks, partly through direct bank shareholdings and partly through stock that the banks hold on behalf of individual clients. It has sometimes been suggested that this pattern helps control agency costs, since the banks have both the power and the incentive to police management carefully.[19] Yet the banks themselves appear to be tied into complex patterns of mutual cross-holdings with the industrial firms they control—cross-holdings that have effectively prevented hostile takeovers and that raise the suspicion of mutual managerial entrenchment.[20] The available evidence on managerial turnover suggests little difference between Germany and the United States in disciplining managers when performance is poor, which may indicate that the entrenchment effects of Germany's concentrated shareholdings counterbalance the potential for improved monitoring.[21]

Moreover, even in the absence of cross-shareholdings that entrench managers, concentration is a two-edged sword: it can provide better incentives for managers to minimize costs, but it also provides stronger incentives and opportunities for the shareholders in control to exploit the shareholders who are not. It is perhaps particularly for the latter reason that the empirical evidence for U.S. firms fails to confirm clearly that concentrated shareholdings are associated with improved corporate performance when they exceed about 5 percent of a firm's stock.[22]

Finally, an important reason for the success of the investor-owned corporation with dispersed shareholdings may well be that, whatever the agency costs of delegated management that are induced by current patterns of shareholdings, the costs that would be incurred in obtaining capital through market contracting are avoided in significant part simply by making the investors the nominal owners of the firm even if, as owners, they are not capable of exercising effective control over their managers. The advantage to the investors in a widely held business corporation from being owners, rather than simply dealing with the firm through market contracting as mere lenders, may be in large part just that their ownership assures them that the firm's management is not serving some other class of owners with interests contrary to that of the investors. Nevertheless, as suggested in Chapter 3, this is in fact meaningful protection whose value plausibly outweighs the costs of managerial opportunism that result from weak owner control.[23] Managers not subject to meaningful shareholder control may fail to minimize costs but, as long as legal or practical constraints effectively keep the managers from misappropriating any substantial fraction of a corporation's net earnings, the managers also lack incentives to exploit the shareholders that are as strong as the incentives an owner has to exploit a lender. This suggests that a key role in keeping the agency costs of dispersed shareholdings to a reasonable level is played by the various institutions—public and private, formal and informal—that have arisen in the United States to enforce the fiduciary duties of managers toward their shareholders. These include, for example, rigorous accounting standards, extensive mandated disclosure, prohibitions on insider trading, procedural rules facilitating shareholder litigation, and a well-developed financial press. The weakness or absence of some of these institutions in other countries, it has been plausibly argued, is in substantial part responsible for the lack of extensive public shareholdings in those countries.[24]

Indeed, as a means of focusing more clearly on the importance of direct owner control of managers in limiting agency costs, it is instructive to ask not only how much agency costs would be reduced by more effective shareholder control—which is the principal focus of much of the rapidly growing literature on corporate governance—but also, conversely, how much higher those agency costs would be if shareholders were formally deprived of any control whatever. More precisely, suppose that the shares of stock in a large publicly traded investor-owned firm, such as General Electric or General Motors, were stripped of voting rights, both in elections to the board of directors and in other corporate decisions. The board of directors, rather than being elected by the shareholders, would then be made formally self-appointing (that is, the directors would simply vote among themselves to choose their successors). Shareholders would continue to receive dividends as and when declared by the board, and shares would continue to trade and be quoted on exchanges. The directors would still be charged, as they are now, with a fiduciary duty to manage the firm on behalf of the shareholders, and that duty would still be supported by the current array of formal and informal sanctions. The only operative difference from present arrangements would be that a proxy fight or a hostile takeover via share acquisition would not be possible, because all shares would be nonvoting.

The result would be a firm that is formally nonprofit. The firm's shareholders would be the beneficiaries of the firm, but not its owners: they would have the formal right to residual earnings, but not to control. Although it may seem strange to think that a business corporation might be organized as a nonprofit firm, there is nothing illogical or contradictory in the concept. The defining feature of a nonprofit organization is not that it is barred from making a profit, but rather that it is barred from distributing that profit to controlling persons. And if the shareholders of the firm have no votes, they are not controlling persons. Rather, they are merely beneficiaries for whom the firm is held and managed in trust by its directors and officers.

Would the behavior of General Motors or General Electric (to take two firms with markedly different performance records), or of most other publicly held business corporations, have been significantly different over recent decades if they had been organized as nonprofit corporations along the lines just described? Without direct experience with such firms, it is impossible to say definitively.[25] Of course, the absence of firms that are beneficially but not formally owned by their investors is presumably evidence that formal shareholder control is a source of efficiency. It may, however, only be evidence, not that shareholder voting is critical to the ascendancy of the modern business corporation as a form of organization, but simply that there are at least potentially *some* benefits to formal shareholder control, while the costs of giving control to the shareholders are modest—something that cannot be said about the costs of giving control to certain other groups of patrons. The experience with various other ownership forms that is recounted in the following chapters suggests that this latter interpretation is not entirely implausible.

Collective Decision Making

Investor-owned firms have the important advantage that their owners generally share a single well-defined objective: to maximize the net present value of the firm's earnings. The costs of collective decision making are thus relatively low for investor-owned firms. This is not to say that there is no room for conflict among a firm's owners. For example, differences in tax status, risk preference, or liquidity may lead investors to differ about the most appropriate financial policy for the firm. To a substantial degree, however, conflicts among investors on such matters can be eliminated by having them sort themselves among firms that have adopted different policies.[26] Whatever differences that remain are likely to be modest in comparison with those that divide other classes of a firm's patrons, such as its employees or customers.

More serious conflicts can arise among a firm's investor-owners where some but not all of them also have another transactional relationship with the firm—for example, as suppliers, salaried officers, customers, or holders of debt securities—and seek to use their voting power as shareholders to advance their interests in these other transactions. Indeed, much of corporate law is concerned with managing such conflicts. (Most of the rest of corporate law is concerned with constraining managerial opportunism vis-à-vis the firm's owners—that is, with the basic agency problem.) But here, too, the existence of a reasonably obvious, simple, and even quantifiable common objective for a firm's investors as investors promotes efficiency by providing a relatively clear standard to employ in constructing legally imposed fiduciary obligations to limit self-dealing by powerful subgroups of shareholders. (The existence of such a simple and quantifiable objective also reduces the agency costs incurred by a firm's shareholders as a whole in policing the firm's management, both by making it easier for them to judge managerial performance and by increasing the effectiveness of indirect—that is, nonvoting—devices for controlling managers such as professionalism, peer pressure, and shareholders' derivative suits.)

It is important to recognize that the very high homogeneity of interest among the owners of a business corporation is neither a necessity nor an accident, but instead the product of design. Although companies often issue several classes of securities to investors of capital, including common stock, preferred stock, and bonds, it is rare for these different classes of investors to share ownership of the firm and therefore to rely on voting mechanisms to resolve conflicts of interest among them. Rather, voting control of the firm is typically placed in the hands of only one of these classes of securities, and that class of voting securities, by its terms, provides that all of its holders will be affected in the same way by any decision made by the firm. The interests of other classes of securityholders are protected primarily by contract and by legally imposed fiduciary duties, not by participation in control.[27]

There are, to be sure, exceptions—situations in which holders of different classes of securities have shared voting control over a company. But experience with these exceptions underlines the problems of shared control. A prominent recent example is offered by companies that have issued "targeted stock," which is a class of common stock whose payouts—dividends and liquidation proceeds—are tied to the performance of a particular subset of the corporation's activities. General Motors was the first prominent firm to make use of the device when, in 1984, it issued a special class of common stock, "Class E" stock, in connection with its acquisition of Electronic Data Systems—and then the following year issued another special class, "Class H," in its acquisition of Hughes Aircraft. In the succeeding decade, several other publicly traded companies also issued targeted stock.[28]

USX (the former United States Steel) offers a typical example of the structure of targeted stock. In 1991, USX divided its common stock into two different classes, a "steel stock" and an "oil stock," tied respectively to the company's two major lines of business, steel and oil. The USX board of directors was authorized to pay a different rate of dividends on the two different classes of stock, and the company announced its intention to base dividends on the steel stock and the oil stock primarily on the earnings and cash flow of its steel and oil businesses, respectively. Earnings and assets for these two lines of business are accounted for separately, but they remain part of the same single corporate entity, and the two classes of stock vote together in electing the corporation's single board of directors. The relative voting power of the different classes of stock is subject to periodic revision to reflect the current relative market prices of the stocks; initially, the oil stock held a clear predominance in voting power.[29]

Proponents of targeted stock have argued that it permits market analysts to evaluate a company's securities more accurately by allowing them to focus on a narrower range of activities when assessing a given issue of stock, and that this in turn leads to higher overall stock prices. Although this might also be accomplished by creating separately incorporated subsidiaries, targeted stock avoids tax costs associated with the latter strategy and also purportedly reduces borrowing costs by pooling all of the company's assets as security for all of its debt, in contrast to the partitioning of security that would occur with separate incorporation.

Yet targeted stock also creates a substantial conflict of interest among the holders of the different classes of the company's common stock. For example, although USX has issued its stock under terms that place broad limits on the corporation's ability to divert assets from its oil business to its steel business and vice versa, and has also constrained its ability to pay out earnings on one of these businesses as dividends on the stock associated with the other, the board nevertheless retains substantial discretion to divert retained earnings from one line of business to another, thus increasing both the financial returns and the voting power of one class of stockholders at the expense of the other. In addition, the corporation can divert value from one class of securities to the other by having one of the underlying businesses incur debt for which the assets of the other business will serve as security.

This conflict of interest has apparently been an important reason why, although the targeted stock concept has been actively promoted by prominent investment bankers, it has not been widely embraced. Only a handful of corporate boards have adopted plans to issue targeted stock, and several of these have been forced to withdraw in the face of shareholder resistance.[30] Even USX, though successful in issuing targeted stock, was subsequently confronted with a proposal by one of its largest institutional shareholders to force the company to appoint an independent director to mediate conflicts of interest between holders of the two classes of common stock.[31]

A Declining Cost of Market Contracting for Capital?

The hostile takeovers and management buyouts that were so conspicuous in the United States in the 1980s were typically financed in large part by debt, with the consequence that they resulted—at least for an interim period—in a marked increase in the target firm's debt-equity ratio. Some observers at the time thought that those high debt levels might become a permanent feature of the capital structure of large firms in mature industries,[32] though more recent experience throws doubt on this.[33] Yet, whether temporary or permanent, these new capital structures brought with them the costs of market contracting for capital described earlier: the incentive for the stockholders to exploit the bondholders, the substantial risk that results from borrowing long term at fixed interest rates, and the potential transaction costs of bankruptcy.

The very large premiums paid in corporate takeovers and leveraged buyouts suggest that the benefits of the new highly leveraged ownership structures exceed their costs—or at least that the financial markets believe they do. But, if so, why was this not true twenty or forty years earlier? A potential explanation is that innovations in the financial markets have led to a substantial reduction in the cost of obtaining a large fraction of a corporation's capital through market contracting. Principal among these innovations has been the high-yield "junk" bond. Several elements seem to be involved. One is perhaps simply a demonstration effect: it has been shown, contrary to the prior conventional wisdom, that the default risks accompanying low-grade corporate bonds are sufficiently low to justify manageable interest rates.[34] Another may be that investment banking firms specializing in such debt staked their reputations on the quality of their offerings and therefore, to protect those reputations, assumed an active role in monitoring the behavior of the firms whose debt they marketed.[35]

The resulting reduction in the cost of borrowed capital, by facilitating corporate control transactions and restructurings, has presumably increased the efficiency of large investor-owned business corporations. But the same development renders feasible the ownership of large firms by classes of patrons other than investors. In particular, by permitting most of a firm's invested capital to be obtained on the market through debt, it has helped to make employee ownership financially feasible even for large industrial firms. This is among the reasons why employee ownership is of special interest today. We turn to it in the next two chapters.

5

The Benefits and Costs of Employee Ownership

Despite the widespread attention given to employee ownership, it is still poorly understood. We begin our analysis with a survey of the pattern of employee ownership actually observed in modern economies. Then, with this pattern as a guide, we examine systematically the form's strengths and weaknesses. The conclusions that emerge, pointing to governance problems as the critical factor, are sharply at odds with most preceding analyses.

The Distribution of Employee-Owned Firms

The United States

Employee-owned firms are rare in the industrial sector of the American economy. If we exclude companies that have adopted employee stock ownership plans in recent years (to which we shall return shortly), employee-owned manufacturing firms have seldom proved viable over the long run. Among contemporary industries, the unique exception is plywood manufacturing, in which worker cooperatives in the Pacific Northwest have maintained substantial market share since the first cooperative was formed in the 1920s.[1] As of 1984 there were fourteen such firms, each with between 80 and 350 members, most of which had been in business for more than twenty years. Together they accounted for more than 10 percent of all plywood produced.[2] In the nineteenth century, there were a few hundred worker cooperatives—whose members were generally skilled artisans—in other industries such as barrel making, shoe manufacturing, and shingle weaving. But those firms largely disappeared early in the twentieth century.[3]

In sharp contrast, employee-owned firms are common in the service sector. In particular, employee ownership has long been the prevailing mode of organization in the service professions, including law, accounting, investment banking, management consulting, advertising, architecture, engineering, and medicine. Although discussions of employee ownership usually focus on industrial firms and rarely make reference to the partnerships and professional corporations common in the service professions, the latter are among the world's purest examples of employee ownership. Moreover, the service professions are virtually the only industries that are dominated by employee-owned firms. Yet this dominance may be nearing its end. In advertising, investment banking, and primary medical care, for example, investor-owned firms have recently come to occupy large shares of the market.

Employee-owned service firms also appear occasionally where the employees involved are not professionals. For example, taxicab companies in large cities are quite frequently employee-owned,[4] and there has long been a group of employee-owned refuse collection companies in the San Francisco Bay Area.[5]

Employee Ownership Abroad

The pattern of employee ownership observed in the United States is roughly duplicated in other market economies: the types of industries in which employee-owned firms are found and the structures those firms assume are remarkably similar everywhere.[6]

Italy and France are the two Western European countries generally regarded as having the largest numbers of successful worker cooperatives.[7] Available estimates (which, however, are dated and apparently do not include partnerships of service professionals such as lawyers) indicate that as of 1983 there were in France several hundred firms organized as worker cooperatives employing a total of roughly 40,000 persons, of whom 61 percent were members;[8] in Italy, as of 1980, there were several thousand worker cooperatives employing a total of roughly 215,000 persons.[9] The average size of these firms is small (in each country around fifty-five workers) and the median size is much smaller still—perhaps no more than a dozen workers.[10] In France roughly half of these cooperatives, in terms of both numbers and aggregate income, are construction companies, and the fraction represented by construction firms is similarly high in Italy.[11] Many of the cooperatives that are not construction companies are firms of artisans, such as printers or locksmiths.[12] In both countries, there are apparently only a handful of manufacturing firms of substantial size organized as worker cooperatives.[13] In Italy, many of the manufacturing firms that are cooperatives were converted from failing investor-owned firms.[14]

The most prominent example of successful industrial worker cooperatives in a market economy is found not in France or Italy but, rather, in the well-established group of closely affiliated worker cooperatives in Mondragon, Spain. The Mondragon group has received considerable attention in recent years, and its success is frequently cited by advocates of employee ownership as the best evidence that this form of organization offers a promising alternative to investor ownership.[15] The performance of the group has indeed been impressive. From a single small cooperative established in 1956, the Mondragon system has grown rapidly to comprise roughly one hundred affiliated firms with a total of approximately 20,000 employee-members.[16] These firms produce a broad range of goods, including home appliances, furniture, heavy machine tools, and agricultural products. They deserve special attention and will be examined more closely in Chapter 6.

Throughout the world, transportation companies are among the types of firms most often organized as worker cooperatives—and it is generally the drivers who are the owners. In Sweden, for example, all taxicab services and 50 percent of truck transport services are provided by worker cooperatives.[17] This is in contrast to the Swedish manufacturing sector, where worker cooperatives account for only 1 percent of all firms and presumably a much smaller percentage of output.[18] Similarly, in Israel, drivers' cooperatives provide nearly all bus transportation[19] and 50 percent of truck transport,[20] while at the same time—and despite strong cultural and institutional support of cooperativism—worker cooperatives have never become well established in manufacturing. In fact, as of 1972 employment in the Israeli bus and truck transportation cooperatives alone was more than four times that in all manufacturing cooperatives combined.[21] More recently, this widespread pattern of driver-owned transportation cooperatives has been extended to airlines: in 1994, the 7,000 pilots of United Air Lines, the world's largest airline company, finally succeeded in their seven-year effort to acquire a majority of the company's stock. Unlike the typical transportation cooperative, however, United is not purely a driver-owned company; to succeed in their acquisition, United's pilots were ultimately led to bring members of the airline's machinists' union into the transaction as well, extending a share in ownership to 54,000 of the firm's 76,000 employees[22]—an important fact that we shall say more about in Chapter 6.

Partial Employee Ownership

The firms just described are, in general, fully employee-owned in the sense that the firm's employees, or some subset of them, share among themselves full rights to control the firm and to appropriate its net earnings. In addition to these instances of full employee ownership, there are many firms that are organized so that employees have a *partial* share in control or earnings. For example, under German co-determination, employees elect half of a corporation's (supervisory) board of directors and have, at least formally, an important but partial share in control. Yet since they remain salaried employees, they do not participate directly in net earnings. Conversely, in most American firms with employee stock ownership plans (ESOPs), employees (through the ESOP) have a claim on some or even all of the firm's residual earnings and assets, yet control over the firm generally remains in other hands. In order to keep the inquiry sharply focused, this chapter will concentrate principally on firms that are fully owned by their employees. We will explore various partial forms of employee participation (including codetermination and ESOPs) in Chapter 6. As that chapter illustrates, an understanding of the strengths and weaknesses of full employee ownership also provides useful perspective on the efficiency of partial forms of employee participation, and vice versa.

The Costs of Market Contracting

A survey of the costs of hiring labor on the market leads to two broad conclusions. First, those costs can be substantial and provide an important incentive for employee ownership. Second, paradoxically, the magnitude of those costs correlates quite poorly with the pattern of employee ownership that we observe, which strongly suggests that they are not decisive in determining the overall efficacy of employee ownership.

Asymmetric Information

Because of the difficulty of monitoring individual employees, a degree of moral hazard necessarily infects market contracting for all but the simplest types of labor. One of the strong attractions of employee ownership is the prospect of mitigating this problem and hence improving the productivity of the firm. To be sure, if there are many employees, each individual employee bears only a small fraction of the costs of her own shirking even with employee ownership. But employee ownership also gives each employee an incentive to monitor her fellow employees and to apply pressure on them not to shirk, an incentive largely lacking in an investor-owned firm.

This logic has led many to argue—most conspicuously Alchian and Demsetz, in a well-known article[23]—that employee-owned firms are particularly likely to arise when monitoring employees is unusually difficult. Alchian and Demsetz, for example, say that "[w]hile it is relatively easy to manage or direct the loading of trucks by a team of dock workers where input activity is so highly related in an obvious way to output, it is more difficult to manage and direct a lawyer in the preparation and presentation of a case."[24] This explains, they claim, why the partnership form is so common among lawyers and other groups of individuals with artistic or professional skills.[25]

In fact, however, Alchian and Demsetz are mistaken about the difficulty of monitoring service professionals, and, more generally, the existing pattern of employee ownership is just the reverse of what one would expect if it were primarily a response to the difficulty of monitoring employees. In the service professions, where employee ownership is the norm, the productivity of individual employees can be, and generally is, monitored remarkably closely, because the quantity and quality of each individual's inputs and outputs can be observed with relative ease. Lawyers in corporate law firms, for example, commonly document the use of their time in intervals of six or ten minutes, indicating whether and to which client the time can be billed and the precise nature of the work done for the client in that interval.[26] Such records yield a close measure of the kind and quantity of work produced by an individual lawyer over the year and of the client revenue that this work has produced for the firm. Moreover, it is relatively easy to assess the quality of a lawyer's work, in part because the work product frequently consists of written documents produced by that lawyer alone.

In contrast, investor ownership is the dominant mode of organization in most firms in which employees commonly work in large teams or have extensive supervisory or managerial tasks—settings in which an individual's productivity is extremely difficult to measure. Thus while it is relatively easy, and in fact a common practice, to compute with some accuracy the marginal contribution to a law firm's net earnings that a given individual lawyer makes each year, it is inconceivable to think of undertaking such a calculation for an assistant vice president, or even a shop foreman, at General Motors.

This is not to say that monitoring can be done perfectly in law firms or in other firms of service professionals. Nor is it to deny that employee ownership improves productivity in such firms by helping to cope with monitoring problems. In fact, improved incentives for productivity are probably a significant reason why employee ownership is so common among these firms (although efforts to establish an empirical correlation between worker ownership and improved productivity have so far offered ambiguous results).[27] The point is simply that there must be other factors that are much more important in determining the distribution of employee ownership, since the types of firms in which employee ownership is most common seem to be firms in which employee monitoring is relatively easy.

Lock-In

Firms rarely occupy a position of monopsony in the labor market. Consequently, simple market power does not provide an important motivation for the formation of employee-owned firms. As we observed in Chapter 2, however, for many employees there may be a substantial problem of ex post market power, or lock-in. After working for a given firm for a number of years, an employee's skills may become specialized to that firm and he may be firmly rooted in the local community. One might expect employee ownership to arise where this type of lock-in is particularly severe.

Yet the distribution of employee-owned firms appears to correlate poorly with the degree of employee lock-in. Although clear data are lacking, it seems a reasonable inference that, in large industrial and service firms, middle- and upper-level managers (and perhaps blue-collar employees as well) often become specialized to their current employer over time and are therefore considerably more productive in that firm than they would be in any alternative employment.[28] These firms also accumulate information about the productivity of their employees that is unavailable to other prospective employers, and this should also reduce the wages the employees can obtain elsewhere. Nevertheless, such firms are rarely employee-owned. Rather, in the types of firms that are employee-owned, the employees appear unusually mobile. This is evidently true for the blue-collar employees who most commonly form worker cooperatives, such as taxicab drivers,[29] refuse collectors, and the semi-skilled laborers in the plywood cooperatives. And it is arguably true as well for service professionals such as lawyers and accountants.

To be sure, a professional such as a lawyer develops a special familiarity with her firm's personnel, procedures, and clients that is considerably more valuable within that firm than in another firm. Yet in part because service professionals typically provide services directly to their firm's clients rather than providing intermediate services to the firm itself, such professionals have mobility advantages that other types of employees lack: their skills are generally highly transferable; they have the option—largely unavailable to other types of skilled individuals—not only of taking a position with another established firm but also of forming a new firm of their own; and they can often take some of their clients with them when they leave their current employer.[30]

The types of employees who are found in employee-owned firms thus appear, if anything, to be less subject to lock-in than are employees in typical investor-owned firms. Again, this is not to say that lock-in does not provide an important incentive for employee ownership. But there must be other considerations that are more important in determining where employee ownership is most viable.

Strategic Bargaining Behavior

With investor ownership, management often has information that labor lacks about the firm's future prospects, including profitability, employment needs, and plant closings or relocations. Similarly, employees have knowledge that management lacks concerning the employees' own opportunities and preferences, including the minimum wages they would find acceptable, the ease with which they can increase their productivity, and changes in workplace organization that will improve productivity but require fewer employees or greater employee effort. The resulting asymmetries in information provide the incentive for both labor and management to adopt bargaining strategies, such as strikes and lockouts, that significantly raise the transaction costs of reaching agreement.[31] One of the strong advantages of employee ownership is its potential to reduce or eliminate these costs.

In the types of firms in which employee ownership is common, however, the potential asymmetry of information between management and employees seems comparatively low. Consider, for example, partnerships of professionals such as law firms. The smallness of such firms and the shallowness of the hierarchy between management and the firm's professionals (indeed, the senior professionals in these firms *are* the firm's management) suggest that the professionals in these firms, even if they were not partners, would among themselves have most of the information available to management and vice versa. It is in large firms with substantial hierarchy and division of labor between management and the rest of the labor force that information asymmetries are likely to be most pronounced. But such firms are rarely employee-owned.

Communication of Employee Preferences

We also observed in Chapter 2 that, because employees in investor-owned firms may have information concerning their preferences that they cannot credibly communicate to management, investor-owned firms may be handicapped relative to employee-owned firms in fashioning the most efficient package of financial compensation and working conditions for their employees. Yet this advantage also fails to explain the existing distribution of employee ownership since, as just noted, employee ownership tends to appear in precisely those settings in which management is likely to have relatively little difficulty understanding employees' preferences.

Responsiveness to Average versus Marginal Employee Preferences

There are many situations in which the preferences of the marginal employee are likely to be different from those of the average employee. Workplace safety is an example considered in Chapter 2. Job security is another, and for similar reasons: the marginal employee may well be a young person who does not have a family and who is easily retrainable, and therefore is less averse to the possibility of layoff than an older employee might be. The organization of work, workplace aesthetics, and employee benefits are also areas in which the interests of the marginal and the average employee may diverge. Thus employee ownership, which should tend to emphasize the preferences of the average employee, may often be more efficient in aggregating employees' preferences than is the hiring of employees through market contracting, which emphasizes the preferences of the marginal employee.

The actual importance of this problem in investor-owned firms is difficult to assess. Collective bargaining presumably mitigates its effects wherever there are unions. In any event, it does not seem important in explaining the distribution of employee-owned firms. As will be discussed at much greater length below, ownership in employee-owned firms is generally shared only among employees who have unusually homogeneous interests, which means that the difference between marginal and average preferences among the employee-owners is unusually small.

Alienation

Finally, it is a familiar argument that market contracting for labor leads to worker alienation. And indeed labor contracting is prototypically the type of setting in which, if anywhere, one would expect to find the problems described under this heading in Chapter 2.

Once again, however, the distribution of employee ownership is arguably the reverse of what one would expect if problems of worker alienation were important. Employee-owned firms tend to arise in industries in which most firms, whether capitalist or employee-owned, are small and have relatively homogeneous work forces with little hierarchy, which is precisely the setting in which one would expect relatively little worker alienation. Moreover, concern about worker alienation generally focuses on blue-collar employees, while it is service professionals that are most commonly employee-owners. (To be sure, the focus on blue-collar workers may simply reflect the strong concern with social class in much of the relevant literature. Whether in fact blue-collar employees resent selling their services through market relationships more or less than do professionals is not obvious a priori.)

Summary

When compared with contracting for labor on the market, employee ownership holds the promise of significant efficiency advantages, including improved employee productivity, avoidance of opportunism associated with employee lock-in, less strategic behavior in bargaining, better communication of employee preferences, and reduction in worker alienation. These advantages presumably explain the success of employee ownership in those industries where it is commonly found. But the magnitude of the potential efficiency gains from these sources correlates poorly with the actual pattern of employee ownership. In general, these potential gains seem greatest in large-scale hierarchical firms, which are typically investor-owned, and comparatively much more modest in the small-scale professional service firms where employee ownership is most common. We must look elsewhere for an explanation of the existing distribution of employee-owned enterprise.

Raising Capital

It is conventional wisdom that employee ownership is poorly suited to capital-intensive industries. While there is some truth in this view, the importance of capital intensity is often exaggerated.

If an employee-owned firm needs capital primarily to purchase assets that are not firm-specific, the firm can usually borrow the capital on reasonable terms. The resulting leverage may impose substantial risk on the employee-owners. But employees are often prepared to bear a relatively large amount of risk. In fact, employee-owned firms are surprisingly common in relatively capital-intensive industries that employ fungible assets. Transportation companies, much of whose capital is invested in vehicles that are easily resold, are among the types of firms in which employee ownership most commonly appears. Investment banking also requires substantial capital per employee, but again, the firms' assets are highly fungible.

The family farms that dominate American agriculture provide yet another example. They are employee-owned firms owned by a single individual or family. And they are often quite capital intensive. But, because the land and equipment are not firm-specific and thus provide good security, individual farmers can borrow extensively to obtain the capital necessary to permit them to be owners.

In contrast, if capital is needed to purchase assets that are firm-specific, the costs of contracting for capital on the market can be heavy, as described in Chapter 4. Where the amount of firm-specific capital per employee is modest, or where the employees are prosperous, these costs can be avoided by having the employees themselves supply the capital. For example, under the ESOP approach to employee ownership, the employees invest their pension savings in their employer's stock. Then both labor and capital are provided by owners, avoiding the costs of market contracting for each factor. But this solution creates two problems of its own.

The first and most familiar problem is that, when employees invest any significant portion of their wealth in the firm that employs them, they increase significantly the amount of risk that they bear. They not only reduce the diversification of their investment portfolio, but also reduce the diversification between their investment portfolio and their source of earned income—that is, their human capital. If the firm goes bankrupt, they lose not only their jobs but their savings as well.

The second problem is that, when the firm's owners are suppliers of capital as well as labor, the opportunities for divergence of interest among them is likely to increase. Generally some employees—often the older employees—will have proportionately more capital invested than others, with the result that the balance between individuals' interests as investors and as employees will vary. This imbalance threatens, in turn, to increase the costs of collective decision making.

In short, if an employee-owned firm requires large amounts of firm-specific capital per employee, the firm may incur substantial costs whether the capital is borrowed or supplied by the employees themselves. This presumably helps explain why employee ownership seldom appears without subsidy in the industrial sector. For those industries, ownership by the lenders of capital has the strong advantages described in Chapter 4.[32]

This point should not be overstated. As we observed before, the success of leveraged buyouts with high debt-equity ratios suggests that today sufficient debt can often be obtained to cover a large fraction of a firm's capital needs. The proliferation of ESOPs in the manufacturing sector indicates that a firm's employees can themselves provide substantial equity capital without crippling costs. The employee-owned firms at Mondragon have not had difficulty obtaining capital even though they are in moderately capital-intensive industries; indeed, by the early 1990s the firms in that group, together with their affiliated bank, had become net lenders.[33] Finally, other types of non-investor-owned firms have had significant success in capital-intensive industries. Consequently there is good reason to believe that capital accumulation is not an insuperable obstacle to employee ownership in most industries.

Conversely, although a relatively low level of firm-specific capital per employee is helpful in making employee ownership viable, it is apparently not sufficient. There are many industries in the service sector that involve low amounts of firm-specific capital but in which employee ownership has remained rare, such as hotel and restaurant services, retailing, and (at least in the United States) the construction trades.

It seems, then, that the costs of obtaining capital cannot by themselves explain prevailing patterns of employee ownership either within or without the industrial sector.[34]

Costs of Ownership

The existing distribution of employee-owned firms clearly cannot be explained just in terms of the costs of market contracting. More particularly, employee-owned firms do not, as one might at first suppose, simply arise where the costs of hiring labor on the market are unusually high and the costs of hiring capital are low. For an explanation we must turn to the costs of ownership.

Agency Costs of Delegation to Management

The problem of the separation of ownership and control—that is, the agency cost of policing management—is potentially much less acute in employee-owned firms than it is in investor-owned firms. Investors of capital are often widely dispersed, have no sources of information about the firm beyond publications, and hold the firm's securities as only one of a number of investments. As a result they are in a poor position to police the firm's management. In contrast, employees know a great deal about the firm simply as a by-product of their employment and are in a good position to learn more; they have a large personal stake in the fortunes of the firm, since most of their income comes from it; and they can be easily assembled for collective action. They have both the opportunity and the incentive to acquire information about the effectiveness of management—or to appoint and hold accountable representatives who will do this for them—and then to act collectively to hold management accountable to their will.

To be sure, investor-owned firms have the benefit of the market for corporate control as an aid in policing management. Yet it is not necessary to forgo the benefits of this market when a firm is employee-owned. The employees can sell the firm to outside investors at any point they wish.[35] In fact, such transactions have occurred frequently (for example, among plywood cooperatives,[36] advertising firms, and investment banking firms).

It follows that one might expect to find employee ownership in those circumstances where investors would be in a particularly poor position to monitor the firm's management. Yet successful employee-owned firms are in most cases sufficiently small that, if investor-owned, they would be closely held firms. They would not experience a significant separation of ownership and control, nor the agency costs associated with such a separation.[37] The potentially high agency costs of investor ownership therefore fail to explain why employee ownership appears where it does.

Risk Bearing

Poor risk sharing is a commonly cited disadvantage of employee ownership. Workers, lacking the ability to diversify risk by taking jobs in a number of different firms simultaneously, are in a worse position than investors to bear the risks of fluctuating residual earnings.

It would be reasonable to conclude from this that risk bearing is a major obstacle to employee ownership in all forms of enterprise, and particularly in capital-intensive enterprise where the risks borne by employee-owners are amplified. Interestingly, however, the observed distribution of employee ownership does not provide much support for this conclusion. The plywood industry is both moderately capital intensive and relatively volatile.[38] Investment banking is highly capital intensive and highly volatile. And farming is often highly capital intensive, as already noted, and also highly volatile. Indeed, the inability of investor-owned firms to gain an appreciable market share in most important crops is dramatic evidence of the relative unimportance of risk bearing in assignments of ownership: farms continue to be owned overwhelmingly by the individuals who work them, despite the large amounts of risk those individuals must consequently bear. Clearly there is a substantial segment of the working population that is quite willing to bear substantial risk in return for other efficiencies.

Moreover, we should not underestimate the amount of risk that employees bear even in investor-owned firms. It would be efficient, if an enterprise were viewed simply in terms of risk bearing, for the investor-owners of an industrial firm to bear the overwhelming share of the risk of the enterprise and to insure employees against the vagaries of the market by providing substantial job security. Yet in the United States, industrial workers have traditionally been hired as employees at will who can be laid off on a day's notice whenever the firm's fortunes take a turn for the worse—and this has been true even in unionized firms.[39] There are presumably several explanations for this seeming anomaly, including the incentives created by the prevailing system of collective bargaining,[40] the reduction in productivity that might accompany greater job security,[41] and the limitation on employees' prospective downside losses resulting from unemployment insurance, social welfare programs, and the prospect of reemployment. But whatever the reason, job security in many industries has traditionally been very low, with the result that a shift to employee-owned enterprise might not cause employees to bear substantially more risk than they do already.

In short, there is good reason to believe that risk bearing is not in itself a major obstacle to employee ownership, and that it plays at best a modest role in explaining the distribution of employee ownership that we observe.

Collective Decision Making

This leaves us to assess the third and final principal cost of ownership, the cost of collective decision making. In fact, this factor seems to play a surprisingly strong role in determining where employee ownership is viable. The next chapter is devoted in large part to exploring this issue. First, however, we must turn to several other considerations that, though not included among the basic costs of contracting and of ownership surveyed in Chapters 2 and 3, are often said to present major obstacles to the success of employee-owned enterprise.

The Horizon Problem

It has been argued that employee-owned firms have too little incentive to invest in projects that will pay off only over long periods of time (the "horizon problem").[42] The source of the problem, it is said, is the employees' lack of transferable residual claims. Because employee-owners freely sell their ownership rights on the capital market, they lack the ability that investor-owners have to realize, in the present, the value of the future returns that their investments will bring.

There may well be a horizon problem in firms, such as those formed in Yugoslavia during the decades of communist rule, in which employees have control but only a limited right to appropriate net earnings and assets—that is, in which firms are employee-managed but not employee-owned. In free enterprise economies, however, most employee-owned firms with any significant amount of invested capital are organized to provide their employees with residual claims that are transferable. In some firms these claims are transferable at all times and in others they are transferable only when the employee leaves the firm. For example, shares in the plywood cooperatives can be freely sold to new employees by departing ones, subject only to a right of first refusal by the firm.[43]

Even if employees could never withdraw capital from the firm, they should have a relatively long time horizon. The median employee's expected tenure with a firm may well be as long as fifteen or twenty years, or even longer if pension payoff periods are included.[44] And a fifteen-year investment horizon is quite long by contemporary industrial standards.

There is thus little reason to believe that the horizon problem has been a major obstacle to employee ownership.

Reversion to Investor Ownership

Successful employee-owned firms frequently convert (or, as advocates of employee ownership say, "degenerate") to investor ownership. For example, there has been gradual attrition from the ranks of the U.S. plywood cooperatives as their members have sold the firms to investors. Similarly, failing investor-owned firms that were bought out by their employees and subsequently succeeded (rather than going bankrupt) have sometimes reverted to investor ownership.[45] And in some of the service professions, such as advertising and investment banking, many firms formerly organized as partnerships have been acquired by outside investors in recent years. Noting this pattern, some scholars have argued that a tendency to convert to investor ownership is an inherent characteristic of employee-owned firms, and that this is an important explanation for the minuscule market share that employee-owned firms occupy in the industrial sector.[46] At least two different mechanisms have been offered to explain this supposed tendency.

A Tendency toward Hired Labor

First, it has been argued that when a successful employee-owned firm takes on additional employees, it has a strong incentive to hire them on a salaried basis rather than to make them owners. For if the firm's net earnings per employee are higher than the market wage rate—which is what "successful" means in this analysis—the existing employee-owners will find it profitable to take on new workers only as mere salaried employees who receive the market wage rate rather than as co-owners who have a pro rata share in the firm's profits. Consequently, over time the ratio of employee-owners to hired employees will steadily decline until ownership is concentrated in the hands of a small number of individuals and the enterprise has essentially assumed the character of an investor-owned firm.[47]

The soundness of this argument, however, depends on the assumption that the productivity of a worker in the worker-owned firm is the same whether she is hired as a salaried employee or made an owner. But in that case worker ownership has no efficiency advantage over investor ownership, and there is no reason why the workers should own the firm. The success of the hypothetical employee-owned firm in this analysis must be due, not to the fact that it is employee-owned, but rather to some other factor such as market power, accumulated reputational goodwill, or possession of an important patent. The firm would then be just as successful, or perhaps even more so, if it were investor-owned, and a tendency to convert to investor ownership would be neither surprising nor inappropriate.

This case is in contrast to those in which the success of an employee-owned firm *is* due to employee ownership, perhaps because the employees are more productive when they are also owners, or because they derive other tangible or intangible rewards from ownership and are hence willing to work for lower cash compensation. In that case, it should be more profitable for the existing members of the firm to add new employees by giving them a share in ownership[48] than by taking them on only as salaried employees, and there should be no tendency toward investor ownership.

In some industries in which employee ownership is the dominant mode of organization, there has been no conspicuous tendency to substitute hired labor for employee-owners. Large law firms, for example, have for generations almost universally followed an up-or-out system whereby an employee must leave the firm if she has not been made a partner within a period of six to eight years. This practice ensures that all but the most junior lawyers in the firm will always be owners. Continued adherence to this system arguably reflects a recognition by all involved that employee ownership is the most efficient system of organization for these firms and that deviation from that system would in the long run be costly. To be sure, in recent years it has been increasingly common for law firms to create a class of hired senior attorneys termed "permanent associates" and in the process abandon strict adherence to the up-or-out system. But, as we shall discuss in the next chapter, this phenomenon seems best explained by considerations other than the theory of inevitable degeneration just described.

Capital Accumulation

The second mechanism alleged to cause successful employee-owned firms to convert to investor ownership is that, owing to the firms' very success, their value per employee becomes so large over time that younger employees cannot afford to purchase a share in the firm from older employees who are retiring. As a result the older employees have a strong incentive to sell their shares to outside investors, thus converting the firm to investor ownership.

The problem with arguments of this type is that they rarely make it clear precisely why the firm's net worth per employee has increased over time. There are, broadly speaking, two possibilities. On the one hand, net worth may have increased because the firm has retained and accumulated net earnings over the years. In that case, the firm should be able to distribute the accumulated retained earnings to the retiring employees (by repurchasing their shares) and replace them with debt, bringing net assets per employee down closer to the original level so that new young employees can afford to purchase shares in the firm.

On the other hand, net assets per employee could have increased because the firm has adopted new technology that requires more firm-specific capital per employee than the technology employed when the employees first acquired ownership, and the firm has used retained or forgone earnings over the years to acquire the required new technology. (Note that goodwill is among the common forms of firm-specific capital that a firm can accumulate over time.) The requisite amount of equity capital per employee may now be much higher than a new employee could or would contribute. Employee ownership is therefore less appropriate, and conversion to investor ownership may be efficient.

In short, financial success need not in itself make it more difficult for a new generation of employees to become owners of the firm than it was for previous generations of employees. If there have been no changes in the industry that make employee ownership less efficient, then it should be possible to rearrange the firm's financing—perhaps by increasing the firm's leverage—so that new employees can afford to purchase shares and the retiring generation of employees can realize the earnings accumulated during their tenure as owners.

Why Are There Conversions to Investor Ownership?

If, as just argued, there is no perverse mechanism that causes successful employee-owned firms to convert to investor ownership simply as a consequence of their very success, then why do conversions from employee ownership to investor ownership occur so frequently? The most likely explanation is simply that employee ownership is not an efficient mode of organization for the firms involved.

In some firms that convert from employee to investor ownership, employee ownership was probably an inefficient way to organize the firm from the start. For example, in some cases employee-owned firms are established out of miscalculation or excessive idealism; conversion to investor ownership is then simply a belated recognition of that fact. In other cases employee ownership, though in itself perhaps inefficient for the firm in the long run, is evidently adopted to facilitate an efficiency-enhancing one-time transaction that could not otherwise be arranged. A common situation of the latter type occurs in investor-owned firms that fall into severe financial difficulties. Selling such a firm in whole or in part to its employees has a variety of potential advantages. It offers a way for the employees, and especially their union, to accept the substantial concessions necessary for the firm to continue—such as layoffs, severe reductions in wages, and changes in work rules —without loss of face and without creating a precedent that will compromise the union's bargaining strategy vis-à-vis other more successful firms. It gives employees a benefit (the stock in the reorganized firm) of uncertain value to set off against their specific reductions in wages and benefits, making the net magnitude of the employees' loss less specifically concrete and hence easier to accept psychologically. It is a credible way for the investor-owners of the firm and their managers to signal credibly to the workers the management's view of the seriousness of the firm's financial difficulties and the consequent necessity for employee concessions, thus averting costly bargaining. Finally, it is a credible way to assure the employees that, if the firm survives and prospers, the fruits of the employees' concessions will not go disproportionately to the firm's current investor-owners.[49] There remains the option that, if the firm succeeds, the employees can ultimately sell it back into investor ownership. This transactional use of employee ownership arguably characterizes the recent employee stock acquisitions in the airline industry, including United Air Lines, as well as the prominent employee buyout of the Weirton Steel Company described in the next chapter.

Finally, there are situations in which employee ownership was once efficient, but has ceased to be so, perhaps because the character of the industry has changed. This is arguably the situation in investment banking, for example, in which the capital required per employee and, perhaps more important, the size and internal complexity of individual firms have increased in recent years to the point where, for most firms, investor ownership may now be the most efficient mode of organization.

Perverse Supply Response

The economics literature on employee ownership shows an almost obsessive fascination with a simple theoretical model, originally developed in the 1950s by Ward, portraying the behavioral incentives facing a worker cooperative.[50] This fascination owes much to the model's prediction of "perverse supply response": when worker cooperatives experience an increase in demand for their product or a decrease in their costs of production, they have an incentive to reduce both the amount of their output and the size of their work force; conversely, when the price at which the cooperatives can sell their product declines, or the costs of their nonlabor inputs rise, they have an incentive to add more workers and increase output. The model likewise predicts that worker cooperatives will be smaller than comparable investor-owned firms and will underemploy labor. The basic reason for this strange behavior is that the firms in the model maximize average profit per worker-member rather than total profit.

Despite the attention given to it, this model does little to explain the observed distribution of employee-owned enterprise. To begin with, the inefficient behavior predicted by the model depends on a variety of unrealistic assumptions—such as that the firm produces only a single product, that the number of hours worked per employee is fixed, that there can be no nonmember employees, and that new employee-owners will always be brought in on the same terms as their predecessors (without, in particular, having to pay anything to the existing members for the privilege of joining). Moreover, as has long been recognized, even if these restrictive assumptions are granted, entry by new cooperatives should ultimately lead to efficient levels of output and employment both for individual firms and for the industry as a whole. Presumably for these reasons, empirical work has failed to uncover clear evidence of the phenomena predicted by Ward's model.[51]

Legal Constraints

It is sometimes suggested that lack of a legal structure well adapted to employee ownership is heavily responsible for the general paucity of employee-owned enterprise in market economies. Yet in the United States, at least, it is hard to argue that the law has been a serious obstacle to the success of employee ownership.

There are no explicit legal prohibitions on employee ownership of enterprise in any industry. On the contrary, there is at least one business—the practice of law—in which employee ownership is explicitly required by law throughout the United States. The American Bar Association's Model Rules of Professional Conduct, like the Model Code of Professional Responsibility and the Canons of Professional Ethics that preceded them, explicitly proscribe any arrangement whereby a lawyer serves as an employee of a profit-seeking organization that sells legal services to the public if that organization is not wholly owned by lawyers who practice in it, as in the conventional law partnership or professional service corporation.[52] Because this provision of the Model Rules, or a close counterpart, has the force of law in virtually very state,[53] employee-owned firms are presently the only available form for organizing the practice of law.[54] Analogous legal restrictions forbade the formation of investor-owned, rather than doctor-owned, medical practice firms in most states before those laws were overridden by the federal Health Maintenance Organization Act of 1973.

More generally, existing organizational law—that is, corporation law and partnership law—is sufficiently flexible to permit the formation of nearly any type of worker cooperative. In some states the cooperative corporation statutes appear suitable for this purpose, and in theory these statutes provide the simplest and most direct approach.[55] In many jurisdictions, however, the business corporation statutes are more workable, owing largely to the rudimentary and sometimes narrowly constricting character of the cooperative statutes.[56] Using the business corporation statutes, to be sure, requires some manipulation to ensure that earnings are distributed according to work contributed. One can argue, therefore, that employee-owned firms have been disadvantaged vis-à-vis investor-owned firms in that statutes embodying a standard form have not been available for the former while they have been for the latter.

The new worker cooperative corporation statutes that have recently been enacted in some states are designed to provide the missing standard legal form. Those statutes do no more than this, however; even their promoters do not claim that they extend the range of available organizations beyond those that can be formed under the existing business corporation statutes. Nevertheless, such a standard form may offer significant advantages. It not only reduces the transaction costs of forming an employee-owned firm (for example, by making the form comprehensible to a broader range of attorneys), but also presumably gives the form a degree of visibility, recognizability, and legitimacy it might otherwise lack. A bank lending officer, for instance, might well feel more secure making a loan to a worker cooperative formed according to a standard pattern set forth in a special worker cooperative statute than to one formed under a business corporation statute by means of complex articles of incorporation, bylaws, and shareholder agreements.

That said, it is nevertheless highly unlikely that the inconvenience of the lack of a standard statutory form has in itself been an important obstacle to the development of employee-owned enterprise. The business corporation statutes generally serve as a standard form only for publicly held corporations, in any case; closely held business corporations, which represent the overwhelming majority of all firms, often require some special drafting. In addition, there have long been conspicuous examples of employee-owned corporations, such as the plywood cooperatives, that have been successful without the benefit of standard statutory forms and whose corporate charters and bylaws are available to serve as organizational models for other employee-owned firms. (Some of the plywood cooperatives are incorporated under cooperative corporation statutes and some under business corporation statutes.)[57] It would be surprising if the adoption of the new worker cooperative statutes were to increase significantly the popularity of employee ownership.

Moreover, tax law is probably more important than organizational law in determining which organizational forms prosper, and tax law has long been biased in favor of, rather than against, employee ownership. At least since 1931, net earnings distributed to members of a workers' cooperative have been able to escape (at least to a substantial degree) the corporate income tax that is levied on net earnings distributed to investors in investor-owned firms.[58] In addition, since 1964, worker cooperatives have qualified for the special regime established for all types of cooperatives in Subchapter T of the Internal Revenue Code— described in more detail in Chapter 7—under which all the net earnings of a worker cooperative, whether distributed or retained, are free from the corporate income tax.[59] Finally, since the early 1970s there has existed a generous package of tax subsidies for employee stock ownership plans.[60]

Ideological Hostility

It has been argued that, whatever the formal legal rules and institutions that bear on the matter, American society in general, or key actors such as bankers in particular, are hostile to employee ownership on ideological grounds and have used their authority to hamper its development and deprive it of cultural legitimacy.[61] Yet while some Americans undoubtedly see employee ownership as socialistic and therefore evil, the evidence makes it hard to argue that ideological resistance to employee ownership is strong or widespread. As was noted in the Introduction, employee ownership has shown broad ideological appeal to the right as well as to the left in the United States, and the advocates of ESOPs have exploited this appeal quite successfully.

Moreover, lawyers, accountants, investment bankers, and management consultants—the actors in society principally responsible for the design of business organizations—have long organized themselves in employee-owned firms. They cannot be unaware of the benefits of employee ownership or opposed to it on principle. At most they can be accused, rather implausibly, of hoarding the benefits of employee ownership for themselves and—whether out of spite or just lack of imagination—denying those benefits to firms in other industries.

To understand the prevailing pattern of employee ownership, we must turn instead to the costs of governance that are the subject of the next chapter.

6

Governing Employee-Owned Firms

A recurrent theme in the voluminous literature advocating employee ownership (or, more broadly, "economic democracy," "worker participation," or "labor management") is that employee participation in control of the firm through democratic processes is of value in itself, quite apart from the quality of the substantive decisions reached by those processes. In Chapter 3 we speculated on three reasons why this might be so: that participation in governance is a consumption good; that it provides a valued sense of control; and that it stimulates and informs participation in political life beyond the boundaries of the firm. The last of these reasons might provide some justification for public subsidy to employee ownership as a means of making workers more responsible citizens in a democratic society. Unfortunately, the available empirical evidence provides little support for it.[1] The employees themselves enjoy the other two potential benefits of employee participation. If those benefits are actually important, they should influence employees' choices about the types of firms in which to work. That is, they should give employee-owned firms a survivorship advantage.

Participation is not free, however. It brings with it all the costs of collective decision making. And there is substantial evidence that these costs can be large.

The Costs of Collective Decision Making

In many respects a firm's employees are often better situated than its investors to oversee management effectively, as we observed in Chapter 5. But there is a compensating disadvantage: employees are far more likely than investors to differ among themselves concerning the firm's policies.

To begin with, employees may disagree about their relative wages. Further, employees often have different stakes in the firm's investment decisions, such as which plants to keep open, which processes to automate, or where to improve safety. The extent to which employees' interests diverge in these respects is likely to increase as the division of labor within the firm increases. Where all employees do essentially the same job, there is little reason for disagreements about pay; moreover, the employees will be similarly affected by most decisions and thus generally in agreement about them.

Employees can also experience conflicts of interest that have other sources besides differences in job assignments. For example, employees can differ substantially in the amount of equity capital they have invested in the firm. This is particularly likely to occur if, as is common, the firm's pension fund is the principal vehicle for employee investments. Older employees, who have disproportionately large amounts of capital invested, will prefer to have a larger amount of the firm's earnings attributed to capital (and hence distributed as earnings on amounts invested in the pension fund) and a smaller amount attributed to labor (and hence paid out as wages) than will younger employees.

Such conflicts might not be troublesome in practice if there were obvious objective criteria to employ when making the decisions in question. For example, if the actual marginal product of both labor and capital within a given firm could be easily measured, then it would be natural to apportion the firm's earnings between wages and return on capital in proportion to those marginal products. Such objective criteria, however, are usually absent or unobservable at reasonable cost. In most firms, for instance, the marginal productivity of labor and capital cannot be accurately measured. Therefore, in important decisions, there is often considerable room for judgment and discretion, and hence for active disagreement. And disagreement, as discussed in Chapter 3, can make governance costly.

We observed in Chapter 4 that, while different groups of shareholders in investor-owned firms sometimes have conflicting interests, corporate law provides means for constraining and resolving the worst of these conflicts in corporate decision making. It is reasonable to ask whether the law could place analogous constraints on collective decisions made by employees. One place where this has been tried is under the "duty of fair representation" that American labor law imposes on unions to prevent the exploitation of the minority by the majority. But in contrast to the analogous doctrines in corporate law, this body of law has been singularly unsuccessful in limiting opportunistic behavior by majorities. In general, the duty of fair representation has been effectively employed only to bar overt discrimination based on conventional personal characteristics such as race or sex.[2] The reason for this is apparently not that the law has had inadequate opportunity to develop, but rather that, unlike the situation with investors, there are no simple objective criteria by which to determine whether a particular subgroup of employees is being treated unfairly.

When we survey the types of firms in which employee ownership has succeeded, the costs associated with collective decision making appear surprisingly important in determining where employee ownership is viable and how it is organized. In fact, these costs seem to go far toward explaining the large residual in the existing pattern of employee ownership that is left unexplained by the other considerations surveyed in Chapter 5.

Which Firms Succeed?

The most striking evidence of the high costs of collective decision making is the scarcity of employee-owned firms in which there are substantial differences among the employees who participate in ownership. Most typically, employee-owners all do extremely similar work and are of essentially equivalent status within the firm. Rarely do they have substantially different types or levels of skills, and rarely is there much hierarchical authority among them. This is evident in the professional service firms, where employee ownership is best established. The partners in a law firm, for example, are all lawyers of roughly equal skill and productivity who work more or less independently of each other; rarely does one partner have substantial supervisory authority over another. Similarly, the employees in the U.S. plywood cooperatives are unspecialized and only semi-skilled, and commonly rotate over time through the various jobs in the mill. They thus have little reason to differ concerning the policies to be adopted by the firm. The manager, who is the only person in the firm with specialized skills and tasks and with substantial supervisory responsibilities, is generally not a member of the cooperative but rather hired as a salaried employee.[3]

The driver-owned transportation cooperatives that are so common throughout the world also fit this mold; the drivers have extremely similar stakes in any decision made by the firm. The predominance of this pattern suggests strongly that employee ownership works best when there is little opportunity for conflict of interest among the employee-owners. Evidently the viability of employee ownership is severely compromised when the employees who share ownership play diverse roles within the firm[4] and consequently will be differently affected by important decisions taken by the firm—a conclusion supported by substantial anecdotal evidence from a variety of different types of employee-owned enterprise.[5]

Conversely, employee ownership evidently is viable when the employees involved all play a similar role within the firm, even if in other respects the net benefits from employee ownership do not appear unusually strong in comparison to situations in which investor ownership is the rule. As we saw in the last chapter, employee ownership does not typically arise where the costs of contracting for labor on the market are unusually high; indeed, quite the contrary. Apparently employee ownership is worthwhile, as a means of reducing the costs of labor contracting, even where those costs are, compared with those of other industries or other types of employees, relatively low—as long as collective decision making is not a potential problem. This remains true, moreover, where the risk-bearing costs associated with employee ownership are relatively high.

The natural conclusion from this pattern is that, if costs associated with collective self-governance were not a problem, employee ownership would be far more widespread than it is.

Structures to Avoid the Costs

Another important indication that collective governance can be costly, and that the costs involved play a critical role in the success or failure of employee ownership, lies in the strong tendency for employee-owned firms to adopt rules and practices that promote homogeneity of interest among the employee-owners.

For example, the plywood cooperatives nearly all adhere rigidly to a scheme under which all members of the firm receive the same rate of pay regardless of task or seniority. The firms explicitly justify this practice as necessary to avoid excessive dissension among the members.[6]

Even more striking, many of America's largest and most prosperous law firms have long followed a practice of sharing the partnership's earnings equally among all partners of a given age, regardless of individual productivity. This is an astonishing fact. As we have seen, law firms not only can, but do, monitor the productivity of their individual lawyers quite closely. It would therefore seem natural to adjust each partner's return to reflect her productivity, and thus provide a strong financial incentive for efficient performance. Yet the equal-sharing firms abandon all such financial incentives. Obviously there must be some strong countervailing value served by equality in distribution of earnings.

One explanation that has been offered for this practice is that it is a mechanism for risk sharing.[7] Yet it is hard to believe that risk sharing is the principal motivation. At the time they enter into the equal-sharing scheme, the lawyers involved have already achieved great prosperity and security. They have proved their professional competence and have become partners, with effective lifetime tenure, in an established law firm. Commonly their expected earnings are at least several hundreds of thousands of dollars per year. Could such individuals nevertheless be so risk averse that they are prepared to relieve their partners of all financial incentives for productivity simply to ensure that their own income will always be the same as that of the other partners their age?

This is highly implausible.[8] It is more likely that these equal-sharing schemes serve principally to reduce the costs of collective decision making. An equal-sharing rule provides a simple focal point for deciding how to divide the pie. Using a political process to decide on a more complex differentiated scheme of division would be time-consuming and divisive for all involved, and there is no reason to believe that a stable outcome could be easily achieved.

Law firms that do not adopt equal-sharing rules commonly employ formulas under which a partner's share is determined according to specified indicia of productivity, such as hours billed or number and value of new clients brought to the firm. Such formulas—as opposed to less formal approaches under which a manager or committee is simply given discretion to set relative shares as seems appropriate, without being bound to a rigid formula—are evidently an alternative effort to establish more or less objective, and hence uncontroversial, criteria for dividing the pie where equal sharing is too difficult to justify. Even so, there is considerable dissension within law firms about the structure of these formulas, and the resulting disagreements are an important source of instability and dissolution among law partnerships.

Indeed, employee ownership generally seems to thrive only where, if equal sharing is not practicable, individual employee productivities are sufficiently easy to measure so that some relatively objective, and hence uncontroversial, method of pay based on that measure can be employed. We find employee cooperatives among taxi drivers and refuse collection crews, where members of the cooperative bill clients individually and can simply be compensated with a fraction of those billings. Employee ownership is correspondingly rare among those firms—which constitute the overwhelming bulk of all large firms today—in which production requires the joint effort of large numbers of employees with different skills performing different tasks, so that the productivity of individual employees is difficult to assess with any precision.

Employee-owned firms also commonly strive to ensure that not only pay, but also amount and even type of work, is equalized among the members of the firm. The employee-owners in the plywood factories, as already noted, commonly rotate through the different jobs over time, so that there is little long-run specialization of work among them. Law firms strongly resist admitting to the partnership any lawyer who is not of roughly the same competence and productivity as the other partners; less-qualified lawyers, if valuable to the firm, are kept on as permanent salaried associates rather than as partners who receive a smaller share of earnings.[9]

Similarly, law firms strongly resist letting some partners work fewer hours than average in exchange for a smaller share. The recent rapid increase in the number of women lawyers, for example, has created considerable pressure for part-time work arrangements to permit time for child rearing. Many law firms now willingly accept such arrangements for salaried "associates" (young lawyers not yet promoted to partnership), and at the same time refuse to permit women to be partners on a part-time basis.[10] This refusal is sometimes explained on the ground that clients demand that attorneys be available full time or that attorneys must practice full time to keep up their skills.[11] But these explanations seem forced. Rather, it appears likely that such inequalities among members of the firm are resisted at least in part because they tend to destabilize the cooperative governance structure. A simple rule under which everyone does essentially the same amount and kind of work, and receives the same pay, is by far the easiest to agree upon and to enforce,[12] and these advantages evidently are often sufficient to outweigh the costs such a simple rule engenders in the form of inflexibility, poor incentives, and lack of diversification among the work force. (This is not to deny, of course, that simple sexism also plays a role in denying partnerships to women under conditions acceptable to them.)

To be sure, it is possible that such egalitarian practices are unusually common in employee-owned firms at least in part for other reasons. In particular, it could be that causation runs the other way from that suggested here: employee-owned firms may be unusually inclined to adopt egalitarian practices simply because they are employee-owned, and not because such practices are necessary to reduce governance costs. For example, there is evidence that employees judge the adequacy of their salaries in relation to the amount paid other employees at the same firm. Consequently, an employee will accept a lower wage if he is among the best paid at the firm, and will require a larger wage if he is among the lowest paid. The result is that the wage structure within a given firm is less dispersed than differences in productivity among employees would predict; the employees at the top of the wage scale compensate the employees at the bottom, as it were, for the privilege of being on top.[13] Perhaps this effect is intensified when employees are co-owners rather than simply salaried employees, because they are then even more inclined to view themselves as a collective reference group for purposes of judging their individual welfare. If so, this would lead employee-owned firms to have less differentiated wage structures than similar investor-owned firms.[14] Such a phenomenon would not, however, explain why it is that employee ownership tends to arise only where the employees involved are highly homogeneous to begin with.

In recent years, the size of corporate law firms has increased dramatically. Firms are now highly departmentalized, and the size of teams that work on major projects has also become large. As a result, there is now substantial horizontal and vertical division of labor within firms. Under such circumstances, norms requiring equal contributions from all senior attorneys become harder to maintain, and equal sharing of earnings becomes harder to justify. These developments presumably help explain the increasing tendency among law firms to hire "permanent associates" who remain with the firm indefinitely as salaried employees rather than as partners. By this device, ownership of the firm can be confined to a relatively homogeneous class of attorneys without cramping the firm's growth or diversification. For similar reasons, it seems predictable that law firms might seek to accommodate as permanent associates rather than as partners the increasing numbers of senior women attorneys who wish to work only part time, although laws and norms concerning sex discrimination may inhibit firms from pursuing this approach.

The ultimate means for a service firm to avoid the governance costs associated with employee ownership, however, is to convert to investor ownership. And this is, in fact, the path being followed in many of the service professions. Advertising firms began converting from the partnership form to investor ownership in the early 1960s, and most of the larger firms are now investor-owned.[15] Similarly, investment banking began abandoning the partnership form in the 1970s, and many of the larger firms there, too, are now investor-owned.[16] Medical practice has been following the same route, as investor ownership has spread rapidly among health maintenance organizations.[17]

Evidently one reason such firms convert to investor ownership is to attract larger amounts of capital than can conveniently be supplied by the professionals who work for them. But there is evidence, too, that the conversions serve to alleviate governance problems. Firms in these industries have been growing larger and more complex, offering a broader range of services and exhibiting more internal specialization and departmentalization. Presumably consensus among the professionals within these firms concerning policies to be followed and division of the firm's earnings has become increasingly difficult to secure. Striking evidence of this appears in the well-documented sale of Lehman Brothers, one of America's oldest investment banking partnerships, to American Express in 1984. Although a need for capital seems to have played a role, the sale was precipitated by a breakdown in internal governance that had its roots in conflicts between the old-line bankers and the newly powerful traders within the firm.[18]

Further evidence comes from the recent emergence of a number of "boutique" investment banking firms organized as partnerships.[19] These firms have only a small number of partners and concentrate on only a portion of the investment banking business (such as mergers and acquisitions), hence reducing opportunities for serious conflicts in decision making. At the same time they are often exceptionally well capitalized.[20] This indicates that the need for capital is not a decisive factor in the choice of ownership in investment banking, and suggests strongly that governance also plays an important role.

What Constitutes Homogeneity of Interest?

The preceding evidence implies that employee ownership works best where the employee-owners are so homogeneous that any decision made by the firm will affect them roughly equally, or where, though the employees differ in ways that cause the burdens and benefits of some decisions to be shared unequally, there is an objective and widely accepted basis for making those decisions. That is, employee ownership is most viable where either no important conflicts of interest exist among the employee-owners, or some simple and uncontroversial means is available to resolve the conflicts that are present.

What constitutes a difference, and what constitutes an objective and legitimate way to resolve a difference, are of course relative things. Formal public choice theory confirms what common sense suggests: that strong homogeneity of interest is not in itself sufficient to eliminate the pathologies of collective choice mechanisms. If the range of available outcomes to choose from is sufficiently large, then majority rule may not yield a stable outcome even if preferences are only very slightly heterogeneous.[21] To take a mundane example, if a majority of the pilots in a pilot-owned airline have brown eyes, they might vote for a policy under which brown-eyed pilots get paid 20 percent more than do blue-eyed pilots. But then, if the pilots over five feet ten inches in height form a majority, they might subsequently vote to eliminate the eye-color-based pay policy in favor of a policy in which pilots over five feet ten inches get paid 30 percent more than do shorter pilots. And so forth.

We must therefore ask why voting ever works. Why doesn't shared decision making among a group of owners always break down, in favor of either chaos or authoritarianism, when there exists any basis for distinguishing among the owners, no matter how trivial—as there virtually always is among a firm's employees? If, as the evidence suggests, substantial (but of course never complete) homogeneity of interest is sufficient to reduce considerably the costs of collective decision making, there must be some special reason why this is so.

One answer, presumably, is that culture and institutions place important limits on the range of legitimate voting outcomes. Where there is substantial perceived homogeneity of interest, as where all workers have essentially the same role within the firm, socially shared norms of fairness, as well as the fiduciary rules that a reviewing court will enforce, place all but a few potential outcomes beyond reach. Thus neither conventional morality nor the courts are likely to sanction a system in which pilots with brown eyes get paid more than do those with blue eyes.

It follows that homogeneity of interest is, in important degree, a social construct. Consequently, what passes for homogeneity in one setting may not in another. There was a long period in which it would have been both morally and legally acceptable in the United States for pilots with white skin to be paid more than pilots with black skin. As we shall see in Chapter 7, an important reason why farmer-owned marketing cooperatives were for a long time much less common in tobacco than in other crops was apparently the presence of much more racial diversity among tobacco farmers than among other types of farmers, with the result that shared governance was less workable among the tobacco farmers.

Ownership by a diverse constituency can be made more viable by creating and maintaining institutions—including shared norms, formal legal and charter limitations on voting procedures and voting outcomes, and review by outside agencies such as courts—that constrain the available range of choices.[22] We have already seen a number of examples. The costs of constructing and sustaining these institutions, which increase as the perceived degree of heterogeneity among the owners increases, are an important component of the costs of collective decision making.

Representative Democracy in Practice: The Case of Mondragon

The firms in which employee ownership is found are, like law firms, often small enough to permit the use of highly participatory forms of direct democracy. This is not to say that such firms are, in reality, usually highly participatory. In partnerships of professionals, such as law firms, although the partners may have substantial nominal rights to participate in collective decision making, governance is often effectively confined to a small group of senior partners who are essentially self-appointing—a practice that itself suggests that collective decision making among employees is costly.

In any event, in larger employee-owned firms, highly participatory forms of decision making are unwieldy, and direct democracy must usually yield to a representative form of governance. The most obvious model is one, analogous to that employed in widely held investor-owned corporations and in other types of large cooperatives, under which the employee-owners elect representatives to a board of directors. The board, in turn, is responsible for appointing and overseeing the firm's managers. Direct voting by the owners is then confined to major "constitutional" changes in the firm, such as merger or liquidation. Where the work force is heterogeneous, indirect representation of this sort could have an advantage over more direct forms of democracy in securing professional management and avoiding high process costs or inefficiently biased decisions. Yet such a system of indirect representation might also insulate management so well as to sacrifice some of the potential advantages of employee control.

Few well-documented examples of large employee-owned firms with heterogeneous work forces exist, and so it is difficult to assess directly and in detail how well a representative system of employee governance can function in such a setting. The case that has been most extensively studied is the affiliated group of worker cooperatives at Mondragon, Spain. Because of the substantial success these firms have achieved (by a variety of measures their average productivity has regularly exceeded that of Spanish industry in general),[23] and because of the extraordinary amount of attention they have received among advocates of employee ownership, they call for special consideration. Unfortunately, even the literature on Mondragon does not focus very carefully on matters of governance. We cannot draw strong conclusions, consequently, but rather can only point to some aspects of the Mondragon experience that offer evidence of the costs of decision making.

In an individual firm within the Mondragon group, direct employee participation in governance is largely confined to annual meetings at which the employees elect representatives, in at-large elections, to a nine-member supervisory board of directors for staggered terms of four years. The board, in turn, is responsible for appointing the firm's managers, who serve for a minimum of four years and cannot be removed during that term except for cause.[24] (In contrast, the members of the board of directors of American business corporations are typically elected for terms of only one year, and managers serve at the discretion of the board.) Each firm also has a "social council" that is elected by the employees separately from the elections to the board of directors and that serves as the principal avenue by which the interests of the employees in a firm are made known to management. In contrast to the members of the board of directors, who are elected at large, the members of the social council are elected by local constituencies within the firm. The social council, however, acts only in an advisory capacity to management and has no formal authority.[25]

In addition to these procedural rules, which blunt the use of electoral mechanisms as a direct means of controlling management, there are limitations on the substantive decisions that the employees can make. In particular, the employees in an individual firm within the Mondragon group are constrained in the extent to which, and the ways in which, they can appropriate the firm's net earnings. They are not free to set their wages at any level they wish; rather, each firm must adopt a system of wages that deviates only within specified bounds from a scale established by the Mondragon system's central bank.[26] Moreover, 10 percent of the net earnings remaining after payment of these wages must be devoted to educational, cultural, or charitable purposes;[27] the rest must be retained and invested in capital accounts. At least 20 percent of net earnings must be put in a collective account that cannot be appropriated by the firm's employees, even upon retirement from the firm, and this percentage increases according to a formula as the firm becomes more profitable. The remaining profits—no more than 70 percent of total profits—are invested in accounts for the individual employees. The amounts in these accounts cannot be withdrawn before retirement but earn interest (which is paid to the workers annually in cash) at 6 percent. These financial restrictions are imposed on the individual cooperatives by a "contract of association" that they enter into, at the time of their formation, with the Mondragon system's central bank; the restrictions are apparently not subject to alteration by a cooperative's employees or management.[28] Other potentially contentious topics, such as precedence in hiring and layoff, are also governed by systemwide rules.[29]

This attenuation of employees' rights to earnings and control in the individual cooperatives is reinforced by other features of the system. Individual cooperatives that are engaged in a given type of production

—consumer goods manufacturing, for example, or furniture making, or agricultural production—are federated into a larger organization whose leadership is effectively appointed by the managers of the constituent cooperatives. These higher-level organizations often have considerable authority over their member firms. In particular, there is substantial pooling of profits among the firms within a given group, so that profitable firms underwrite the losses of unprofitable ones. Similarly, individual workers can be reassigned from one firm to another within the group.

In addition, each individual cooperative must affiliate itself with the system's central bank. The bank, whose own board of directors is largely composed of managers of the constituent cooperatives, exercises substantial authority over the individual firms. The bank's wage-setting authority has already been mentioned. Each firm must also obtain whatever additional capital it needs from the bank and must invest any capital surplus with the bank.[30] The bank also retains and exercises the authority to replace an individual cooperative's management, or to take over the firm's operations directly, in case of poor performance.[31]

This system, with its strong delegation to management and its centrally imposed restrictions on individual firms' decision making, has evidently been designed self-consciously to mute the play of political forces among the firm's employees, preempting opportunities for costly conflict. Not surprisingly, given this structure, the Mondragon firms have a somewhat managerial character. It appears that leadership comes largely from the top; for the most part, the electoral mechanisms are employed largely to ratify proposals made by management.[32] The powerful bank at the center of the system itself appears distinctly managerial; as late as 1987, the two individuals who had long served as chairman of the bank's board of directors and as its chief executive officer were both among the five persons who had founded the Mondragon group more than thirty years before, and the chairman of the bank's board was also chairman of the board of the oldest and largest individual firm in the Mondragon system and of the federated group to which that firm belongs.[33] An eight-day strike of workers against managers at the latter firm, in 1974, is indicative of the managers' independence from their workers.[34]

In short, workers' rights to control and to participation in earnings are attenuated in the Mondragon system, and the individual firms cannot really be said to be fully owned by their workers. Rather, the system has something of the character of a large nonprofit holding company that delegates to the employees of each subsidiary the right to elect the subsidiary's management. More particularly, Mondragon bears some resemblance to the more decentralized American private universities, such as Harvard, whose constituent schools and departments have substantial budgetary autonomy and are largely self-governing but are subject to the right of the central administration to intervene when it feels necessary.

None of this is to deny that the employees at Mondragon participate meaningfully in control. An indication of that control (though perhaps also of some instability in governance) is the departure from the group of at least four of the cooperatives through conversion to investor ownership, and the departure of at least another twelve firms as independent cooperatives. All of these departures took place despite the opposition of the central administration.[35]

The wage structure has been among the most contentious issues at Mondragon. Initially, the systemwide top pay index—the maximum permissible ratio of highest to lowest rate of pay—was three to one. Over the years, this ratio has been increased to attract and hold talented executives. Thus in 1988 the top pay index was raised from 4.5 to 6. The new top index was imposed only as a ceiling, however; individual cooperatives were left free to adopt a lower ratio if they wished. The change was unpopular with the rank and file, which repeatedly voted down acceptance of the higher top index at individual firms. Five years later, in 1993, only 8 of 125 affiliated firms had adopted the new top index of 6, and nearly three-quarters remained at 4.5 or below. (Even the latter firms appear liberal as cooperatives go: three-quarters of Spain's other—generally much smaller—producer cooperatives report that, as with the American plywood cooperatives, all their members receive the same wage.)[36]

In sum, Mondragon does not offer a straightforward demonstration of the feasibility of adopting full employee ownership in a large firm with a heterogeneous labor force. But it does show that an attenuated form of employee ownership, in which the firm is managed on behalf of its employees though not fully owned by them, can sometimes be successful in industrial enterprise.

The representativeness of the Mondragon experience, as many have noted, remains unclear. There are reasons to be cautious in concluding that replication will often be feasible. Among these reasons are the ethnic homogeneity, insularity, and low mobility of the Basque population from which the Mondragon system draws its work force.[37] After forty years in operation, and despite substantial publicity, Mondragon has still spawned few successful imitators on a similar scale, either in Spain or elsewhere.[38]

In any event, examination of Mondragon reinforces the inference that the costs of collective decision making are significant in employee-owned firms, and that structures to constrain those costs are a strategic element in the design of those firms.

Other European Experience

Mondragon aside, the characteristics of worker cooperatives throughout Europe—for all one can tell from the literature, which tends to be scanty on significant details—seem to follow a consistent pattern that reinforces the observations made above concerning the efficiency of employee ownership.

Among European countries, as we have noted, Italy and France apparently have the highest concentrations of successful worker cooperatives.[39] In the case of Italy, this may be at least in part because that country (like Spain) subsidizes worker cooperatives in general through tax exemptions and special credits.[40] In addition, both France and Italy grant construction cooperatives special advantages in bidding for government business, which may be quite important in explaining the high concentration of cooperatives in that industry.[41] The construction companies and artisanal firms that constitute the bulk of the worker cooperatives in these countries seem to conform roughly to the type of firm in which employee ownership has proved most viable elsewhere, with relatively little internal hierarchy, although the Italian cooperatives evidently include some construction companies and manufacturing firms of substantial internal complexity.[42]

The Italian worker cooperatives are generally affiliated with one of three associations, each of which has traditionally been connected with one of the nation's political parties. In particular, well over half of the cooperatives, including most of the largest and most successful firms, are members of an association (the "Lega") historically affiliated with the former Italian Communist Party (now the Democratic Party of the Left). Although it is difficult to obtain a clear view of these cooperatives from the available literature, there is some reason to believe that their decision-making autonomy is constrained to an important degree by control exercised from the top down through the Lega.[43] Moreover, the cooperatives' members are represented by a national labor union also affiliated with the former Communist Party, and wages in the cooperatives, like those in similar investor-owned firms, are determined by industrywide bargaining—with the Lega serving the role of the employers' representative for the cooperatives in these collective negotiations. Furthermore, in Italy (as in France), the statutes governing worker cooperatives impose on them a quasi-nonprofit structure, requiring that a substantial fraction of net earnings be retained in accounts not distributable to the worker-members and prohibiting the distribution of net assets to members upon dissolution.[44] Profit-sharing bonuses are limited by law to 20 percent of wages. In practice, these bonuses are commonly paid to nonmember employees as well as to members, are often small or nonexistent, and (like wages) do not exceed those paid in investor-owned firms.[45] In sum, although the evidence suggests an important degree of real employee governance in the most successful Italian worker cooperatives, those cooperatives operate in an environment of favoritism and constraints that make it difficult to draw general conclusions from them about the behavior and viability of fully worker-owned firms.

England has far fewer employee-owned firms than France or Italy. Omitting partnerships of service professionals, such as solicitors, the firms that have been successful over the long run can be divided into two groups. The first group has its origins in the labor and cooperative movements of the late nineteenth century. The number of these firms has been declining throughout this century; by one count there were only sixteen remaining in 1973. The firms in this group are typically small artisanal cooperatives; more than half are in printing or bootmaking.[46] The second group consists of more recently founded firms associated with the Industrial Common Ownership Movement (ICOM). There were eleven of these firms as of 1977. They include some moderate-sized industrial enterprises with a fair record of success. The ICOM firms, however, are not truly employee-owned. The employees have no claim on the firms' net assets, their rights to participate in current net earnings are constrained, and ultimate authority over important aspects of the firms' affairs are in the hands of trustees who are not elected by the employees.[47] These firms are, like many other firms called worker cooperatives, essentially nonprofit firms that are managed on behalf of their workers and not actually owned by them. They have also benefited from some generous subsidies. Four of the eleven ICOM cooperatives, for example, were essentially donated to their employees by their former owners.[48]

The experience in these countries thus does not provide clear evidence of the viability of large firms with heterogeneous work forces under full employee ownership.

Experience with Partial Employee Participation

The importance of governance costs relative to the other costs and benefits of employee ownership is further underscored by the accumulated experience with various forms of partial employee participation in earnings and control that fall short of full employee ownership.[49]

Employee Stock Ownership Plans

Since the 1970s many American firms have adopted employee stock ownership plans under which most or all of the firm's employees receive a portion of their compensation in the form of stock in the firm. Typically ESOPs are structured as deferred compensation plans in which the employer deposits stock in a trust fund that holds the stock for the benefit of the participating employees, often as the reserve for the employees' pensions. By 1986 approximately 4,700 companies had adopted such plans. Roughly 25 percent of these plans owned more than 25 percent of the stock in their firms, and somewhat less than 2 percent owned all of the stock.[50] By 1990 the number of companies with ESOPs had grown to roughly 10,000,[51] and estimates suggest that the ESOP owned a majority of the stock in more than 1,000 of these companies.[52]

The rapid proliferation of ESOPs is not an unbiased indicator of their efficiency. Although the ESOP concept has been actively promoted since the 1950s,[53] it did not become popular until ESOPs were granted substantial federal tax subsidies beginning in 1974—tax subsidies that have since been broadened and deepened[54]—and until it was discovered that creation of an ESOP could be a useful defensive tactic for management in an attempted corporate takeover.[55] It is entirely possible that, without these special advantages, ESOPs would remain rare. The numerous studies of ESOPs that have been undertaken to date, while not conclusive, have failed to present clear evidence of improvements in either employee productivity or firm profitability once allowance is made for tax subsidies.[56]

Whatever the motivation for adopting ESOPs, one of the most striking facts about them is that they generally provide for participation only in earnings and not in control. Only rarely have they been structured to give the employees a significant voice in the governance of the firm. A substantial fraction of the stock held by ESOPs is nonvoting stock.[57] Further, the power to vote any voting stock held by an ESOP is commonly not exercised by the employees who are the beneficiaries of the plan. In the latter regard, the tax law plays a significant role. For a privately held corporation to obtain the tax benefits provided for ESOPs, the power to vote stock held by the corporation's ESOP need not be passed through to the employees, but can be voted by the plan's trustee.[58] The trustee, in turn, can be appointed by the firm's management without consultation with the employees who are the plan's beneficiaries. In publicly traded corporations, in contrast, voting power must be passed through to the employees on all ESOP stock actually allocated to the employees—which is to say, not purchased through borrowing, as in the popular "leveraged" ESOP.[59]

These tax law provisions are evidently important in understanding the pattern of ESOPs that has evolved. If we exclude so-called tax credit ESOPs—that is, ESOPs created under a special (and now repealed) provision effectively giving a 100 percent tax subsidy to the plan—roughly 90 percent of all ESOPs are in privately held firms. Moreover, there are very few publicly traded firms in which an ESOP has more than 20 percent of the firm's stock, and perhaps none in which the plan has a majority of the stock.[60] Firms in which a majority of the stock is held by an ESOP are, it appears, almost exclusively privately held. And, although the law permits (but does not require) that votes on ESOP stock be passed through to employees in privately held firms, this is done in only a distinct minority of such firms.[61] Thus ESOPs generally do not permit much employee participation in control of the firm in either publicly or privately held firms. In fact, an extensive 1986 survey found that only 4 percent of sampled firms with ESOPs had any nonmanagerial employee representatives on their boards of directors and found no firms with ESOPs in which employee representatives constituted a majority of the board of directors.[62]

What is particularly interesting is that voting rights have not been passed through to employees even in some firms—including, for most of its young life as an employee-owned firm, the much-publicized Weirton Steel Company[63]—in which the ESOP owns 100 percent of the firm's stock. Instead, voting rights are commonly held by the ESOP's trustee, who is appointed by a self-perpetuating board. In effect, these firms are operated as nonprofit institutions in which directors with control but no claim on residual earnings are charged with managing the firm as fiduciaries for the benefit of the employees.

A commonly held view is that employee participation in corporate governance is highly desirable but that the risk and the high cost of capital that employees face when they participate in ownership are serious liabilities. From this, one would expect employee ownership to be structured to maximize employees' participation in control but to minimize their contribution of capital. ESOPs, however, have just the opposite character. Since they provide for participation in residual earnings through the purchase of stock (rather than, for example, through a simple profit-sharing plan), they amplify employees' problems of illiquidity and risk bearing. Yet at the same time they typically give employees no voice at all in the management of the enterprise.[64]

If the advantages of employee participation in control exceeded its costs, then one would surely expect to see much more employee control in firms with ESOPs, and particularly in the thousand or more firms in which the ESOP owns a majority of the firm's stock. These firms, or their employees, are already incurring most of the principal costs of employee ownership—particularly the high costs of bearing undiversified risk that employee ownership imposes on employees. The fact that employees typically do not participate in the governance of these firms suggests strongly that the persons responsible for structuring them believe that any reduction in agency costs that might result from making management directly accountable to the firm's employees, even though the employees are already the firm's *beneficial* owners, would be outweighed by the costs—whether in the form of inefficient decisions or high process costs—that would be engendered by the political process required for such accountability.[65]

To be sure, the creation of ESOPs in which votes are not passed through to employees can probably be explained at least in part as an effort by corporate managers to preserve or increase their own autonomy—that is, as a means of protecting the managers both from hostile takeovers and from direct accountability to the employees. But managerial opportunism alone seems insufficient to explain the virtually complete absence of employee control even in firms in which an ESOP holds a majority of the firm's equity. If creation of an ESOP with pass-through of votes to the employees would be more efficient than either no ESOP or an ESOP without pass-through of votes, then one would expect to see hostile takeovers initiated with the aim of creating such a structure—or at least to see such ESOPs put in place upon the successful completion of hostile takeovers attempted for other reasons. In fact, one would expect to see employees themselves, perhaps through their unions, participating in such hostile takeovers.

Beneficial Ownership

As just noted, firms in which an ESOP owns a majority of the company's equity are typically controlled not by their employees but by trustees who manage the firms as fiduciaries for the employees. Thus these firms are not fully employee-owned but rather, in a sense, are nonprofit firms that are operated on behalf of their employees. Indeed, a number of often-cited instances of "employee ownership" in the United States—including, for example, the car rental company Avis, the publisher Norton, and the now-defunct airline People Express[66]— have not, in fact, put voting control of the firm in the hands of their employees; on the contrary, they have given voting rights only to a small group of top managers, leaving most employees to participate only in earnings and not governance.

Similarly, the most successful large-scale experiments with employee-owned industrial enterprise in Britain, the ICOM cooperatives, have also been structured with only beneficial employee ownership. The same is apparently true to a substantial degree of many French and Italian worker cooperatives, and one can even argue that this characterization has some application to Mondragon. In short, examples of successful employee ownership in industrial enterprise frequently involve not true worker control but rather firms that are only beneficially owned by their workers, with actual authority exercised by fiduciaries.

A plausible inference to be drawn from this pattern, as already noted, is that full employee control tends to bring serious inefficiencies with a work force as heterogeneous as those to be found in most industrial firms. One might concede this point, however, and nevertheless argue that even firms that are only beneficially owned by their employees are often preferable to investor-owned firms. Indeed, many advocates of employee self-governance explicitly call for giving employees only attenuated property rights in their firms' earnings and assets.[67]

Some of the most important benefits of employee ownership discussed in Chapter 5 could presumably still be realized with only beneficial ownership instead of full employee ownership. The problems of monitoring employees, employee lock-in, strategic bargaining behavior, and poor communication of employee preferences arise principally because of the conflict of interest between employees and owners that characterizes an investor-owned firm. Even beneficial employee ownership promises to eliminate that conflict of interest in substantial part.

At the same time, serious countervailing inefficiencies may result if industrial firms are structured, to an important degree, as nonprofits in which employees have beneficial ownership but lack essential elements of full ownership, such as ultimate authority to replace top management or to compel distributions of earnings or assets. We will explore the nonprofit form more carefully in Chapter 12, and here simply note that such a structure largely insulates the firm's management from any direct incentives to perform efficiently. Further, such firms are subject to special problems in adjusting their capital stock. When nonprofit firms need a rapid infusion of capital, they often have difficulty raising it since they cannot sell equity shares. Conversely, when market conditions permit, nonprofit firms tend, by retaining earnings, to accumulate capital well beyond the amount needed for efficient operation.

For these reasons, only under two conditions does it make sense to organize an industrial firm as a nonprofit, managed in substantial part on behalf of but not by its employees: (1) if severe inefficiencies in contracting for labor would result if the firm were investor-owned; and (2) if collective governance by the employees would be extremely costly. In such circumstances, the inefficiencies of the nonprofit form might be smaller than either the costs of labor market contracting that would accompany investor ownership or the costs of collective decision making that would accompany true employee ownership.

The fact that employee ownership in the industrial sector is confined largely to firms that are only beneficially owned by their employees rather than being fully employee-controlled suggests that condition (2) holds. The fact that even beneficial employee ownership rarely appears in complex industrial firms where it is not heavily subsidized suggests that condition (1) does not hold. Taken together, these conclusions imply two things. First, if employees are to be given some form of ownership interest in an industrial firm, it is most efficient to structure the firm as a fiduciary entity managed on behalf of, but not fully controlled by, its employees. Second, the costs associated with contracting for labor on the market—that is, the inefficiencies of investor ownership—are nevertheless insufficient to justify the costs of adopting the nonprofit form to avoid them. As a general matter, industrial firms that are only beneficially owned by their employees may be more efficient than fully employee-owned firms, but are evidently less efficient than investor-owned firms.

It should be kept in mind that we are talking here only of what we have loosely termed "industrial" firms—that is, firms with sufficient hierarchy and division of labor to have a work force with significantly heterogeneous interests. As we saw in Chapter 5, employee ownership can be, and is, quite successful when the employee-owners can be drawn from a relatively homogeneous group for whom the costs of collective decision making are not an important issue.

Codetermination

German-style codetermination, providing for substantial worker participation in corporate governance but no direct participation in net earnings, has roughly the opposite characteristics from ESOPs.[68] More particularly, under legislation adopted for the coal and steel industry in 1951 and extended to German industry in general by stages in 1952 and 1976, German workers are entitled by law to elect half of the members of the supervisory board of directors in all large German firms, though workers otherwise remain salaried employees with no equity stake in the firm.[69]

If all workers were homogeneous, and if the workers had complete parity on the corporation's board, then codetermination would yield a structure roughly like a two-person partnership, in which the two parties must continually bargain between themselves over all relevant matters concerning the operation of the firm. It would also have something of the character of ordinary collective bargaining, except that it would have the advantage that information would be fully shared and that the terms of the agreement might be more easily adjusted as time goes along.[70]

Such a structure is, arguably, roughly what one finds in the German coal and steel industry. The worker representatives there have been granted substantial parity on the board of directors. Moreover, those worker representatives arguably speak with a roughly unitary voice as a consequence of the heavily blue-collar nature of the work force and, probably much more important, of the substantial role given to the union in representing the workers on the board. The highly centralized structure of union authority in Germany presumably tends to yield a common policy for the worker representatives vis-à-vis the investor representatives on the boards in these firms.

The industries covered by the Co-Determination Act of 1976 (namely, all firms outside of coal and steel in which there are more than 2,000 employees) present a somewhat different picture. These firms evidently exhibit all the work-force heterogeneity typically encountered in modern industry. And the unions have not been given a central role in the process of selecting worker representatives to the supervisory board. As a result, the worker representatives on the board represent constituencies with diverse interests. The legally mandated system for selecting worker representatives reinforces this, because it requires that there be included at least one representative from each of three classes of workers: wage earners, salaried employees, and managerial employees. From all that has been said above, one would not expect that this system of representation would be highly viable as a means of governing the firm. Given the apparent difficulty of making collective self-governance workable for employees alone when the labor force is heterogeneous, it would be surprising if a firm's electoral mechanisms, including voting for and within the board of directors, could effectively be employed not only to resolve conflicts among different groups of employees but also to deal with the more serious conflicts of interest between labor and capital.

The German experience does not clearly belie that expectation. To begin with, codetermination has been imposed upon German firms by force of law; no similar system seems to have been adopted by any significant number of firms either inside or outside of Germany in the absence of compulsion.

In addition, a variety of elements in the German system of codetermination seem well designed to prevent politics at the board level, both among workers and between workers and shareholders, from yielding instability and inefficient decisions. First, outside the coal and steel industry, labor lacks full parity on the board: if there is deadlock between the worker and the shareholder representatives, a tie-breaking vote is effectively granted the shareholder representatives. Second, German firms have a dual board structure in which the higher "supervisory" board, on which the worker representatives sit, is distant from all but the broadest decisions of policy. Third, the provision for separate managerial representatives among the employee representatives creates the likelihood that one or more of the worker representatives will often side with the shareholder representatives. Fourth, the matters of most direct importance to workers are not decided at the level of the supervisory board. Either they are decided higher up, at the industry level, through collective bargaining between the unions and the employers' associations, or they are decided at a lower level in dealings between management and the legally mandated works councils. As a consequence, the board is not used for making the particular types of decisions where workers and shareholders have the most strongly conflicting interests, and where the workers have the most strongly conflicting interests among themselves.

Indeed, it appears that codetermination has not had a substantial impact on firm decision making at the board level, which continues to be dominated by shareholder interests in firms outside the iron and steel industry. The worker representatives to the supervisory board arguably play a largely informational role, providing a credible source of information from the firm to the workers (and vice versa) in support of collective bargaining by the unions and decision making in the works councils, where the real worker influence takes place and where shared information presumably reduces the incentive for, and hence the costs of, strategic bargaining. This suggests, in turn, that there may not be much difference between the regime imposed on those firms covered by the 1976 law and the smaller firms still covered by the 1952 law, which provides for only one-third of the directors to be worker representatives, and indeed that both these systems may be little different in practice from the regimes imposed in the Scandinavian countries and elsewhere, under which workers have the right to have only one to three members on the board—enough to serve as informational conduits, but not enough to exercise meaningful control.

Unionization

In those firms in which employees bargain collectively through labor unions, employees already employ a political process for the purpose of aggregating their individual interests. The difference between such an arrangement and the type of collective representation involved in employee ownership, of course, is that the union's political process is used not to select the firm's management but to select representatives to bargain with a management chosen by the firm's shareholders.

It might seem that unions have most of the costs and few of the benefits of employee ownership. On the one hand, because unions do not involve full employee ownership, they do not entirely remove the possibility that the management of the firm will behave opportunistically toward the employees (or vice versa). Yet, on the other hand, they potentially have all the costs of collective decision making among employees.

There is surely some truth to this view, and it presumably helps explain the near abandonment in the contemporary United States of the adversarial model of collective bargaining that was adopted in American law in the 1930s.[71] Whatever the overall efficiency of that model of employee representation, however, there are many ways in which it adapted to the problems of collective representation on which we have been focusing.

For one thing, employees with managerial or supervisory responsibilities are generally not unionized; it is usually only the employees who make up the lower, more horizontal strata among the firm's employees who belong to a union. (Where more senior employees form unions, they tend to be highly homogeneous, as in the case of teachers or pilots.) Where the jobs held by the unionized employees are particularly diverse, the employees are frequently split up into separate bargaining units. As a consequence, there is commonly a fair degree of homogeneity of interest among the employees represented by any given union.[72]

Further, unions typically bargain with management only over a relatively narrow range of issues immediately touching on the employees' interests, such as wages, hours, and job classifications.[73] Other issues, such as the firm's investment policies or even its policy on layoffs, are seldom bargained over even though in theory it might be more efficient if employees were more actively involved in deciding them.[74] Indeed, unions themselves seem to avoid broader involvement of this sort, intentionally keeping the scope of bargaining narrowly confined.[75] There may be a variety of reasons for this. But whether it is cause or consequence, with this strategy a union averts certain possibilities for costly internal conflict. By confining themselves to such matters as wages, hours, and job classifications, unions avoid the necessity of making a variety of hard choices where the interests of their members conflict. They leave that task to management and stay focused on the less controversial aim of generally pressing for greater equality with respect to the subjects they bargain over.

Finally, it is often observed that unions are seldom democratic.[76] This is commonly deplored in both the social science and the policy literature, much as the general absence of genuine shareholder democracy in publicly held business corporations was deplored several decades ago. But it may be that greater democracy would bring much higher governance costs without a corresponding improvement in the accuracy with which the union members' preferences are represented. Michels's iron law of oligarchy[77] may in fact be an economic law, at least where unions are concerned.

Similar considerations may help explain why it is that bargaining between a union and a firm is often conducted in large part by representatives from the union's national office and not just by local union officials: this helps defuse even further the problem of local internal politics.

Experience with collective bargaining thus does not provide strong evidence that democratic processes can be effectively employed to represent the interests of a heterogeneous class of employees in general corporate decision making.

Other Problems with Employee Governance

One might concede that the high costs of employee governance have been a critical constraint on employee ownership but nevertheless believe that these costs have some source other than conflicts of interest among the employees or that, whatever the source of the costs, they can be made manageable through experience and organizational innovation. Two such arguments deserve special attention.

Employees May Lack Managerial Skills

It is sometimes argued that employee ownership is common among service professionals but rare among industrial employees simply because the latter lack the skills necessary for governance of a firm. For example, blue-collar employees may have insufficient knowledge of management or finance to select or police the firm's managers effectively. Or such employees may be inclined to be short-sighted in planning; the high salience of wages and working conditions may make the employees focus on those concerns to the detriment of new investment. Perhaps there is some truth in this view. The prevailing patterns of ownership suggest, however, that the skill level of employees is much less important than their homogeneity of interest in making employee ownership feasible. Employee ownership is evidently viable among blue-collar employees where there is little diversity of interest, as with the drivers in the transportation cooperatives or the semi-skilled employees in the plywood manufacturing cooperatives. Conversely, employee ownership is rare among white-collar employees who are not highly homogeneous, such as those employed in retailing, hotel and restaurant services, health care other than physician services, or computer programming.

An individual employee need not herself have the expertise to make managerial decisions in order to exercise her voice effectively as an owner. She need only be able to vote intelligently in electing the firm's directors. Consider, for example, a firm like General Motors. It is quite believable that even an assembly line worker at GM is in a position to act more thoughtfully in electing directors than are most of that firm's public shareholders, since she is likely to be more willing and able to obtain relevant information about the candidates and to act on it. Furthermore, many of GM's employees are not assembly line employees but financial planners, design engineers, and marketing executives—employees who have a great deal of information relevant to an assessment of the firm's management and who are likely to influence less-informed blue-collar employees in deciding whom to elect as directors. Consequently, it is quite plausible that, if the employees owned General Motors, they would elect a more effective board of directors and hold them more accountable than do the firm's current public shareholders—or at least it is quite plausible that this would be the case if, contrary to fact, there were no important conflicts of interest among the firm's employees.

Employees Lack Experience with Governance

It has also been argued that a major obstacle to widespread employee ownership is simply the absence of the customs, mores, and standard procedures necessary to make employee governance effective.[78] According to this theory, employees must first become accustomed to the notion of managing the firm where they work and develop the experience and methods needed for the task. This is presumably a cumulative process; employees in one firm can benefit from the example of another. Once the proper institutions and procedures are well established and there is substantial accumulated experience in working with them, employee ownership will compete effectively with investor ownership in a broad range of settings, including those in which there is substantial heterogeneity of interest among the employees.

We cannot easily dismiss this argument. Organizational innovation and its diffusion have sometimes proceeded slowly in other settings. But there is strong reason to be skeptical.

Institutions for collective governance play a central role in American culture and are familiar to most citizens in a broad range of settings, from presidential elections to the student council and the local Moose Lodge. Employees, in particular, have long been familiar with collective governance in unions. In such a cultural environment, it is hard to argue that lack of experience with collective decision making in general is a major obstacle to the viability of employee ownership. At most, one can argue that the obstacle is lack of knowledge about, or experience with, the specific types of governance mechanisms that are needed to permit employees to act collectively in managing industrial enterprise.

The experience with ESOPs and at Mondragon suggests that the most suitable forms for employee self-governance in large-scale enterprise may involve a complex combination of representative and fiduciary mechanisms. Further experimentation and experience in developing these organizational forms may therefore help to reduce their costs. Perhaps there are sufficient gains yet to be had in this respect to yield important improvements in the viability of employee ownership. But this seems unlikely. Even in the United States there has already been considerable experience with forms of employee self-governance in service enterprise and in small-scale industry. Further, as later chapters will discuss, there has accumulated over many decades substantial experience with consumer cooperatives and with other types of producer cooperatives (such as farmer-owned processing and marketing cooperatives), some of which rank among the nation's largest industrial firms. These firms provide obvious models for the governance of worker cooperatives. Their success suggests strongly that where there are substantial gains to be had from collective ownership, its development will not long be inhibited simply by lack of experience with institutions for collective governance in the particular setting involved.

The experience with housing cooperatives and condominiums, which is explored in detail in Chapter 11, is instructive in this regard. Prior to 1961 the condominium form was essentially unknown in the United States, and its close cousin, the housing cooperative, was largely confined to the wealthy. Since then, however, changes in property law have made the condominium form feasible, and developments in taxation have made it financially attractive for a broad range of individuals. As a consequence, the condominium form has now spread rapidly and widely through the housing market even though it requires, at its core, a mechanism for collective self-governance by the owner-occupants. There is reason to believe that collective governance in housing condominiums is costly and that, in part for that reason, without substantial tax subsidies the condominium form would be far less common than it is. It also appears that the mechanisms for collective governance in condominiums are continuing to evolve—for example, by delegating increasing authority to hired management—in ways that reduce these costs. Nevertheless, the basic governance mechanisms necessary to make condominiums viable in competition with investor-owned (that is, rental) buildings developed quite rapidly. If so many individuals can so quickly become accustomed to collectively governing the apartment building where they live, why can they not also quickly become accustomed to collectively governing the firm where they work? Evidently more is required to make employee self-governance viable than simply additional time to get accustomed to it.

A Test Case: United Air Lines

The employee buyout of United Air Lines in 1994 promises to provide an illuminating test of the importance of governance problems and of the potential mechanisms to cope with those problems. Originally the company's 7,000 pilots sought to purchase the firm by themselves, and in fact reached a preliminary agreement with the company's shareholders for such a transaction in 1989. If that transaction had succeeded, the result would have been very much the type of employee-owned firm that has proved successful elsewhere, with ownership shared by a single highly homogeneous group of employees. The pilots' 1989 buyout ultimately failed, however, in part because of the strong opposition of United's 23,000-member machinists' union, reflecting the serious conflicts of interest between these two quite different groups of employees.

In the successful 1994 buyout, the pilots brought the machinists in as participants. The participating employees acquired, through ESOPs, 53 percent of United's stock, with the remaining 47 percent left in the hands of public shareholders. The consequence is a conspicuously heterogeneous set of owners, with potential conflicts of interest not only between the employees and the public shareholders but also, among the employees, between the pilots and the machinists. In addition, the machinists are themselves, in comparison with the pilots, a highly heterogeneous group. In an apparent effort to cope with these potential conflicts, United's governance mechanisms were revised, as part of the buyout, to provide for selection of the company's board of directors in a complex and highly constrained fashion that involves no direct voting for any of the board members by either the pilots or the machinists. Rather, majority control of the board is in the hands of quasi-self-appointing outside directors who are apparently intended to serve as fiduciaries simultaneously for all of the factions among the owners.[79] (In addition, both the pilots' and machinists' unions committed themselves, as one of the terms of the buyout, to six-year no-strike agreements.)

United's new governance structure reflects the general pattern we have seen elsewhere, with substantial muting of electoral democracy and heavy reliance on control by fiduciaries. The size, economic importance, and potential profitability of the airline make this an important experiment. It will be interesting to see whether this complex ownership structure proves viable in the long run, suggesting that participation in ownership is a promising route for restructuring labor relations across the economy in general, or whether it ends up being simply a temporary expedient to resolve the bargaining impasse reached under the old regime of adversarial collective bargaining, with the company ultimately reverting to a more homogeneous class of patron-owners.

Conclusion

The classical model of the business firm, under which formal control is confined to suppliers of capital while management in turn deals with employees through market contracting, leaves room for considerable inefficiency in the form of agency costs between owners and managers and opportunistic or strategic behavior between the firm and its employees. In theory, employee ownership promises substantial efficiency improvements in these respects. And in practice it appears that, when the employees involved are highly homogeneous, employee ownership often is more efficient than investor ownership. The evidence suggests, however, that with a heterogenous work force direct employee control of the firm brings substantial costs—costs that are generally large enough to outweigh the benefits that employee ownership otherwise offers. For similar reasons, true sharing of control between labor and capital does not appear promising as a route to efficiency. Paradoxically, the aspect of employee ownership often extolled as its principal virtue—active participation in governance of the firm through democratic institutions—appears in fact to be its greatest liability.

Consequently, forms of employee participation that fall short of true ownership may offer better prospects for improving on the efficiency of the classical model. For example, simple profit-sharing plans may be a better approach to increasing incentives for productivity, while quality circles, shop floor committees, works councils, labor-management committees, and informational seats for labor on the board of directors may be more workable means of improving the flow of information between management and employees.

To be sure, all such conclusions must be tentative. Organizational innovations may yet make employee ownership viable in circumstances where it has previously failed to make headway. But for the present, it seems most reasonable to predict that successful instances of employee ownership will remain largely confined to firms with highly homogeneous classes of employee-owners.

The chapters that follow, which explore other forms of producer and consumer-owned enterprise, strongly reinforce the conclusion that the problems of collective decision making play a key role in determining patterns of ownership. Indeed, that role is often much easier (and less controversial) to identify in other forms of shared ownership than it is in employee ownership.

7

Agricultural and Other Producer Cooperatives

There are three common types of producer-owned enterprise: investor-owned, worker-owned, and farmer-owned. In this chapter we turn to the last of these three, farmer-owned cooperatives that process and market agricultural products. At the end of the chapter we shall also examine other types of producer cooperatives and ask why they are so rare—that is, why there are only three principal forms of producer-owned enterprise.

Farm Marketing Cooperatives

Farmer-owned cooperatives are enormously important in marketing agricultural products. In the United States, as of 1991, there were 2,400 cooperatives primarily engaged in marketing farm products for their members, with an aggregate annual business volume of $56 billion and a total membership of 1,840,000 farmers.[1] These cooperatives marketed 28 percent of all farm products, and their market share reached as high as 81 percent for dairy products, 38 percent for grain and oilseeds, and 36 percent for cotton.[2] The share of the overall market for agricultural products accounted for by the cooperatives has increased substantially over the course of the twentieth century, advancing from 6 percent in 1913 to 15 percent in 1929 and 20 percent in 1950, and achieving a peak of 30 percent in 1982.[3]

Farm marketing cooperatives differ markedly in the scope of their activities. Some are simply bargaining cooperatives that negotiate on behalf of their farmer-members with purchasers of agricultural commodities. These bargaining cooperatives often do not take possession of their members' produce. They simply negotiate a common price for the commodity, leaving purchasers to deal directly with individual farmers to arrange delivery at that price. In the United States, bargaining cooperatives are particularly prominent among producers of milk for fluid consumption and, in the Pacific coast states, among growers of tree fruits and tomatoes and producers of raisins.[4]

Much more numerous and more important than the pure bargaining cooperatives are the cooperatives that actually handle their members' crops. Often the amount of processing done by the cooperative is relatively modest. For example, farmers in a locality who produce a given type of grain—particularly wheat, corn, or soybeans—will often own a local cooperative grain warehouse or elevator company that dries, sorts, and stores their grain prior to sale. The cooperative may simply hold the grain on behalf of its members, selling it on the member's order and charging for its services, or it may purchase the grain from the member and then resell it. These local grain cooperatives are often federated into regional cooperatives that operate large-scale elevator facilities for aggregating grain in greater bulk.[5]

There are also many farmer cooperatives that, like the cheese factory described in Chapter 1, not only take possession of their members' commodities but process them into finished products and even, in many cases, market those products to consumers. The brand names used by some of these cooperatives are quite familiar to American consumers. They include, for example, Sunkist (California orange growers), Sun Maid (California raisin producers), Land O'Lakes (midwestern dairy farmers), Ocean Spray (New England, midwestern, and Pacific Northwest cranberry growers), Welch's (nationwide Concord and Niagara grape growers), Diamond (California walnut growers), and Gold Kist (southern poultry producers). Many of these firms are impressively large. As of 1992, Land O'Lakes, Gold Kist, and Ocean Spray were among the leading fifty firms in the prepared food industry[6] and were also on *Fortune* magazine's list of the five hundred largest U.S. industrial corporations.[7]

The processing cooperatives are sometimes vertically integrated far downstream into manufacturing, marketing, and distribution, and some are highly innovative. Ocean Spray, for example, has developed a succession of new fruit products based both on cranberries and on other fruits, and has also been a leader in packaging.[8]

Just as the market share of the cooperatives has been steadily growing, so has the relative size of many of the individual firms. In 1962, for example, there were only five agricultural cooperatives among the Fortune 500 largest industrial firms;[9] thirty years later, in 1992, there were fourteen.[10] The cooperatives' degree of vertical integration also appears to have increased steadily over time. The regional grain cooperatives, for example, developed substantial grain export facilities that permitted them to increase their share of total grain exports—previously dominated by several large investor-owned firms—from roughly 5 percent in 1965 to 15 percent in 1985.[11]

Farm marketing cooperatives play a similarly large role in other developed market economies. By the early 1970s, for example, cooperatives accounted for 45 percent of the agricultural market in France, 48 percent in Germany, 60 percent in the Netherlands, over 70 percent in Denmark, and 80 percent in Sweden—in each case a substantial increase from just a decade earlier. Moreover, among these and other European Community countries the areas of concentration roughly parallel those in the United States, with cooperatives having especially large market shares in dairy products and grains and somewhat smaller, though still important, shares in meat and vegetables.[12] In less-developed countries, it appears that agricultural producer cooperatives generally play a distinctly smaller but rapidly expanding role.[13]

There is thus nothing quaint, old-fashioned, or local about agricultural producer cooperatives. They find their most extensive development in those economies that have the most sophisticated and competitive agricultural sectors, and the cooperatives themselves are often large, complex, and dynamic firms. As a consequence, they offer a useful application and test of our theories of ownership.

Costs of Market Contracting

Monopsony

Farming, with its highly homogeneous commodities and numerous producers, is one of the most competitive of all industries. In contrast, the middlemen—handlers and processors—who purchase farm products are often highly concentrated and hence have the potential for exercising a degree of monopsony power over the farmers they deal with.

This monopsony power can sometimes be accentuated by the seasonality or perishability of agricultural commodities. An individual farmer who simply harvests his crop and then takes it to market risks encountering prospective purchasers who offer only a very low price—perhaps below the cost of production—in the realization that the farmer has very little time in which to market his crop and therefore cannot credibly threaten to hold out for long or to engage in an extensive search for other purchasers. A purchaser, in contrast, can often realistically threaten to turn to other farmers to satisfy his needs.

The result is to give farmers an incentive to form cooperatives through which they can bargain collectively with middlemen, or with which they can displace the middlemen entirely. That incentive has apparently played an important role in the formation of farm marketing cooperatives.[14]

Cooperatively owned grain elevators, which were among the earliest forms of farmer cooperatives to be widely successful in the United States, provide a conspicuous example. Economies of scale are such that generally only one or two elevators are needed to collect, store, and transfer to a railroad all the grain produced by farmers within a given locality. In the 1890s, the elevators were nearly all operated by proprietary firms, each of which commonly owned many—sometimes hundreds—of elevators. In the major grain-producing states these firms succeeded in forming highly effective cartels, through which they collectively set the price they would pay farmers for grain. In direct response, farmers established their own local grain elevators organized as cooperatives. After a period of overt economic warfare that lasted roughly through the first decade of the twentieth century, cooperatives were established over a large fraction of the market and broke the cartels. The result was a substantial increase—perhaps between 6 and 12 percent—in the price farmers received for their grain, and a correspondingly larger percentage increase in the price of farmland.[15]

There is good reason to believe that the elevator cooperatives would not have become widespread without the stimulus of monopsony. There had been many efforts to establish cooperative grain elevators prior to the 1890s. These cooperatives typically failed after a few years, apparently because local markets for grain were then competitive. It was only after the cartels succeeded in suppressing effective competition[16] that viable cooperatives were formed by the farmers—the same farmers who had failed in forming cooperatives twenty years earlier.[17]

Outside of the staple grains, marketing cooperatives in the United

States seldom seem to have formed in response to explicit cartels. They do, however, appear to be particularly prevalent where the business undertaken by the cooperative has some degree of natural monopsony power. For example, high transportation costs combined with economies of scale have resulted in high local concentration among the processors of dairy products, which helps explain why dairy processing, like the grain elevator business, is an area in which cooperatives are particularly common.[18]

Monopsony is evidently also an important reason why proprietary processing firms tend to convert to farmer cooperatives in declining industries. For example, in the California fruit and vegetable canning industry, which has been declining since the 1950s owing to better distribution of both fresh and frozen foods, a number of failing proprietary firms have been reorganized as farmer cooperatives.[19] An important incentive for such transactions, presumably, is that once the industry has declined to the point at which local farmers have only a single cannery as a likely purchaser for their produce, they face potential price exploitation. And this possibility is aggravated by the fact that growers often have substantial crop-specific investments in their farms (fruit orchards being the most obvious example) and in their human capital, the value of which is available for expropriation by a monopsonist. The farmers are in a situation similar to that of workers in a declining firm in a declining industry.

The increasing degree of concentration in the canning industry, however, seems to be an exception to the overall trend in agriculture. In general, although markets for farm products remain fairly concentrated, the market power exercised by middlemen appears to have declined over the past hundred years. Explicit cartels among purchasers of agricultural commodities, such as those that prompted the formation of the grain elevator cooperatives at the end of the nineteenth century, have long since disappeared and would be unlikely to arise again under modern antitrust policy. At the same time, the development of futures markets for many agricultural commodities over the course of the twentieth century has reduced the strategic disadvantage that farmers face in dealing with middlemen. With a futures market, a farmer can sell his crop at his leisure long before it is harvested, or even before it is planted.

Nevertheless, as already noted, farm marketing cooperatives have not only continued to thrive but have significantly expanded their market share over the course of the century. Evidently there have also been other factors that have encouraged the success of agricultural cooperatives.

Cartelization

When farmers form a cooperative to displace a monopsonistic purchaser of farm products—that is, to actually own and operate a middleman processing or handling operation that would otherwise face the farmers as a monopsonist—the result promises to be an unambiguous improvement in social welfare, making farmers better off without making consumers worse off.[20] When, alternatively, farmers form a cooperative not to displace a monopsonistic purchaser but rather just to serve as a vehicle through which to negotiate collectively with the monopsonist, offsetting his market power with monopoly power of their own, the consequences for social welfare are more ambiguous. Although it has been argued that the exercise of such "countervailing power" is an important public policy justification for encouraging the formation of farm marketing cooperatives,[21] the issue is debatable. Undoubtedly farmers themselves will be better off if they can form an effective cartel with which to confront a monopsonistic purchaser. And, under some market conditions, consumers will benefit too. But it is also quite possible that consumers will be worse off as a result of the farmers' collective action—that the effect on consumers of putting another layer of market power in the chain of distribution will be cumulative rather than countervailing.[22]

In any event, if a farm marketing cooperative is to exercise countervailing power it must be able to function effectively as a farmers' cartel. That is, it must be able to control the aggregate supply, and hence the price, of the farmers' products. (In contrast, if the objective of the cooperative is not to bargain with a monopsonist but to displace it, as in the case of the grain elevators, then it is not necessary that the cooperative be able to function as an effective cartel.) And indeed, whether for good reasons or bad, farm marketing cooperatives in the United States have been permitted to exercise this power by the Capper-Volstead Act of 1922, which gives the marketing cooperatives a partial exemption from the antitrust laws.

On its face, the Capper-Volstead Act simply provides that setting prices collectively through a farmer cooperative is not an antitrust violation per se, and thus arguably leaves cooperatives exposed to the threat of prosecution if they should seek to exercise monopoly power. But the exemption has been given a broad interpretation. Farmers have generally been allowed to form both bargaining and processing cooperatives freely, and to use those cooperatives as means to set common prices for their products, so long as the cooperatives do not use "predatory tactics" (such as selective boycotts) to compel either farmers or purchasers to deal with them, and so long as they do not enter into anticompetitive agreements with other organizations that are not cooperatives. The formation of cooperatives, and mergers among existing cooperatives, has been freely permitted.[23] Even agreements among separate cooperatives to fix prices have been upheld, on the theory that they were doing nothing more than would be permissible if the cooperatives involved were to merge into a single organization.[24]

This long-standing antitrust exemption raises the prospect that the marketing cooperatives may have been used to establish market power, not just to counter monopsony, but further to extract monopoly profits for the farmers themselves from ultimate consumers. We must consider, therefore, to what extent farm marketing cooperatives are just cartels, formed not because they are more efficient than investor-owned enterprise but because they provide a means of fixing prices.

There are, in fact, some industries in which farmers have succeeded in using marketing cooperatives as mechanisms for cartelization. Milk is an example. Through an elaborate system of federal and state regulation that has been in place since the 1930s, legally mandated minimum prices for Grade A fluid milk have been established and enforced in most parts of the United States. These prices are well above the prices that would prevail in a competitive market, and they result in a substantial shift of wealth from consumers to dairy farmers.[25] Nevertheless, milk marketing cooperatives have regularly succeeded in raising prices even further, above the legally mandated minimum prices, throughout much of the country.[26]

The success of the milk cooperatives in fixing prices, however, is heavily dependent on the milk regulatory regime, which—among other things—places severe restrictions on the ability to take milk produced in one part of the country and sell it in another, higher-priced market.[27] Producers of most other agricultural commodities do not have the benefit of such an extensive regulatory regime. And it appears that, as a consequence, cooperatives in other areas generally have not been markedly successful in functioning as cartels.

This is not for lack of trying. Raising prices by restricting the amount produced or marketed has been an explicit objective of many farmer cooperatives handling various agricultural commodities, particularly in the 1920s and 1930s.[28] But most crops are produced by a large number of farmers, each of whom can vary his individual production substantially. Moreover, new entry into production of most agricultural commodities is relatively easy—most obviously, by farmers who had previously been growing other crops. This makes it very difficult for a cooperative to control aggregate production, and hence to exercise monopoly power.[29] If a cooperative succeeds in raising prices above cost, it creates a strong incentive for expanded production that threatens to drive prices back down. This was what happened to the cooperatives that tried to act as cartels in the 1920s and 1930s. They sought to raise prices to monopolistic levels by withholding product from the market. But the resulting surplus production hung over the market and kept prices low, often leaving the members of the cooperatives even worse off than if they had behaved competitively.

Strong evidence that marketing cooperatives generally do not succeed in establishing monopolistic prices comes from their membership policies. Some cooperatives have closed memberships (that is, additional farmers can join the cooperative only with the explicit agreement of the existing members). But the great majority have open membership policies under which any farmer who produces the crop in question is free to join and market his crop through the cooperative. Either policy makes it difficult to control the amount of crop marketed. With closed membership, excluded farmers have a strong incentive to expand production freely to take advantage of any increase in price the cooperative succeeds in arranging. With open membership, higher prices will encourage an expansion of membership and hence of product to dispose of. The evidence suggests that market power is generally sustainable, if at all, only with closed membership. Consequently, the fact that most marketing cooperatives have open membership is substantial evidence that they are unable to control prices. Indeed, a careful 1964 study could locate only four marketing cooperatives that appeared to exercise any substantial market power.[30]

The preceding observations concern cooperatives that engage in processing. One might think that pure bargaining cooperatives would provide stronger evidence of market power, since they would seem to exist for little other reason. And indeed, some of the more successful bargaining cooperatives represent a very large portion of the market. Yet there is reason to believe that they exercise only a modest degree of market power. For example, the California tomato bargaining cooperative has a very large share of the nation's total crop. Yet it is not clear that the organization has much market power. Entry into tomato growing is easy, and contracts with the cooperative bind the growers only for two years. If there is any market power, it probably derives from California legislation that imposes collective bargaining on the industry.[31] Overall, there is only modest evidence of monopoly power among the various California bargaining cooperatives.[32]

Further structural evidence of low market power comes from the relatively short length of the membership contracts in most marketing cooperatives. Cooperatives commonly employ contracts that bind their members to market their produce through the cooperative. These contracts are enforceable, and typically provide for liquidated damages sufficiently high to discourage breach. The nut growers' cooperative (Diamond), which is one of the few marketing cooperatives that apparently have substantial market power,[33] has contracts of this sort that bind its members to the cooperative for a period of five years. But contracts of this duration are rare. Most marketing cooperatives, including bargaining cooperatives, employ contracts of only one year's duration.[34] Thus farmers can decide annually whether to market their crops through the cooperative, leaving the cooperative with little control over long-run supply.[35]

Ocean Spray is an interesting example in this respect. Although it has about 85 percent of the American cranberry crop, its profitability evidently comes from marketing, not monopoly. For years it was in a position of chronic oversupply. It ultimately succeeded in rescuing its members from this condition, not by cutting back on production, but by developing and marketing new cranberry products.[36]

The preceding evidence is drawn entirely from experience in the United States. But there is good reason to believe that similar conclusions apply in other countries. In Britain, for example, concentration is lower among agricultural marketing cooperatives than among agricultural supply cooperatives, suggesting little effort at monopolization by the former. Also, levels of concentration among marketing cooperatives in Britain are low in comparison with those of the processors to whom the farm products are sold.[37]

The evidence indicates overwhelmingly that cooperatives are not simply a creature of antitrust exemption, and that they would continue to exist in large numbers even if they were effectively barred from raising prices above competitive levels.

Costly Information

Asymmetric information about crop attributes and prices has sometimes served as a stimulus to the formation of farmer marketing cooperatives. Again grain elevators and warehouses in the late nineteenth century provide an example. Proprietary operators, who understood the grading methods employed in the terminal markets better than did local farmers, would assign grain they purchased from a farmer an inappropriately low grade (for example, classifying it as Number 3 Northern Wheat rather than as Number 2), paying the farmer only the price appropriate for that grade and then reselling it at the price prevailing for the higher grade. Or, similarly, when receiving grain from a farmer for storage they would grade it too low and then substitute for it other grain that they owned that was actually of the lower grade.[38]

More generally, farm marketing cooperatives economize on a variety of information costs for their farmer-members. If each farmer in a given locality were to decide separately when and at what price to market his crops, there would be substantial duplication of effort in gathering information about market conditions, prospective purchasers, transportation, and other matters. Cooperatives allow farmers to share these costs.[39]

Risk Bearing

Farming is a risky business. Markets for most crops show large year-to-year fluctuations, and this is accentuated by the large amount of leverage farmers generally undertake in order to meet their substantial needs for capital. It is sometimes said that an important role for cooperatives is to help farmers to deal with this risk.[40] And cooperatives might indeed play such a role if they were organized to pool the returns from different crops. But in fact cooperatives are generally organized to handle only a single crop. And in those cooperatives that handle more than one crop, the returns from the different crops are typically kept separate. Thus there is no risk diversification, and the typical marketing cooperative does not reduce the amount of risk borne by its member farmers. Indeed, as noted further below in discussing the costs of capital, membership in a cooperative may substantially increase a farmer's exposure to risk.

Marketing Externalities

If there are barriers to entry into agricultural production, but processing is relatively competitive, then there may be opportunities for promoting the commodity through advertising that are available to a cooperative but not to an investor-owned intermediary. This may help explain the success of the fruit and vegetable cooperatives. Entry into (and exit from) production for many fruits, and perhaps some vegetables, is relatively inelastic in the short run because the trees take time to mature and represent a substantial crop-specific investment with a long expected life. The Sunkist orange growers' cooperative, which successfully promoted fresh orange consumption nationwide early in the twentieth century, offers an example.[41]

Tax and Credit Subsidies

In addition to the preceding more or less natural advantages that marketing cooperatives have offered farmers in reducing the costs incurred (or raising the prices received) from contracting, there have been important tax and credit subsidies offered to farm marketing cooperatives. This naturally raises the suspicion that many or most marketing cooperatives may be solely a response to these subsidies, and would not exist in their absence.

Tax Preferences

Under the United States federal corporate income tax, farm marketing cooperatives have the benefit of two favorable regimes that are not available to their investor-owned competitors. First, nearly all farm marketing cooperatives can qualify for the special rules for taxing cooperatives that are contained in Subchapter T of the Internal Revenue Code. Second, as long as they meet some slightly more stringent requirements, farm marketing cooperatives can also qualify for special tax "exemption" under Section 521.

In essence, Subchapter T permits a cooperative to escape the double taxation that is imposed on business corporations. The special privileges of Subchapter T are not confined to farm marketing cooperatives. Rather, they are available to any firm organized as a producer or consumer cooperative, with the exception of lenders' cooperatives (that is, ordinary business corporations). For example, as noted in Chapter 5, Subchapter T is also available to worker cooperatives. Because it has such general importance, it is worthwhile examining briefly how Subchapter T works.

Under Subchapter T, earnings that a cooperative pays out in cash as patronage dividends in the year they are earned are not subject to corporate taxation at all; rather, they are taxable only to the member who receives them, at her personal tax rate. Earnings that are retained rather than paid out can be treated in either of two ways, as the cooperative and its members choose. The first alternative is for the cooperative to pay tax on those earnings at the corporate tax rate. Then, if the earnings are paid out in cash as patronage dividends in a subsequent year, the corporation can deduct them for tax purposes (effectively getting a rebate of its earlier tax payment) and the earnings will be taxed to the members who receive them at their personal tax rate. The second alternative is for the cooperative's members to include their pro rata share of the retained earnings in their personal taxable income in the year they were earned, paying tax on them at their personal rate just as if they had received them as a cash dividend. If, in a later year, the earnings are then distributed as cash patronage dividends, the members receive them free of tax.

Subchapter T thus provides that a cooperative's net earnings are subject to tax only once, rather than being subject to the double taxation imposed upon business corporations. And as long as those earnings are retained rather than distributed, the cooperative can effectively choose whether that tax will be paid at the corporate tax rate or at the personal rates applicable to the cooperative's members.

More precisely, this is true of earnings to be paid out as patronage refunds and not as stock dividends. A cooperative can issue nonvoting capital stock and still qualify for Subchapter T treatment as long as dividends on the stock are limited to a rate of 8 percent. But even under Subchapter T, dividends paid on such stock remain subject to the dual-level system of taxation applied to earnings in business corporations, under which earnings are taxed both at the corporate rate when earned and again at the shareholder's personal tax rate when actually paid out.

Under Subchapter T, a cooperative need never be taxed more heavily than a comparable business corporation and may well be taxed much less. This is not to say that Subchapter T is either exceptional or unprincipled. The tax regime it establishes is roughly the same as that applied to sole proprietorships, to partnerships, and to the small business corporations that fall within Subchapter S. From the standpoint of economic efficiency, moreover, that regime is substantially more rational than the standard corporate tax regime. In fact, the major inconsistency of Subchapter T is simply that one particular type of cooperative is arbitrarily excluded from it—namely, the lenders' cooperative. Consequently, Subchapter T does not subsidize cooperatives in a general sense but only relative to investor-owned corporations that are subject to the corporate income tax.

In addition to being eligible, like other cooperatives, for the general benefits of Subchapter T, farm marketing cooperatives have the special opportunity of qualifying for status as an "exempt" cooperative under Section 521 of the federal tax code—an opportunity they share only with farm supply (purchasing) cooperatives, which will be examined in Chapter 8. Cooperatives qualifying under Section 521 have all the benefits of Subchapter T. In addition, they are exempt from corporate level taxes on any stock dividends they pay and they are also exempt from corporate taxation on income they derive from business they do with nonfarmers—income that is taxed to other Subchapter T cooperatives just as if they were ordinary business corporations.

But this additional "exemption" that Section 521 offers over the ordinary Subchapter T tax treatment of cooperatives is often marginal. As we shall see, capital stock in farm cooperatives, if present at all, is generally held by the farmer-members of the cooperative in amounts roughly proportional to their levels of patronage. As a result, even a nonexempt cooperative can avoid all corporate level tax on its patronage earnings simply by paying no dividends on its capital stock and instead paying out larger patronage refunds. Because the money distributed will go to the same individuals in any case, there is no particular disincentive to do this. And in fact this is what most farm cooperatives do. Indeed, to qualify for Section 521 status, a cooperative cannot derive more than 15 percent of its income from nonfarm business. Section 521's exemption for nonfarm income is therefore not a major benefit either.

Indeed, a cooperative that pays no stock dividends and has no nonfarm business would not be taxed any differently whether it qualified for Section 521 or not. And in fact, because the benefits of Section 521 are so modest and its restrictions can be confining, many farm cooperatives do not seek to take advantage of it.[42]

In short, farm marketing cooperatives get roughly the same tax benefits that are available to producer or consumer cooperatives in any other industry. Although those tax benefits may have led to a larger market share for farmer cooperatives than they would otherwise have had, they cannot explain why it is that producer cooperatives are so much more common in agriculture than in other industries.

Credit Subsidies

Beyond tax preferences, the federal government has aided farm marketing cooperatives with credit subsidies. These subsidies began as early as 1916 but achieved more substantial scope with the formation of a system of federally sponsored Banks for Cooperatives in 1933—a system that continues today. For many years these banks had the benefit of capital invested by the federal government without interest and also had the authority to issue tax-free bonds. Prior to 1944 they received some direct interest subsidies as well. By 1968, however, all subsidies to the Banks for Cooperatives had been eliminated.[43] As a result, although the Banks for Cooperatives remain an important source of capital for cooperatives, they are not the exclusive source,[44] and in fact it appears that the terms on which they have offered loans to cooperatives since the late 1960s have not been noticeably different from those offered by commercial banks.[45]

Have the Subsidies Been Important?

How important have these tax and credit subsidies been, overall, in promoting the cooperative form? Some authors have argued that the tax preferences, which provide the only continuing subsidy of importance, are a significant inducement to the adoption of the cooperative form, and that without these subsidies cooperatives would have trouble competing with investor-owned firms.[46] The existing empirical evidence does not permit strong conclusions.[47] Clearly the tax system gives cooperatives an advantage over their investor-owned counterparts at the margin,[48] and presumably the cooperatives' market share is larger as a consequence.

Yet there is good reason to believe that cooperatives would have assumed an important role in the marketing of agricultural commodities in the United States even in the absence of the tax and credit subsidies. Perhaps the best evidence is that cooperatives were well established before any of these subsidies were enacted. For example, both grain cooperatives and dairy cooperatives were already widespread by the time the federal corporate income tax was adopted in 1912 and the first elements of the federal farm credit system were established in 1916. In particular, of the 2,614 grain cooperatives existing in 1936, about 60 percent had been established before World War I.[49] Of the California citrus crop, over half was already being marketed by cooperatives as of 1906.[50]

Costs of Ownership

The preceding discussion suggests that, while market contracting for agricultural products has some costs that offer an incentive for farmer ownership, those costs are not conspicuously high. Moreover, neither antitrust exemption nor tax and credit preferences seem able to account for the unusually large role that cooperatives play in this sector. Apparently much of the explanation is to be found in unusually low costs of ownership.

Monitoring

The farmer-members of agricultural marketing cooperatives are in an unusually good position to exercise effective control over the firm. The result is that agency costs are, from all the evidence available, unusually small in these organizations.

Farmers have both the incentive and the opportunity to monitor marketing cooperatives actively and intelligently. The crops that the cooperatives market represent a major, and often the only, source of income for the farmer. Farmers commonly produce the same crop, and deal with the same cooperative, for many years and sometimes for generations. Farmers of a given crop tend to be geographically concentrated, making participation in governance relatively easy. And where a cooperative covers a large region, it is both possible and a common practice to structure the cooperative in ways that continue to permit active and informed member control. For example, many large cooperatives in the United States, including those that handle basic grains such as wheat, have a federated structure in which a number of small and highly responsive local cooperatives serve as members of regional or national cooperatives. Similarly, in many cooperatives directors are elected by district rather than at large.

The high degree of control that members are able to exercise over farm marketing cooperatives is reflected in the composition of their boards of directors. The elected members of the boards in these cooperatives, in contrast to a typical large business corporation, do not include the firm's managers but rather consist exclusively of members who are active producers. The elected directors may in turn appoint a few other individuals to seats on the board. These appointed directors may include the cooperative's chief executive officer. That is not common, however, and in any case the CEO does not chair the board. More commonly included among the appointed directors are individuals, such as academics or persons prominent in public affairs, who can serve as "public" directors. Typically the cooperative's management plays no role in the nomination of directors, and sometimes even the board itself does not participate in nominations.[51]

As these board structures suggest, the farmer-members of the marketing cooperatives are commonly well informed about the cooperative's affairs and take an active interest in them. Members usually know one or more directors personally. The directors play an important role not only in conveying the members' views to management but also in conveying information from management to the members. Managers pass important or potentially controversial issues to the board for decision. Boards scrutinize managerial performance closely and not uncommonly replace managers who are not performing well. In this and other ways, management in the cooperatives is highly responsive to members' interests.[52]

This is not to suggest that management of the cooperatives is amateurish or parochial. The larger and more extensively integrated cooperatives, such as Ocean Spray, hire professional managers and give them substantial discretion in running the business.[53]

There is good reason to believe that the resulting low agency costs play a significant role in the success of the cooperatives vis-à-vis investor-owned firms. Important evidence of this is the fact that marketing cooperatives are most common among farmers who produce only one or a very few commodities,[54] and who therefore have the focused incentive and knowledge to exercise their voice in the cooperative effectively. The geographical distribution of the cooperatives also supports this conclusion. The market share of the dairy cooperatives, for example, is highest in those regions in which dairy farming is most heavily concentrated.[55] This suggests that the effectiveness of farmer monitoring, which is presumably greater when the members of the cooperative live in close proximity to one another, is more important in making the cooperative form viable than is the monopsony power of the milk purchasers, which is presumably greatest when dairy farmers are least concentrated geographically. In similar fashion, the grain marketing cooperatives are strongest in those areas devoted to one or two field crops[56] and the fruit and nut marketing cooperatives span only a single region confined to one, two, or three states.[57]

Of course, farmers located in close proximity to one another are likely to have more interests in common than those located in different regions. The tendency for the farmer-members of a cooperative to be geographically concentrated may thus also reflect another important element of governance costs—the homogeneity of interest among the cooperative's members—to which we now turn.

Collective Decision Making

A critical advantage for farm marketing cooperatives, it appears, is the extreme homogeneity of interest among the typical cooperative's members. Most cooperatives handle only a single agricultural commodity. This commodity is itself exceptionally homogeneous, to the point where the produce of the various members is commonly fungible. This means that the members of the cooperative all share the relatively simple goal of maximizing the value of the commodity involved. Costs of collective decision making, as a consequence, can be kept to a minimum.

The scarcity of cooperatives that handle more than one commodity is strong evidence of the importance of this homogeneity of interest. Cooperatives handling multiple commodities can potentially derive substantial gains from risk diversification and common marketing. Nevertheless, they are rare. Presumably this is because it is difficult to find an objective basis for apportioning costs and revenues. Growers of the different products are likely to disagree about important aspects of the firm's operations, raising haggling costs and leading to decisions that exploit one commodity for the benefit of another or are otherwise inefficient.

Indeed, the few cooperatives that handle more than one commodity give evidence of just such problems. For example, canneries in California commonly pack more than one crop in order to realize economies of scale and scope. In the canneries operated as cooperatives, this creates conflicts among growers of the different crops in apportioning costs and revenues. Initially these cooperatives operated on a "single pool" system, under which, instead of accounting for costs and revenues separately by crop, each cooperative's aggregate annual profits were simply divided up among growers of the different crops according to a measure of the value of the raw crops they supplied. The measure chosen was the "field price" of the crop, which is the market price paid by proprietary canners. An important reason for choosing this method was its objectivity. But the field price was sometimes ambiguous and was often not an accurate index of the relative profitability of the crop to the cooperative, inducing growers of individual crops to argue that the crop's current field price was "unrealistic" or "unfair." The result was significant conflict among the board members representing growers of different crops as to whether there should be deviation from a specific crop's field price as a measure of value or whether the allotment for a given crop (that is, the aggregate amount purchased by the cooperative) should be increased or decreased because of the crop's current profitability to the cooperative. Moreover, for some crops there was no field price because the cooperative was the only packer. In these cases, the cooperative's board, which was dominated by growers of other crops, would treat growers of the crop the way a proprietary canner would, paying them no more than was necessary to induce supply.[58]

These conflicts consumed substantial amounts of energy from board members and managers and finally led the cooperatives to abandon the single pool system in favor of the "multiple pool" system, under which the cooperative's revenues and costs are accounted for separately for each crop.[59] Yet the apportionment of overhead and other common costs among different crops is necessarily a very subjective process. In addition, under multiple pooling the returns to growers of a given crop can depend heavily on the cooperative's allocation of resources to processing and marketing that crop. Consequently this method, like single pooling, intensely politicizes many operational decisions, breeding substantial conflict for board members and managers and leading to much second-guessing of management by the board of directors. Indeed, one suspects that the difficulties of governing multiple-crop canneries as cooperatives is important in explaining the strong dominance of investor-owned canneries before the industry fell into decline in the 1960s.

It is not only the canneries that have elected the multiple pool system. The relatively few cooperatives of other types that handle more than one commodity commonly do the profit accounting for each crop separately.[60] For example, Land O'Lakes, which primarily markets milk products, also markets turkeys, but makes the latter operation a separate profit center so that turkey growers internalize all their own costs and benefits.[61] Similarly, in order to gain important economies of scope in marketing, Ocean Spray added grapefruit and guava products to its traditional business of cranberries. But the grapefruit growers were formed into their own separate pool, and the guavas are purchased on a commercial basis rather than making the growers members of the cooperative.[62]

Even in the single-crop cooperatives, the conflicting interests of different growers can be significant. For example, although Ocean Spray is dominated by the cranberry growers, "on the board there is a lot of politics," particularly involving the disparate interests of cranberry growers from different geographical regions.[63] In the California fruit bargaining and marketing cooperatives, grading of members' fruit by quality and condition is such a sensitive issue that the cooperatives' managers are reluctant to get involved and commonly contract out the evaluation to independent third parties.[64] Indeed, even among growers of a single crop, accommodation of conflicting interests through collective governance can sometimes bring important efficiency costs.

For example, Hetherington describes a situation in which a strike closed the California fruit and vegetable canneries for eleven days at the peak of the 1976 peach canning season. The investor-owned canneries, observing that the industry inventory of canned peaches was already substantial and demand was weak, simply invoked the force majeure clauses in their contracts and declined acceptance of the fruit that would otherwise have been processed during the period involved, letting the fruit be lost at the expense of the growers. The cooperatives, in contrast, stored the fruit that would have been packed during this period and operated overtime to pack it rapidly at the end of the strike.

By this means they managed to save nearly all the fruit that ripened during the strike. But they also incurred substantial additional costs and packed excessive amounts of fruit for which there was weak demand.

The cooperatives chose this inefficient course to avoid imposing disproportionate costs on some of their members. This norm of equality of treatment—so common as a means of avoiding the costs of conflict in collective decision making, as we saw in Chapter 5—could have been preserved at much lower cost by allowing the fruit in question to spoil while still letting its growers share in the profits from the pool as if it had been packed. But the growers whose fruit had been canned before the strike were unwilling to accept this solution, evidently in part because of the difficulties of deciding, for purposes of determining shares in the pool, the quantity and quality to impute to fruit left unpicked.[65] The equality norm has also led to continued inclusion in the cooperatives of growers that deliver inefficiently small volumes or that are located in areas that have become uneconomical.[66]

The extreme importance of homogeneity of interest also seems a likely explanation for the fact that cooperatives tend to have a larger market share in those crops that are particularly simple to grade, such as grains and milk, than in those that are not, such as vegetables and livestock.[67] Among fruits and vegetables, for similar reasons, the cooperatives have not had much success with highly perishable varieties and have concentrated on the less perishable varieties.[68] This is apparently because, as in the canning cooperatives, perishability makes crops more difficult to grade and also creates disparities in value based on the time the crops ripen—the crops ripening at the peak of the season generally being less valuable than those that ripen at other times, for example. The ease of resolving conflicting interests among the owners seems to be a more important consideration, in determining the assignment of ownership, than are the costs of contracting that arise when investor-owned purchasers try to exploit the pressure to sell that faces growers of perishable crops.

Finally, although various attempts have been made, there have been no successful nationwide bargaining cooperatives. An important reason for this, it has been argued, is that it would be too difficult to reconcile the divergent and conflicting interests of all the farmers involved.[69] This suggests, in turn, that the governance costs of such an organization would be substantial enough to outweigh the potential gains from increased market power and the economies in information and bargaining costs that the organization could offer its members.

Homogeneity of interest clearly plays a critical role. Where interests among potential members conflict even modestly, marketing cooperatives do not experience much success. Conversely, where the farmers involved have nearly identical interests, marketing cooperatives thrive even when the costs of contracting with investor-owned firms appear relatively modest.

The homogeneity of interest emphasized here, as elsewhere in the book, involves similarity in the types of transactions that members have with the cooperative—or, more precisely, similarity in the effect that any decision by the cooperative will have upon transactions between the cooperative and each of its various members. But there is evidence that homogeneity among the members along other, more personal dimensions can also be important. For example, cooperatives seem to have been particularly successful when the local farmers have shared unusual cultural homogeneity, as where they are mostly of Scandinavian descent. And in spite of strong incentives to form tobacco cooperatives in the South—incentives that arose from both monopoly and asymmetric information—these cooperatives were slow to form and grow, evidently owing in substantial part to the black-white split among farmers.[70]

Capital Supply

For the reasons discussed in Chapter 4, the equity capital required by farm marketing cooperatives must generally be raised from the cooperatives' farmer-members.[71] There are obvious costs to having farmers provide this capital. Modern farms, though predominantly family-owned businesses, are relatively capital intensive. Therefore farmers are unlikely to have substantial amounts of liquid capital available to invest elsewhere. In addition, the returns to a farmer from investing in a marketing cooperative are likely to be positively correlated with the returns to his farm. Since farming is a volatile business in itself, this means that a marketing cooperative is a highly risky investment for a farmer.

Nevertheless, it is not apparent that difficulty in raising capital has substantially inhibited the formation and growth of farmer cooperatives. Many marketing cooperatives are relatively heavily capitalized.

Some of this capital is obtained by borrowing. Much of it, however, is equity capital raised from members.[72] For example, as of 1992 the members of the National Grape Co-operative (Welch's) had each invested an average of $54,000 in the firm, or more than $1,900 per acre contracted to the cooperative, making this investment close to the members' total investment in production assets.[73] Even more impressively, in 1989, the book value of equity in Ocean Spray Cranberries— surely an underestimate of the actual value—was $242,000 per member.[74] And the California canning cooperatives commonly require that members maintain an investment in the cooperative well in excess of 100 percent of the average value of their total annual crop.[75]

In fact, interviews with managers of agricultural cooperatives have not reflected any general sense that their organizations have suffered from serious capital constraints, or even that the cooperatives have found it harder to raise capital than have their investor-owned counterparts.[76] For farmer-owned enterprise, as for worker-owned enterprise, risk bearing and liquidity constraints are evidently far less important constraints than one might expect a priori.

The methods used by the marketing cooperatives to raise equity capital are often highly refined and carefully designed. The same methods are used by farm supply cooperatives, which also are often heavily capitalized. We shall examine those methods with care in Chapter 8.

Why Not Vertical Integration?

An obvious alternative to farm marketing cooperatives is simple vertical integration, in which the marketing firm owns the farms that supply it. Why is it that Ocean Spray, for example, does not simply own its own cranberry bogs? Or why does Land O'Lakes not own its own dairy farms? Vertical integration would presumably serve just as well as farmers' cooperatives, and perhaps much better, in avoiding the costs of market contracting. Moreover, vertical integration would provide easier access to capital and would avoid the cumbersome constraints and costs imposed on cooperatives by potential conflicts of interest among their farmer-members.

The reason is clearly that, in growing most crops, the family-owned farm remains the most efficient unit of production. Economies of scale are not substantial,[77] and individual ownership provides strong incentives for working when and how it is most effective. It is not for lack of imagination that General Mills does not meet its needs for wheat by owning and operating huge corporate farms as subsidiaries. Large-scale corporate farming was experimented with extensively as early as the late nineteenth century, but has never been able to compete with family farms in most basic crops.[78]

Marketing cooperatives allow farmers to achieve economies of scale where they are significant—namely, in marketing—and to accomplish some economies from vertical integration, while at the same time leaving individual ownership in place where its incentive effects are most important. The flexibility thus afforded by the cooperative form will become even more apparent in Chapter 8, where we examine the farm supply cooperatives from which farmers obtain a large fraction of their farming inputs. Through appropriate use of both consumer and producer cooperatives, small family farms have remained the basic unit of agricultural production while, at the same time, those farms have been vertically integrated with very large firms both above and below them in the stream of production. This neatly articulated system of ownership manages to economize on the costs of market contracting while simultaneously providing effective monitoring of managers where economies of scale are large and, where economies of scale are small, maintaining the strong incentives of owner-entrepreneurship.

The Scarcity of Other Types of Producer Cooperatives

We observed, at the beginning of Part II, that there are only three common types of collectively owned enterprise that are owned by their suppliers: investor-owned firms, worker-owned firms, and farmer-owned firms. Other types, to be sure, can occasionally be found. For example, the owners of independent oil wells located in a given oil field sometimes collectively own the oil pipeline to and through which they sell their oil.[79] Some of the business-owned service cooperatives described in the next chapter, although classified there as consumer cooperatives, could instead be labeled producer cooperatives. For example, Allied Van Lines, the largest firm in the United States providing long-distance moving of household possessions, was from 1928 to 1968 a cooperative owned by the many local moving companies that actually provided the firm's services.

As this example indicates, the line between supplier-owned and consumer-owned enterprise is often vague. When Allied Van Lines was organized as a cooperative, was it a producer cooperative owned by the local firms that provided the company with the trucks and personnel it used to perform its services? Or was it a consumer cooperative, owned by local moving firms that purchased marketing and dispatching services from the central organization? Similarly, worker-owned firms might often be characterized, not as producer cooperatives, but as consumer cooperatives in which workers collectively own the firm that supplies them with the capital and coordination services they need to work effectively. As the analytical framework offered in Part I suggests, very little depends on whether we label the patrons who own a given firm suppliers or customers. It is principally for simplicity of exposition that firms have been separately grouped here, in Parts II and III, into producer-owned and consumer-owned enterprise.

Nevertheless, regardless of how we choose to classify the borderline cases, there are few examples of producer-owned collective enterprise where the owners are not investors, workers, or farmers. In contrast, there are many different types of consumer-owned enterprise. Why, then, are there only three common types of producer-owned enterprise?

The answer is evidently that there are few inputs other than financial capital, labor, and agricultural crops that meet the essential characteristics, namely: (1) the input is highly homogeneous; (2) the input is provided by a number of different suppliers, none of which is large enough in itself to supply all the needs of a purchaser of efficient scale; (3) there is a compelling efficiency reason to keep the suppliers separate as producing entities rather than merging them under unified control (as would happen if a purchasing firm simply acquired all its suppliers); and (4) a firm's purchases of the input would be attended by some degree of market failure if those purchases were conducted just by means of market contracting.

Our survey of farm marketing cooperatives has reaffirmed the conclusion suggested by our earlier discussion of worker-owned firms, a conclusion that will be further underlined in the chapters that follow: condition (1) is more important than condition (4). Where the input is not highly homogeneous, collective supplier ownership generally does not succeed even in the presence of substantial market failure. Conversely, if the input is highly homogeneous, collective supplier ownership is often viable even if the costs of contracting with an independently owned purchaser would be relatively modest.

Condition (3), however, also deserves attention. In the case of labor, it is satisfied because of the degree of decision-making autonomy that is characteristic of every human being, and because the social prohibition of slavery reinforces this autonomy. For agricultural commodities it is satisfied because the family-owned farm remains the most efficient production unit for most crops.

Why is condition (3) satisfied for the independent oil producers in a given oil field? Presumably the reason is that, although the oil produced by the different properties is essentially the same (since they are generally all situated on top of the same pool of oil), the parcels of land themselves are not homogeneous with respect to the amount of oil believed to lie under them or the ease of extracting the oil from them. This heterogeneity often prevents the owners of the individual parcels in an oil field from forming a single cooperatively owned production firm for the field as a whole, even though they would achieve substantial efficiency advantages from doing so.[80] With cooperative production of that sort, there would be no occasion for collective ownership of pipelines. These observations further underscore the importance of homogeneity of interest: the parcel owners are capable of coming together in cooperative ownership of a pipeline to ship their oil, an enterprise in which the homogeneity of interest is high but the potential efficiency gains are modest; yet the same parcel owners are incapable of organizing a jointly owned production firm, where there is less homogeneity of interest but the potential efficiency gains are large.

Conclusion

Farm marketing cooperatives thrive even where the potential costs of market contracting appear relatively low. The success of the cooperatives does not seem to depend importantly on their own exploitation of monopoly power or on governmental tax preferences or subsidies. Risk bearing and accumulation of capital have apparently not been important obstacles.

These observations reinforce the general conclusions suggested by our earlier study of investor-owned firms and employee-owned firms: where the costs of ownership are low—and, in particular, where the potential producer-owners have highly homogeneous interests—producer cooperatives can succeed even in the absence of serious market imperfections that would make market contracting costly for the producers. This presumably accounts for the impressive growth in the overall market share of farm marketing cooperatives in the United States and other countries over the course of the twentieth century: although the monopsony power of farm product purchasers has evidently decreased over this period, the costs of ownership for farmer cooperatives have apparently decreased even faster.

To be sure, these general inferences are slightly clouded by the fact that each of the types of producer-owned enterprise examined in Part II exists, in the United States and in most other countries, in a relatively complex and specialized legal and institutional environment that obscures somewhat the importance of competing efficiency considerations. When we turn to consumer-owned enterprise, we shall find that such biases play a smaller role (or at least a less ambiguous one), making it easier to draw conclusions about relative efficiency.

PART III
Customer-Owned Enterprise

8

Retail, Wholesale, and Supply Firms

In the popular mind, the image of a customer-owned enterprise is typically a retail firm such as a cooperative grocery store. Yet consumer cooperatives have an insignificant share of the market for nearly all retail goods in the United States and, with a few exceptions, in other developed nations as well. This does not mean that customer-owned enterprise is a rarity. On the contrary, once we move beyond markets for retail goods, we discover that firms that are collectively owned by their customers are surprisingly common and play an important role in a variety of markedly different industries.

We begin our examination of customer ownership in this chapter by considering firms that market standard producer and consumer goods. The following three chapters then focus on industries that provide particular services—utilities, social affiliation, and housing—that have special characteristics.

Farm Supplies

In the United States, as of 1990, there were roughly 1,700 consumer cooperatives whose primary business was farm supplies. The gross value of their sales amounted to $26 billion and represented 27 percent of all farm production expenditures—up from 23 percent in 1973. The cooperatives have been particularly important in supplying the farm market with fertilizer (43 percent in 1990), petroleum products (38 percent), farm chemicals such as pesticides (30 percent), livestock feed (19 percent), and seeds (16 percent).[1]

Most farm supply cooperatives serve only a local area of one or several counties and are tightly controlled by their farmer-members. Often these local cooperatives are federated into much larger regional cooperatives, which have the local cooperatives as members and which supply many of the goods sold by the local cooperatives. The regional cooperatives, in turn, are sometimes federated into national cooperatives that manufacture or wholesale major lines of supplies. The regional and national cooperatives are often quite large; six of them appear among the Fortune 500 listing of the largest U.S. industrial corporations for 1992.[2]

Costs of Contracting

Market power has apparently provided an important incentive for customer ownership in the farm supply business. In the period when cooperatives first established a significant market share in most lines of farm supplies—primarily the two decades immediately following World War I—the markets involved were not highly competitive. Investor-owned firms in the fertilizer industry, for example, were repeatedly the subject of investigation and prosecution for restrictive agreements concerning prices and sales territories.[3] Petroleum supply cooperatives achieved their most important growth in regions of the country, such as the Midwest, far removed from areas of oil production. Oil distribution in those regions was dominated by several large companies that had a monopoly on low-cost means of transportation (chiefly pipelines) and avoided price competition in favor of service and advertising competition. In contrast, cooperatives achieved little market share in those regions, such as the Southwest, that were characterized by surplus oil production and consequent stiff competition among oil producers and refiners.[4]

In addition, problems of asymmetric information played a role in the growth of farm supply cooperatives. Early in the twentieth century, for example, when commercial livestock feeds were first coming into use, their ingredients were largely unknown to the buyers and, as a consequence, their quality was generally low. The same was true of commercial fertilizers. The cooperatives therefore had an advantage in gaining the farmers' trust in their products.

This informational advantage seems to have diminished substantially, however, after the cooperatives' formative stage. Both livestock feed and fertilizer were from an early date the subjects of "open formula" campaigns that promoted the disclosure of ingredients on labels—campaigns in which the cooperatives themselves took part. By 1916, for example, all states in which large amounts of fertilizer were sold required labels listing active ingredients by percentage.[5]

We see here an important phenomenon that we shall meet again in later chapters when we examine other industries such as banking and life insurance. Governmental regulation to protect consumers can substantially improve the viability of investor-owned firms in industries where they would otherwise have difficulty competing with consumer cooperatives. In effect, regulation can be a substitute for customer ownership in protecting consumers from market failure. Or, to put it the other way around, customer ownership serves as a substitute for governmental regulation in addressing problems of market failure, and may lose its comparative advantage when effective regulation is enacted.

Costs of Ownership

Costs of ownership are highly favorable to agricultural supply cooperatives, just as they are to the farm marketing cooperatives discussed in Chapter 7. Each of the commodities in which farm supply cooperatives have significant market share regularly constitutes a substantial fraction of a farmer's budget. A farm is likely to be in business, and hence in a position to continue to patronize the same supplier, for decades or even generations. Farms growing a given crop, and consequently having similar demands for supplies, tend to cluster geographically for reasons of soil and climate, and can be easily organized as members of a local cooperative that they can govern effectively. Federation of the local cooperatives, whose activities are largely confined to distribution, in turn permits efficient operation of large-scale wholesale and manufacturing operations while maintaining workable customer control.

By confining the cooperatives principally to relatively simple, homogeneous commodities, such as petroleum, feed, seed, and fertilizer, conflicts of interest among members are kept to a minimum. To capture economies of scope, a given supply cooperative often handles more than one commodity; in that case, however, it is common for patronage refunds to be computed separately for different product lines. For example, Land O'Lakes, the large midwestern dairy farmers' cooperative that operates both as a marketing cooperative and as a supply cooperative, not only computes patronage refunds separately for its marketing and its supply businesses but, within its supply business, has refined its patronage refund accounting to the point where, for instance, it computes a separate rate of patronage dividend for each of its six different types of fertilizer.[6] This is done—at some accounting expense, and with a loss in risk diversification—precisely because it reduces the potential for conflict among members concerning the amounts to be invested in developing different product lines and the relative prices to be charged for the different products.

Problems Associated with Capital

Many farm supply cooperatives have integrated upstream into manufacturing, and these operations sometimes require substantial capital. For example, farm petroleum cooperatives own, singly or jointly, refineries that provide roughly half the cooperatives' needs, oil wells that produce close to 90 percent of those refineries' crude oil input, and pipelines that transport most of the oil from the cooperatives' wells to their refineries. Similarly, farm supply cooperatives have integrated upstream into the manufacture of feed, seed, fertilizer, and other agricultural chemicals.[7] The extent of these upstream investments provides further evidence—beyond that which we have seen in the context of worker-owned firms and farm marketing cooperatives—that capital supply, and the attendant problems of liquidity and risk bearing, need not be critical obstacles to non-investor-owned firms.

The methods by which farm supply cooperatives obtain and account for equity capital—which, as noted in Chapter 7, are the same as those used by farm marketing cooperatives—are among the most well-developed, widely used, and time-tested approaches to capital accounting found in any form of cooperative enterprise. We shall examine those methods here, not just for what they tell us about agricultural cooperatives, but also for what they tell us about the problems and prospects of capital formation in collectively owned enterprise generally.

Raising and Accounting for Equity Capital

A farmer cooperative typically uses one or more of three different methods to raise capital from its members. The first method is to issue shares of capital stock in the cooperative[8] and sell them to the cooperative's members. The second method is for the cooperative to retain a portion of its net earnings rather than paying them out as patronage dividends. These retentions may be either "allocated" or "unallocated." Allocated retentions are credited to the capital accounts of individual members; unallocated retentions are simply added to the surplus of the cooperative as a whole. The third method is for the cooperative to employ "per-unit capital retains," which are amounts added to the price the member would otherwise pay for supplies he purchases from the cooperative, and which are credited to a capital account that the cooperative maintains for the member. The amount retained is computed without reference to the cooperative's net earnings, and is based only on the volume or value of transactions with the particular member. (In a marketing cooperative, the per-unit capital retains are funds withheld from the amount otherwise payable to a member for the crops he has delivered to the cooperative.) In practice, the second and third methods described here have been by far the most important sources of equity capital for the cooperatives.[9]

If members' capital investments in the cooperative are not proportional to the amount of business they do with the cooperative, then, as we noted earlier with worker-owned firms, there is potential for a conflict of interest among the members. In particular, the division of the firm's net earnings between the return paid to capital investments and the return paid as patronage dividends, which necessarily involves matters of judgment, can become a matter of contention between those members whose capital investments are large relative to their current level of patronage and those whose capital investments are small. These conflicts of interest can evidently be an important problem in farmer cooperatives, since the more capital-intensive cooperatives commonly structure their financing in ways that are designed to avoid those conflicts.

To begin with, the cooperatives issue relatively little capital stock, and thus avoid creating, either symbolically or in reality, a class of stockholders that has interests distinct from those of the patron-members.

Moreover, the cooperatives typically do not pay dividends or interest on members' equity investments, and they generally redeem equity at book or net value, whichever is lower.[10] The only return that a member gets on his equity is in the form of lower net (that is, after-dividend) prices for products he purchases from the cooperative (or, in the case of a marketing cooperative, higher net prices for items sold to or through the cooperative).[11] In some cases this may reflect the incentive that Subchapter T of the tax code gives cooperatives to distribute as much as possible of their earnings as patronage dividends rather than as dividends on capital stock, since dividends on capital stock, unlike patronage dividends, are subject to both corporate and personal taxes. Yet many farm marketing and supply cooperatives are exempt from taxation on capital stock dividends under Section 521 of the tax code, and even these firms generally do not pay dividends on capital.

Perhaps a more persuasive reason for not paying dividends on capital investments is that this practice helps to bond members to the cooperative. As we shall see, members must generally wait a number of years after leaving a cooperative before all of their invested capital is returned to them. If the member could receive a reasonable rate of return on that capital, this delay would not be an important disincentive to leave. But because the return on that capital is included in patronage dividends, rapid exit—which immediately drops a farmer's patronage dividends to zero—is costly.

Finally, any positive rate of dividends on capital will necessarily involve an arbitrary and contentious choice. It is simpler to choose zero as the default rate of dividend, and seek to keep each member's total invested capital proportional to his current level of patronage. As long as this proportionality is maintained, the division of earnings between capital dividends and patronage dividends is a matter of indifference, and all earnings can simply be paid out as patronage dividends without generating conflict.

The cooperatives employ various different schemes, of different levels of sophistication, to maintain such proportionality.[12] Not surprisingly, the most elaborate and finely tuned approaches are found in the largest and most capital intensive of the cooperatives. The latter firms typically begin by determining the overall amount of equity capital that they wish to maintain. From this they then compute the necessary ratio between invested capital and current patronage. Then, when a new member joins the cooperative or when an existing member increases his level of patronage, the cooperative requires that the member make new capital investments until his aggregate capital investment reaches the desired ratio to his average level of patronage (the average being computed over the past several years). These investments are commonly extracted by increasing the member's per-unit capital retains for several years. Then, when a member retires (or otherwise decreases his level of patronage), the process is reversed, with the cooperative redeeming some portion of the member's capital investment annually until it has all been returned.

Any such system involves an obvious trade-off. If the number of years over which new members' capital contribution is paid in and old members' is paid out is relatively long, then liquidity problems for both the new members and the cooperative are minimized; retiring members are in effect lending a portion of the required capital contribution to new members for the period involved, and the cooperative is unlikely to be faced with a sudden run on its capital when retirements are unusually concentrated. The longer the payin and payout periods are (and they need not be equal), however, the greater the conflict of interest between old and new members. Members close to retirement will wish to see the cooperative minimize its aggregate capital investment and maximize its patronage dividends; new members will prefer the opposite. In addition, the length of the payin period and, especially, the payout period will itself be a source of disagreement between younger and older members. Cooperatives are in fact often quite leisurely about refunding retired members' capital, and this has resulted in extensive discussion in the trade press, in proposals for legislation mandating the period within which capital contributions must be refunded, and in more litigation than any other aspect of the cooperatives' operations.[13]

There is nothing unique about agricultural cooperatives in these respects. When designing schemes for raising capital from the members of any type of cooperative, there is necessarily a tension among three competing considerations: the total amount of capital that can be accumulated per member, the speed with which that capital can be accumulated, and the degree to which each member's share of the invested capital can be kept proportional to his patronage. This tension is least where patrons remain members of the cooperative over long periods of time, and where the members' level of patronage remains fairly constant. It is therefore not surprising that capital-intensive cooperatives are most commonly found where these conditions are met, as they are in providing many farm supplies, in marketing most agricultural products, and in other situations, such as those described below, where the cooperative's members are reasonably stable and long-lived businesses.

Why Not Machinery?

Although farm machinery accounts for a significant portion of farm budgets,[14] consumer cooperatives play an insignificant role in its marketing or manufacturing. This is difficult to explain if we simply look at the costs of contracting. Farm machinery is an extremely concentrated industry. As of 1989, just two companies (Deere and Case) together had 82 percent of the U.S. market, and Deere alone had more than 50 percent.[15] Market power of this degree would seem to be a strong incentive to entry by cooperatives. Moreover, the complexity of farm machinery, and the infrequency with which a farmer purchases any given type of machine, presumably put purchasers at a substantial informational disadvantage to the sellers. Evidently the reason cooperatives have such a small presence in farm machinery as compared with other farm supplies is not that the costs of market contracting are unusually low, but that the costs of consumer ownership in farm machinery are unusually high.

What are the sources of those high costs of ownership? The capital intensity of the farm machinery business may be among them. Yet petroleum is also a capital-intensive business, and this has not prevented cooperatives from supplying a third of the farm market. Farm supply cooperatives could enter the machinery business the same way they did the petroleum business, beginning at the retail distribution stage (which does not require much organization-specific capital) and then integrating upstream into manufacturing—by internal expansion, by purchasing an existing firm, or both—only after establishing themselves at the distribution level. In fact, from the mid-1940s to the mid-1950s, the Cockshutt Farm Equipment Company distributed a portion of its farm machinery through regional farm supply cooperatives. This equipment was painted a distinctive color and bore the "Co-op" name. But instead of expanding this operation—perhaps by purchasing Cockshutt—the cooperatives discontinued it in the late 1950s, and Cockshutt was subsequently acquired by White Motor Company, which continues to manufacture farm machinery.[16]

Most likely, the critical factor is that the costs of exercising customer control are much higher in the farm machinery business than in other farm supplies. The sporadic nature of equipment purchases removes both the incentive and the opportunity for farmers to engage in continuous monitoring of vendors. The widely varying types and vintages of equipment used by different farmers also make for heterogeneity of interest, creating the potential for substantial disagreements among members of a cooperatively owned vendor about such matters as the types of inventory to carry, the type of service facilities to maintain, and the type of financing to offer.[17]

Conversely, it is noteworthy that it is the most homogeneous of farm supplies, petroleum, in which cooperatives have the largest market share. This underlines the importance of costs of ownership relative to costs of market contracting in determining ownership patterns. Petroleum markets today, like the markets for other standardized agricultural supplies such as fertilizer and feed, seem to display relatively little market failure. The ability of cooperatives to compete effectively with investor-owned firms in these businesses therefore cannot be explained on the basis that the cooperatives avoid significant costs of market contracting. Rather, the cooperatives must be succeeding because their costs of ownership are as low or lower than those of the investor-owned firms. More particularly, the success of the cooperatives in distributing homogeneous products such as petroleum suggests that, in the absence of significant conflicts of interest among the members of farmer-owned cooperatives, the overall costs of ownership are no higher for cooperatives than they are for investor-owned firms. Any relative disadvantages that the cooperatives suffer in access to capital and risk bearing are apparently more than overcome by lower agency costs of policing management.

Wholesale and Supply Firms

Agriculture is not the only industry in which small businesses obtain their supplies through consumer cooperatives. Customer-owned wholesale and supply firms are common throughout the U.S. economy. For example, retailer-owned wholesale cooperatives account for 80 percent of the hardware market[18] and 14 percent of the grocery market (or nearly one-third if one excludes chain stores with integrated wholesale and retail operations),[19] and they play an important role as well in supplying drugs to drug stores and dry goods to department stores.[20] Similarly, a substantial share of the nation's bakeries obtain their baking supplies from firms that they own as cooperatives.[21]

Business-owned consumer cooperatives are also important suppliers of services. The largest international news service, Associated Press, has long been cooperatively owned by the thousands of newspapers and broadcasting stations it serves. From 1929 to 1967 Railway Express Agency operated as a railroad-owned cooperative through which the member railroads provided nationwide express shipping services. Over the same forty-year period, as noted in the last chapter, Allied Van Lines was organized as a cooperative owned by numerous local moving companies.[22] And both MasterCard and Visa are cooperatives that are owned by the hundreds of local banks that sell and service the credit cards carrying the cooperatives' names, with the cooperatives themselves simply providing, in addition to the license to use their trademark, collective advertising and clearinghouse services.

Costs of Contracting

Simple market power appears to provide an incentive for customer ownership in many of these cases. The grocery business, for example, is highly competitive at the retail level. If independent stores are to compete with the large chains, which maintain their own wholesale distribution systems, they cannot afford to pay inefficiently high prices to a wholesaler. Yet economies of scale at the wholesale level apparently leave room for at most a few firms to serve the independent retailers in a given area, a situation that leaves wholesalers with a degree of market power. Retailers then have an incentive to avoid price exploitation by owning the wholesaler that serves them. The Associated Press is another obvious example. Economies of scale led to a market that was long occupied by only two substantial news services in the United States, United Press International and Associated Press, the former investor-owned and the latter a cooperative.

An equally important incentive for customer ownership, however, is probably the lock-in that derives from the brand names that wholesale and supply firms license to their customers. For example, independent hardware dealers belonging to the same wholesale cooperative generally use a common store name and insignia, and also market products that bear that same brand name. True Value, Ace, and Servistar, each of which is a cooperative with thousands of independently owned local hardware stores as members, are examples familiar to American consumers.[23] Most members of the largest bakery supply cooperative market bread under the common brand name "Sunbeam."[24] With these brand names, wholesalers are able to offer economies in packaging and advertising to their customers. Similarly, the MasterCard and Visa brand names are an important part of what those two cooperatives offer their member banks. All these arrangements are essentially franchises. They differ from other familiar franchise operations, such as fast food chains, only in that the franchisees collectively own their franchisor.

Franchisees commonly face a serious lock-in problem. If a franchisee leaves the franchise, it risks losing both its investment in franchise-specific buildings and equipment and the value of the local goodwill it has built up under the franchisor's brand name. Thus franchisors are often in a position to behave opportunistically toward their franchisees, expropriating some or all of the value of the franchisees' sunk costs.[25] Neither contracting nor regulation has been highly successful in mitigating the threat of this kind of opportunism.[26] (Although a franchisor's concern for its reputation may restrain it from acting opportunistically while it is still seeking new franchisees, the same may not be true when the system is no longer expanding or when the franchisor decides it would prefer to own its new outlets directly rather than run them as franchises.) The great advantage of collective ownership of the franchisor by the retailers is its virtual elimination of this difficult problem.

Costs of Ownership

The costs of ownership are highly favorable to these retailer-owned cooperatives, just as they are to farmer-owned supply cooperatives. A retail grocery or hardware store, for example, generally purchases a significant fraction of its goods from a single wholesaler with which it transacts continuously for many years. The store is then in a position to oversee the affairs of the wholesaler without incurring substantial costs beyond those involved in market contracting. Moreover, the capital equipment involved in the supply business, such as warehouses and trucks, is not highly organization-specific. Consequently, although organizing wholesalers as cooperatives necessarily increases both the capital requirements and the risk facing retailers, these burdens are relatively modest.[27] In addition, the retail hardware stores or grocery stores patronizing a given wholesaler are likely to stock similar arrays of merchandise, so that their interests with respect to the wholesaler will be reasonably homogeneous.

Why Are Some Franchise Systems Not Cooperatives?

Given the conspicuous advantages to franchisees of collectively owning their franchisor, it is interesting to ask why there are any franchisors that are not organized this way. For example, why are franchisors in fast food chains characteristically organized as investor-owned firms and not as franchisee-owned cooperatives? Surely lock-in is much greater in fast food retailing than it is in hardware or groceries, since in fast food a local franchisee's facilities and goodwill are more closely tied to the products of a particular franchisor.

A likely explanation is that franchisors that are investor-owned find it easier than those that are franchisee-owned to discipline errant franchisees by terminating their franchise. As we have seen in our study of producer cooperatives, with collective ownership there commonly arise, presumably as a means of avoiding conflicts of interest among the owners, strong norms that require either that all members be treated equally or, if they are not, that any differences of treatment follow clear rules that are established ex ante. Such norms make it difficult to grant the central administration of a cooperative the discretion to punish, rapidly and rigorously, the wayward behavior of an individual member.

Thus while franchisee cooperatives are more successful than investor-owned franchisors in controlling opportunism by the franchisor, they may be significantly less successful in controlling opportunism by the franchisees. As a result, cooperatives are handicapped vis-à-vis investor-owned franchisors in businesses where the franchisees can impose substantial damage by opportunistically skimping on quality while free riding on the brand name. Fast foods are such a business, for two reasons. First, since a major element of the business is to offer a standardized service to travelers, it is important to hold all local stores tightly to detailed systemwide standards. Second, in fast foods, much of the important product preparation is done at the franchisee level, so that ensuring the quality and uniformity of the franchisees' products requires close supervision. Hardware and grocery stores, in contrast, cater to a much less mobile population, so that deviations from one store to another are less important, and the brand-name goods sold by the stores generally require little or no local preparation.

Cooperatives versus Integrated Firms

So far we have been focusing on the relative advantages of customer ownership and investor ownership for supply firms. An alternative to both these forms, however, is to have a fully integrated firm in which the supplier and the retailers to which it sells are commonly owned (or, put differently, in which the wholesaler owns the retailers rather than vice versa). This approach is common in the grocery business, where a number of fully integrated chain stores together account for half of the overall market.[28] In hardware the fully integrated Sears chain has long held a prominent position.

The fully integrated firm solves the same problems with market contracting between retailers and wholesalers that the cooperative form solves. Moreover, the fully integrated firm can economize on common planning and services in ways that are difficult for the independently owned retailers in a cooperative, and it can ensure, more easily than can a cooperative, a high degree of homogeneity of services and products among its associated retail stores.

At the same time, the fully integrated firm has the obvious disadvantage that it sacrifices the strong incentives for cost minimization and customer responsiveness at the store level that characterize independently owned retailers. In those businesses where the cooperatives have substantial market share, such as hardware and groceries, these incentives are evidently at least as important as any advantages that would derive from tighter central control.

Retailers of Consumer Goods and Services

Consumer cooperatives are far less common at the retail level than at the wholesale level. In the United States, consumer-owned retail stores account for only one quarter of 1 percent of the consumer goods market. Even in groceries, where cooperatives account for a substantial share of the wholesale market, their share of the retail market is less than half of 1 percent. Outside of financial services such as banking and insurance, the focus of Chapters 13 and 14, consumer cooperatives also play a very small role in retail markets for services.[29]

The small market share held by retail cooperatives is easy to understand. The costs of customer ownership for many retail goods and services are high, because the customers of any given retail firm are commonly too numerous, transitory, and dispersed to organize easily or effectively. The costs of market contracting are commonly low: retail markets for most ordinary items are sufficiently competitive to keep prices close to cost, and the goods and services themselves are sufficiently simple or standardized, or are purchased so repetitively, that asymmetric information about quality is not a serious problem.

An Example: Food Cooperatives

Food retailing provides a good example of both the limits and the strengths of consumer ownership. The relatively insignificant share of the retail food market represented by consumer cooperatives is not easily explained in terms of the costs of ownership, which appear moderately favorable for grocery cooperatives. For many customers, the costs of information gathering and decision making should be small relative to the value of their transactions with the firm: groceries are a large budget item for most people; customers commonly patronize the same store regularly over long periods of time; and customers frequently live in close proximity to the store where they shop. Risk sharing does not seem to be a major problem: the amount of invested capital in a grocery store is relatively low as a fraction of annual sales volume, and the major capital investments—a store, refrigeration equipment, and the like—are not highly firm-specific.

To be sure, there is a question about the homogeneity of interest among customers. Grocery stores carry a wide variety of different products, leaving room for conflicts of interest among members who generally purchase different items. Since most consumers purchase roughly similar market baskets of goods, however, this may not in itself be a fatal disadvantage to the cooperative form.

Rather, the obvious explanation for the general absence of retail grocery cooperatives is that the costs of market contracting are so low. Asymmetric information is not an important problem with groceries. A large fraction of the products sold by grocery stores are widely marketed brand-name packaged goods available from a variety of competing stores. For those items that are not packaged, like meat and vegetables, the customer can either judge quality simply by inspection prior to purchase or quickly obtain experience about the quality of a store's offerings by a few trial purchases. Nor is market power a problem. Grocery retailing is an extraordinarily competitive business in which profit margins are exceptionally narrow. As a consequence, there is no meaningful opportunity for efficiency gains from consumer ownership.

Bookstores

Books are the single retail item for which consumer cooperatives have been important, accounting for as much as 9 percent of the market in the 1960s.[30] This is a consequence of the presence of cooperative bookstores on many university campuses, where a significant fraction of the nation's books are sold.

Market power is presumably an incentive for adopting the cooperative form on university campuses: it is generally efficient to have only one major seller of textbooks on a campus, owing to the substantial information and coordination economies in ordering and handling assigned texts. Yet the degree of market power involved here is presumably rather modest; other booksellers can, and do, enter the textbook market at the margin reasonably cheaply when they see an opportunity. And in addition to books, most student cooperatives sell a variety of other ordinary consumer items for which the market is more competitive, suggesting that market power in textbooks is neither necessary nor sufficient for the success of the student cooperatives.

Rather, the key to the success of the university cooperatives is probably the low costs of ownership facing the students. Expenditures on books and other items are a significant fraction of a student's budget; students typically continue to patronize the same store for four years or so; student demand is relatively homogeneous; and students can be easily organized through their common affiliation with, and residence near, the university.

Experience in Other Countries

Consumer retail cooperatives occupy a somewhat larger share of the market in many Western European countries than they do in the United States. For example, in West Germany cooperatives account for roughly 3 percent of the retail market,[31] in England 4.6 percent,[32] and in Sweden 18 percent.[33] It is possible that this is in part the consequence of different histories of institutional innovation and development in these countries—a factor to be explored more closely in subsequent chapters, and especially in our discussion of housing and insurance. But there is reason to believe that the principal explanation for these variations in market shares lies in national differences in the costs of ownership and of market contracting.

Some of these differences are general. At least until recently, for example, prepackaged and nationally merchandised goods accounted for a smaller share of retail goods in European countries than in the United States,[34] raising information costs and perhaps inhibiting price competition. Similarly, the low rates of residential mobility in Europe compared with the United States[35] have presumably resulted in lower costs of consumer ownership.

Other, more specific factors are also at work, however. The exceptionally large market share held by consumer cooperatives in Sweden, for example, is a direct response to the anticompetitive practices that have long been common in Swedish industry. Swedish antitrust laws have always been weak: prior to 1953 there were few legal constraints on anticompetitive activity, and even after that date agreements to fix prices were not per se violations of Swedish antitrust law.[36] As a consequence, the manufacture and importation of consumer products has been highly cartelized. This has created a strong incentive for consumers to form cooperatives both to achieve countervailing market power vis-à-vis the cartels and to integrate backward into manufacture in competition with the cartels. In fact, Swedish consumer cooperatives have played an explicit "cartel busting" role in a number of industries, from margarine and coffee to shoes and light bulbs.[37]

Anticompetitive practices in Sweden have extended down from manufacturing and wholesaling to the retail level, creating an even stronger incentive for consumer cooperatives. For example, beginning in the early 1930s, the existing food retailers conspired with food processors and food wholesalers to inhibit, through threat of collective boycott, the establishment of new retail grocery outlets. Further, prior to 1953, one-third of all Swedish foodstuffs and housewares were subject to binding resale price maintenance. Although this was subsequently made an antitrust violation, wholesalers and retailers simply responded with an informal system of "suggested" retail prices; it was consumer cooperatives that were primarily responsible for initiating price competition under the new law by failing to conform to these suggested prices.[38]

Incentives for an Inappropriate Choice of Scale

Economic analyses of consumer cooperatives often impute to them a conventional U-shaped average cost curve.[39] They then argue that if—as is common—the cooperative maintains open membership, it will operate at too high a membership level: new members will keep joining until average cost is as high as the nearest competitor's price. If the cooperative has closed membership, the existing members have an incentive to operate at suboptimal scale, keeping membership and purchases down to the level that minimizes average cost, which is less than the level at which total welfare is maximized. (The latter problem is the consumer cooperative analogue to the problem of perverse supply response in worker cooperatives discussed in Chapter 5.) In sum, consumer cooperatives will operate at a scale that is either too large or too small.

The proponents of such analyses, however, offer little evidence that an inappropriate choice of scale is actually a problem among consumer cooperatives.[40] In fact, there is good reason to believe that it is not.

To begin with, in the industries in which consumer cooperatives are most common, it is not apparent that there are substantial diseconomies of scale. On the contrary, consumer cooperatives often arise where there is a degree of natural monopoly. Thus rather than having a U-shaped average cost curve, most cooperatives probably face a cost curve that, within the relevant range, is either continually declining or relatively flat.

Moreover, consumer cooperatives have incentives to adopt policies that will avoid an inefficient choice of scale, and they appear to act on these incentives. Farm supply cooperatives, for example, have chosen to remain fairly small in scale at the local retail level while federating to achieve the larger economies of scale available in wholesaling and manufacturing. Also, by not paying dividends on members' capital investments, the farmer cooperatives have effectively established a two-part pricing scheme: first, members pay a fixed price annually, in the form of the forgone interest on their capital contribution, that covers fixed costs; second, they then pay a net price (nominal price less patronage refund) for the cooperative's goods and services that covers variable costs. The result is that goods are sold to members at per-unit prices that approximate marginal rather than average cost, which avoids incentives for an inappropriate choice of scale and for inefficient utilization of the scale chosen.

Tax Incentives and Other Subsidies

In the United States, nonfarm wholesale and supply cooperatives benefit from no important subsidies or other special privileges beyond the right, shared with all other producer and consumer cooperatives, to be taxed according to Subchapter T of the Internal Revenue Code (which, as described in Chapter 7, essentially applies to cooperatives a single tax rather than the dual-level corporate and personal income taxes applicable to investor-owned enterprise). Since this tax subsidy is available to consumer cooperatives in all industries, it cannot be responsible for the peculiar distribution of consumer cooperatives across industries that we have described here. Rather, at most this tax subsidy may have had the consequence that, throughout the economy in general, there are more cooperatives vis-à-vis investor-owned firms than there would be under a system of taxation that is entirely neutral between these two organizational forms.

To be sure, farm supply cooperatives, like the farm marketing cooperatives examined in Chapter 7, have the further benefit of exemption from the corporate-level tax on stock dividends and on certain forms of nonpatronage income. But since farm supply cooperatives often do not pay stock dividends, and since many farm supply cooperatives choose not to qualify for the exemption,[41] it is not apparent that this exemption is important in explaining the unusually prominent role of cooperatives in the farm supply industry.

Similarly, farm supply cooperatives, like farm marketing cooperatives, have at times enjoyed the benefit of government credit subsidies. Yet these subsidies do not seem to have been fundamental to the success of the farm supply cooperatives, which existed in large numbers long before the subsidies came into existence, and whose market share continued to grow after the last of these subsidies were eliminated in 1968.

Culture and Ideology

In the popular mind, it is common to attribute the development of cooperative enterprise, and consumer cooperatives in general, to peculiar patterns of culture or ideology that have little to do with the underlying costs and benefits of the cooperative form. Cooperatives are the peculiar institutions of Scandinavians, it is said, or of individuals with a peculiarly strong political antipathy to capitalism. The pattern of customer-owned enterprise that we observe, however, strongly belies such notions. It is not individual consumers, but businesses and businesspeople, who make up the membership of most consumer-owned enterprise. The businesspeople involved are drawn from a broad cross-section of the population both ethnically and regionally. Moreover, it is difficult to think of a more intensely commercial, individualistic, and politically conservative class of individuals than the small entrepreneurs, such as hardware store owners, who make up the membership of most wholesale and supply cooperatives. And nobody could accuse the banks that belong to the MasterCard cooperative of being anticapitalist.

Conclusion

The patterns of customer-owned enterprise among retail, wholesale, and supply businesses appear largely unaffected by conspicuous legal, ideological, or historical biases. As a consequence, those patterns permit a relatively unclouded assessment of the factors determining the relative efficiency of alternative forms of ownership.

That assessment reinforces the principal conclusions suggested by our study of producer-owned enterprise in Part II. In particular, it is striking that most of the industries in which wholesale and supply cooperatives have been successful exhibit a relatively modest degree of product market failure compared with industries in which investor ownership is the norm. High costs of market contracting thus do not seem to be critical to the success of customer-owned enterprise. At the same time, high costs of market contracting do not appear sufficient in themselves to foster consumer ownership. Rather, the costs of ownership, and particularly the costs of monitoring managers and of collective decision making among the owners, seem to be decisive. One does not encounter customer ownership where those costs of ownership appear high. Conversely, and more interestingly, when customers have homogeneous interests and are in a good position to exercise effective control, it is apparently efficient to abandon investor ownership in favor of customer ownership even if the degree of product market imperfection is quite modest.

9

Utilities

In the United States, most electricity is supplied by investor-owned firms whose rates are regulated by public agencies to avoid monopoly pricing. This is not, however, the only form of ownership found in that industry. There are also approximately one thousand electric utility companies organized as consumer cooperatives and fifteen hundred that are municipally owned.

Consumer cooperatives also account for a substantial share of telephone service provided in rural areas. As of 1989 there were 244 telephone cooperatives, collectively serving roughly one million subscribers. These telephone cooperatives coexist with the 22 operating companies from the former Bell system and with approximately 1,000 other independent telephone companies that are investor-owned.[1] In contrast, consumer cooperatives appear to play no significant role in supplying households or businesses with the two other common utilities, water and natural gas, which are dominated by investor-owned and municipal firms. In seeking to understand these patterns, we shall focus primarily on the electric power industry, though we shall briefly examine the other utilities as well.

The Rural Electric Cooperatives

The electricity cooperatives are located almost exclusively in rural areas of the country. They supply electric power to approximately half of all farm households and also to a substantial percentage of nonfarm households and commercial and industrial users located in nonmetro-

168

politan areas.[2] Although they serve only 10 percent of the nation's population, cooperative utilities appear in forty-six of the fifty states, serve roughly two-thirds of the nation's continental land area,[3] and own nearly 45 percent of all electricity distribution lines.[4]

Most of the electricity cooperatives only distribute electricity to retail customers. They do not generate the power they distribute, but rather purchase it from another firm. That other firm is sometimes an investor-owned company and sometimes a publicly owned hydroelectric power facility such as the Tennessee Valley Authority. Frequently, however, the supplying firm is another cooperative, an electricity generating and transmission (G&T) cooperative, whose members are the local distribution cooperatives that purchase its power. The result is a federated structure, much like that of the farm supply cooperatives examined in the last chapter. The percentage of the local distribution cooperatives' power supplied by G&T cooperatives has increased steadily over the years, growing from 16 percent in 1959 to 45 percent in 1983. As of 1980, G&T cooperatives accounted for 2.8 percent of the nation's overall generation of electric power.[5]

Costs of Contracting

The large market share of the rural electricity cooperatives fits comfortably with the cost considerations discussed in Part I. Most fundamentally, local electricity and telephone networks are natural monopolies. Consumers would therefore be exposed to serious price exploitation if they were to rely on market contracting with an investor-owned firm. For this reason, the investor-owned firms that provide most of the electric power and telephone service in the United States have their rates regulated by governmental agencies. Yet since no agency can perfectly monitor the firms it regulates, rate regulation has some familiar costs of its own. If the regulatory agency sets the permissible rates too low to permit a market rate of return on the firm's invested capital, there will be an incentive for the utility to underinvest; the reverse will be true if rates are set too high. Also, if there is no slack in the regulation—that is, if the rates that the utility is allowed to charge are constantly adjusted to reflect the firm's actual costs—then the firm will have little incentive for cost reduction. Yet providing for slack permits the utility's prices to become, over time, higher or lower than necessary to ensure a market rate of return on capital.

By aligning the firm's interests with those of its customers, cooperatives can avoid not only the costs of monopoly but also the costs of rate regulation. Indeed, of the forty-six states in which rural electric cooperatives are located, only eighteen regulate the cooperatives' rates, and ten of the latter states employ a streamlined procedure for cooperatives.[6]

Costs of Ownership

The costs of ownership are also quite favorable for utility cooperatives, much as they are for farm supply cooperatives. In fact, one can view the rural utility cooperatives as just another form of farm supply cooperative. Electricity and telephone service are highly homogeneous commodities with few important quality variables that affect different users differently. To be sure, in the electricity cooperatives there might well be a divergence of interests among residential, commercial, and industrial customers. But farm and nonfarm residential households account for over 90 percent of the membership and 60 percent of the demand for electricity in the rural electric cooperatives,[7] thus creating a dominant group of patrons with relatively homogeneous interests, while market forces and other factors, discussed below, provide protection for the interests of the commercial and industrial customers.

Capital

The capital intensity of utilities might seem a substantial obstacle to customer ownership. In fact, given the wide dispersion of farm households, the capital cost of constructing and maintaining a distribution network is far higher in rural areas than it is in cities.[8] Several factors, however, help make the problem of capital supply manageable.

To begin with, local cooperatives need not own their own generating and long-distance transmission facilities. Rather, they can purchase those services from another firm, thereby restricting their capital requirements to those needed to finance the local distribution network. Backward integration by the local electric cooperatives into G&T cooperatives has occurred only after the local distribution cooperatives have become well established.

The local distribution networks themselves are highly firm-specific, and for this reason might seem difficult to finance with debt. But the local utility's monopoly position in the market, together with the dependability of the demand for electricity, provides substantial assurance that a market for the firm's assets (that is, for the firm as a whole) will continue to exist. The assets consequently make good collateral for debt. Moreover, both because of the firm's monopoly position and because of the relative constancy of consumers' demand, electricity supply is a relatively low-risk business, which both enhances the feasibility of borrowing and reduces the residual risk that the firm's customer-owners must bear. As a result, debt can be used to meet a substantial share of a local utility's capital requirements. Indeed, in the early stages of rural electric cooperatives, it was apparently common for them to borrow 100 percent of their fixed and working capital. Although government loan programs—discussed below—were commonly the conduits for this debt,[9] those programs did not absorb significant risk; of the $47 billion lent through these programs up to 1980, less than .001 percent was lost through foreclosure or failure.[10]

Where the local electricity distribution cooperatives have joined to form G&T cooperatives, the latter have secured their access to debt capital by piggybacking on the monopoly position of their members. This has been accomplished by having the distribution cooperatives enter into thirty-five-year requirements contracts with the G&T cooperatives. That thirty-five-year term has been chosen to match the term of the G&T's own loans, thus allowing the G&T to pledge a secure income stream as security for its debt.[11]

Subsidies

A further reason that the need for capital has not crippled the rural electric and telephone utility cooperatives is their receipt of various public subsidies. Prominent among these have been interest subsidies and loan guarantees administered by the federal Rural Electrification Administration. For the first fifteen years after the creation of the REA in 1935, the interest rate on REA loans to cooperatives was roughly equal to the rate paid by the government on marketable Treasury issues, and as a consequence did not involve a significant subsidy. After 1950, however, the interest rate charged the cooperatives, which was fixed at 2 percent in 1944 and raised to 5 percent in 1973, fell below the government's cost of borrowing. From 1945 to 1985, the interest rate on REA loans averaged 2.3 percentage points below the annual interest rate on marketable Treasury issues.[12]

In addition to the federal interest subsidies, the cooperative utilities have had the benefit of exemption from the federal corporate income tax. Further, the electricity cooperatives have also been given preferential access to power generated by federally owned hydroelectric facilities. Finally, the REA has historically played an important role in promoting the formation of cooperatives—that is, in playing an entrepreneurial role—and in providing them with technical assistance in their formative stages.

These subsidies have undoubtedly been important in encouraging the formation and growth of cooperative utilities, and therefore the great proliferation of rural electric cooperatives does not provide an unbiased test of the viability of the cooperative form. Evidently, however, the federal subsidies have not been critical to the success of cooperatives in the electric power industry. Even before the federal programs were enacted, there already existed forty-six rural electric cooperatives operating in thirteen different states.[13] Also, as already noted, there was no net interest subsidy to the cooperatives for the first fifteen years of the REA.[14] And in its early years, the REA also offered low-interest loans to investor-owned utilities that wished to extend service into rural areas, but found little interest in these loans among the latter firms.[15]

Risk

Even if a cooperative is able to borrow sufficient capital, its consumer-owners must still bear the risk of the enterprise. Indeed, the greater the amounts borrowed, the greater the amount of risk they must bear. Yet there are reasons why risk, too, is not a particular burden to utility cooperatives. There is relatively little risk, of course, from fluctuations in demand. And while costs—such as the cost of fuel or of environmental protection—might change dramatically over time, these are generally passed on to customers by regulated investor-owned utilities. As a result, it is not apparent that customers must bear substantially greater risk with a cooperatively owned utility than with one that is investor-owned.

Conflicts of Interest

Cooperatives, as we have seen, have a tendency to shift capital values from one generation of members to the next. For a capital-intensive enterprise such as an electric utility, such shifting might be particularly pronounced and could discourage accumulation of equity capital. With a rural electricity or telephone distribution network, however, much of the value of invested capital is presumably capitalized into the market value of the farms that the utility serves. This means that, on average, when a farmer stops patronizing the cooperative (which will in general happen only when he sells his farm), any discrepancy between the amount that the farmer has invested in the cooperative (whether through stock or through retained earnings) and the amount he can receive by cashing in his shares or selling them to the new owner of the farm will be reflected in a higher sale price for the farm.

To be sure, while this capitalization process may help prevent large shifts of capital value among members over time, it will not prevent— and it may even accentuate—transfers of capital value among current members according to their physical location. The capital cost of serving customers is inversely proportional to their geographic density, and that density can be very low in rural areas.

Why Are There No Urban Utility Cooperatives?

The most interesting question about the ownership of utilities is not why there are so many electricity and telephone cooperatives in rural areas, but rather why there are virtually no utility cooperatives in urban areas. Why is cooperative ownership not, in urban areas as in rural areas, an attractive alternative to the conventional system of public utility rate regulation?

Surprisingly, there is virtually no discussion of this question in the extensive literature on public utilities.[16] Rather, that literature largely confines itself to exploring the relative merits of four other methods of organizing public utilities: (1) unregulated investor ownership; (2) investor ownership subject to rate regulation; (3) governmental ownership;[17] and (4) "franchise bidding," in which competing investor-owned firms submit competitive bids for the exclusive right to provide the service—that is, to obtain a franchise—from a governmental agency.[18] The absence of urban electric cooperatives is intriguing, however, and in seeking an explanation we can shed some light not just on the role of consumer ownership but also on the role of governmental enterprise.

Subsidies

One tempting explanation for the absence of urban cooperatives is simply that federal subsidies for electricity cooperatives have been confined to rural areas. But that explanation appears inadequate. First, the success of the rural cooperatives seems not to have depended critically on federal subsidies: many cooperatives were successfully established prior to the advent of the federal support programs, and those programs themselves provided little net subsidy in their early years. Moreover, if cooperatives had substantial efficiency advantages in urban areas, one would expect that the federal government, or at least some state or local governments, would have extended capital subsidies or loan guarantees to urban cooperatives. For municipalities, especially, this would seem a more modest step than establishing a publicly owned utility, which many local governments have done.

Conflicts of Interest

A second, more fundamental reason for the absence of urban utility cooperatives is probably that utility cooperatives face higher costs of ownership in urban markets as compared with rural markets.

To begin with, in urban areas, it is likely that both residential and commercial customers are much more transient than are customers in rural areas, and transiency increases the costs of ownership. In particular, transiency reduces the effectiveness of consumer control. And as we observed in Chapter 8, high transiency makes capital accumulation more difficult for a cooperative, necessitating substantial flows of capital from patrons to the firm when they join and similar flows in the other direction when the patrons leave. These capital payments place a financial burden on the cooperative and its consumers if made in their entirety at the time the customer joins or leaves the cooperative. Yet if they are spread out over time, they tend to shift wealth between successive generations of patrons. This latter problem is accentuated by the fact that a large proportion of urban utility customers are renters rather than owners, for whom capitalization of the firm's value into real estate can do little to alleviate such shifting. In fact, since it is commonly the tenant who pays the utility bills while the landlord experiences the capitalization, with widespread tenancy the cooperative form has the additional disadvantage of potentially shifting capital values between tenants and their landlords: landlords will benefit if the utility accumulates capital from charges levied on tenants, while landlords will correspondingly suffer if the utility incurs debt to build excessive plant or incurs debt whose lifetime is longer than that of the plant it is used to finance.

To the extent that capital accounting does not suffice to eliminate such shifts of value between classes of residents, a cooperative may experience important conflicts in its decision making and may be used by one group of members to exploit another. Conflicts among classes of customers in an urban cooperative are likely to extend well beyond landlords and tenants. As Table 9.1 shows, residential (and particularly farm) electricity customers do not dominate in urban areas as they do in rural areas. Rather, urban customers are relatively evenly divided among residential, commercial, and industrial customers. Conflicts of interest among these groups could be substantial, and almost any voting scheme for the members of the cooperative could easily lead to a rate structure that would subsidize one class of customers at the expense of another. For example, under a one-customer-one-vote scheme, voting would be dominated by residential customers, who might seek to impose rates on commercial and industrial customers that were well above cost and thus cross-subsidize residential service. Conversely, one-kilowatt-one-vote would lead to the dominance of the utility's commercial and industrial customers, who might then seek to subsidize themselves at the expense of the residential customers. In fact, under any type of voting scheme there might well be substantial struggle among residential, commercial, and industrial customers for control of the utility.

As a consequence, if an urban electric utility were established as a consumer cooperative, external public rate regulation might still be needed to prevent any one group of customers from taking advantage of the others. And once that regulation is imposed, a consumer cooperative loses its most conspicuous advantage over an investor-owned utility.

Interestingly, there is little evidence that, in rural electric cooperatives, residential customers use their dominance to discriminate against

Table 9.1   Distribution of demand by customer category in electric utilities, 1985

Customer category	Distribution cooperatives	Total utility industry
Residential	61%	34%
Commercial	19	27
Industrial	16	35
Other	4	4

Source: "Our Vital Statistics," *Rural Electrification,* November 1986.

commercial or, particularly, industrial customers.[19] Rather, different classes of customers are generally assigned rates that, within the limits of the available systems of accounting, reflect the customers' varying marginal impact on the utilities' capital and operating costs. One reason for this is apparently that industrial customers are quite welcome in the rural cooperatives as sharers of capacity costs, and consequently have substantial bargaining power in establishing rates. The effectiveness of this bargaining is evidently enhanced by the relatively small size of the rural distribution cooperatives, which makes each industrial customer relatively more important to the utility while also lending credibility to an industrial customer's threat to turn to a competing source of electricity if it is charged exploitative rates.

In short, in the rural cooperatives collective control protects the interests of the dominant class of customers, who are farm and residential, while market contracting protects the other customers. Both collective governance and market contracting may be facilitated by the fact that farms are not typical household users of electricity, but rather have a substantial commercial or industrial character, and hence may identify to a considerable degree, both psychologically and in actual interest, with the utility's commercial and industrial customers.

Municipal Utilities

Another likely reason for the absence of urban electricity cooperatives is that municipally owned utilities play much the same role in urban areas that cooperatives do in rural areas.

Municipally owned electric utilities have been common in the United States since the formative days of the electricity industry. Although their numbers were greater in the first half of the twentieth century, there remain today, as already noted, approximately 1,500 local municipally owned firms that distribute electricity to retail customers. These firms are generally located in small (often very small) towns,[20] although they also appear in a few large cities, including Los Angeles and Seattle.[21]

Municipal electric utilities are not organized like most other municipal services—such as education, police protection, or even garbage collection—which are usually financed through general taxation and made available to all residents free of charge. Rather, the organization of a municipal utility strongly resembles a consumer cooperative. The finances of the utility are generally separated from those of the city as a whole. Revenues are derived solely from user charges for electricity. (Most municipal utilities in fact provide a positive revenue flow to their parent municipality.[22]) In terms of financial flows, municipal utilities differ from cooperatives principally in that they do not require capital investments of individual customers. But this distinction may be a major advantage, since it avoids the high transaction costs of maintaining separate capital accounts for as diverse and transient a population as is found in urban areas, and particularly for a population with substantial numbers of tenants. Because a municipality's credit can be used to help a municipal utility borrow nearly all of the capital that it needs, there is little reason for a municipal utility to accumulate equity capital in any case.

Governance of municipal utilities takes various forms. Sometimes control of the utility is exercised directly by the municipality's city council; sometimes it is in the hands of an independent utility board. Independent utility boards, in turn, are sometimes elected directly by the residents of the municipality, but more often are appointed by the mayor or the city council.[23] Because nearly all of a city's voters are residential consumers of electricity, all of these forms of governance effectively place ultimate voting control over the utility in the hands of its residential customers. The relative homogeneity of interest among this class of customers presumably helps avoid serious internal conflicts in the governance of the firm.

There remains the possibility that residential customers use their control over the utility to the disadvantage of its commercial and industrial customers. As suggested above, this may well be an important reason why investor ownership is so much more common in urban areas than in rural areas. There are, however, some checks on the incentive and ability of a municipal utility to overcharge its commercial and industrial customers, particularly in the small towns where the municipal utilities are most often found. Commercial utility customers, such as shops and offices, will commonly have usage patterns similar to those of residential customers, thus making any effort to establish rates that discriminate against them relatively transparent. Moreover, higher electricity rates for commercial firms are likely to be reflected in higher prices for locally procured goods and services, as firms either raise their prices or move outside the municipality. Industrial customers, in turn, will often have substantial bargaining leverage with a municipal utility, just as they do with rural cooperatives. This may help explain why public ownership has tended to survive longer in small communities than in large ones: the smaller the community, the more credible the threat that industrial customers will respond to high electricity charges by exiting the community or by purchasing their power from a source outside the community.

Finally, the small numbers, focused interests, and financial resources of both commercial and industrial customers commonly give them influence in local politics, and hence protection from exploitation by a municipal utility, that is disproportionate to the number of votes their owners can exercise in local elections. In this respect, it may be an advantage that municipal electric utilities are often controlled either by the city council or by a board appointed by city politicians rather than (as in a true cooperative) by a board elected directly by the residential customers, and that, even when the board *is* directly elected, the city council sometimes retains a degree of control over it.[24] Political control of this sort may help to check excessive favoritism toward residential customers. In any case, recognition that municipal utilities in fact treat all classes of customers with reasonable equity can be found in the fact that, like cooperative utilities, municipal utilities in most states are exempted from the rate regulation that is applied to investor-owned utilities.[25]

In sum, a municipal utility has much of the character of a consumer cooperative, though a cooperative in which both financing and control are buffered by the municipality's financial resources and political mechanisms. Given the transient and heterogeneous character of urban utility customers, this buffered form may have advantages over the pure cooperative form; what it loses in direct responsiveness to its customers it gains in mitigation of the capital financing complexities and conflicts of interest among owners that a pure cooperative would face in an urban environment. There have been numerous empirical studies of the relative efficiency of municipal and investor-owned electric utilities. Taken together, they fail to establish any significant differences in efficiency between the two organizational forms.[26] Nevertheless, since the 1920s there has been a long-term tendency for investor ownership to displace municipal ownership. One reason for this shift is apparently that, as technology has increased the efficient scale of generation, municipalities, unlike the rural electric cooperatives, have failed to integrate or confederate to form efficient-scale consortia for generation and transmission. Rather, municipalities have tended first to go out of the generation business, retreating to ownership of only the local distribution network, and then to sell their distribution network as well to the investor-owned generating firm that supplies their power.[27] This suggests that municipalities have more difficulty than do rural distribution cooperatives in forming a G&T cooperative among themselves, perhaps because differences in size and composition among municipalities make collective ownership awkward for them.

Cooperatives in Other Types of Utilities

The nearly complete absence, in the United States, of consumer cooperatives in the provision of utilities other than electricity and telephone service is probably a reflection of the same considerations we have surveyed in the case of electricity. These other utilities—including water, gas, sewage disposal, and (more recently) cable television—are generally provided centrally only in urban areas, where population densities justify the costs of installing a connected network of pipes or wires for distribution. Rural households commonly get their water from wells, their gas in bottles and tanks, and their television by broadcast (including direct reception from satellites), while they dispose of their sewage in septic tanks. As a consequence, there is no occasion to form cooperatives for these services in rural areas. And in urban areas, these utilities are typically organized as regulated investor-owned firms or as municipally owned firms rather than as consumer cooperatives for, one presumes, the same reasons that lead urban electric utilities to adopt those forms.

Is Rate Regulation Any Better?

A rate-regulated private utility, like a municipal firm or a cooperative, seeks to prevent monopolistic exploitation of the firm's customers by giving the customers a degree of control over the firm's operations. Under rate regulation, however, that control is much more attenuated and disciplined than it is under the other two forms.

To begin with, the regulatory body is not directly elected by the firm's customers, but rather is typically appointed by government at the state level and given substantial independence. Any direct effort by consumers to influence regulatory policy must take place in formal public hearings. In addition, the management of the firm itself has a voice in such hearings. Because the management represents the firm's investor-owners, it has an incentive to resist any effort to set rates that would exploit one class of the firm's customers for the benefit of another, since that would be likely to interfere with overall profitability. Finally, the orders of the regulatory agency are subject to judicial review according to a standard that is far more exacting than that which would be applied to the pricing policy of a consumer cooperative or of a municipal firm.

These constraints on consumer control of the firm's policies presumably buffer and balance, even more than does municipal ownership exercised through an independent board, any pathologies that might result from factionalized politics among a utility's customers, and help account for the relative success of regulated investor-owned firms in heavily urbanized areas.

Utility Organization in Other Countries

Although the mix of ownership forms for utilities varies significantly from one country to another, the general pattern has distinct similarities to that found in the United States. Electricity generation and distribution—the service in which consumer cooperatives have the largest market share in the United States—provides an example.

In some countries, such as France, Greece, and Ireland, nearly all electricity generation and distribution is undertaken by a single state-owned enterprise. In other countries, distribution is largely handled by local municipal utilities, while generation may be principally in the hands of private firms (as in Belgium and Germany) or governmental firms (as in the Netherlands).[28] Although consumer cooperatives for distributing and generating electricity evidently arose first in the United States, the cooperative form has since spread to a number of other countries as well.[29] For example, in Denmark, where generation of electricity is undertaken by 10 private and 2 municipal firms, distribution is carried out by 111 firms, of which 5 are also generating companies, 54 are municipal, and 52 are cooperatives or private foundations.[30] Likewise, in Indonesia, a total of 118 rural electric cooperatives had been organized by 1990.[31]

It is interesting to ask why, although municipal utilities play a large role in both Europe and the United States, full consumer cooperatives are apparently more common in the latter. Europe's generally more urban character may be partly responsible. The large number of cooperatives in heavily rural Denmark is consistent with this view.

Conclusion

As with the industries examined in earlier chapters, the form of ownership that predominates for utility firms in any given setting appears to be determined more by the relative heterogeneity and transiency of the firm's customers than by other considerations such as risk bearing or access to capital. Consumer ownership is found in predominantly rural areas, where the capital costs per user are high but the customer base is relatively stable and homogeneous. Investor ownership plays its most important role in heavily urbanized areas, where capital intensity is lower but the customer base is highly heterogeneous and transient. Municipal ownership is most heavily concentrated in small towns, which display an intermediate level of homogeneity and stability among customers.

10

Clubs and Other Associative Organizations

Membership organizations of a social character, such as country clubs, urban athletic and dining clubs, and fraternal lodges, are commonly either collectively owned by their patrons or organized as member-controlled nonprofits. Although this may at first seem unsurprising, upon examination the reasons for this pattern of ownership are subtle and complex. An understanding of ownership in these organizations, furthermore, sheds important light on the patterns of ownership that appear in other types of firms examined in preceding and succeeding chapters, including schools and colleges, law firms, insurance companies, housing cooperatives and condominiums, and residential communities. Consequently, although social clubs themselves account for only a modest fraction of overall economic activity, the determinants of ownership in clubs are worth special attention.

The Easy Cases

We begin with a brief examination of those clubs in which patron control is easiest to understand. These include organizations in which participation is an end in itself, and organizations that are dedicated to charity or the provision of public goods. We shall then concentrate our attention more closely on membership organizations in which the rationale for patron control is less immediately obvious—namely, those that principally offer services, such as athletic facilities and restaurants, that are also commonly provided by investor-owned firms.

Control as an End in Itself

In some membership organizations, exercising control over the organization is an end in itself: making decisions collectively is an excuse to have a meeting, which is in turn an opportunity for socializing. Some fraternal lodges, for example, seemingly have this character. More commonly, however, patron control appears to be a means to some other end rather than an end in itself.

Protecting Charitable Transfers

Organizations that collect philanthropic contributions to finance public goods or (more rarely) charitable services are often member-controlled. The National Audubon Society is a prototypical example. Severe asymmetric information is evidently an important factor here: by controlling the organization, the donors gain additional assurance that their contributions are being used for their intended purposes.

Such organizations are usually formed as nonprofits and have much in common with other types of nonprofit organizations. We shall postpone detailed discussion of them to Chapter 12, which focuses on nonprofits in general.

Lock-In

Members of social organizations often form close personal bonds; indeed, such fellowship is often among the organizations' most important purposes. But these bonds lead to lock-in: after a person has long been a member of a club, other clubs are no longer good substitutes, and hence offer poor competition. This has been offered—in one of the few essays that address the question of club ownership[1]—as an important reason for ownership by the members: the proprietor of an investor-owned club might try to increase membership fees over time to capture, as economic rents, the value to the members of retaining these bonds.

There are good reasons to believe, however, that lock-in is not a serious problem in most social organizations, and thus not an important reason for consumer control. Social organizations must generally admit new members from time to time, and the new members, not yet having forged close personal bonds with the other members, cannot be exploited. If, as is common, new members are charged a price at least as high as that charged the existing members, then those prices cannot be exploiting the existing members. And if an investor-owned social organization did try to charge new members less than current members, this would be likely to discourage applicants by signaling to them what the future would hold if they were to join.

Exclusivity

Not all social organizations are controlled by their patrons. Rather, patron ownership and patron control are concentrated particularly in those social organizations that are exclusive in selecting their members.

Golf clubs provide a good example. There are approximately 13,000 golf courses in the United States. Roughly 6,000 of these are investor-owned, 2,000 are municipally owned, and 5,000 are owned by their members.[2] The investor-owned courses, like the municipally owned courses, are virtually all "public" in the sense that anybody can play at them if he or she is willing to pay the stated fee. The 5,000 member-owned courses, however, are virtually all "private" clubs. This means that, in order to play at these courses, it is not sufficient to be willing to pay the organization's membership fee; an applicant must also be socially acceptable to the club as an individual.[3]

The same phenomenon can be seen among urban athletic clubs: those that sell memberships to the general public are commonly investor-owned; those that are socially exclusive are owned by their members.

The facilities that the member-owned golf clubs provide are not different in kind from those offered by the investor-owned clubs: a golf course, and perhaps also a pro shop, tennis courts, a swimming pool, a dining room, and a bar. The reason for the difference in ownership form must therefore be tied to the question of exclusivity.

The explanation is not that investor-owned firms are incapable of being socially discriminatory. On the contrary, they frequently select their clientele on social criteria. For example, prior to the passage of the federal Civil Rights Act of 1964, it was common for proprietary service firms of all types, including not only public golf clubs but also restaurants and hotels, to refuse to serve individuals on racial or religious grounds. Studio 54, a chic New York disco, set a trend in the late 1970s with its conspicuous policy of admitting only customers that management considered sufficiently attractive, famous, or otherwise appealing. And even at the peak of their popularity, some of the leading English men's clubs, though highly exclusive, were proprietary.[4]

Nor is the strong correlation between social exclusivity and member control simply a product of the civil rights laws. To be sure, since the civil rights laws can be avoided by organizing as a member-owned private club, they have created a strong incentive to adopt that form among organizations that wish to discriminate on grounds of race, religion, or sex. But organizations can be, and often are, highly exclusive without overtly discriminating on any of those particular grounds. More to the point, even before the enactment of the Civil Rights Act in 1964, there was a strong correlation between member control and social exclusivity among social and athletic clubs.

In short, if exclusive clubs are generally member-controlled, it is not simply because it would be illegal or otherwise infeasible for them to have any other organizational form. The link between exclusivity and member control evidently lies elsewhere. A plausible explanation for that link can be found in the properties of associative goods.

Associative Goods

There are many instances in which an individual's decision to patronize a firm depends not just on the quality and price of the goods or services offered by the firm but also on the personal characteristics of the firm's other patrons. Social clubs, such as private golf clubs, are conspicuous examples. A potential applicant to a club of this sort is likely to be quite as interested in the other members' personal attributes—such as their athletic ability, personality, wealth, family pedigree, profession, and business contacts—as in the quality of the club's golf course, tennis courts, and dining facilities. Even if two golf clubs have identical facilities and charge identical fees, prospective members may not be at all indifferent in choosing between them. Typically, they will prefer the club whose members they consider more attractive.

Educational institutions provide another example. Students commonly select an undergraduate college not just on the basis of the quality of the instructional program but with an eye to the intelligence, previous education, social attractiveness, athletic ability, and future promise of its other students.

In part the attraction of joining a social club or attending a college with a particularly high-quality clientele lies in the opportunity to enjoy the other patrons' company or—especially in the case of colleges—to learn from them. In part one joins or attends for the sake of developing contacts that will be useful elsewhere in life. And in part the appeal is not just in associating with such people but in being associated with them in the eyes of others.

For convenience we can label such organizations "associative organizations" and the services that they supply "associative goods." This class of organizations encompasses many types of firms beyond social clubs and colleges, some of which will be discussed below. To focus clearly on the incentives for patron ownership, however, for the moment we shall continue with the example of golf clubs.

Association and Stratification

In particular, let us think of the group of golf clubs—or "country clubs," as they are commonly called—that serve the prosperous residents of some suburban region, such as the Main Line suburbs of Philadelphia or the North Shore suburbs of Chicago. As noted, there may be a variety of different factors—family pedigree, athletic ability, business contacts, and so on—that contribute to an individual's attractiveness as a fellow member in one of these clubs. Although individuals may differ in their assessments of the relative importance of these various attributes in determining an individual's desirability as a fellow club member, in any given social milieu—such as that of Philadelphia Main Line country clubs—there is likely to be a fair degree of agreement on this matter. As a consequence, club members and potential club members can be roughly ranked according to their desirability as a fellow club member, on the basis of the aggregate of their personal attributes. We shall refer to an individual's position in this ranking as his "status." What we are saying, then, is that, given any two individuals, there will commonly be general agreement, among the members or potential members of the clubs in the region, as to which of the two individuals is the more desirable as a fellow club member—that is, who has the higher status.

Whether a club is owned by its members or by a profit-seeking entrepreneur, it has an incentive to charge higher fees to lower-status members than to higher-status members, since the latter contribute more to making the club attractive to its other members. In practice, however, country clubs and other social clubs generally charge the same fee to all their members. There are probably a number of reasons for this practice. One is simplicity. Another is to bond the club not to exploit members after they have become locked in. Yet another, undoubtedly, is that fees that vary according to members' perceived status would fuel invidious comparisons and resentments that would be destructive of a club's atmosphere of fellowship.

Given that all members must be charged the same fee, a club— whether member-owned or investor-owned—that has one opening in its membership and two applicants of different status will always choose to admit the higher-status applicant. Conversely, if a given individual is offered admission at two different clubs, both of which charge the same membership fee but one of which has a higher-status membership, the individual has an incentive to join the higher-status club. The result is a natural tendency for individuals to become stratified across clubs according to their status, with all the highest-status individuals belonging to one club, the next-highest status individuals belonging to a second club, and so forth. The following section explores this tendency in more detail.[5]

The Logic of Hierarchical Competition

The tendency toward stratification among clubs is most pronounced, and easiest to see, where the clubs involved are all member-owned. Such clubs must, over time, charge their members fees that are roughly equal to cost. Clubs of similar size and facilities will charge similar fees, leaving prospective members to choose between them principally on the basis of the status of the clubs' other members. This means that, as between any two clubs, all applicants will prefer to join the club with the higher-status members. The club that begins with the highest-status members will be in a position to pick and choose among applicants, admitting only those that it prefers—which will be the highest-status among them. The highest-status club will thus have an incentive to be exclusive, admitting all and only the highest-status individuals among those who wish to join a club. And the highest-status club will succeed in attracting all the highest-status applicants who, like everyone else, will prefer that club to all others.

In effect, since any given club charges all applicants the same fee, the only commodity with which applicants can compete for admission to the most desirable (that is, highest-status) clubs is with their own personal status. The highest-status applicants will be able to out-compete lower-status applicants for admission to the highest-status clubs.

The result will be a self-perpetuating and very stable hierarchy of clubs ranked according to their members' status. Members in all of the clubs will pay a fee that is just sufficient to cover the club's costs. In return for that fee, however, the members of the higher-status clubs receive greater benefits than do the members of the lower-status clubs—namely, the ability to associate with higher-status persons.

Now consider what would happen if one or more of the clubs were owned by a profit-seeking entrepreneur (that is, were investor-owned) rather than being owned collectively by their members. The easiest way to see this is to ask what would happen if, in the stratified system of member-owned clubs just described, ownership of only the highest-status club (which we will call "Club 1") were to be turned over to an entrepreneur.

The owner of Club 1 could be expected to raise his club's fee well above cost. Since he could offer his members a group of fellow members with higher status than those at the next-highest-status club ("Club 2"), he could charge them a higher fee than is charged by Club 2. More particularly, the fee at Club 1 can be raised to a level just below that at which the members of Club 1 would be indifferent between the high status and high fee of Club 1 and the lower status and lower fee of Club 2. If both Club 1 and Club 2 have the same size membership and similar facilities, they will have a similar cost of operation per member. And if, as assumed, Club 2 is member-owned, its fee will just equal that cost. Since Club 1 can charge a higher fee, it can earn a pure profit from its members without encouraging them to leave for Club 2. And since other clubs—Club 3, and so on—have lower-status members than Club 2, they will be even less attractive alternatives for the members of Club 1 than is Club 2.

Even if all the other competing clubs are charging their members a fee that is no higher than the clubs' cost, as they would if they were member-owned, Club 1's owner can charge his members a fee well above cost and earn pure profits. Although all other clubs would happily admit Club 1's members, they could not succeed in attracting those members without a fee that is much lower than Club 1 charges. In this environment competition among clubs does not drive price down to cost, because the various clubs are not offering a homogeneous product, but rather a highly differentiated one—differentiated in terms of the status of the club's members. The result is that the owner of Club 1 has a monopoly of sorts—namely, a monopoly on the highest-status fellow club members in society. And he can charge a monopoly price as a result.

Although this analysis has only asked what would happen if the *highest*-status club (termed Club 1) were proprietary, the analysis would be much the same if any other club in the hierarchy—say, Club 5—were to be proprietary, while the others remained member-owned. The owner of Club 5 could raise prices to the point at which its members are indifferent between remaining in Club 5 or leaving it to join the next-highest-ranking club, Club 6. The presence of the higher-status Clubs 1–4, meanwhile, would have no effect on the price that Club 5 could charge since, even if Clubs 1–4 were all charging a fee just equal to their cost, none of them would be willing to admit Club 5's members, and thus none of them would offer effective competition to the lower-ranking Club 5.

Nor is it important that we have been assuming that only one of the clubs is proprietary. For example, if both Club 1 and Club 2 were proprietary, then Club 1 could charge an even higher membership fee than it could if Club 2 were member-owned. The owner of Club 2 would have an incentive to raise Club 2's price above cost, to the point at which Club 2's members were indifferent between remaining in Club 2 and abandoning it for Club 3. As a consequence, Club 1 could raise its fee to the point at which its members were indifferent between paying that higher fee and leaving for Club 2, with its now-higher fee.

If clubs could freely vary their fees according to the personal status of each of their members, then competition among clubs would largely eliminate the potential for monopoly pricing. Without this ability to engage in price discrimination, however, each member's status has the quality of an externality for other members of the club. The result is to create a strong incentive for exclusivity in admissions policies, which in turn leads to stratification of clubs by status. And stratification, in turn, breeds market power.

The Incentive for Member Ownership

Thus if each club is constrained to charge all its members the same price regardless of their status, the clubs will tend to become stratified according to the status of their members. This stratification, in turn, will give market power to the clubs that have the highest-status members: those clubs can charge a premium to their members for the privilege of associating with other high-status individuals. And if the clubs are owned by investors or entrepreneurs rather than by their members, they can be expected to charge such a premium.

The members of a club, and particularly of a high-status club, therefore have a strong incentive to own the club, since by that means they can avoid price exploitation. Indeed, the monopolistic exploitation to which they would be subject in a proprietary club would be particularly galling, and the incentive to avoid it particularly strong, because the commodity that the proprietor would be selling to the members at a monopoly price would be the members' *own* high personal status. Moreover, the incentive for member ownership goes beyond just price exploitation. The profit-maximizing owner of a proprietary club has an incentive not only to charge a price above cost but also to make the membership of the club larger, and hence less exclusive (lower in average status), than the members would choose if they were in control.[6]

Other Associative Organizations

The preceding analysis does not apply solely to country clubs. The logic is perfectly general. In any industry in which firms provide associative goods, and the firms cannot engage in price discrimination (that is, each firm must charge all its customers the same price), there is an incentive for customers to own the firms to avoid monopolistic exploitation.

Private colleges are one example that we have already mentioned. Although there are about 3,400 colleges and universities in the United States, roughly one-fifth of which are private, the industry is far less competitive than these numbers alone would suggest. An important reason for this is that colleges are highly stratified in terms of the status (academic, athletic, and social) of their students. This stratification, though always apparent, has become more pronounced in recent decades as a result of nationally administered aptitude tests (which provide a commonly shared metric for judging the status of applicants) and as a result of the practice, common since the 1950s among elite institutions, of offering financial aid only on the basis of need and not on merit—that is, of not charging a lower price to more talented students.[7] As a consequence, if a group of informed individuals (such as families of talented college-age students) were today asked to name the nation's twenty-five best colleges, and to rank them from 1 to 25, the content and ordering of the lists would undoubtedly show substantial agreement. And the rankings would be based, in considerable part, upon the perceived quality of the students who attend the institutions rather than just upon the quality of the institutions' facilities and faculties.

The market power that elite colleges obtain as a result of this status hierarchy is presumably one reason why these institutions are organized not as proprietary firms but, rather, as nonprofit firms over which alumni—which is to say, former customers and continuing contributors—often have substantial control. About 10 percent of the institutions of higher education in the United States are, in fact, investor-owned. Most of these institutions are trade schools (including some law schools), although some are junior colleges providing general education. But whatever the type of education they offer, they tend to be concentrated in the lower ranges of the quality spectrum where the status hierarchy is less pronounced. Of course, there are other reasons for elite educational institutions to adopt the nonprofit form, the most obvious of which is their heavy dependence on donative income (discussed in Chapter 12). But market power would continue to offer an incentive for avoiding investor ownership even if the institutions involved derived all of their income from the tuition they charge their students.

An apartment building is also an associative organization, since its occupants are generally concerned about the personal characteristics of the other people who share the building. As we shall see in the next chapter, this evidently helps explain why cooperative ownership of apartment buildings in the United States originated among buildings catering to a prosperous elite. Insurance companies, too, are associative organizations to the extent that they are unable to adjust the prices of their policies according to the degree of risk presented by individual policyholders. This may have contributed to the widespread use of the mutual (policyholder-owned) form in this industry, discussed further in Chapter 14.

Even residential suburbs are associative organizations. Individuals have a strong incentive to patronize—that is, to reside in—a community composed of people who build expensive residences. This incentive derives not simply from a taste for attractive surroundings and affluent friends but also from the fact that expensive houses raise the community's property tax base and reduce the effective price of municipal services. As a consequence, suburbs use their zoning authority to set "admission requirements" in terms of the minimum quality and maximum density of new residences that can be constructed. The result is stratification of suburban communities in terms of the wealth of their residents. And this provides another incentive—beyond that provided by the monopolistic or public goods character of many municipal services—for these communities to be organized as territorial cooperatives (that is, as resident-controlled municipal corporations).

A firm can have an associative character not only for individuals who are purchasing services *from* it, but also for individuals who are selling services *to* it. A scholar, for example, will commonly choose employment with a particular university not only, or even primarily, on the basis of work conditions such as salary and teaching load, but also on the basis of the professional accomplishments of the other members of the faculty. A lawyer will typically seek to sell her services to a law firm in which the other lawyers are as competent as possible. In this latter case, as with suburbs, the motivation is in part directly pecuniary: because income within law firms is generally pooled to some extent, each lawyer's income is dependent upon the productivity of her colleagues. The result is the stratification of universities in terms of the quality of their faculties and of law firms in terms of the quality of their lawyers. And this stratification, in turn, gives the firms market power in the labor market and consequently reinforces incentives for avoiding investor ownership in these industries.

To be sure, some of the stratification of employees by talent that appears in organizations such as law firms is probably more a consequence than a cause of worker ownership. As we observed in Chapter 6, worker ownership creates an incentive for an egalitarian pay structure. This egalitarian pay structure then accentuates the incentive for stratification of workers among firms according to ability. While the market power resulting from this stratification presumably reinforces the incentive for worker ownership, it may not be an important exogenous motivation for that form of ownership.

Costs of Ownership

There are many associative goods that are not supplied by customer-owned firms. A ride on a subway or a railroad train, for example, is an associative good: there are some people one would rather share a car with than others. Nevertheless, the trains generally are not collectively owned by their riders. Restaurants, bars, resorts, hotels, and ocean liners are also associative institutions, but are commonly investor-owned. A decisive reason for investor ownership in these cases is the prohibitively high costs that patron ownership would entail. The individuals who patronize these firms are so dispersed and transitory, and the value of their transactions with the firm sufficiently small, that the costs of organizing them as owners would far exceed the value to them of any improvement in the quality and cost of the services they could derive from such a reorganization. In most social clubs, in contrast, the costs of ownership are relatively low. The members of a country club, for example, generally live in the same community and make the club a regular part of their social and athletic life for many years. The homogeneity of members that gives a club its market power also helps constrain the costs of collective decision making.

Low costs of ownership are not sufficient in themselves, however, to encourage patron control. The patrons of many of the nation's investor-owned public golf courses, for example, could probably also organize themselves as owners at relatively low cost. But the customers of these golf courses evidently place relatively little importance on the personal characteristics of the other patrons. They wish to use the course primarily to play golf. Such a golf course is then not in a position to establish market power through exclusive membership policies. Rather, it can compete with other golf courses only in terms of physical facilities and prices. If the local market is sufficiently large to support at least several such golf courses, competition among them is likely to be sufficient to keep fees close to costs, so that there is no strong incentive for customer ownership. And, in fact, investor-owned golf courses are often found in these circumstances. (In those communities in which the market is too small to support more than one golf course for persons who do not wish to mix golf with exclusive socializing, a golf course may have monopoly power based on economies of scale alone. In this case it is common for the golf course either to be consumer-owned, in the form of a nonexclusive club that anybody is free to join upon payment of a fee, or to be municipally owned—that is, to be organized, like the municipal utilities described in the preceding chapter, as a consumer-owned entity with ownership extended to the citizenry at large.)

The trade-off between the costs of ownership and the costs of contracting can also be seen at play in situations where, although the facilities involved are investor-owned, some portion of their use is licensed through an exclusive customer-controlled organization. Ocean and river cruises are a familiar example. Such cruises are highly associative goods. Nevertheless, the costs of customer ownership are high. As a result the ships themselves are investor-owned, and the cruises are generally either marketed directly by the owners or brokered through investor-owned travel agents. Sometimes, however, a member-controlled nonprofit group, such as a university alumni association or the members of an art museum, will serve as the broker for such a cruise. The nonprofit contracts with the owner of the ship for all the space on a given cruise and then in turn makes the cruise available exclusively to the organization's members. The result is that the members of the group get a high-quality associative good (since it is confined to the group's members) without paying a monopoly price (since the broker is nonprofit, and is controlled by its members).

A similar arrangement occasionally arises in railroad travel. For example, for many years a group of businessmen who commuted daily between the wealthy suburb of Lake Forest, Illinois, and their offices in downtown Chicago joined together to rent their own private car on a commuter train of the Chicago and Northwestern Railroad—thus creating, quite literally, an exclusive "club car" on the otherwise investor-owned train.

Mixed Motives

In sum, associative organizations such as social clubs fit the pattern seen in other industries where consumer ownership is common: substantial market power on the part of the firm combined with low costs of consumer control. What is particularly interesting about these organizations is the unusual source of their market power vis-à-vis their consumers, which often derives from the personal characteristics of the consumers themselves.

11

Housing

In the United States in 1960, more than 99 percent of all residential apartments in multi-unit buildings were rented from commercial landlords. Since then, a rapidly increasing number of apartment buildings have come to be owned collectively by their occupants through a cooperative or, more commonly, a condominium. By 1991 cooperatives and condominiums accounted for 16 percent of all multi-unit housing.[1] A similar tendency for cooperatives and condominiums to displace investor-owned apartments developed in Europe earlier in the twentieth century and has apparently gone much further there. This recent and rapid shift in ownership is intriguing, and invites a search for the causative factors.

The Organization and Evolution of Housing Cooperatives and Condominiums

In a housing cooperative, the building's occupants lease their individual units. The arrangement is distinguished from an ordinary landlord-tenant relationship by the fact that the tenants collectively own the building by holding shares in a corporation that has title to the property. That is, the tenants act collectively as their own landlord. In a condominium, in contrast, the occupants own rather than rent the individual units they occupy. There remains an important element of collective ownership in a condominium, but it is confined to the common elements of the property such as the hallways, elevators, exterior shell, roof, and grounds.

In a cooperative apartment building, debt financing is generally obtained collectively by the cooperative corporation under a single blanket mortgage that covers the building as a whole. In a condominium, each unit owner obtains his own mortgage financing, pledging his individual unit as security. In most other significant operational respects, the two forms are quite similar. In particular, the lease in a typical cooperative is not a standard lease for a fixed term of years, but rather is a "proprietary lease" that entitles the tenant to perpetual occupancy of the unit. The lease, and the associated shares of stock in the cooperative corporation, can be sold by the tenant at whatever price the market will bring. As a consequence, a member of a cooperative, like the owner of a condominium, effectively has a perpetual, exclusive, and freely transferable[2] property right in the apartment unit he occupies. Both forms will sometimes be referred to together as "owner-occupied apartment buildings."

In the United States, cooperatives long antedate condominiums. New York City's first cooperative apartment building, and perhaps the first in the United States, was built in 1876.[3] By 1929 there were at least 125 cooperative apartment buildings in New York City, most of which were luxury buildings.[4] Cooperative apartments also spread to other American cities during this period.[5] Chicago, for example, had over 100 cooperative apartment buildings by 1930.[6]

There are no accurate figures on the numbers of cooperatives in existence between 1930 and 1975. However, an estimate for 1960, which may be generous, suggests that there may have been as many as 150,000 cooperative units in existence then, amounting to roughly 1 percent of all multifamily dwellings; about one-third of these units were in New York City.[7] More systematic data, available from 1975 onward, indicate that the market share of cooperatives reached its historical peak in 1976, when cooperatives accounted for 2.2 percent of all multi-unit housing. By that year, the condominium had replaced the cooperative as the preferred form for owner-occupied apartment buildings in most of the country. New York City is the only significant jurisdiction where new cooperatives have remained an important part of the market.[8]

Prior to 1961, there was no enabling legislation for housing condominiums in the United States. For this reason, and because condominiums were difficult to create with the devices of common law conveyancing, almost no condominium housing was created in the United States before that date. Between 1961 and 1963, however, thirty-four states enacted enabling statutes for housing condominiums, and by 1967 all but one state had followed suit.[9]

The enactment of these statutes did not immediately lead to the large-scale formation of condominiums. In fact, relatively few condominium units were created prior to 1970. After that, however, condominiums began to be formed at an accelerating pace, both by new construction and by conversion from rental units, and they quickly came to represent a substantial portion of the housing market in metropolitan areas throughout the nation.

Costs of Contracting

Market Power

Although simple market power often provides important impetus for consumer ownership of enterprise, it is not a plausible stimulus to the formation of housing cooperatives and condominiums. In urban areas of sufficient density to have multi-unit apartment buildings, there are typically large numbers of reasonably fungible apartments under diverse ownership. The market for apartment rentals is thus quite competitive.

Lock-In

More particularly, the market for apartment rentals is competitive when an individual is looking for a new apartment. After an individual has begun to occupy a particular apartment, however, he or she becomes locked in to a degree, since the costs of searching for another apartment, moving possessions, and changing neighbors and neighborhoods can be substantial. Tenants may therefore be subject to expropriation by the landlord, not when they sign their initial lease, but when they renew their lease.

At the same time, landlords also become locked in to their tenants. If a tenant fails to renew her lease, the landlord faces the costs of refurbishing the apartment, advertising it, and forgoing rent while awaiting a new tenant. The available data indicate that landlords typically charge renewing tenants roughly the same rental[10] that new tenants are charged for similar units, suggesting that on average the tenant's ex post market power is at least equal to the landlord's. At most, then, ex post market power results in a degree of bilateral monopoly between tenant and landlord, and as a consequence perhaps some costly haggling over lease renewals, that might be avoided by tenant ownership.

Exclusivity

In some cases, the owner of an apartment building may also have market power that derives, not from the uniqueness of the apartments, but from the uniqueness of the tenants who occupy them. This is the type of market power, found in many types of socially exclusive institutions, that was analyzed in Chapter 10.

A landlord who secures a group of tenants who are attractive neighbors can charge more for apartments than he could otherwise. For most classes of tenants, competition among landlords should limit any such increase in rental to no more than the costs incurred by a landlord in searching and screening for desirable tenants. In buildings occupied by social elites such as the prominent rich, however, a landlord may be in a position to extract large monopoly rents from his select clientele. Such tenants often place a substantial premium on having neighbors of comparably high status. Yet as with the elite colleges and country clubs discussed in Chapter 10, there may be too few prospective tenants of any given social stratum to induce effective competition among landlords. As a consequence, tenants who desire social exclusivity may be able to avoid paying large monopoly rents by collectively owning their own building.

This may help explain why, among the well-to-do, social exclusivity has long been considered an important reason for living in a cooperative apartment building,[11] and there is evidence that it was a significant inducement for the cooperative housing created prior to the Second World War, much of which was in luxury buildings.[12] Yet it is probably an unimportant factor today in most cooperative and, particularly, condominium housing. The market for owner-occupied apartments now extends well beyond social elites. And condominiums, in contrast to cooperatives, generally do not screen prospective unit owners on social criteria.[13]

Moral Hazard

An apartment rental is a complex long-term transaction that, owing to the high cost of writing and enforcing contractual provisions that cover all contingencies, provides an opportunity for moral hazard. Tenants have an incentive to underinvest in maintenance whose benefits will extend beyond the end of their lease, or that will affect units other than their own. Landlords, in turn, have an incentive to underinvest in improvements (such as rapid repairs) whose benefits will be experienced primarily by a current tenant. Occupant ownership can mitigate these incentive problems.[14]

These incentive problems undoubtedly play an important role in explaining why such a large proportion of single-family detached houses (85 percent in the United States[15]) are owned by their occupants. In rented apartments, however, these problems seem much less severe. The most important systems in an apartment building that require long-term investments, such as the exterior shell and the utility systems, are not under the tenant's control and thus not subject to the tenant's incentive to underinvest. The apartment units themselves generally do not require substantial maintenance by the tenant. Few residential tenants desire substantial physical alterations to the unit they occupy even when such alterations are feasible; those who do can seek to negotiate them separately with the landlord. In turn, the landlord's incentive to behave opportunistically is constrained by the advantage of having a good reputation when seeking lease renewals and new rentals.

Nevertheless, at least for those tenants who wish to modify their apartments substantially to suit their own taste or convenience, contracting with a landlord can be costly in terms of complex negotiations and misaligned incentives, and this undoubtedly provides an important part of the incentive for occupant ownership.

Changes over Time

For all but the luxury end of the housing market, the costs of contracting just surveyed were insufficient to induce collective occupant ownership of apartment buildings in the United States prior to 1960. Nor is it apparent that these costs of contracting became noticeably higher after that date. To explain the rapid spread of cooperative and condominium housing since then, we must turn to changes in the cost of ownership, in subsidies, and in regulation.

Costs of Occupant Ownership

Collective Decision Making

The occupants of an apartment building are in many ways well positioned to exercise collective control over the building. They commonly occupy the building for a number of years and devote a substantial portion of their income to it. They obtain a good deal of information about the building's management without extra effort simply because they live there. They reside in very close proximity to one another, making meetings easy to arrange. And, by virtue of the fact that they have all chosen to live in the same building, the occupants are likely to be unusually homogeneous in terms of preferences, wealth, and even social background. These unusually low costs of collective governance presumably go far toward explaining why housing is one of the few retail goods or services in which consumer ownership is common.

This does not mean, however, that collective decision making is costless in an apartment building. The residents must still take time to attend meetings and to inform themselves on matters that would otherwise be outside their knowledge (or bear the costs of decisions in which they are unrepresented or uninformed).[16] Further, the interests of the various occupants of an apartment building can diverge substantially. Some occupants will be satisfied with wood-grained vinyl for the lobby walls; others will strongly prefer spending what is necessary to have real wood. Some will want better laundry facilities in the basement; those who take their laundry out or have their own machines will not. And residents of the ground floor may be less eager than those on the top floor to refurbish the elevators. As a consequence, there is substantial room for costly haggling and for outcomes that fail to maximize the aggregate welfare of the occupants.

Although it is difficult to obtain direct empirical observations on the costs of collective decision making, substantial anecdotal and case-law evidence suggests that conflicts among members are a serious problem in the governance of cooperatives and condominiums[17] and that homogeneity of membership is an important aid to viability.[18] The much lower rate of owner-occupancy in apartments than in single-family houses may also be a reflection, in part, of the relative absence of the costs of collective decision making in the latter.

Liquidity

On the one hand, buildings provide good collateral, making debt financing readily available for owner-occupied housing. Undoubtedly this also helps account for the exceptionally high degree of consumer ownership in housing as compared with other consumer goods and services. On the other hand, a house or apartment does not provide perfect security for a loan for its full purchase price, and that price is typically large relative to the occupant's income. As a result, an owner-occupant must usually invest substantial equity in his residence, and this may exceed his wealth or at least leave him highly illiquid, pushing him toward rental.

It might be supposed that the growing popularity of owner-occupied apartments in recent decades is attributable, at least in part, to an increase in liquidity among apartment dwellers that has permitted a greater proportion to invest the equity necessary for ownership. But the evidence seems quite contrary to this conclusion. In the middle and late 1970s, when apartment ownership first began to spread rapidly, there was virtually no overall growth in real family income, in sharp contrast to the preceding two decades.[19] At the same time, housing prices increased in the 1970s more rapidly than inflation in general, in contrast to the experience of the two preceding decades, thus increasing the price of housing relative to household income.[20] And the inflation rate itself increased dramatically in the late 1970s, substantially increasing nominal interest payments on mortgages and effectively making new purchasers of homes repay the principal on their loan much faster than they would otherwise, aggravating liquidity problems.[21]

Finally, throughout the twentieth century there have been substantial numbers of apartment dwellers who were quite prosperous and yet, until the recent past, rented; for these individuals, at least, liquidity must not have been constraining.[22]

Risk Bearing

Risk bearing is a related problem. Because, for most individuals, the value of the residence they occupy is large relative to their total wealth, home ownership results in poor diversification of investments relative to rental. In addition, the market value of an individual's residence is likely to be positively correlated with important nonfinancial investments they have made. In particular, deterioration in the local job market is likely to be reflected in a decrease in housing prices, with the result that an individual who loses his job may find that the value of his house has decreased at the same time.

However, the extraordinarily high rate of owner-occupancy in single-family homes suggests that, here as elsewhere, risk does not act as a strong determinant of forms of ownership. Where, as in single-family homes, important incentive considerations weigh the other way, individuals are prepared to assume ownership even in the face of substantial risk. In any case, during the 1970s and early 1980s, when the great expansion of condominium and cooperative housing took place, the risks of homeownership for the average family seem actually to have increased as a consequence of the liquidity problems just discussed.

There are some cases in which risk bearing favors occupant ownership of housing. In particular, retired persons with fixed nominal incomes from pensions are exposed to serious risk from changes in the inflation rate. By purchasing their residence they can hedge against this risk as far as expenditures on housing are concerned. This may help explain the spread of condominiums and cooperatives among the elderly, an increasing number of whom have retired on substantial pensions since the 1960s. It cannot, however, explain the great spread of these forms among the population at large.

The Importance of the Legal Environment

From the preceding, it appears that neither the basic costs of market contracting nor the basic costs of consumer ownership have shifted in ways that provide a convincing explanation for the great expansion in condominium and cooperative housing in the United States since the 1960s. This suggests that the reason for that expansion lies in changes in the organizational, regulatory, or tax law that govern housing. Three particular changes seem likely candidates: the spread of rent control, the increase in tax subsidies to homeownership, and the promulgation of new statutes for organizing condominiums.

Rent Control

By driving down the rate of return on rented apartments, rent control creates a strong incentive for forming cooperatives and condominiums. There is good reason to believe that rent control is in large part responsible for the extensive spread of cooperative and, especially, condominium housing in Western Europe. Rent control had its first widespread appearance in Europe during World War I, though it was repealed in many jurisdictions during the interwar years. Then, during the Second World War, rent control was widely reimposed and largely left in place afterward; it has remained in effect throughout much of Western Europe since then. The spread of condominium and cooperative housing largely follows the same pattern. The first extensive use of the condominium form for multi-unit apartment buildings in Europe came after the First World War, and it was only after the Second World War that condominiums and cooperatives achieved their current dominance.[23] Moreover, although good data on the market share of condominiums and cooperatives for most European countries seem to be lacking, it appears that this market share is largest in those countries with the most extensive rent control regimes. In Italy, for example, where rent control has been universal since the Second World War, the market for rental apartments seems to have virtually disappeared; condominiums and cooperatives appear to be nearly universal in multi-unit buildings.

In the United States, in contrast, rent control can quickly be dismissed as a direct cause of the initial spread of cooperatives and condominiums. Only a small minority of those American cities that have experienced a recent surge in cooperatives and condominiums have rent control.[24] Indeed, at least as far as conversions from rental to ownership are concerned (as opposed to new construction), jurisdictions with rent control seem to experience less activity than noncontrolled jurisdictions.[25]

It is possible, however, that the fear of rent control has provided at least some of the incentive for the surge in condominiums. In 1970, New York City was evidently the only American city with rent control. (It had never repealed its rent control statute after the Second World

War.) But by 1979, rent control had been adopted in at least 250 local jurisdictions—including Los Angeles, San Francisco, Boston, and Washington, D.C.—and was continuing to spread rapidly.[26] This development, following the earlier adoption of rent control in Western Europe, may have discouraged many potential landlords even in those jurisdictions to which rent control had not yet come.

Tax Subsidies

The federal personal income tax has, at various times and for various classes of taxpayers, contained large subsidies for both rental housing and owner-occupied housing. The subsidies for owner-occupancy have generally been larger, however, creating a net tax bias in favor of owner-occupied as opposed to rental housing. In contrast to the tax biases considered in earlier chapters, the net tax subsidy to owner-occupied housing is both large and relatively easy to quantify.

We begin by considering separately the tax preferences provided to owner-occupants and to renters, respectively, describing the general structure of those preferences and then estimating their magnitude as a fraction of the total cost of housing. These are then put together to obtain a quantitative estimate of the net tax subsidy to owner-occupancy, and hence to the condominium and cooperative forms for multi-unit housing.

Tax Preferences for Owner-Occupancy

Although, in the popular mind, the tax subsidy to homeownership vis-à-vis rental is often associated with the ability to deduct mortgage interest and property taxes when computing taxable personal income,[27] these deductions are in fact not a source of subsidy. Landlords can also take these deductions, and in competitive markets—which rental markets presumably are—the value of the deductions will be passed through to tenants. Rather, the principal source of the subsidy lies in the failure to include the imputed rental value of owner-occupied housing in taxable personal income.[28] The value of this tax subsidy is offset somewhat by the fact that owner-occupants, in contrast to landlords, are not permitted a deduction for depreciation.[29] The absence of the latter deduction, however, is generally far from sufficient to offset the value of the exclusion of imputed rental income.[30]

In addition, since 1951 owner-occupied housing has benefited from a special rule that defers taxation of capital gains on the sale of a residence as long as the proceeds of the sale are reinvested in another owner-occupied residence. This rule was supplemented in 1963 by another provision granting a one-time forgiveness of accumulated capital gains from the sale of a personal residence when the taxpayer is over fifty-five years of age.

The full benefit of these tax preferences for owner-occupancy has been extended to housing cooperatives since 1942, when tenant-stockholders in housing cooperatives were first permitted to deduct their proportionate share of the mortgage interest and property taxes paid by the cooperative.[31] Prior to that time, no such deduction was permitted.[32] This does not mean that cooperatives could not take advantage of the full tax subsidy to owner-occupied housing prior to 1942. To get the full subsidy before that year, the building could not be financed with a mortgage, but instead had to be owned outright by its members[33]—which is probably the way that the luxury buildings that then accounted for most cooperatives were generally financed.

There is no special provision in the Internal Revenue Code that permits owner-occupants of condominium units to take deductions for property taxes and mortgage interest; the deductions are allowed under the same provisions that apply to homeowners in general. Allowance for these deductions was only first explicitly recognized by the Internal Revenue Service in 1964,[34] but it is unlikely that owners of condominium units prior to that date would have doubted the availability of the deductions.[35]

The value of these tax subsidies for owner-occupancy is roughly proportional to the owner's marginal tax rate (or, more precisely, the tax rate that would be applicable to the owner's imputed rental income if it were taxed). An individual in a high tax bracket receives a substantial subsidy, while an individual who pays no taxes receives no subsidy at all (that is, pays the same taxes whether he owns or rents).

Because tax rates have changed over time, the value of the tax subsidy to owner-occupancy has changed too. In general, average tax rates have increased through the years, and they jumped especially sharply at the time of the Second World War. To provide some sense of this, Table 11.1 gives an estimate, for a series of years between 1936 and 1988, of the marginal tax bracket facing persons at different points in the income distribution. The first column, for example, gives the marginal tax bracket of a person whose income falls at the twentieth percentile (from the bottom) of the income distribution; the seventh column gives the marginal tax bracket confronting a person in the ninety-ninth percentile (that is, the top 1 percent of the income distribution). The eighth column gives the highest marginal rate applied to anyone in the year in question. Although until the 1960s the top rate was very high, it applied to very few individuals. In 1936, for example, the top rate applied only to incomes in excess of $5 million.

Table 11.1 shows that the tax subsidy to owner-occupied housing was nonexistent for everyone except those in roughly the top 1 percent of the income distribution in 1936, and even for many households in the top 1 percent the tax rate was so low as to make the subsidy quite modest. After the Second World War, however, tax rates became large enough to make the subsidy significant for the great majority of households, and increasingly so through the mid-1970s.

Tax Preferences for Rental

The federal tax code provides a subsidy to rental properties vis-à-vis other investments to the extent that it permits the owner of a rental building to take depreciation deductions that exceed the real rate of economic depreciation. In particular, between 1954 and 1986 the tax code made depreciation deductions extremely generous by permitting them to be computed according to the double declining balance method.[36] Until 1986, moreover, landlords were allowed to finance rental

Table 11.1   Marginal tax rates

Year	\multicolumn{8}{c}{Household's position in income distribution}
	20%	40%	50%	60%	80%	95%	99%	Top
1936	0%	0	0	0	0	0	6	79
1946	17	17	19	19	19	27	35	86
1956	20	21	24	24	26	32	43	91
1966	18	20	22	22	27	36	46	70
1976	19	25	27	28	36	45	58	70
1985	17	24	28	32	42	45	48	50
1988	15	15	15	28	28	28	28	28

Source: Henry Hansmann, "Condominium and Cooperative Housing: Transactional Efficiency, Tax Subsidies, and Tenure Choice," 20 Journal of Legal Studies 25, 55 (1991).

buildings through limited partnerships that permitted outside investors (serving as the limited partners) to shelter income they received from other sources by offsetting against it the large tax losses that the depreciation rules generated in the early years of the real estate investment. The result was that the depreciation deductions could effectively be sold to taxpayers in high tax brackets, thus permitting landlords to extract maximum value from the deductions.[37]

The tax subsidy to rental housing, though substantial in some periods, was largely eliminated after 1986 by new legislation that severely reduced depreciation deductions for real estate and that imposed strict constraints on investors' ability to use depreciation deductions to shelter other income from taxes.[38]

The Value of the Net Subsidy to Owner-Occupancy

Table 11.2 gives the annual capital cost of housing for both rental and owner-occupancy for selected years, stated as a percentage of the market value of the building. The computations are presented for selected decades, beginning in 1936. Because 1986 was a transition year between two very different tax regimes, figures for 1985 and 1988 have been included instead.

For each year, the row labeled "own" gives the amount of the annual after-tax cash flows that an individual would reasonably have expected if he had bought his living unit in that year.[39] The row labeled "rent" gives the after-tax cost to a landlord of renting out a unit that a landlord would reasonably have expected if she had purchased a building in that year. This becomes the cost for renters if competition induces the landlord to charge a rental equal to the landlord's cost, which here includes a market rate of return on capital. (Because, in 1976 and 1985, the landlord's after-tax costs depend significantly on whether the landlord is subject to the "minimum tax" that was applicable to some individuals in those years, Table 11.2A gives alternative calculations for those two years.)

The costs included in the computations in Table 11.2 (and 11.2A) are the costs of invested and borrowed capital and the cost of depreciation, plus net taxes. Other costs of housing—such as maintenance of the building, utilities, and other services—are not included here, since their after-tax cost should be the same whether an individual owns or rents. In effect, the figures in Table 11.2 give the annual capital cost of

Table 11.2   After-tax cost of housing as a percentage of building value (no minimum tax)

	Landlord/owner-occupant's position in income distribution							
Year	20%	40%	50%	60%	80%	95%	99%	Top
1936: Rent	5.08%	5.08	5.08	5.08	5.08	5.08	5.03	6.70
Own	5.08	5.08	5.08	5.08	5.08	5.08	4.77	1.63
1946: Rent	4.21	4.21	4.13	4.13	4.13	3.78	3.35	−7.45
Own	3.73	3.73	3.61	3.61	3.61	3.12	2.64	−0.11
1956: Rent	7.13	7.09	6.99	6.99	6.91	6.67	6.10	−3.92
Own	6.16	6.08	5.85	5.85	5.70	5.23	4.39	1.43
1966: Rent	6.76	6.68	6.60	6.60	6.38	5.92	5.50	3.85
Own	5.89	5.73	5.57	5.57	5.17	4.44	3.78	2.32
1976: Rent	3.22	2.69	2.50	2.41	2.02	1.45	0.18	−1.95
Own	2.51	1.86	1.65	1.54	0.98	0.34	−0.58	−1.43
1985: Rent	8.08	7.62	7.44	7.23	6.61	6.38	6.12	5.93
Own	7.12	6.19	5.65	5.12	3.79	3.43	3.16	2.97
1988: Rent	8.88	8.88	8.88	8.83	8.83	8.83	8.83	8.83
Own	7.39	7.39	7.39	5.65	5.65	5.65	5.65	5.65

Source: See Table 11.1.

Table 11.2A   After-tax cost of housing as a percentage of building value (minimum tax applied to landlord)

	Landlord's position in income distribution							
Year	20%	40%	50%	60%	80%	95%	99%	Top
1976: Rent	3.87%	3.41	3.25	3.17	2.87	2.44	1.48	−0.14
1985: Rent	8.74	8.34	8.20	8.05	7.56	7.38	7.18	7.03

Source: See Table 11.1.

owner-occupancy and of rental, respectively, per dollar spent on the initial purchase price of the building. In the long run, the purchase price of a building should be determined by the cost of construction, and should therefore be the same whether the purchaser is a landlord or a condominium association. By comparing the figures yielded by these calculations we obtain a measure of the difference in cost that results, by virtue of the tax code alone, from operating the same building on a rental basis on the one hand or as a cooperative or condominium on the other.

Because the cost of housing for an owner-occupant depends on the owner's tax bracket, and the cost of rental housing on the landlord's tax bracket, the columns in Table 11.2 give a series of eight different cost figures for both ownership and rental for each year to reflect different tax brackets. The tax brackets chosen for each year were those given in Table 11.1, corresponding to different points in the income distribution. The columns of Table 11.2 correspond to the columns in Table 11.1. For example, the first column gives figures for individuals who are in the tax bracket corresponding to a household income representing the twentieth percentile of the income distribution; the last column gives figures for individuals who are in the top marginal tax bracket.

To find an individual's cost of being an owner-occupant for a given year from Table 11.2, one looks at the column corresponding to the individual's position in the income distribution. On the other hand, while the rows labeled "rent" in Table 11.2 similarly give the landlord's cost as a function of her tax bracket, this does not necessarily become the tenants' cost. If, as seems plausible, the market for rental apartments is reasonably competitive, then market forces will drive rents to equal the cost (as given in Table 11.2) for the marginal landlord—that is, the landlord with the highest cost among those who remain in the market when supply equals demand. And the landlord with the highest cost is the one in the lowest tax bracket.[40] The cost of rental to the renter for a given year is thus given by the figure in Table 11.2 for that tax bracket which is the tax bracket of the marginal landlord. Landlords in higher tax brackets will be earning pure profits, while those in lower brackets will be driven from the market.

Unfortunately, we have no reliable empirical data on the tax bracket of marginal landlords. Because of the ease of syndicating investments in real estate through limited partnerships, however, it is reasonable to assume that, at least for large or luxury apartment buildings prior to the Tax Reform Act of 1986,[41] this bracket was relatively high.[42]

The figures in Table 11.2 permit us to observe the value of the net tax subsidy to owner-occupied as opposed to rental housing by comparing the after-tax cost to an individual of occupying the same apartment when it is (a) in a building organized on a rental basis and (b) in a building organized as a condominium or cooperative. To make the

Table 11.3 Difference between rental cost and owner-occupancy cost as a percentage of building value (no minimum tax)

Owner's position in income distribution	Marginal landlord's position in income distribution							
	20%	40%	50%	60%	80%	95%	99%	Top
1936								
20%	0.00%	0.00	0.00	0.00	0.00	0.00	−0.05	1.62
40	0.00	0.00	0.00	0.00	0.00	0.00	−0.05	1.62
50	0.00	0.00	0.00	0.00	0.00	0.00	−0.05	1.62
60	0.00	0.00	0.00	0.00	0.00	0.00	−0.05	1.62
80	0.00	0.00	0.00	0.00	0.00	0.00	−0.05	1.62
95	0.00	0.00	0.00	0.00	0.00	0.00	−0.05	1.62
99	0.31	0.31	0.31	0.31	0.31	0.31	0.26	1.93
Top	3.45	3.45	3.45	3.45	3.45	3.45	3.40	5.07
1946								
20%	0.48%	0.48	0.40	0.40	0.40	0.05	−0.38	−11.18
40	0.48	0.48	0.40	0.40	0.40	0.05	−0.38	−11.18
50	0.60	0.60	0.52	0.52	0.52	0.17	−0.26	−11.06
60	0.60	0.60	0.52	0.52	0.52	0.17	−0.26	−11.06
80	0.60	0.60	0.52	0.52	0.52	0.17	−0.26	−11.06
95	1.09	1.09	1.01	1.01	1.01	0.66	0.23	−10.57
99	1.57	1.57	1.49	1.49	1.49	1.14	0.71	−10.09
Top	4.32	4.32	4.24	4.24	4.24	3.89	3.46	−7.34
1956								
20%	0.97%	0.93	0.83	0.83	0.75	0.51	−0.06	−10.08
40	1.05	1.01	0.91	0.91	0.83	0.59	0.02	−10.00
50	1.28	1.24	1.14	1.14	1.06	0.82	0.25	−9.77
60	1.28	1.24	1.14	1.14	1.06	0.82	0.25	−9.77
80	1.43	1.39	1.29	1.29	1.21	0.97	0.40	−9.62
95	1.90	1.86	1.76	1.76	1.68	1.44	0.87	−9.15
99	2.74	2.70	2.60	2.60	2.52	2.28	1.71	−8.31
Top	5.70	5.66	5.56	5.56	5.48	5.24	4.67	−5.35
1966								
20%	0.87%	0.79	0.71	0.71	0.49	0.03	−0.39	−2.04
40	1.03	0.95	0.87	0.87	0.65	0.19	−0.23	−1.88
50	1.19	1.11	1.03	1.03	0.81	0.35	−0.07	−1.72
60	1.19	1.11	1.03	1.03	0.81	0.35	−0.07	−1.72
80	1.59	1.51	1.43	1.43	1.21	0.75	0.33	−0.33
95	2.32	2.24	2.16	2.16	1.94	1.48	1.06	−0.59
99	2.98	2.90	2.82	2.82	2.60	2.14	1.72	0.07
Top	4.44	4.36	4.28	4.28	4.06	3.60	3.18	1.53

1976								
20%	0.71%	0.18	−0.01	−0.10	−0.49	−1.06	−2.33	−4.46
40	1.36	0.83	0.64	0.55	0.16	−0.41	−1.68	−3.81
50	1.57	1.04	0.85	0.76	0.37	−0.20	−1.47	−3.60
60	1.68	1.15	0.96	0.87	0.48	−0.09	−1.36	−3.49
80	2.24	1.71	1.52	1.43	1.04	0.47	−0.80	−2.93
95	2.88	2.35	2.16	2.07	1.68	1.11	−0.16	−2.29
99	3.80	3.27	3.08	2.99	2.60	2.03	0.76	−1.37
Top	4.65	4.12	3.93	3.84	3.45	2.88	1.61	−0.52
1985								
20%	0.96%	0.50	0.32	0.11	−0.51	−0.74	−1.00	−1.19
40	1.89	1.43	1.25	1.04	0.42	0.19	−0.07	−0.26
50	2.43	1.97	1.79	1.58	0.96	0.73	0.47	0.28
60	2.96	2.50	3.32	2.11	1.49	1.26	1.00	0.81
80	4.29	3.83	3.65	3.44	2.82	2.59	2.33	2.14
95	4.65	4.19	4.01	3.80	3.18	2.95	2.69	2.50
99	4.92	4.46	4.28	4.07	3.45	3.22	2.96	2.77
Top	5.11	4.65	4.47	4.26	3.64	3.41	3.15	2.96
1988								
20%	1.49%	1.49	1.49	1.44	1.44	1.44	1.44	1.44
40	1.49	1.49	1.49	1.44	1.44	1.44	1.44	1.44
50	1.49	1.49	1.49	1.44	1.44	1.44	1.44	1.44
60	3.23	3.23	3.23	3.18	3.18	3.18	3.18	3.18
80	3.23	3.23	3.23	3.18	3.18	3.18	3.18	3.18
95	3.23	3.23	3.23	3.18	3.18	3.18	3.18	3.18
99	3.23	3.23	3.23	3.18	3.18	3.18	3.18	3.18
Top	3.23	3.23	3.23	3.18	3.18	3.18	3.18	3.18

Source: See Table 11.1.

comparison for a given year, one compares (a) the figure in the "rent" row in the column corresponding to the marginal landlord's position in the income distribution with (b) the figure in the "own" row corresponding to the individual's position in the income distribution.

Tables 11.3 and 11.3A give these differences for the years and the tax brackets reflected in Tables 11.2 and 11.2A. To take an example, consider the figures in Table 11.3 for 1976; they show that an individual who is in the eightieth percentile of the income distribution would face an annual cost of housing that is lower by .47 percent of the market value of the living unit if he were to own the unit rather than rent it and if the tax bracket of marginal landlords were that of persons in the 95th percentile of the income distribution. Since, from Table 11.2, the

Table 11.3A   Figures for Table 11.3 when alternative minimum tax is applicable to marginal
landlord

Owner's position in income distribution	Marginal landlord's position in income distribution							
	20%	40%	50%	60%	80%	95%	99%	Top
1976								
20%	1.36%	0.90	0.74	0.66	0.36	−0.07	−1.03	−2.65
40	2.01	1.55	1.39	1.31	1.01	0.58	−0.38	−2.00
50	2.22	1.76	1.60	1.52	1.22	0.79	−0.17	−1.79
60	2.33	1.87	1.71	1.63	1.33	0.90	−0.06	−1.68
80	2.89	2.43	2.27	2.19	1.89	1.46	0.50	−1.12
95	3.53	3.07	2.91	2.83	2.53	2.10	1.14	−0.48
99	4.45	3.99	3.83	3.75	3.45	3.02	2.06	0.44
Top	5.30	4.84	4.68	4.60	4.30	3.87	2.91	1.29
1985								
20%	1.62%	1.22	1.08	0.93	0.44	0.26	0.06	−0.09
40	2.55	2.15	2.01	1.86	1.37	1.19	0.99	0.84
50	3.09	2.69	2.55	2.40	1.91	1.73	1.53	1.38
60	3.62	3.22	3.08	2.93	2.44	2.26	2.06	1.91
80	4.95	4.55	4.41	4.26	3.77	3.59	3.39	3.24
95	5.31	4.91	4.77	4.62	4.13	3.95	3.75	3.60
99	5.58	5.18	5.04	4.89	4.40	4.22	4.02	3.87
Top	5.77	5.37	5.23	5.08	4.59	4.41	4.21	4.06

Source: See Table 11.1.

annual cost of renting from such a landlord would be 1.45 percent
of the market value of the unit, this represents a saving of 32 percent
over the cost of rental. (Again, we are speaking here of capital costs;
the savings as a percentage of the total market rental cost would be
smaller.) Or, put in dollar terms, the annual savings on an apartment
with a market value of $100,000 would be $470.[43]

A clear measure of the pure tax subsidy to owner-occupancy is offered by the figures on the diagonals in Tables 11.3 and 11.3A, giving
the cost difference when the occupant and the marginal landlord are in
the same tax bracket. The first column in Table 11.4 restates these
figures for the tax bracket corresponding to the ninety-fifth percentile
of the income distribution. The third column in Table 11.4 gives the
cost savings from owner-occupancy as a percentage of the capital cost
of renting (given in the second column, from Table 11.2). The fourth
through the sixth columns give the corresponding figures under the

assumption that the minimum tax applies. From the figures in the third column of Table 11.4, we see that the percentage savings in the capital cost of a building when it is occupant-owned rather than rented goes from zero in the 1930s to a peak of at least 77 percent in 1976, and then falls off somewhat after that. The absolute dollar savings from owner-occupancy, on the other hand, reaches its peak in 1988, when (as shown by the first column) it amounts to an annual savings equal to 3.18 percent of the value of the housing unit (or $3,180 on a unit costing $100,000).[44] If the minimum tax is binding on marginal landlords, then the savings are even more dramatic in 1976 and 1985, as the last three columns show.

One way to judge the magnitude of this tax subsidy for cooperatives and condominiums is to imagine that a new apartment building was constructed in 1985 with 100 units, at a cost of $100,000 per unit (or $10 million in total). Using the figures from Table 11.4, aggregate tax savings of $295,000 per year ($395,000 if the minimum tax were applicable) would have been expected for the building as a whole if the developer had sold off the apartments as condominium units rather than retaining title to the building and renting out the apartments.

Implications for the Spread of Cooperatives and Condominiums

Over the fifty-year period from the 1930s to the 1980s, there was a clear progression toward stronger tax subsidies for owner-occupied as

Table 11.4 Savings from owner-occupancy when marginal landlord and owner-occupant are both in 95th percentile

	Without minimum tax			With minimum tax		
Year	Savings from Table 11.3	Rent from Table 11.2	Savings as % of rent	Savings from Table 11.3A	Rent from Table 11.2A	Savings as % of rent
1936	0.00%	5.08%	0%			
1946	0.66	3.78	17			
1956	1.44	6.67	22			
1966	1.48	5.92	25			
1976	1.11	1.45	77	2.10%	2.44%	86%
1985	2.95	6.38	46	3.95	7.38	54
1988	3.18	8.83	36			

Source: See Table 11.1.

opposed to rental housing. In 1936, there was a net tax subsidy in favor of ownership only for housing occupants in the top 1 percent of the income distribution,[45] and that subsidy was substantial only for the very small number of individuals in the highest marginal brackets. By 1956, there was a net subsidy in favor of ownership in nearly all cases except when the landlord was in the top tax bracket. By 1966 and 1976, if we assume the minimum tax was generally binding, this net subsidy had broadened further to include all cases in which the potential landlord and occupant were in the same tax bracket. Finally, by 1988 there was a substantial net tax subsidy in favor of ownership regardless of the tax bracket of the occupant or the landlord.

This pattern of development corresponds, in general terms, with the evolution of cooperative and condominium housing. In the 1930s, cooperatives were largely confined to the luxury market. The market share of cooperatives then grew, though at a modest pace, through the 1950s, and was supplemented by the condominium form in the 1960s. Thereafter, cooperatives and condominiums spread with increasing rapidity. From this we might infer that tax subsidies have been an important inducement to the spread of housing cooperatives and condominiums, and that cooperatives and condominiums would account for a much smaller share of multi-unit housing in the absence of these subsidies.

When we look at some shorter time intervals, however, the rate of formation of cooperatives and condominiums correlates poorly with the magnitude of the net tax subsidy to ownership. In particular, although the major increase in the rate of formation of cooperatives and condominiums occurred in the mid-1970s, the net tax subsidy was not generally stronger then than it was in 1966 and, excluding landlords in the very top tax bracket, was not markedly stronger than it was even in 1956. If we look at annual data for more recent years, the correspondence is even worse. Figure 11.1 shows, for each year from 1973 to 1986, both the net tax subsidy to ownership and the percentage of new construction of multi-unit housing represented by cooperatives and condominiums. As that figure illustrates, the rate of formation of cooperatives and condominiums during that period appears, if anything, to correlate inversely with the net subsidy to ownership (unless, that is, we credit builders with anticipating changes in after-tax costs roughly four years in advance of their realization). This is confirmed by statistical analysis, which shows a negative co-

Figure 11.1 Net tax subsidy and new construction, 1973–1986. (From Henry Hansmann, "Condominium and Cooperative Housing: Transactional Efficiency, Tax Subsidies, and Tenure Choice," 20 *Journal of Legal Studies* 25, 55 (1991).)

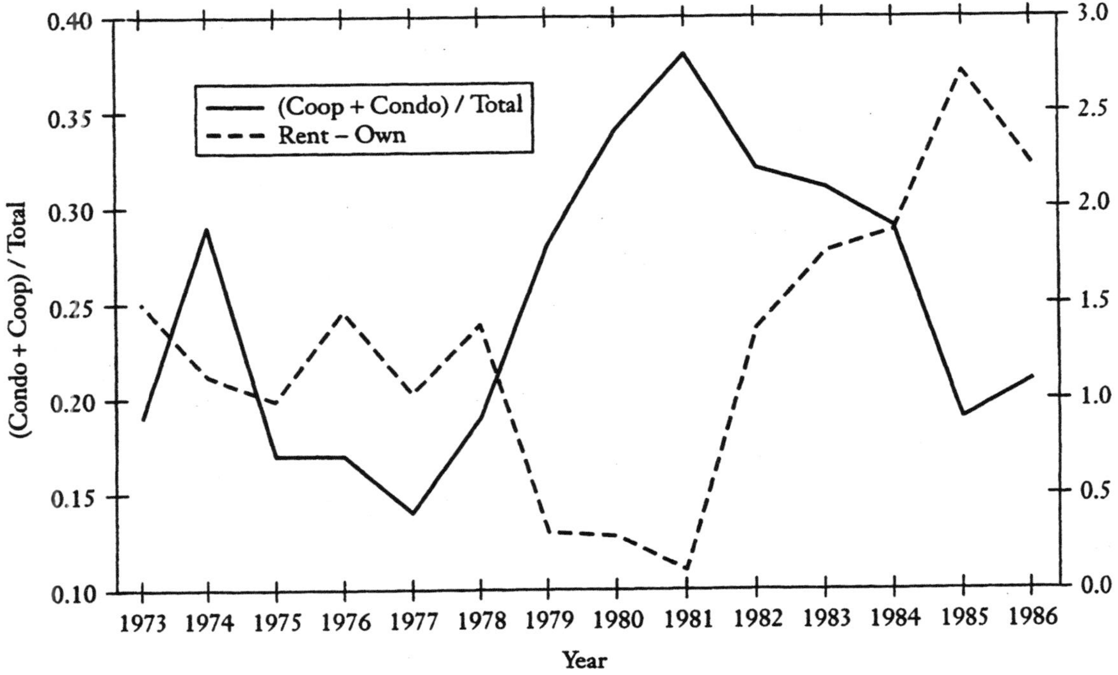

efficient when the rate of formation of cooperatives and condominiums is regressed against either current or lagged figures for the net tax subsidy.

Consequently, if tax subsidies have been an important inducement to the development of condominium and cooperative housing, the effect has evidently been long-term and slow-acting.

Organizational Innovation

Another possible explanation for the recent spread of condominiums in the United States is that the condominium form, when first introduced to American law in the early 1960s, constituted an organizational innovation that reduced the cost of owner-occupancy in multi-unit dwellings significantly below that afforded by cooperatives, thus making owner-occupancy cost-effective for a much larger segment of the apartment market than it had been previously.

This explanation, which for convenience can be labeled the "organizational innovation theory," has some plausibility. By minimizing the common-property element in ownership and leaving each occupant to seek separate financing for her individual unit, a condominium, in contrast to a cooperative, reduces the extent to which the occupants of a building must serve as financial guarantors for each other. A condominium is then less prone than a cooperative to the prospect that default by some of the building's occupants will force default and dislocation for the rest. Such domino-like defaults had occurred among cooperative apartment buildings during the depression of the 1930s, and gave cooperatives a reputation as being risky for several decades afterward.

Moreover, in a cooperative as opposed to a condominium, a member is (or was until recently) constrained to the same level of debt financing as the other members. If the collective mortgage represents only 40 percent of the current market value of the building, then a new tenant can in effect borrow no more nor less than 40 percent of the cost of purchasing her unit.[46]

Whether for these or other reasons, the condominium form must be at least marginally more efficient than the cooperative form for most purposes. Otherwise it would be hard to explain why, from the time that the condominium form was introduced to American law, condominiums have been formed far more rapidly than cooperatives in all parts of the United States outside New York City. There are, however, several objections to the organizational innovation theory—objections that might lead one to suspect that the efficiency advantages of condominiums over cooperatives are no more than marginal, and insufficient in themselves to account for the rapidly growing popularity of owner-occupied apartments.

Why Was the Condominium Form Not Adopted Earlier?

The condominium form is an import from Europe, where it has been known for centuries. If condominiums are significantly more efficient than cooperatives, why was the form not imported to the United States much earlier than the 1960s?

There may be a response to this objection. Arguably it is only since the First World War that European nations have refined their condominium statutes sufficiently to provide an adequate model for importation to the United States.[47] However old the general concept, modern enabling statutes for condominiums effectively came to Europe only a little earlier than they did to the United States, constituting a more or less simultaneous legal innovation on the two continents.

The actual circumstances surrounding the enactment of condominium statutes in the United States shed surprisingly little light on the economic advantages of the form. The statutes were, in fact, not directly imported from Europe, but came to the mainland United States by a slow and circuitous path that led from Spain through Latin America and Puerto Rico and that appears to have been largely fortuitous. The critical event that stimulated the adoption of condominium statutes by the American states—namely, the extension of federal mortgage insurance to condominium units in 1961—was a response to lobbying by interests in Puerto Rico, which had long had the condominium form; it was not actively supported by housing developers, financiers, or consumers in the continental United States, thus suggesting that the condominium form was not then perceived by the real estate community as offering important efficiency advantages (although this might, of course, simply have reflected their inexperience with the form).[48]

Why the Lag in Condominium Development?

If the condominium form constituted a conspicuous reduction in the cost of owner-occupancy for apartments, one might wonder why a decade elapsed between the enactment of the condominium statutes and the time when condominiums began to be developed in substantial numbers.

To be sure, even industrial process innovations, whose diffusion rates have been widely studied, commonly exhibit a lag of some years between introduction and widespread adoption.[49] In addition, an organizational innovation such as condominium housing, in contrast to industrial process innovations, requires not only that producers (in this case, developers) learn the advantages of the new form and the means of implementing it, but also that lenders, brokers, and consumers come to understand and trust it. Consumers, in particular, must come to believe that there will be a resale market for their units, which requires a substantial act of faith before that market has actually developed. A delay of a decade between the appearance of the innovation and its widespread adoption is therefore not necessarily evidence that the innovation did not represent a significant reduction in costs.

Why So Many Cooperatives in New York City?

A final and more telling objection to the organizational innovation theory is that in New York City, as late as 1986, there were still nearly five times as many cooperative units as there were condominium units,[50] and new cooperatives continued to be formed, through new construction and (more important) conversion, in significantly larger numbers than condominiums.[51] Presumably an important explanation for this is that New York consumers, lawyers, lenders, and real estate agents accumulated substantial experience with cooperatives through their uniquely extensive development there—evidently as a response to rent control—between 1945 and 1965. This experience, which was lacking in other jurisdictions, apparently gave cooperatives a continuing transaction cost advantage over condominiums even after the latter form became available. If condominiums were significantly more efficient than cooperatives as an organizational form, it seems unlikely that such familiarity would in itself have been sufficient to cause cooperatives to continue to dominate the market for a quarter of a century after condominiums became available. This conclusion is reinforced by the fact that, as discussed below, in New York City cooperatives and condominiums have appeared in roughly equal numbers among commercial buildings even though nearly all of them were formed since 1978, by which time the condominium form was quite well established in the New York residential market. If condominiums were significantly more efficient than cooperatives, one would have expected only condominiums among these commercial buildings.

These developments in New York City suggest that, had condominium statutes never been adopted in the United States, many of the buildings organized as condominiums in the past two decades, not only in New York but throughout the country, might well have been organized as cooperatives instead, and that the total market share of owner-occupied apartments would still have grown roughly as it did.

Commercial Condominiums and Cooperatives

Even more persuasive evidence that the recent spread of cooperatives and condominiums is primarily a response to tax incentives, and not to organizational innovation or other factors, comes from the remarkable paucity of commercial buildings organized as cooperatives or condominiums.

In the 1960s, when condominiums were still new to the United States, it was widely thought that they would see their greatest growth in the commercial sector.[52] Yet this has not occurred. Commercial cooperatives and condominiums remain a rarity; multi-unit commercial buildings are still almost universally organized on a rental basis.[53] In New York, for example, despite the extensive development of both cooperatives and condominiums in the residential sector, there was evidently only one office building organized as a condominium before 1978, and there were none organized as cooperatives. Since then, the rate of formation (primarily through conversion) of office cooperatives and condominiums has increased; nevertheless, as of December 1984 there were still only sixty such buildings in New York in total, divided roughly equally between cooperatives and condominiums. And this was true despite the fact that office cooperatives and condominiums escape New York City's commercial rent tax.[54]

Tax Incentives

For commercial buildings, the Internal Revenue Code is essentially neutral between owner-occupancy and rental when both the landlord and the tenant are in the same tax bracket. This is in contrast to residential buildings where, as we have seen, the tax law favors owner-occupancy. When tax brackets differ between occupants and potential landlords, the tax code is not neutral for commercial buildings. Rather—at least when depreciation deductions exceed economic depreciation, as has historically been common—it has been advantageous to have a commercial building owned by someone who is in a high tax bracket and can use the depreciation deductions to shelter other income from tax. Occupants in low tax brackets, consequently, have had an incentive to rent rather than own.

An estimate of the magnitude of this incentive can be derived from Table 11.2. In 1976, for example, there was a potential annual tax saving of 1.2 percent of the building's value if an occupant in a tax bracket corresponding to the fortieth percentile in the income distribution decided not to own but rather to rent from a landlord in the ninety-fifth percentile, and 4.6 percent if the landlord was in the top tax bracket. The paucity of commercial cooperatives and condominiums indicates that these forms have insufficient organizational efficiency advantages over rental, if any, to overcome a subsidy in this range.

In sum, while the growth of income taxation in the course of the twentieth century has created an incentive for owner-occupancy over rental in residential buildings, it has had the reverse effect in commercial buildings.

Costs of Contracting and of Ownership

If we put tax considerations aside, and simply consider organizational efficiency, in many respects there seems as much or more incentive for owner-occupancy in commercial buildings as in residential buildings. Many commercial tenants occupy their space for relatively long periods of time. Further, businesses commonly seem to need, as much or more than households, to modify the space they occupy to suit their special requirements: shops frequently remodel their display space elaborately, and even law firms and other consumers of office space commonly move walls, install paneling, or reconfigure utilities to meet their individual needs. Likewise, businesses seem as well suited as households to bear the risks associated with ownership—perhaps rather better suited, on average. Nor is it apparent that businesses suffer from greater liquidity problems than do households.

When it comes to the costs of collective decision making, the comparison with residential buildings is more ambiguous. Like households, businesses frequently own the building they occupy if they are the sole occupant. This suggests that the lack of commercial cooperatives and condominiums may be attributable in substantial part to the costs of collective governance where interests are heterogeneous. Further evidence of this comes from observing the types of situations in which commercial condominiums typically arise. Doctors' offices seem to be among the most common.[55] One reason for this is presumably that doctors are frequently in high tax brackets, and thus can make good use of the tax shelter advantages of owning commercial real estate. Many types of tenants other than doctors, however, are in high tax brackets, yet still rent rather than own their commercial space. Perhaps the more important characteristic of doctors is that they have relatively homogeneous interests when it comes to renting office space, so that serious conflict in decision-making is relatively infrequent in a building occupied only or primarily by doctors. Other types of commercial tenants, in contrast, can be quite heterogeneous in their needs, and in general are probably more so than residential tenants. (For example, some commercial tenants may wish the building to be open, heated, and attended at night or on weekends while others do not, or some tenants may wish to expand their space into that currently occupied by other tenants.)

Tax Forms versus Contractual Forms

If we compare the choice of ownership forms in multi-unit residential buildings with that in commercial buildings, we see that in both cases the incentives created by tax law run counter to the underlying contractual logic. In residential apartment buildings, tax subsidies strongly encourage owner-occupancy although, in general, rental is probably the more efficient contractual regime. Conversely, in multi-unit commercial buildings the tax law has (at least until 1986) favored rental, although the need of many commercial tenants to customize their space suggests that occupant ownership might often be advantageous. Not surprisingly, the contractual arrangements employed in residential and commercial settings have adjusted accordingly. In residential condominiums, there appears to be an increasing trend toward delegation of management to hired management companies; the range of decisions that condominium boards reserve for themselves has been shrinking, presumably to reduce the costs associated with collective decision making.[56] This move toward a single decision maker whose interests (as a hired agent) are in some respects at odds with those of the residents mimics rental to a degree, while maintaining the nominal form of owner-occupancy for tax purposes.

Conversely, commercial leases often have many of the attributes of ownership. They are commonly written for relatively long terms (such as ten years), leave the tenant bearing virtually all the costs of maintaining and remodeling his space, and pass through to him all utility and service charges. The owner of the building frequently agrees to do little more than maintain the shell of the building, and even for this service commonly takes a rental fee that is indexed for inflation. As a consequence, commercial buildings achieve many of the characteristics of condominiums while retaining the nominal form of a leasehold, with its accompanying tax benefits.

Interpreting the Historical Experience

The clear dominance of rental over occupant ownership in multi-unit residential housing in the United States before 1960 suggests strongly that, at least as long as the only available form for tenant ownership is a cooperative, the costs of market contracting (principally lock-in and moral hazard) are generally smaller than the costs of collective ownership (principally illiquidity, risk bearing, and coping with conflicts of interest among the owners), although for prosperous individuals the balance has sometimes gone the other way. The appearance of the condominium form in the 1960s shifted this calculus more in favor of occupant ownership, but the magnitude of that shift is unclear. The continuing vitality of the cooperative form in New York City and the failure of condominiums to achieve much popularity in commercial buildings both throw some doubt on the significance of the condominium form as a cost-reducing organizational innovation.

More important, perhaps, in encouraging occupant ownership of apartment buildings have been the growth of tax subsidies and the threat of rent control. Again, however, the precise strength of these effects is difficult to determine. Although the boom in cooperatives and condominiums was preceded by the advent of large net tax subsidies to owner-occupied housing, the precise timing of the sudden surge in cooperatives and, particularly, condominiums in the mid-1970s is difficult to explain on the basis of taxes alone. Similarly, while for the nation as a whole the condominium boom coincided neatly with the beginning of the rent control explosion, there is little correlation between the adoption of rent control and the market share of condominiums across individual jurisdictions.

Critics of the tax subsidy to homeownership commonly point to overinvestment in housing as a principal cost of that subsidy. Critics of rent control, in turn, point to its tendency to induce underinvestment in housing. The analysis here suggests yet another inefficiency that can be induced by both these policies: incentives for inappropriate choice of organizational form. In particular, both the tax subsidy and rent control encourage occupant ownership of multi-unit buildings where investor ownership might be less costly.

PART IV

Nonprofit and Mutual Enterprise

12

Nonprofit Firms

In the United States, private nonprofit firms play a prominent role in the production of human services. As of roughly 1990, nonprofits accounted for 64 percent of all hospital care, 56 percent of day care for children, 48 percent of primary medical care provided by health maintenance organizations, 23 percent of nursing care, 20 percent of college and university education, and 10 percent of primary and secondary education.[1] Producers of high-culture live performing arts (symphonic music, opera, ballet, and repertory theater) are also overwhelmingly nonprofit, as are museums.

The economic importance of nonprofit firms in the United States has increased steadily throughout the twentieth century. In 1929, nonprofits accounted for only about 1.1 percent of GNP. That figure had grown to 2.8 percent by 1974, and to 3.6 percent by 1988.[2] Moreover, because nonprofit firms are heavily concentrated in labor-intensive services, their share of employment is substantially larger than their share of GNP.

Nonprofit firms play a much smaller role in most other developed market economies than they do in the United States. An important reason for this is that higher education, health care, and other human services are more heavily socialized in many other societies, and particularly in Europe. This pattern is not universal, however. For instance, while nonprofit institutions account for 20 percent of all college and university education in the United States, and public institutions provide the other 80 percent, in Japan these figures are roughly reversed, with public universities accounting for less than 25 percent of total enrollment while private nonprofits serve the rest.[3]

227

As noted in Chapter 1, nonprofit firms are not barred from earning profits. Indeed, many nonprofit firms consistently show an annual accounting surplus. Rather, the critical characteristic of a nonprofit firm is that it is barred from distributing any profits it earns to persons who exercise control over the firm, such as its members, officers, directors, or trustees. This does not mean that a nonprofit cannot pay reasonable compensation to anyone who supplies labor or capital to the organization; it is only residual earnings that cannot be distributed. All residual earnings must, instead, be retained and devoted to financing the services that the organization was formed to provide. As a result of this "nondistribution constraint," a nonprofit firm, by definition, has no owners—that is, no persons who have a share in both control and residual earnings.

In Chapter 3 we observed that these firms without owners typically arise where there is at least one class of patrons for whom both the costs of contracting and the costs of ownership are quite high, with the result that there is no class of individuals to whom ownership of the firm can be assigned without severe inefficiencies. This class of patrons is usually a significant group of the firm's customers. The high costs of contracting facing those customers are typically the result of severely asymmetric information. More particularly, nonprofit firms commonly arise where customers are in a peculiarly poor position to determine, with reasonable cost or effort, the quality or the quantity of the services they receive from a firm. As a consequence, assigning ownership to anyone other than these customers would create both the incentive and the opportunity for the customers to be severely exploited. Yet at the same time, the customers are so situated that the costs to them of exercising effective control over the firm are unacceptably large relative to the value of their transactions with the firm. The solution is to create a firm without owners—or, more accurately, to create a firm whose managers hold it in trust for its customers. In essence, the nonprofit form abandons any benefits of full ownership in favor of stricter fiduciary constraints on management.

Sources of Contracting Costs

To make this general analysis more concrete, it helps to survey several of the most characteristic sources of contracting costs that give rise to nonprofit firms.[4]

Third Party Purchases

Many nonprofits serve customers who are purchasing services to be delivered to third parties with whom the customers have little or no contact. The most conspicuous examples are traditional charities—such as Oxfam, CARE, and the American Red Cross—that provide relief to the poor and distressed. Customers of these firms are usually referred to as "donors." These customers are making a donation not to the firm itself, however, but to the individuals to whom the firm provides services. The firm is simply an intermediary for the donation. Individuals who contribute money to Oxfam, for example, are essentially buying, from Oxfam, food and other supplies to be delivered to hungry people in the third world.

In principle, charitable intermediaries such as Oxfam could be organized as for-profit firms. They could simply offer to deliver, in return for a customer's payment of a specified amount, a certain quantity of relief services to needy people. CARE, the American charity that was first organized to aid distressed Europeans after the Second World War and now provides relief services worldwide, has long marketed its services in just this way. A typical CARE solicitation states that "$5 serves 100 children a daily bowl of nourishing porridge for a week. $10 gives 2,000 children each a glass of fortified milk. $25 provides wheat flour for 3,000 nutritious biscuits in a school feeding program." A for-profit counterpart to CARE could make a similar offer. And if a donor could be assured that the firm would in fact perform the services as promised, presumably the donor would have no reason to prefer channeling his donation through the nonprofit CARE rather than through its for-profit competitor. After all, for-profit firms regularly serve as charitable intermediaries in other circumstances. People will frequently pay a department store to send a wedding gift to a friend, or call up a florist to have flowers sent to their mother for her birthday.

The problem with the services delivered by organizations such as CARE and Oxfam, however, is that the individuals to whom the services are provided are far removed from, and generally unknown to, the contributors who pay for the services. The contributors are in a poor position to judge the quantity or quality of the services that the firm delivers, or even to discover whether the firm performs the service at all. A florist's customer is likely to hear whether her mother received the flowers ordered for her birthday, and whether they were pleasing.

But a contributor of $5 to CARE is unlikely to discover whether, as a result of her contribution, 100 children in Africa actually received a bowl of nourishing porridge each day for a week. The result is a radical case of asymmetric information. The usual means of enforcing contracts—legal action or loss of reputation—are ineffective in such circumstances. An investor-owned counterpart to CARE or Oxfam would have great difficulty convincing prospective contributors that it could be trusted to perform the services it promises rather than diverting most or all of its contributions directly to its owners.

If the firm were owned by its customers, its incentive to exploit its informational advantage would be largely eliminated. But contributors to firms such as Oxfam, CARE, and the Red Cross are so numerous, dispersed, and transitory, and their contributions are typically in such small amounts, that any effort to organize the contributors for effective governance would cost more than it would be worth. Meaningful patron ownership is not a possibility. The solution commonly chosen is therefore to organize the firm as a fiduciary entity that is operated on behalf of, but not by, its customers. Although we often think of such firms as being operated on behalf of their beneficiaries, this is true only indirectly. The organizations are designed to serve their beneficiaries well in order to serve their contributors well, since it is the welfare of the beneficiaries that the contributors are, in a sense, buying.

Purchases of Public Goods

Another common role for nonprofit firms is in the private production of public goods. For whatever reason, many individuals are willing to ignore the incentive to free-ride, choosing instead to make a contribution toward the purchase of a good that will serve a large public. Listener-supported radio and television stations, which have been among the principal suppliers of high-culture broadcasting in the United States for several decades, are a conspicuous example. In this case, the contributors are also beneficiaries of the service, and in fact typically contribute in order to ensure the production of the service for their own consumption. A contributor can then accurately judge the quality and quantity of the service that is provided. Because the service is indivisible, however, a contributor cannot observe the marginal increment to the service that is purchased by her individual contribution. Thus she cannot know from direct observation whether the same quantity and quality of service would have been provided even without her contribution. An investor-owned firm could therefore be expected to solicit payments far beyond what is needed to cover the cost of its broadcasts. With a nonprofit firm, in contrast, the patron has some assurance that her payment will actually be used to produce more or better programming.

Again, patron ownership would be an alternative solution. But as with redistributive charities like Oxfam, most private suppliers of public goods, such as listener-supported broadcasters, are supported by patrons who are too dispersed, and who make individual contributions that are too small, for effective patron ownership to be feasible.

Price Discrimination

In the United States, as already noted, nonprofit firms play a dominant role in the high-culture performing arts. The apparent reason for this is that the institutions involved do not receive sufficient income from ticket sales alone to support themselves; consequently, they depend on voluntary donations to survive. To be sure, most contributors to the performing arts attend performances of the organizations they support, so they can determine for themselves the quantity and quality of the organization's performances. As with public goods such as broadcasting, however, the contributors cannot easily judge the marginal increment financed by their own contribution. A firm owned by anyone other than the contributors would thus have an insurmountable credibility problem when soliciting contributions.

In contrast to the types of philanthropies already discussed, however, performing arts institutions commonly have a geographically compact group of contributors who contribute substantial sums of money repeatedly over many years. In such cases, consumer ownership appears feasible. We shall return to this issue below, and discuss why these institutions are organized as nonprofit firms rather than as consumer cooperatives.

Another interesting question is why the performing arts are donatively financed in the first place. The overwhelming majority of individuals who make donations to an opera company, symphony orchestra, or nonprofit repertory theater are also regular subscribers to seats for the organization's performances. Why do the organizations solicit donations from these individuals, rather than simply raising ticket prices?

The apparent explanation is that donative financing in the performing arts serves as a form of voluntary price discrimination, the need for which is dictated by the unusual cost and demand structure in that industry.[5] Fixed costs (primarily those of preparing a show prior to the first performance, including the cost of rehearsals, costumes, and stage sets) are a large proportion of the total costs of a production. Once a production has been staged, the marginal cost of adding another performance to the run, or of admitting another person to the audience for a performance that has not been sold out, is relatively small. This high ratio of fixed costs to marginal costs is also a reflection of the fact that the audience for the high-culture performing arts is quite limited, even in the largest cities, so that any given production will have only a few performances over which the fixed costs can be spread.

As a consequence, for many productions there is no structure for ticket prices that can cover total costs. If costs are to be met, some form of price discrimination must be employed so that high demanders pay more than low demanders for a given performance. Transferability of tickets limits the amount of price discrimination that can be enforced through ticket pricing. Yet voluntary price discrimination has proved possible here: ticket purchasers with unusually high demand for performing arts productions can simply be asked to contribute voluntarily some portion of the consumer surplus they would otherwise enjoy at the nominal ticket price—and, interestingly, a large proportion of the audience is willing to do so.

The audiences for the popular performing arts, such as the movies and Broadway theater, are large enough so that fixed costs can be spread over a large number of performances, and thus fixed costs are low relative to marginal costs. Voluntary price discrimination is unnecessary for the viability of such productions, and they are usually produced by for-profit firms.

Although the performing arts offer the best illustration of voluntary price discrimination, it also appears to be an important function played by donatively supported nonprofits in other industries with fixed costs much higher than marginal costs, such as museums, libraries, and higher education.

Implicit Loans

The substantial role of donative financing in higher education may serve to finance public goods, such as research, or to pay for the provision of education to the poor. These explanations do not seem compelling, however, in the case of private primary or secondary schools or in the case of four-year private colleges, many of which emphasize teaching rather than research and have (at least until recently) served almost exclusively the relatively well-to-do. Further, such explanations do not entirely square with the fact that donations to any given institution come almost entirely from its own alumni.

An alternative explanation, more consistent with such phenomena, is that donative financing in private education serves at least in part as a system of voluntary repayment under an implicit loan system that has arisen to compensate for the absence of adequate loan markets for the acquisition of human capital. There are many individuals for whom the present value of the potential long-run returns from postsecondary education exceeds its costs, but who are unable to finance that education out of their own or their family's current income and assets. If these individuals could take out long-term loans against their future earnings, then this would be a worthwhile strategy for financing their education. Yet for reasons both legal and practical, an individual cannot pledge human capital as security for such a loan, with the result that private lenders offer an inadequate supply of such loans. Private nonprofit educational institutions provide a crude substitute for these loans. They supply education to many students at rates below cost, in return for an implicit commitment on the part of the students that they will "repay" their loan through donations during the course of their lives after graduation.

This analysis suggests that, if government were to provide a more generous system of grants, loans, and loan guarantees to deal with students' financing problems, for-profit institutions would compete more effectively with nonprofit institutions in education. In fact, in response to the existing governmental grant and loan programs, investor-owned firms are already rapidly expanding their market share in postsecondary education in the United States.[6]

Complex Private Services

So far we have just been considering "donative" nonprofits—that is, nonprofit firms whose income depends heavily on voluntary contributions that are not closely conditioned on the delivery of specific goods or services to the patron. Sometimes, however, the development of nonprofit firms has been stimulated by the less obviously severe problems of asymmetric information involved in purchasing private goods or services for the patron's own consumption. Savings banking in the early nineteenth century is among the clearest examples of this, and that industry will be examined closely in Chapter 14. But savings banks are not the only example of what might be called "commercial" nonprofits—that is, nonprofits that receive no significant amount of donations, but derive their income almost exclusively from prices charged for private goods and services they deliver to paying customers. In the United States, most nonprofit hospitals, nursing homes, day care centers, and health maintenance organizations fall into the category of commercial nonprofits.

It is possible that these commercial nonprofits, too, are serving as a response to high contracting costs resulting from asymmetric information. The types of services that commercial nonprofits provide, such as health care and education, are often complex and difficult for the purchaser to evaluate. Moreover, the actual purchaser of the service is often not the individual to whom the service is directly rendered—parents buy day care for their children, and relatives or the state buy nursing care for the elderly—with the result that the purchaser is at a further disadvantage in judging the quality of performance. Finally, the services of many commercial nonprofits, such as nursing homes and colleges, are provided over a prolonged period, and the costs to the customer of switching from one provider to another can be considerable, leading to a degree of lock-in. For all these reasons, customers might rationally prefer to patronize an institution whose incentive to exploit them is smaller than it would be in an investor-owned firm.

At the same time, where commercial nonprofits are concerned, the costs of market contracting—and, in particular, the costs resulting from asymmetric information—are clearly less serious than they are for the types of services provided by donative nonprofits. As evidence of this, commercial nonprofits, in contrast to donative nonprofits, nearly always share their market with for-profit firms providing similar services. For example, roughly 12 percent of private (that is, nongovernmental) hospitals, 37 percent of private day care centers, and 69 percent of private nursing homes are investor-owned.[7]

Indeed, there is good reason to believe that problems of asymmetric information in themselves are inadequate to explain why investor-owned firms do not have an even larger market share in these industries than they already do. The nonprofit form is a very crude consumer protection device. It does not create strong positive incentives for serving customers well; it simply reduces the incentives to serve them poorly. The inefficiencies of the nonprofit form, discussed below, are presumably worth suffering in the case of donative nonprofits, where the costs of contracting are so obviously high that they would probably lead to the complete breakdown of the market if only proprietary firms were available as suppliers. But where individuals are purchasing private goods and services for their own consumption, as they are with the services provided by commercial nonprofits, it is less clear that nonprofits generally offer a degree of consumer protection, beyond that available from for-profit firms, that is sufficient to justify the inefficiencies of the nonprofit form.

Hospitals, which (in terms of GNP) constitute by far the largest class of nonprofit institutions in the United States, are a case in point. Hospital patients might at first seem to suffer severely from problems of asymmetric information. They often know little about the illnesses they have or the appropriate way of treating them, and when they are most in need of hospital services they are often in poor condition and have little time to make judgments about alternative suppliers. Yet there are reasons to believe that, in fact, asymmetric information is not a terrible handicap for hospital patients. The hospital itself does not provide the patient care services that are the most sensitive and difficult to evaluate—namely, the services of attending physicians. Rather, the physicians are usually independent contractors who deal separately with the patient. The hospital itself is largely confined to providing relatively basic services such as room and board, nursing care, and medicines. The patient herself does not order the hospital services she receives and often does not even choose the hospital; they are selected and monitored for her by a knowledgeable purchasing agent: her physician.[8] Many consumers purchase hospital services through health plans of various sorts that have both the incentive and the capacity to make informed decisions in choosing the hospitals that serve their members. Finally, since hospitals are large, visible, and long-lived institutions, reputation can serve as an important aid to monitoring. The effectiveness of reputation as a control increases substantially, moreover, when a particular hospital is part of a large commonly controlled chain of institutions, as is typically the case today with the investor-owned hospitals. A newspaper exposé about shoddy treatment at a hospital is likely to have costly repercussions for that hospital and for all others affiliated with it. Perhaps for these reasons, empirical studies have failed to detect a lower quality of care at investor-owned hospitals than at nonprofit hospitals.[9]

Why, then, are most U.S. hospitals nonprofit? Problems of asymmetric information ultimately provide an explanation, but only if we allow for some historical lag. Until the end of the nineteenth century, hospitals were almost exclusively donative institutions serving the poor; prosperous persons were treated in doctors' offices or in their own homes. The nonprofit form was therefore efficient for the reasons discussed above with respect to donative institutions in general. Then, however, a revolution in medical technology turned hospitals into institutions where people of all classes went for treatment of serious illness. The subsequent development of first private and then public health insurance made it possible for the great majority of patients to pay their hospital bills without the aid of charity. The result is that, at least since the advent of federal health insurance for the elderly and the poor in 1965, most nonprofit hospitals have become more or less pure commercial nonprofits, receiving no appreciable portion of their income from donations and providing at best a very modest amount of charity care—an amount not appreciably different from the amount of uncompensated care provided by typical investor-owned hospitals. These nonprofit hospitals arguably have no efficiency advantages over for-profit hospitals. Large chains of investor-owned hospitals in fact began entering the U.S. hospital industry in force in the late 1960s. Yet presumably because of the forces of inertia discussed below, nonprofit hospitals have continued to maintain a dominant presence in the industry.

Arguably much the same story helps explain the large numbers of commercial nonprofits in other industries, such as nursing care, day care, and prepaid group medical practice (health maintenance organizations). These are relatively new industries, having grown up largely during the latter half of the twentieth century as services moved out of the family and into specialized institutions. Many of the initial entrants into these businesses were supported by charitable donations, which made the nonprofit form essential. Moreover, in the early days of these industries, even consumers who were simply purchasing services for themselves or for members of their family might well have been doubtful about relying on a profit-seeking provider for such novel services, given the consumers' lack of experience with the industry, the scarcity of suppliers in operation long enough to have built up a significant reputation, and the absence of meaningful public regulation. Finally, perhaps for much the same reasons that consumers might have been hesitant at first to trust proprietary firms, the regulations that were initially adopted in these industries were often strongly biased against the for-profit form. As a result, these industries were heavily populated with nonprofit firms in their formative years. As the industries matured, their services became more familiar and more standardized, suppliers built reputations, and regulation became more effective—all of which significantly reduced the costs of market contracting. The nonprofit form then became increasingly anachronistic, and for-profit firms began entering these industries in large numbers. Yet the original nonprofit firms, having already become well established, were slow to exit and maintained a presence in these industries beyond that which could be explained by any continuing efficiency advantages the nonprofits offered in mitigating the costs of contracting.

Producer Nonprofits

Nonprofits generally arise in response to contracting problems facing consumers. Sometimes, however, they are formed to protect patrons who sell services *to* the firm. That is, just as there are both consumer and producer cooperatives, there are both consumer and producer nonprofits.

Firms that are organized as nonprofits for the benefit of their workers are the most common example of producer nonprofits. As was noted in Chapter 6, a number of firms, in both the United States and Britain, that are called worker cooperatives are not in fact owned by their workers, but rather are nonprofit firms that are managed on behalf of their workers. Producer nonprofits are, however, relatively rare. One reason for this is the same as that given above for the relatively small variety of producer-owned firms as compared with consumer-owned firms: there are relatively few situations in which a firm purchases inputs from a large number of suppliers all of whom are affected by high costs of contracting. In addition, in the types of situations in which this in fact occurs, the suppliers are commonly capable of organizing themselves effectively for actual ownership, and need not resort to the nonprofit form with its truncated incentives for cost-efficient operation.

It is somewhat surprising to find any producer nonprofits at all. Presumably an important reason they exist is that, as we speculated in Chapter 6, the nonprofit form has the advantage of mitigating problems of collective decision making where the patrons involved are heterogeneous in their interests, as in the case of workers in an industrial firm.

Costs of Ownership

We have already noted that nonprofits tend to arise where the costs of monitoring management are prohibitive for the only class of patrons to whom ownership could be efficiently assigned—namely, those facing exceptionally high costs of market contracting. There are, to be sure, many nonprofits that are patron-controlled, in the sense that the patrons elect the nonprofit's governing board. In some nonprofits this control is really only formal: in practice, the organization's board of directors nominates their own successors. In other nonprofits, however, the elections to the board are not formalities, and the members exercise effective control. We shall discuss nonprofits of the latter type in a separate section below, and consider their relationship to consumer cooperatives, which they strongly resemble. For the present, we shall confine our discussion to nonprofits whose patrons are not capable of exercising effective control.

Managerial Incentives

A nonprofit firm with a self-electing board of directors represents the ultimate in separation of ownership and control; the management is under no effective supervision by anyone with an interest in residual earnings. Thus one would expect that managerial agency costs would be at their maximum in such organizations.

It is interesting to observe, therefore, that these costs do not seem to be exceptionally high. There have been a number of attempts to develop empirical estimates of the difference in efficiency between nonprofit and for-profit firms. Most of these studies have focused on the hospital industry. While these studies provide some evidence that nonprofits are less likely to minimize costs than are for-profit firms, they do not clearly demonstrate a striking difference between the two types of firm in this respect.[10] This is all the more impressive given that the for-profit firms in the hospital industry are presumably relatively efficient, since they are mostly either small closely held firms (commonly owned by the doctors who practice in them) or else owned by large national chains that have been aggressively managed.

This result should perhaps not be surprising. Managers of nonprofit firms are not much differently situated than managers of large publicly traded investor-owned firms in which shareholders exercise no meaningful voting control. As we observed in Chapter 4, firms of the latter type are, in an important sense, effectively producer nonprofits: they are managed on behalf of their shareholders, but not by their shareholders.

Indeed, if investor-owned firms are in fact managed more efficiently than are nonprofit firms, and in particular are better at cost minimization, in large part this may not be because the managers of the investor-owned firms are more effectively monitored, but because their organization's stated goal is clearer. Investor-owned firms are charged only with maximizing return on invested capital, which is a simple numerical objective on which progress can be easily measured. It is far less clear, in contrast, what constitutes success for a nonprofit hospital or university.

This is not to say, of course, that nonprofit firms are as efficient as firms owned by a class of patrons who have homogeneous interests and are well situated to monitor management effectively. The point is simply that ownership in investor-owned firms is often so attenuated that those firms come very close to being, and behaving like, firms that are formally nonprofit.

Conversely, nonprofit firms often appear to be managed with substantial efficiency when, as is often the case, they operate in a competitive environment. A case in point is the hospital industry. Despite vigorous entrepreneurship, the investor-owned hospital chains that began entering the industry in the late 1960s succeeded in increasing the market share of proprietary hospitals only from 6 percent of all short-term general hospital beds in 1971 to 12 percent in 1992. Moreover, most of the growth of the proprietary hospital chains came at the expense, not of nonprofit hospitals, but of governmentally owned hospitals and of small independently owned proprietary hospitals. In fact, far from being driven out of business by the new investor-owned chains, nonprofit hospitals actually increased their market share slightly, from 63 percent to 64 percent, between 1965 and 1992.[11] This resilience of the nonprofits in the face of competition surely owes much to capital immobility—discussed below—and to subsidies. But it also appears that the survival of the nonprofit hospitals has resulted in part because, in the face of an ever more challenging environment, they have become increasingly efficient in cutting costs and increasing revenues, often by adopting many of the same managerial techniques employed by their investor-owned competitors.

Capital Immobility

In determining the relative efficiency of nonprofit and investor-owned firms as alternative forms of organization in any given industry, managerial inefficiency—the minimization of costs in the short run—may be much less important, in general, than the sluggishness of nonprofit firms in accumulating capital when demand is growing and in reducing capital investment when demand declines. Even if nonprofit firms produce their services at minimum cost, they may produce too few or too many services.

Nonprofit firms, by definition, are incapable of obtaining equity capital. Instead, they must rely upon debt, donations, and retained earnings as sources of capital. These sources are generally less responsive than equity capital to rapid increases in demand. As a consequence, when demand increases rapidly for the services of an industry—such as nursing care or hospital care—that is populated with both nonprofit and investor-owned firms, the nonprofit firms generally expand, through new entry and through the growth of existing firms, much less rapidly than the investor-owned firms.[12]

Conversely, when demand declines, nonprofit firms have much less incentive and opportunity than investor-owned firms to reduce their investment in the industry. A nonprofit firm need not—indeed, cannot—pay any return on its net capital (that is, the capital that the firm has acquired over time through donations and retained earnings). Consequently, even in the absence of any direct or indirect subsidies (such as tax exemption), a nonprofit firm can remain in operation at its current scale as long as its revenues are sufficient to cover depreciation—that is, sufficient to earn just a zero net rate of return. Any positive rate of return on the nonprofit's net capital, even if it is well below the rate of return required by the capital market, will actually permit the firm to expand. And a nonprofit's management—whose employment is at stake, who has no ownership interest in the firm's assets, and who may feel a professional commitment to supplying the type of services produced by the firm—has a strong incentive to avoid liquidating the firm in whole or in part, and to keep it going at the largest scale possible regardless of the rate of return on its invested capital. The result is that forces of competition in the product market can be quite slow in weeding out inefficient nonprofit firms; even in the absence of subsidies, nonprofits can survive and even grow when they are earning a rate of return so low as to cause an investor-owned firm to scale back or exit.

In short, capital tends to get locked into nonprofit firms. This phenomenon probably goes far toward explaining why, despite the rapid and aggressive entry of well-capitalized investor-owned chains into the hospital industry after 1965, the market share of nonprofit hospitals did not decline. If nonprofits could and would disinvest as rapidly as for-profit firms, then nonprofit hospitals, which account for a large share of the GNP produced by all nonprofits in the United States, would probably have a much smaller presence in the economy. Much the same may be true for other service industries in which commercial nonprofits have a large presence, such as prepaid group medical practice (health maintenance organizations), day care, most forms of education, and banking (the latter of which we shall examine in Chapter 14). As each of these industries has expanded and matured, the severe informational problems and the supply-side subsidies that initially prompted the use of the nonprofit form have been mitigated. Nevertheless, the nonprofit firms that originally populated these industries have remained and even expanded.

This is not to deny that informational asymmetry may continue to provide a justification for a significant nonprofit presence in some of these industries. Nursing care, in particular, is arguably an industry where the potential for customer exploitation is large and is not always adequately dealt with by regulatory and reputational constraints on for-profit firms. This may help explain why, even as the nursing home industry roughly doubled in size between 1971 and 1985, the market share of nonprofit nursing homes actually increased, from 18 percent to 23 percent, over the same period.[13]

Risk Bearing

Relative to owned enterprise, and particularly to investor-owned enterprise, nonprofit firms are poor bearers of risk. Because they cannot sell equity shares, they are constrained in their ability to raise capital to invest in risky projects, and they lack the most effective mechanism—the stock market—through which the risk of an enterprise can be diversified. Fluctuations in cash flow must largely be absorbed within the individual nonprofit firm itself. Moreover, the managers of nonprofit firms, lacking a class of owners to whom they are responsible, have unusual autonomy and thus are unusually free to indulge their personal aversion to the risk that the firm might fail, costing them their jobs. As a consequence, nonprofits are generally found in industries that present relatively low levels of risk, such as basic health and educational services.

Member-Controlled Nonprofits versus Cooperatives

Nonprofit firms, we have argued, tend to arise where both the costs of contracting and the costs of ownership are unusually high for an important class of the firm's customers. This might seem to be contradicted by the fact that many nonprofits are membership organizations, and that the members of these organizations often have the power to elect the organization's board of directors. For the latter organizations, then, the costs of monitoring and decision making must not be so high as to make patron control absolutely impossible. It is natural to ask what distinguishes these firms from the consumer cooperatives discussed in earlier chapters.

The formal distinction is that in a member-controlled nonprofit, unlike a cooperative, net earnings cannot be distributed to the members as cash dividends. But should that matter? The nondistribution constraint, as commonly interpreted, does not prevent a nonprofit from effectively distributing its net earnings to its members by using those earnings to subsidize the services that the nonprofit provides in the future.

There are, nevertheless, differences between distributing earnings as cash dividends and distributing earnings through subsidized services, and those differences are related to the distinctly different circumstances in which nonprofits and cooperatives are generally found. Nonprofits tend to arise where the consumer is more concerned that the firm will skimp on quality than that it will charge an excessively high price. Indeed, nonprofits rarely serve as a response to monopoly. The industries in which nonprofits are typically found—such as nursing care, day care, primary health care, education, or even hospital care—seem to have relatively low economies of scale, with the result that most consumers have at least several different providers, and often very many, from which to choose. Cooperatives, in contrast, tend to arise in the reverse circumstances, where high price rather than low quality is the evil most to be feared from an investor-owned firm. This difference is presumably a reflection of the fact that cooperatives are well designed to return to their patrons any excess of price over cost through cash dividends, whereas nonprofits are committed to keeping all their receipts and devoting them to production of services, and therefore have a bias in favor of high quality over low cost.

Also, nonprofits commonly serve a group of patrons who are relatively heterogeneous, not necessarily in terms of the services they consume but in terms of the payments they make for those services. In particular, as we observed above, nonprofits commonly engage in substantial price discrimination, both voluntary and involuntary. Different contributors to listener-supported radio and television stations may make donations of greatly varying amounts even though they listen to or watch the same amount of the station's programs. Students who receive equivalent educations at a private college may receive very different amounts of scholarship aid (and thus pay very different net tuitions), and contribute very different amounts as alumni. If the patrons of such organizations, like the members of a cooperative, had the power to declare dividends to themselves, or to liquidate the firm and divide its net assets among themselves, there would be enormous difficulties in determining the appropriate proportions for the distributions, and there would be the palpable risk that one group of patrons would gain control and benefit themselves disproportionately with these distributions.

Yet the nonprofit and cooperative forms clearly blur into each other at the margins. In the next two chapters we shall see that many mutual firms in the insurance and banking business, though formally structured as consumer cooperatives, in fact both behave like nonprofit firms and perform an economic role that is very similar to that played by typical nonprofits.

Subsidies

In the United States, most nonprofit firms of any financial significance are exempt from the federal corporate income tax, and often from state corporate, property, and sales taxes as well. Further, at various times most nonprofit firms have been exempt from, or received specially favorable treatment under, Social Security taxes, unemployment insurance taxes, postal rates, the minimum wage, securities regulation, bankruptcy, copyright, laws on antitrust and unfair competition, and tort liability. These exemptions and privileges have presumably resulted in a larger nonprofit sector than would otherwise have developed.[14] Even in the absence of these subsidies, however, nonprofit firms would probably still have a significant presence in the economy. Indeed, nearly all of the special legal benefits accorded nonprofits were first granted in the late nineteenth or twentieth centuries,[15] when nonprofits were already well established in important sectors such as education and health care.

Moreover, the extension of special privileges to nonprofits in any given industry has generally occurred as a response to the development of a significant nonprofit presence in that industry, and not the other way around. That is, as nonprofits have developed in new industries, such as the performing arts, health insurance, and nursing care, the scope of exemptions and other benefits has subsequently been expanded to include those classes of nonprofits. Subsidies have evidently had little role in determining the distribution of nonprofits across industries.

Finally, the range of subsidies granted nonprofit firms reached its peak about 1950, and has steadily eroded since then. Nearly all the privileges and exemptions mentioned above have been scaled back or have simply been withdrawn entirely from some or all nonprofits.[16] And although these changes will presumably have some impact in the long run, they have not immediately resulted in an obvious reduction in the scope of the nonprofit sector.

Conclusion

We observed in Chapter 3 that, where one group of a firm's patrons faces very high costs of market contracting, it may be efficient to make those patrons the owners of the firm even if they cannot exercise their nominal right of control very effectively. The critical point in such situations is not so much that the patrons in question own the firm as that nobody else owns it—and especially nobody capable of exercising effective control. The extensive role played by nonprofit firms in important sectors of the U.S. economy underlines this point. These firms have no owners at all. Yet that fact is a critical advantage for at least those nonprofits that are donatively funded; the absence of owners gives donors the assurance they need to patronize the firm. At the same time, the costs imposed on nonprofit firms by the absence of owners appear to be relatively modest: nonprofits operate with a fair degree of efficiency, and compete effectively with owned enterprise, even in industries in which the nonprofit form is apparently anachronistic and confers no special advantages beyond qualifying firms for a dwindling group of indirect subsidies.

These observations are consistent with the other principal point to be made here about nonprofits: that nonprofit firms are not sharply different from firms that are investor-owned, or that are owned by some other class of patrons, but rather are at the end of a continuum of owner monitoring. At the other end of that continuum are those firms that are tightly controlled by one or more owners who are strongly involved in the conduct of the firm's business. In between are those firms that, though nominally owned by some class of the firm's patrons, are not very effectively controlled by those patrons, but rather are operated by a self-perpetuating group of managers largely free of owner interference. As owner control becomes increasingly attenuated in a formally owned firm, the difference between such a firm and one that is formally unowned (that is, nonprofit) tends to vanish. This is illustrated in the following two chapters.

13

Banks

In the United States today, investor-owned firms account for most consumer banking. There are, however, three other forms of ownership that also occupy a significant share of the market in that industry: mutual savings banks, which are nonprofit firms; mutual savings and loan associations, which are consumer cooperatives; and credit unions, which are also consumer cooperatives.[1] In the nineteenth century, when consumer deposit banking was in its formative stages, these nonprofit and cooperative firms dominated the industry. Investor-owned firms began to play a significant role in consumer banking only late in the nineteenth century, and did not rise to ascendancy until well into the twentieth century.

To understand the roles of different ownership forms in the banking industry, we must therefore examine that industry in historical perspective. Most of this chapter is devoted to offering that perspective. At the end of the chapter we look at banking institutions in other countries, and see that forms of ownership have evolved elsewhere along much the same lines that they have followed in the United States.[2]

Mutual Savings Banks

Consumer deposit banking first appeared in the United States in the form of mutual savings banks. Although the term "mutual" suggests that these banks are consumer cooperatives that are owned by their depositors, this is not the case. The depositors in a mutual savings bank

246

have no voting rights or other means of exercising direct control over the organization, and are not members or owners in any proper sense. Instead, control over mutual savings banks lies in the hands of a self-perpetuating board of directors that holds the bank's assets in trust for its depositors. In a mutual savings bank, "[t]he term 'mutual' only indicates that all distributed earnings must be shared by the depositors."[3] Thus mutual savings banks are true nonprofit organizations rather than cooperatives. In contrast, mutual savings and loan associations, discussed below, are (at least formally) true consumer cooperatives that are collectively owned by their depositors.

Mutual savings banks arose in the United States early in the nineteenth century, following earlier English models. The first mutual savings bank was chartered in Massachusetts in 1816; by 1849, 87 mutual savings banks were in operation, primarily in urban centers in the northeastern and mid-Atlantic states. They were typically founded as philanthropic institutions, with their initial capital donated by wealthy businessmen. The founders' motivation, it is said, was to help prevent pauperism and to relieve the burden on public charity by encouraging thrift among the working class.[4]

Given this early history, one might conclude that mutual savings banks were established simply as a vehicle whereby the rich could provide charitable services to the poor, in the form of subsidized interest on the latter's savings. Indeed, this was long the conventional view of mutual savings banks. Under this view, the banks presumably assumed the nonprofit form, rather than being established as proprietary organizations, for the same reasons that lead donative institutions in general to be formed as nonprofits: to provide some degree of fiduciary protection for the organization's donors, who otherwise would have little assurance that their contributions were being used for the purposes they intended rather than going into the pockets of the organization's proprietors.

Yet the theory that mutual savings banks were created to serve as vehicles for philanthropy is unsatisfying for several reasons. To begin with, although hard data appear to be lacking, the amounts of capital contributed by the founders were probably inadequate to yield more than a trifling subsidy per individual depositor. It seems implausible that mutual savings banks were established merely as charitable intermediaries through which the rich could redistribute some of their income to the frugal poor. Likewise, the subsidy per investor must surely have been too small to provide a meaningful additional incentive for the working class to save.

Further, and more important, investor-owned banks at that time did not serve as places where individuals could deposit their savings. Although investor-owned banks were numerous in the early nineteenth century—there were over three hundred in the United States in 1820[5]—they did not serve as a repository for small deposits made by individuals[6] and generally dealt only with businesses. They served primarily a monetary function, creating money in the form of bank notes, which were then the principal circulating currency.[7] These bank notes were issued in exchange for notes from merchants, which the bank purchased at a discount:

> neither the merchant, nor the saver, of [the early nineteenth century] thought of banks in connection with deposits. A bank ... meant primarily a place of discount for [a merchant's] notes. He owed bills ... [but] [h]is own note would not suffice to pay those bills, even though his credit were excellent, because it would not pass acceptably from hand to hand. But if he exchanged it for the note of some bank, paying for the privilege, through a discount, he would obtain something which would pass acceptably.[8]

Investor-owned banks obtained their working capital, not from deposits, but from selling stock in the banks. And the savings that went to purchase this stock were the earnings accumulated by successful merchants, not the meager weekly savings of the working class.

In the early nineteenth century, then, there was no convenient vehicle through which persons of modest income could invest. It follows that mutual savings banks were founded, not simply to provide a place where the working poor could get a more attractive rate of return on their savings, but rather as the only place where such individuals could deposit their savings. To understand the role of the early mutual savings banks, we have to understand why it was that there were no investor-owned savings banks until well into the nineteenth century.

The principal reason, it seems, is that investor-owned banks were too untrustworthy to serve as a repository for the savings of persons of modest means. That is, the problem was not on the supply side but on the demand side. If individuals had been willing to entrust their savings to investor-owned banks, the latter might well have taken them; but willing depositors were probably too few to make the activity worthwhile.

Investor-owned banks were so untrustworthy in the early nineteenth century because they were largely unregulated; they were not required to maintain minimum levels of net assets or reserves and there were no restrictions on the ways in which they could invest their funds. Investor-owned banks therefore had both the incentive and the opportunity to behave opportunistically toward their depositors. In particular, they had an incentive to invest depositors' savings in highly speculative ventures that would pay off handsomely if successful, but that also ran a substantial risk of not paying off at all. If the bank were lucky in such investments, it would earn a large profit; if it were unlucky, it would go bankrupt, leaving its depositors to bear most of the losses. Further, investor-owned banks had an incentive to maintain only minimal net assets. That way, if the bank's investments went sour, the owners would not be much exposed; most of the losses would fall on the depositors. Depositors would, of course, have had an incentive to try to bind banks by contract to maintain adequate net assets and not to undertake excessively speculative investments with their savings (and banks, in turn, would have had an incentive to bind themselves in this way in order to attract more business). But under the circumstances, it was probably impossible to draft a contract of this type that was both effective and enforceable.

In fact, the early investor-owned banks often engaged in speculation, and not infrequently behaved opportunistically even toward holders of their notes (for example, by making it difficult for them to be redeemed in specie).[9] And the banks were, indeed, highly risky ventures: nearly 50 percent of all investor-owned banks formed between 1810 and 1820 had closed by 1825, and the same proportion of banks formed between 1830 and 1840 failed before 1845.[10] For these reasons, investor-owned banks were popularly viewed with distrust during the first half of the nineteenth century.[11] Individuals would, with reason, have been very hesitant to permit such institutions to hold their life savings for any length of time. The activities of the investor-owned banks were therefore confined to short-term transactional services, such as discounting notes, that exposed a bank's customers to only limited losses in case the bank failed.

In short, consumer deposit banking was characterized by a high degree of asymmetric information in its early years: depositors could not know, or control, what investor-owned banks were doing with the depositors' funds. There was consequently a demand for savings banks that would provide a higher degree of fiduciary protection for depositors than investor-owned banks could offer. This demand grew particularly strong in the early nineteenth century, when for the first time there was a large class of urban industrial workers who received their income in the form of wages rather than in kind, and who lacked the traditional supports of the farm communities to tide them through periods of unemployment.[12] The mutual savings banks met this need. By organizing as nonprofit institutions, they provided an essential element of fiduciary protection to their depositors.

As nonprofit institutions, however, the mutual savings banks could not obtain equity capital, and they turned to wealthy philanthropists to gain the needed funds. The banks' nonprofit form was of course important in providing assurance to these donors that their contributions would be devoted to the intended purpose. But it appears that, in contrast to most other types of donative nonprofits, such as traditional redistributive charities, mutual savings banks were not established as nonprofit firms principally to provide fiduciary protection to donors. Rather, it was the reverse: the mutual savings banks sought donative financing for their capital needs because they were nonprofit—a form they adopted to protect their "commercial" customers, namely, their depositors. Further evidence for this conclusion comes from the fact that donative financing seems to have been confined largely to the initial formation of mutual savings banks; once established, they tended to become purely commercial nonprofits.

We remarked in Chapter 12 that, although there are a number of industries in which commercial nonprofits have a large presence in the United States today—including hospital care, nursing care, day care, and education—it is not clear that consumers are at such an informational disadvantage in these industries that the crude protection from opportunism afforded by the nondistribution constraint makes commercial nonprofits more efficient, overall, than investor-owned firms. Most of these commercial nonprofits are probably just the residue from an earlier stage in the evolution of these industries, when donations were an important source of financing. They were formed as nonprofits to protect donors rather than to protect the recipients of the organizations' services. Now that donors are no longer an important source of income, these institutions survive as nonprofits largely owing to capital lock-in, continuing subsidies, and regulatory favoritism. If these industries were to be re-created anew today, nonprofits would play a much smaller role in them; the services now provided by commercial nonprofits would be provided by investor-owned firms instead. For this reason, the savings bank industry is unusually interesting: it is a uniquely clear example of an industry in which nonprofits arose, from the beginning, primarily as a response to asymmetric information on the part of paying customers rather than to protect donors or other third-party payors (such as the government).

The mutual savings banks continued to be highly successful throughout the nineteenth century. They reached their peak in total number of banks around 1900, when there were 652 mutual savings banks with a total of $2.1 billion in deposits.[13] By then, however, they were beginning to meet serious competition from mutual savings and loan associations and, more important, from investor-owned banks. Before we examine the development of these latter institutions, it is instructive to look briefly at trust companies.

Trust Companies

Although investor-owned banks did not take consumer savings deposits until the middle of the nineteenth century, there existed before then a number of investor-owned trust companies that administered private and charitable trusts. Why did these investor-owned trust companies develop and survive in this period, while investor-owned savings banks did not?

The answer presumably lies in the size of the individual trusts and the method of remuneration devised for trust managers. The trust companies, then as now, took a percentage of the total assets as their form of compensation. This reduced their incentive to behave opportunistically; indeed, it essentially made each individual trust into a small nonprofit firm. The trust managers could not keep any fraction of the gains from speculating irresponsibly with the trust assets, so they had little incentive to engage in such activity. In a savings account, the depositor receives a fixed rate of return on his savings, and the bank keeps all profits (or absorbs all losses) that result from its investment of these funds. The incentive for the bank to behave opportunistically is thus much higher than in the case of a trust account.

Of course, the nineteenth-century investor-owned banks could have arranged a method of remuneration for savings accounts that looked more like that of trusts. An individual savings account is generally too small to permit a bank to segregate and account separately for the investments it makes with the amounts deposited in the account; the funds from a number of such accounts must be pooled for efficient administration. Nevertheless, a bank could simply have confined itself to a fixed rate of compensation for the entire pool of savings, such as a percentage of the total assets. All earnings beyond this would be returned pro rata to the depositors as interest on their accounts.

Yet this approach would essentially turn the bank into a nonprofit entity. Such a method of compensation makes the bank a trustee of the depositors' funds. The pool of assets administered by the bank would be held by it in trust for the beneficial owners, who are the depositors. In effect, this is the type of contractual relationship that was established between the managers of the mutual savings banks and their depositors. (Alternatively, the pooled assets could be owned by the depositors as a group not just beneficially, but directly; acting as a group, they would simply hire the bank's management. This is the arrangement employed in the mutual savings and loan associations.)

Interestingly, the early mutual savings banks were often closely associated with stock banks, having overlapping directors or officers and sometimes sharing the same offices.[14] This suggests an arrangement similar to the organization of the trust companies (and much like a modern mutual fund), in which an investor-owned firm sets itself up as a trustee, managing a pool of funds for individuals on a commission basis.

Mutual Savings and Loan Associations

Unlike the mutual savings banks, mutual savings and loan associations (MSLAs) are true cooperatives: their depositors have formal voting control over the organization as well as the sole claim to residual earnings.

MSLAs first arose in the United States in the 1830s, although similar institutions had appeared in England in the eighteenth century. Originally called "mutual building and loan associations," they responded not just to the need for a place for small savers to deposit their funds but, more important, to individuals' need for credit with which to acquire a home. When MSLAs first developed, investor-owned banks were generally unwilling to make consumer loans. The MSLA arose as an institution in which a small group of working people would pool their savings, and from which they would then take loans, by turns, with which to finance the construction or purchase of a house. When all of its members had acquired a home, the MSLA would be dissolved.[15]

Presumably part of the impetus for the formation of MSLAs was the same as that for the formation of mutual savings banks: asymmetric information in the management of savings accounts by investor-owned banks. Depositor ownership, like the nonprofit form of the mutual savings banks, mitigated the hazards of opportunistic conduct by the bank. But another important impetus for the formation of the MSLAs evidently came from the unwillingness of investor-owned banks to make loans to individuals.

What permitted the mutuals to make such loans successfully where the investor-owned banks feared to tread? Adverse selection and moral hazard are the obvious explanations. A group of workingmen presumably had better information than an investor-owned bank about which of their friends and fellow workers would be good risks for a loan, and they could use this information to determine who should be permitted to join the mutual. Further, when times are hard a borrower will be less inclined to default on a loan when he knows that his friends and neighbors will bear the loss.

Thus while the mutual savings banks arose principally in response to the customers' lack of information about the actions of the bank, the MSLAs arose principally to deal with the reverse problem of asymmetric information: the banks' lack of information about its customers.

From their beginnings as time-limited pools among discrete groups of individuals seeking to finance their homes collectively, MSLAs evolved through stages. First, rather than dissolving after the members of the founding group had all financed their homes, MSLAs began to deal with successive or overlapping groups of members, with each group's finances managed as a separate pool. Later the MSLAs ceased to differentiate among different groups of members, and simply admitted individuals as members whenever they wished to join. Borrowers and depositors then came to be distinct classes of individuals: some individuals joined primarily to save; others joined primarily to borrow. The extent of member participation in the management of MSLAs, which was substantial in the early stages, diminished as the institutions evolved. Ultimately the MSLAs came to have self-perpetuating boards of directors subject to no meaningful degree of member control.[16]

Today there is little operational significance to the formal difference between MSLAs and mutual savings banks. Although the MSLAs nominally remain consumer cooperatives, both types are effectively commercial nonprofits, controlled by their managers.[17] We see here a clear case of the phenomenon described in the preceding chapter, in which the distinction between owned and unowned firms becomes essentially meaningless—that is, in which there are no practical differences between firms that are owned by a given class of patrons and nonprofit firms that are established as fiduciaries for that same class of patrons.

For savers, MSLAs evidently served much the same fiduciary role as mutual savings banks, particularly after the MSLAs evolved into permanent institutions in which the savers need not also be the borrowers. A strong indication of this can be found in the regional and temporal concentration of the two forms. Mutual savings banks, which arose in the first half of the nineteenth century, concentrated primarily in the New England states, which is where the nation's commercial activity was then concentrated. MSLAs, in contrast, initially developed in the southern and western parts of the country, where commercial activity had begun to take root by the mid-nineteenth century when the MSLA model first became popular. Mutual savings banks never arose in those parts of the country, presumably because the MSLAs served the same needs more effectively. MSLAs ultimately began to form in the northeastern states as well, and by the early twentieth century had become more numerous there than were the mutual savings banks, offering further evidence that the MSLA was at least marginally the more efficient form, perhaps because it was not dependent on philanthropy for its initial capital.

The number of MSLAs in the United States peaked in 1928, at 12,600.[18] From then on, their numbers gradually dwindled, declining to 4,100 in 1980,[19] as investor-owned firms came increasingly to dominate consumer banking.

The Development of Investor-Owned Savings Banks

Toward the end of the nineteenth century, investor-owned banks began actively entering the savings field. In 1880 investor-owned banks held 12 percent of all time deposits, as compared with 87 percent held by mutuals savings banks and 1 percent held by MSLAs. By 1925 the share of the investor-owned banks had increased to 52 percent, while the mutual savings banks and MSLAs held 32 percent and 16 percent, respectively.[20]

The increasing importance of the investor-owned banks reflected important changes in the organization of the banking industry. By the early twentieth century, the evolutionary changes affecting MSLAs—in particular, the adoption of a fluid mass membership and the atrophy of effective member control—had probably eliminated any particular advantage that MSLAs had over investor-owned banks in avoiding moral hazard and adverse selection on the part of borrowers. These changes, which effectively converted MSLAs from cooperative to nonprofit entities, would not have prevented MSLAs, like mutual savings banks, from offering their depositors, and particularly depositors with savings accounts, a degree of fiduciary protection from opportunistic behavior higher than that to be expected from investor-owned banks. Other developments, however, also reduced the mutuals' advantage in attracting savings deposits.

The first of these developments was the imposition of governmental regulation on the management of bank assets. In the middle of the nineteenth century—and most conspicuously with the passage of the National Banking Act of 1864—the states and the federal government began requiring, for the institutions that they respectively chartered, that banks adhere to certain practices designed to provide greater security to their depositors. These regulations included minimum capital requirements, the maintenance of liquid reserves equal to a stated percentage of deposits, and limitations on the types of investments that could be included in bank portfolios.[21] Moreover, many states and the federal government chartered investor-owned banks only on the condition that their shareholders bore double liability under which, if a bank's assets proved insufficient to pay off its depositors, shareholders could be personally assessed an additional amount equal to their initial investment in the bank.[22] These measures gave depositors some assurance that investor-owned banks would not speculate excessively with the funds entrusted to them. This form of regulation was evidently sufficiently effective to deprive the mutual banks of their decisive competitive advantage over investor-owned banks in attracting consumer savings deposits, and permitted investor-owned banks to come to dominate savings banking just as they had always dominated shorter-term banking services.

Despite governmental regulation of bank assets, MSLAs and mutual savings banks remained safer institutions, as far as the depositors were concerned, than were investor-owned banks. For example, during the period 1921–1928, the annual failure rate for investor-owned banks varied from a low of 1.24 percent to a high of 3.65 percent, while the failure rate varied between .04 percent and .22 percent for savings and loan associations (nearly all of which were mutual),[23] and remained virtually at zero for mutual savings banks. In 1933, the worst year of the Great Depression for banks, 27.7 percent of all investor-owned banks failed, but only .8 percent of SLAs and .01 percent of mutual savings banks.[24] The continuing expansion of the investor-owned banks vis-à-vis the mutuals, despite this higher rate of risk, is probably attributable to the fact that, with regulation, they could generally offer a degree of assurance to depositors at least close to that offered by the mutuals,[25] while at the same time having the advantage of better access to capital for their formation and growth and stronger incentives for entrepreneurship.

In 1933 the federal government imposed mandatory deposit insurance on all federally chartered banks, whether investor-owned or mutual. This measure decisively eliminated any remaining advantage that mutual banks had over investor-owned banks in offering safety to their depositors, at least so far as federally chartered institutions were involved.

At the same time, the government still had a motive for preferring consumer-owned and nonprofit banks. Because deposit insurance shifted the risk of bank default from depositors to the federal government, the problem of asymmetric information that previously faced a bank's depositors now confronted the government instead. To be sure, the Federal Deposit Insurance Corporation, which provided the insurance, was in a much better position to police bank behavior than were the banks' customers, so the problem of asymmetric information was presumably much reduced through this change. Nevertheless, the government has not been a perfectly informed patron (or at least has not acted like one), and its deposit insurance has led to a degree of moral hazard on the part of banks.

The extent of this moral hazard became evident in the wave of insolvencies that swept savings and loan associations in the 1980s. By the time that crisis occurred, there were many savings and loan associations that were organized, not as mutuals, but as investor-owned corporations. During the 1980s, the failure rate among these investor-owned SLAs was significantly higher than it was among the MSLAs. The insolvencies were clearly associated, as one would expect, with a tendency on the part of the investor-owned SLAs to pursue more speculative investment policies than did the MSLAs.

In fact, the best empirical evidence from the 1980s tends to confirm what one would expect about the relative efficiency of mutual banks and investor-owned banks. If we hold constant the portfolio of assets in which the banks invest, mutual banks tended to be somewhat less efficient than investor-owned banks—that is, they were less likely to minimize costs. Investor-owned banks, however, were more likely than mutual banks to invest in an inefficient portfolio of assets—and particularly in a portfolio of assets that was excessively speculative. The higher rate of insolvency among investor-owned than among mutual SLAs is evidence that the inefficiency in portfolio choice exhibited by investor-owned banks outweighed their efficiency in management.[26] (In an overall assessment of the relative efficiency of investor-owned versus mutual ownership, however, one must also consider that investor-owned banks, with their more flexible access to equity capital, have not only the incentive but also the ability to respond more rapidly than do mutual banks to changes in demand for their services—an advantage not well captured by existing studies.)

In its role as insurer of deposits, the government benefited from the reduced incentives for opportunistic behavior, and consequent lower failure rate, exhibited by the mutual form of organization. If the government had responded by charging lower premiums on deposit insurance to mutual banks than to investor-owned banks, the mutual banks might still have been able to translate their advantages as fiduciaries into a competitive advantage vis-à-vis investor-owned banks. The government, however, charged all banks, regardless of type, the same flat premium rate for deposit insurance. After 1933, it was consequently only the government, and not customers, that had a reason to prefer MSLAs and mutual savings banks over investor-owned banks on account of their greater safety.

Whether for this reason or for others, for a substantial period the federal government gave favored regulatory treatment to mutual savings banks and MSLAs. From 1935 until 1980, investor-owned banks were subjected to a ceiling on the interest rates they could pay on consumer deposits; the mutual savings banks and MSLAs, however, were exempt from this limit until 1966 and, thereafter, allowed a rate

.25 percent higher than that permitted investor-owned banks. Furthermore, mutual savings banks and MSLAs were exempt from federal corporate income tax from 1913 until 1952, and until at least 1962 continued to benefit from a highly preferential tax regime.[27]

Because of the important and conflicting effects of governmental regulation, survivorship has been a very uncertain index of the comparative efficiency of mutual versus investor-owned banks since 1933. From that date until 1980 there were in fact few new mutual banks formed, while at the same time there was a relatively slow but steady exit of existing mutuals from the industry. As a consequence, in 1980 there were only a third as many mutual banks in the United States as there had been in 1933. Then, in the 1980s, there was a marked increase in the rate of exit of the mutuals, primarily through conversion to investor-owned banks.

The conversions of the 1980s were clearly a response to a series of regulatory developments. In the late 1970s and early 1980s, the federal government, while maintaining a system of deposit insurance that implicitly favored investor-owned banks, eliminated rate regulation from which the mutuals had benefited, removed restrictions on the conversion of MSLAs to investor-owned SLAs, and substantially increased the range of assets in which SLAs could invest. The result was a strong incentive to convert mutual banks into investor-owned banks—an incentive that was reinforced by the ability of insiders to capture, in the process of conversion, a substantial portion of the net assets that the mutuals had accumulated over their many years of existence. Ironically, this acceleration in conversions took place just when, as noted, investor-owned savings banks were giving evidence of being less efficient, overall, than their mutual counterparts, and when in particular the failure rate among investor-owned savings banks was twice that for the mutuals.

Credit Unions

Credit unions are consumer banks that are organized as depositors' cooperatives. As their name suggests, they not only take deposits from their members but use those deposits primarily to make loans to their members. Credit unions are distinguished by the requirement, imposed on them by the chartering statutes, that their members must all share a "common bond." Although this common bond can take a number of forms, such as residence in the same community or membership in a local church, most frequently the common bond is employment at the same place of work.

The first credit union in the United States was formed in New Hampshire in 1909, following Canadian models that, in turn, had been inspired by European, and particularly German, experience. In that same year, Massachusetts adopted a general statute for chartering credit unions. Most other states subsequently enacted similar statutes, and in 1934 the federal government enacted legislation for federal chartering of credit unions.[28]

The market share of credit unions grew relatively steadily after their original appearance, and especially after World War II. In 1982—the last year for which figures are available—credit unions accounted for 4.5 percent of all consumer savings held at financial institutions and 13.8 percent of all consumer credit (down from 18.4 percent in 1976). In the 1970s, credit unions were the fastest-growing financial intermediary accepting deposits until regulators approved money market mutual funds in 1977. Since then, credit unions have had the second-highest rate of growth in assets, behind the money market mutual funds.[29]

Credit unions play a role similar to that played by the original MSLAs: they provide their members with better access to credit than could be obtained from an investor-owned bank. The members' common bond serves to mitigate the risks of adverse selection and moral hazard in making consumer loans. Moreover, since the common bond requirement is maintained by law, credit unions have generally avoided the fate that befell the MSLAs: to evolve into institutions in which there are no personal ties between the institutions' borrowers and its depositors, and which therefore impose little more restraint on borrowers' opportunistic behavior than could an investor-owned bank.

Employment at the same place of work—the most usual common bond—is evidently an effective means not only of avoiding moral hazard on the part of borrowers, but also of lowering the transaction costs of banking. A workplace-based bank has good access to information about prospective borrowers' creditworthiness (through the employee's reputation with fellow employees and with the employer); it has a convenient means of securing repayment (through payroll deductions); and it has effective policing mechanisms (through social pressure from fellow employees and sanctions from the employer).[30]

Employers can also benefit from having a credit union for their employees. The credit union ties the employees more tightly to the employer, improves the employees' financial situation (and consequently their effective wage), and helps keep the employees out of financial difficulties that may interfere with their work or create bother for the employer (such as garnishment of wages). For these reasons employers have often helped promote the formation of credit unions, for example, by providing free office space and free time off to the employees who administer them. Indeed, Edward Filene, the Boston department store magnate, was the first great advocate of credit unions in the United States and was instrumental in the adoption of the 1909 Massachusetts credit union statute.

If the employer actually owned and operated the credit union, however, his employees might well believe he would be tempted to use it to exploit the employees, just as company stores have a reputation for doing—and this would defeat the bank's effectiveness in overcoming employee moral hazard. So it is important that, though the credit union is supported by the employer, it is controlled by the employees.

Unlike mutual savings banks and MSLAs, credit unions have continued to form at an appreciable rate and to expand their role even after the enactment of extensive state and federal banking regulation. This is perhaps because banking regulation has been aimed principally at preventing opportunism on the part of banks, while credit unions serve to mitigate opportunism on the part of borrowers—although the development of private credit rating services and other improved means of determining creditworthiness may have reduced the comparative advantage of credit unions over investor-owned banks both in obtaining information about prospective borrowers and in sanctioning them through reputation.

In any case, survivorship is no longer an unambiguous test of the relative efficiency of credit unions, since in the course of the twentieth century credit unions, even more than mutual savings banks and MSLAs, have benefited from various forms of governmental favoritism. In particular, credit unions were exempt from the interest rate ceilings that were imposed on investor-owned banks for many decades, and (unlike mutual banks after 1962) they have always been exempt from federal corporate income taxes.[31]

Early Mercantile Banks

Interestingly, the earliest investor-owned banks in the United States— namely, the mercantile banks that were incorporated at the end of the eighteenth century, shortly after the Revolution—also had roughly the character of credit unions. But they were credit unions among merchants, not among workers. In effect, they were associations through which merchants pooled their savings to provide themselves with credit. Their stockholders were principally merchants and, although they did not restrict their loans to stockholders, stockholders had preference.

As with all of the other collectively owned institutions we have surveyed, these early banks' charters commonly included provisions regulating their activities and governance in ways designed to prevent one group of members from using the bank to exploit others. For example, regressive voting systems, under which the number of votes cast by a stockholder increased with the amount of stock held but less than proportionately to the amount of stock, were commonly employed to prevent either large or small shareholders from gaining undue influence in the affairs of the bank. The banks were also commonly barred from engaging in trade. The latter restrictions, which appear to be the historical beginnings of the separation of banking from commerce in the United States, were clearly adopted, not (as in the case of their modern descendants) to protect the banks' customers by preventing the banks from engaging in excessively speculative activities, but to keep the banks from competing with some subset of the merchants who formed them.[32]

Bank Ownership in Other Countries

In developing countries making the transition from a traditional agricultural economy to a more modern commercial economy, rotating credit associations, similar to the earliest American mutual savings and loan associations, have been common throughout the world.[33] These associations generally have a relatively small number of members—perhaps twenty or thirty—all of whom are bound by kinship or other close personal ties. In a typical arrangement, the members all contribute the same fixed sum each week (or, alternatively, month) for as many weeks as there are members in the association. Each week, the entire amount collected is given to one of the members, with each member receiving the pot in this way only once. The order in which the members receive the pot is determined by lot, by bidding, or by some other system of priorities. Once all the members have received the pot once, the organization is dissolved, though another one may be immediately started up again with the same or different members. In their simplest forms, these associations make no provision for interest payments. More elaborate associations provide for interest, and can involve substantial sums of money; the monthly pot in an association of merchants can reach $1 million.[34]

The rotating credit associations allow the saving and borrowing of funds for large purchases while using social ties to avoid the problems of moral hazard that would otherwise affect lending and borrowing in a society without developed financial institutions. The fact that all members of the association are typically both savers and borrowers, and participate on equal terms, avoids conflicts of interest that could interfere with the associations' smooth functioning.[35]

In societies that are more developed commercially, but that still lack a well-developed system of banking regulation, nonprofit and cooperative banks similar to those found in the United States have commonly played an important role in consumer banking. In the brief period 1810–1825, nonprofit savings banks made their first successful appearance, not just in the United States but also in many European countries, including Denmark, England, France, Ireland, Italy, and Scotland. By the middle of the nineteenth century, these nonprofit savings banks were numerous throughout Europe, as they were in the United States. Then, also as in the United States, the second half of the nineteenth century saw the formation in Europe of banks organized as consumer cooperatives. These cooperatives achieved their most intense and systematic development in Germany, but became widespread in many other European countries as well. Like the original mutual savings and loan associations and the credit unions in the United States, the European cooperative banks were established primarily to provide better access to credit for their members and not, like the nonprofit savings banks, to serve just as a place to accumulate savings.[36] Thus in Europe as in America, the nonprofit banks arose principally as a means of protecting customers from opportunism on the part of the bank, while the cooperative banks arose to protect the banks from opportunism on the part of their customers.

Like their counterparts in the United States, European nonprofit and cooperative banks have tended to lose market share to investor-owned banks in the course of the twentieth century. Nevertheless, they continue to play a substantial role—and arguably a role that is larger, owing to inertia from capital lock-in and regulatory favoritism, than can be justified on the basis of their efficiency vis-à-vis contemporary investor-owned banks.[37]

Conclusion

The evolution of ownership forms in the banking industry underlines several themes that have by now become familiar from our discussion of other industries.

First, identity of interest among owners is critical to success. The unusual prominence of cooperatives in consumer banking is evidently due in considerable part to the homogeneity of the services that the banks perform. There is very little conflict of interest among the depositors in a bank: they all want the highest rate of interest possible on their deposits, and there is an obvious formula for dividing a customer-owned bank's earnings among its owners (that is, proportionally to the amounts deposited). Where, as in the rotating credit associations, the members of the bank are borrowers as well as depositors, and there is a potential for substantial conflict of interest between members who are primarily depositors and those who are primarily depositors, strong measures are often taken to assign all members equally to both roles and thus eliminate the conflict.

Second, so far as the behavior of the firm toward its customers is concerned, the line between customer-owned and nonprofit firms is quite indistinct, and the choice of one or the other of these two forms seems to make little difference. From the consumer's point of view, mutual savings and loan associations behave much like mutual savings banks, despite the fact that the former are customer-owned and the latter are unowned. But there is a clear behavioral difference between customer-owned and nonprofit firms on the one hand and investor-owned firms on the other hand. This is most obvious in the contrast between the relatively high failure rates of investor-owned commercial banks and savings and loan associations and the very low failure rates experienced by mutual savings banks, mutual savings and loan associations, and credit unions. Evidently the managers of investor-owned firms are much more willing to speculate with their depositors' funds than are the managers of customer-owned and nonprofit firms.

When we consider, not the behavior of the firm toward its customers, but the behavior of customers toward the firm, the picture changes. To the extent that customer ownership is used, not (as is usual) to protect the customers from opportunism on the part of the firm, but to protect the firm from opportunism on the part of its customers, effective customer control evidently is important. Thus where customer ownership is used principally to prevent moral hazard on the part of the banks' borrowers, as in rotating credit associations and credit unions, membership is typically confined to a small and closely linked group and management is highly participatory, for the obvious reason that this maximizes both the incentive and the opportunity for the owners to police one another's conduct. In such situations, merely organizing the firm as a nonprofit that is managed on behalf of its customers, but not by them, is apparently not as satisfactory as true customer control.

Finally, governmental regulation permits investor-owned firms to thrive where nonprofit firms or consumer cooperatives would otherwise have a decisive efficiency advantage. Effective regulation has permitted investor-owned banks to bond themselves not to exploit their customers unduly, while leaving those firms free to take advantage to their superior access to capital. We shall see another clear example of this phenomenon in the next chapter, when we examine the insurance industry.

14

Insurance Companies

In the United States, mutual companies account for almost half of all life insurance in force and a quarter of all property and liability insurance. Moreover, the annual volume of business done by the mutual life insurance companies, which are formally organized as policyholders' cooperatives, far outweighs the volume of business done by consumer cooperatives in any other line of business. And it is not just in comparison with other cooperatives that the mutual insurance companies appear large; the assets of the largest of the mutuals, Prudential, exceed those of any industrial corporation.[1]

If we are to understand this pattern of ownership, we must not only understand the costs of contracting and the costs of ownership that presently characterize the insurance industry, but even more important we must also, as in the case of banking, understand the origins of the industry in the nineteenth century. The factors that have given rise to such a large role for mutual firms also differ considerably between the life insurance industry on the one hand and the property and liability insurance industry on the other.[2]

Life Insurance

In the United States, life insurance first began to be sold to the public around 1810. From then until 1843, a number of companies, all investor-owned, offered life insurance policies. Of these, the only ones that had any success in selling policies were roughly half a dozen large firms, organized after 1830, that combined the sale of life insurance with the management of trusts. These life and trust companies were all well capitalized, conservatively managed, and of unquestioned financial soundness. Nevertheless, although they tried hard to market life insurance, none of these companies sold more than a few hundred life insurance policies in total; their primary business always remained the management of trusts.[3]

In 1843, the first mutual life insurance company serving the public at large was formed. By 1847, six more mutual life insurance companies—but no new stock companies—had also entered the business. These mutual companies proved much more successful than their proprietary predecessors. All seven companies remain in business today and are among the largest of the mutuals; in contrast, all but two of the stock companies that were selling life insurance in 1843 had withdrawn from the business ten years later, and the activities of the remaining two had been substantially curtailed.[4] By 1849 nineteen mutuals were in business.[5]

With the rise of the mutual companies, there came a change in the types of policies written. Prior to 1843, most life insurance policies were for relatively short terms of between one and seven years. By 1859, when the mutuals had become well established, whole life policies accounted for more than 90 percent of the business.[6]

The reasons for the success of the mutual life insurance companies in the first half of the nineteenth century strongly parallel the reasons for the success of mutual savings banks in the same period. This is not surprising since, in important respects, a life insurance policy is like a savings account. In fact, the advantages of the mutual form in life insurance are even stronger than they are in savings banking.

Long-Term Contracting under Uncertainty

A life insurance policy is a long-term contract between the insurance company and the insured that typically has a duration of several decades and often is in force for more than half a century. In such a long period of time, many contingencies can arise that affect the value of the bargain to one or both parties. Writing an enforceable contract that will anticipate and deal with such contingencies adequately is a difficult task. And because the contract is for insurance, it is obviously important that the contract deal effectively with contingencies in a way that imposes minimal risks on the insured.

Since a life insurance contract is a promise to pay a specified sum of money, the central problem lies, as with savings banking, in providing assurance to customers that the firm will maintain financial reserves to meet its future commitments. But the problem of reserves for life insurance companies is even more complicated than it is for savings banks.

The fundamental risk against which a life insurance policyholder seeks protection is, of course, that he will die an unusually early death. An insurance company can largely eliminate this risk, so far as its own finances are concerned, by writing a sufficiently large number of policies. But if the company does not have a sufficiently large group of policyholders—and many of the early insurance companies did not—then the company needs to maintain sufficient reserves to protect against the possibility that the company's experience will be different from that predicted by the actuarial tables.

In addition, there is the risk that the actuarial tables themselves will turn out to be wrong—that is, that the average lifespan of a given segment of the population will be different from what was expected at the time that the insurance policies were written. This was a particularly serious problem in the first half of the nineteenth century, when actuarial data were extremely crude. Such a risk could not be reduced through diversification simply by writing more policies.

Finally, there is the risk that the return on the insurance company's investments will be different from what was expected when its policies were written. This is another risk that cannot be reduced by writing a larger number of policies, although with more policies the company has a larger and hence more easily diversifiable pool of funds to invest. Two basic factors contribute to the riskiness of an insurance company's investments. First, there is the difficulty of predicting the real rate of return that the company's investments will produce over the term of its policies. This remains a problem today; it was clearly worse in the early nineteenth century, when diversification of investments was more difficult and economic forecasting was a much cruder discipline than it is even now. Second, there is the difficulty of predicting the long-run rate of inflation, which is important because life insurance policies have generally been written in terms of nominal dollars.

If a life insurance company is to make its policies attractive to potential customers, it must provide them with substantial assurance that it will always maintain, over the many years that the policy is likely to remain in force, adequate reserves to ensure the company's solvency in the face of these various risks. Even if the company's policyholders were financially quite sophisticated and in a position to remain closely informed about the company's affairs, it would be extremely difficult for them to know what level of reserves a company should maintain in all possible situations, much less to write an effectively enforceable insurance contract that would ensure that the company maintained such reserves. The amount of reserves required, after all, varies appreciably with the age, health, and occupation profile of the company's policyholders, with the types of assets in which the company has invested its funds, and with the best current wisdom about the future performance of the economy. Writing a contingent contract that would deal effectively with such variables over a period of decades would be a heroic task. Some evidence of just how heroic can be found in the fact that, in the mid-nineteenth century, even the managers of both the mutual and the stock life insurance companies evidently had very little idea about the prices they should charge or the amount of reserves they should maintain if they wanted to stay in business.[7]

Moreover, life insurance policyholders, then as now, presumably were *not* well informed about the financial affairs of insurance companies, including the ones they dealt with, and were unsophisticated in general about the financial, actuarial, and legal factors involved in insurance contracting. Even today, prices vary widely for equivalent life insurance policies,[8] which suggests that substantial consumer ignorance exists about even the most basic factors relevant to their choice of policies. And undoubtedly the level of consumer information was worse in the early nineteenth century.

Customer Lock-in

Not only does the policyholder have to be assured that the insurance company will keep its promise to pay off on the policy when it comes due, but, conversely, the insurance company must also receive assurance that the policyholder will keep his promise to continue making payments on the policy even if, in future years, the policy becomes less advantageous to him.

If premium payments on life insurance policies were designed so that each year's payment just covered the cost to the company of insuring the policyholder's life for the year in which the payment was made, the company would experience serious problems of adverse selection. As the years pass, life insurance policyholders that remain relatively healthy would have an incentive to drop their original policies and either go without insurance (if the purposes for which they needed the insurance, such as support of a spouse or child, were no longer present), or seek a new policy with a different company at a lower annual premium. The policies a company was left with would then become losing policies for the company. (This assumes that, as is usual, the policies oblige the company to continue providing insurance to the policyholder as long as the latter continues to pay premiums at the originally contracted rate. Any other approach would, of course, provide undesirable incentives for the insurance company to drop policyholders whose health began to look frail.)

To avoid such adverse selection, life insurance policies typically have a heavy front-end load: premium payments in the early years of the policy are substantially in excess of the cost to the company of providing insurance for those years, so that the policyholder stands to lose considerably if he abandons the policy at any point. In fact, the conventional life insurance policy, whether for term insurance or for the whole of life, has always provided for level premiums throughout the duration of the policy. To be sure, life insurance policies today offset this front-end load somewhat by offering cash surrender values. To avoid adverse selection, however, these values are typically well below the accumulated value of the premiums already paid[9]—and in the mid-nineteenth century, when the market share of the mutuals was at its maximum, life insurance policies had no cash surrender value.[10]

Front-end loading of premiums effectively copes with the adverse selection problem. But by locking the policyholder into the policy, this tactic eliminates the use of exit as a means of policing the behavior of life insurance companies. Life insurance companies thus have even further scope in which to behave opportunistically toward their policyholders.[11]

The Mutual Form as a Solution

Given the preceding problems, consumer ownership has offered an attractive alternative to market contracting in policing insurance companies.

With the policyholders as owners, there is little incentive for the company to behave opportunistically in setting the level or riskiness of its reserves. A mutual company can simply establish a nominal premium for its policies that is high enough to provide reserves adequate for the most pessimistic forecasts of mortality, rate of return on investments, and inflation; then, if and when events turn out better than a worst-case forecast, the excess reserves can be liquidated and returned to the policyholders as dividends. The difficulty of market contracting between companies and policyholders is eliminated by eliminating the market and replacing it with an ownership relationship.[12]

Creating Risk with Long-Term Contracts

The principal function of life insurance contracts is, of course, to eliminate risk through pooling. But because the contracts involved must have such a long term, they also create risk. In particular, as already noted, they create risk that the average mortality rate, the real rate of return on investments, and the rate of inflation will be different from those forecast at the time that the policy was written.

This is most obvious with the rate of inflation. A life insurance contract denominated in nominal dollars—as they were, and as they virtually had to be in the mid-nineteenth century, given the absence of reliable price indices—creates a pure gamble between the policyholder and the insurance company on the future rate of inflation. This gamble imposes costs on the policyholder in two forms. First, he must bear the risk that the real value of his policy will turn out to be different from its expected value. Second, he must pay a higher price for the policy to the insurance company to compensate the company for bearing its side of the same gamble—a risk that the company cannot easily reduce through diversification. In short, the purchaser must bear all of the costs, to both parties to the transaction, of a gamble that has no social value. And much the same is true, as well, of the risks that the average mortality rate and the average rate of return on investments will differ from their expected value.[13]

With a mutual company, a policyholder can purchase pure life insurance without having to bear the cost of these additional risks. Since the policyholder is on both sides of the transaction, there is no gamble. If the inflation rate, the real rate of return on investments, or the mortality rate turn out to be different than forecast, then what the member of a mutual insurance company loses on his policy he gains as owner of the company, and vice versa. A mutual insurance company can regularly adjust its policyholder dividends, which can be paid either in cash or in the form of further insurance, to ensure that the company's policyholders always have in force the appropriate amount of insurance and pay only the actual cost of providing that insurance.

The mutual company's advantage in avoiding the large risks of long-term contracting may explain in significant part why the investor-owned life and trust companies of the 1830s charged premiums for life insurance that were 50 percent higher than those charged by the mutuals that were established a decade later.[14] That these high prices did not simply reflect market power is indicated by the fact that, as we have noted, nearly all of the investor-owned companies abandoned the life insurance business, rather than simply lowering their prices, when the mutuals came on the scene and forced prices down.[15] Moreover, the lower premiums charged by the mutual companies do not seem explainable by advantages in avoiding moral hazard or adverse selection on the part of the company's policyholders: the mutual companies, from the beginning, were not really consumer-controlled entities, but rather were established and run by managers who were essentially autonomous and self-perpetuating, and who simply sold insurance policies on the market to strangers as did the investor-owned companies.

The mutuals' advantage in eliminating the large gambles created by long-term contracts presumably also encouraged the switch from writing predominantly short, term life policies, as the early investor-owned companies had done, to writing predominantly whole life policies, as the mutual companies did.

Regulated Investor-Owned Firms as an Alternative to Mutuals

Today there is a well-established system of state regulation of life insurance companies. This system, which is relatively uniform among the states, does not attempt to control prices for life insurance policies, but concentrates on controlling reserves. Insurance companies are required to maintain reserves adequate in amount to cover their foreseeable liabilities for claims, and to invest these reserves in assets of sufficiently low risk to minimize the probability that the reserves might fall substantially in value. Because of the great difficulty of writing an unambiguous formal rule that clearly defines an acceptable reserve policy, state insurance commissioners maintain substantial discretion to use their judgment in determining the minimum reserve level for individual companies.

Such a system of regulation did not exist in the first half of the nineteenth century, when mutual companies came to dominate the industry. New York enacted the first general insurance law in 1849, requiring that life insurance companies have a minimum capital of $100,000, limiting the types of investments that companies could make, and requiring annual publication of accounts. It was not until the period 1859–1867 that effective regulation of this sort spread widely among the other states.[16] Evidently this regulation served as a workable substitute for the mutual form in assuring consumers that insurance companies would not behave too opportunistically: 1859 was the last year in which mutual life insurance companies outnumbered stock companies, and after 1866 the ratio of stock to mutual companies began increasing at a substantial rate.[17]

Participating Policies

Stock life insurance companies also began to compete more effectively with the mutuals by developing contracts that mimicked some of the features of the mutual form. In particular, stock companies early on came to offer "participating" policies, under which the policyholder shares with the company some of the net returns that the latter obtains from investing the premiums received under the policy.[18]

Participating policies reduce the amount of risk created by a life insurance contract, and hence reduce the cost of writing such a contract with an investor-owned firm. Participating policies are themselves difficult for policyholders to evaluate and police, however, and for that reason are today the subject of regulation in many states. Indeed, strong evidence that participating policies are insufficient in themselves to make stock companies competitive with mutual companies can be found in the fact that the first stock company to issue participating policies did so in 1836, before the advent of the mutuals, but was not particularly successful.[19]

The Costs of the Mutual Form

So far we have been speaking of the relative advantages of mutual and investor-owned life insurance companies in terms of the costs of contracting. But we must also consider the relative costs of control by customers as opposed to investors.

One factor that makes the life insurance business viable for customer-owned firms is that the amounts of organization-specific capital needed in the industry are modest. Indeed, the earliest mutuals were founded with no net capital at all. One company began operations by borrowing $100,000 in long-term subordinated debt. Another simply wrote policies that would not come into force until the company had received subscriptions for at least one million dollars of insurance.[20]

Customer ownership is also facilitated by the fact that the customers of a life insurance company all purchase a single, relatively simple, and homogeneous product from the firm—and this was especially true in the early days of the life insurance business, when the terms of policies were generally quite uniform. The result is a strong identity of interest that, as we have repeatedly seen, seems to be the hallmark of all successful forms of widely shared ownership.

At the same time, the number and geographic dispersion of the policyholders in a life insurance company effectively ensure that the policyholders will not exercise meaningful direct control over the company's management. In fact, since their very first appearance in the 1840s, mutual life insurance companies have been entirely managerial entities, founded and controlled by officers and directors who are essentially self-appointed. As in banking, however, it is not obvious that this clear separation of ownership from effective control has in itself disadvantaged the mutual companies vis-à-vis their stock competitors: empirical studies have failed to find a significant difference in average costs between mutual and stock life insurance companies.[21]

This suggests that if mutual life insurance companies are in any way less efficient than stock companies (as is implied by the gradual decline in the mutuals' market share that began in the late nineteenth century), it is not owing to weaker incentives to minimize costs,[22] but instead to problems involving capital. These problems take two somewhat conflicting forms.

First, mutuals have more restricted access to capital than do stock companies, which hampers the rate at which they can be founded and grow.[23] Moreover, since the capital that a mutual company uses to expand must generally come from retained profits on existing policies, fast growth is likely to be strongly against the interests of current policyholders, and to be undertaken at their expense.[24]

Second, the evidence suggests that the mutuals often accumulate financial reserves—likewise at the expense of their policyholders—that substantially exceed what is necessary to ensure solvency. Although these reserves are evidently accumulated in part to finance future growth, in part they apparently serve simply to satisfy management's desire for a very comfortable margin within which to maneuver and for a large investment portfolio to oversee.[25] This tendency to accumulate excessive net assets, as we noted in Chapter 12, is familiar among large nonprofit institutions such as universities, museums, and hospitals. That mutual life insurance companies behave the same way is not surprising, given that, with the absence of meaningful policyholder control, the managers of the mutuals are in essentially the same position of autonomy as the managers of the nonprofits.[26]

Subsequent Historical Experience

Although the enactment of public regulation made stock life insurance companies viable competitors, the balance of costs and benefits was evidently such that the stock form still did not have a decisive advantage over the mutual form in the late nineteenth and early twentieth centuries. Thus while many new stock companies were formed in the 1860s—so that by 1868 there were 205 stock companies and only 61 mutual companies in business—61 percent of these stock companies had failed by 1905, as opposed to only 22 percent of the mutuals. As a consequence, by 1906 there were only 110 stock companies as compared with 52 mutuals.[27]

The mutual form continued to show substantial strength in the first third of the twentieth century. In the period 1900–1936, at least fifteen stock life insurance companies were converted into mutual companies.[28] These included three of the largest stock companies—Metropolitan, Equitable, and Prudential—all of which converted between 1915 and 1918 and today are among the largest of the mutuals. The latter mutualizations were evidently inspired to some degree by journalistic muckraking and governmental investigations (including, most notably, New York's Armstrong Commission of 1905) that exposed dubious marketing practices and managerial self-dealing in the life insurance business and called for the mutualization of all stock companies—even though it was not entirely clear that abuses were much more prevalent among stock than among mutual companies.[29] The extent to which those exposés reflected, or stimulated, public opinion against stock companies and thus indicated that mutuals would find it easier than stock companies to sell policies in the ensuing years is difficult to judge.[30] At least in the case of Equitable, there is evidence that conversion to the mutual form was motivated in substantial part by the managers' desire to avoid being displaced by a corporate take-over[31]—a motivation that may also have played a role in other mutu-alizations that took place in those years.

In any case, there were also a number of conversions of mutual life insurance companies into stock companies during the same period. Indeed, between 1900 and 1936 there were at least seventeen such "stockings"—more than the apparent number of mutualizations. These conversions were evidently motivated in part by the desire to achieve greater access to capital or by the desire to diversify.[32] They may also, like the mutualizations, have been motivated to some extent by the self-interest of the companies' managers, who found it easy, in the course of such conversions, to obtain stock for themselves repre-senting a substantial fraction of the company's net worth.[33] In any event, such conversions suggest that the market was no longer working strongly to select for the mutual form by the first third of the twentieth century.

Finally, in the second half of the twentieth century, investor-owned companies achieved clear ascendancy. The mutuals' share of life in-surance in force fell from 69 percent in 1947 to 43 percent in 1983.[34] The total number of mutual life insurance companies reached its his-torical maximum of 171 in 1954, and then declined to 117 by 1991, while the number of stock life insurance companies increased from 661 to 2,078 during the same period.[35]

Tax Incentives

It is possible that the mutual companies would have lost market share to the stock life insurance companies even more rapidly in the twen-tieth century had it not been for tax preferences enjoyed by the mu-tuals, although it is not at all apparent that taxes have been important in this respect. Since there was no corporate tax throughout most of the nineteenth century, federal taxation obviously played no role in the initial shaping of the industry. But for several decades preceding the enactment of the Life Insurance Company Income Tax Act in 1959, the federal corporate income tax may have provided an implicit subsidy to the mutual versus the stock form. This was not clearly the case, however, and if such a subsidy existed it must have been quite modest, since the taxes collected from the life insurance industry in general were small in that period. The 1959 act was designed to increase the taxes collected from the industry, but was also apparently designed to ensure equality in the tax treatment of stock and mutual companies. As events unfolded, the latter act may even have inadvertently led to some tax bias against the mutual form.[36]

Property and Liability Insurance

The problems of long-term contracting responsible for the presence of mutual companies in the life insurance business do not explain the important role of mutuals in property and liability insurance. Most property and liability insurance is sold under relatively short-term contracts, commonly with a duration of a single year. To be sure, changes in technology have caused some of the risks now covered by property and liability insurance to become long-term ones. A company that writes liability coverage for a chemical plant for a given year may find that it is called upon to pay claims for cancers that only appear decades later. But the technological and legal changes responsible for this situation are relatively recent ones and are long antedated by the development of mutual companies offering property and liability insurance. To understand the role of mutuals in this industry we must turn to other types of contracting costs, both natural and governmentally induced.

The Evolution of the Mutuals

In property and liability insurance, as in life insurance, the nineteenth century was the high point for the formation of mutual companies. The circumstances in which the successful mutuals arose were remarkably uniform.

The stylized facts are roughly as follows. Owners of firms within a particular industry and a particular region—say, cotton textile mills in Rhode Island, or flour mills in Iowa, or farms in a township in Indiana—who believed they presented unusually low risks of fire, would find themselves paying fire insurance premiums to stock companies that seemed excessive. After trying unsuccessfully to persuade the stock companies to lower their fire insurance premiums, they would finally band together to form a mutual company to insure themselves. The resulting net premiums would be far below those charged by the stock companies. Unlike the stock companies, the mutual would only insure the better risks in the industry and would have a regular program of inspecting the firms they insured, both to assess the risk and to recommend loss prevention measures.[37] This pattern suggests several likely explanations for the success of the mutual companies.

Asymmetric Information

It was suggested above that the development of mutual life insurance companies was attributable in part to the fact that prospective policyholders have difficulty in obtaining the information necessary to distinguish among insurance companies that differ in their riskiness. In the case of property and liability insurance, the situation seems to be the reverse: mutual companies evidently arise in part because insurance companies cannot distinguish easily between prospective insureds that differ in the risks they present.

The prospective customers for any given line of insurance—for example, fire insurance for textile factories—are likely to vary considerably in the degree of risk they present. Moreover, the customers themselves are often likely to have better information than the insurance companies on this matter. If this were all there was to the problem of asymmetric information here, then, although one might expect adverse selection to undercut the viability of the market, there would still be no particular reason to expect mutual companies to evolve in place of stock companies. It seems plausible, however, that one textile company, by virtue of what it knows about the business, will commonly be in a better position to assess the risk of fire presented by another textile company than will any firm, including any insurance firm, that is not itself in the textile business. Or at least it seems probable that this was the case in the mid-nineteenth century, when the formation of mutuals was at its relative peak. Long-term experience tables and other systematic means of estimating expected losses were then generally unavailable to insurance companies. The firms that joined to form the mutuals, in contrast, were commonly owned and operated by individual entrepreneurs, who necessarily were already quite familiar with the available technology in the industry and the risks that it presented. This situation provided an incentive for those firms within an industry that knew themselves to be unusually good risks to join together to form a mutual insurance company to insure themselves: the firms could recognize one another as good risks but would have difficulty convincing an insurance company from outside the industry that they deserved especially low premiums. Or, put differently, the cost of information about the riskiness of individual insureds was lower to firms within the industry than to those outside of it.

To be sure, this theory in itself does not explain why a single firm within a given industry would not exploit its inside information about the industry by going into the insurance business itself rather than by joining with other firms to form a mutual. To understand this, we need to explore some additional considerations.

Limited Competition

In the nineteenth century, property and liability insurance seems to have been a relatively local business, presumably owing to the costs of communication. This fact, together with the necessity of writing a large number of policies to yield adequate diversification of risk, presumably left insufficient room for the creation of a substantial number of competing insurers with detailed knowledge of any given industry. Thus even if a stock company had succeeded in developing the expertise needed to rate accurately the risks presented by a given type of local industry, it would have had little or no competition. And this, in itself, would create an incentive for the firms buying insurance to form a mutual.

The absence of competition may have been reinforced by the relative absence of price discrimination that characterizes the insurance industry. For various reasons—presumably including the costs of information and administration, and the problem that price rationing can aggravate adverse selection[38]—insurance companies commonly do not adjust their rates to the specific risks presented by individual customers, but charge the same rate to all customers who fall within a given broad category. Indeed, there is evidence that at the time that the mutuals were formed, a given stock insurance company would commonly charge the same rate to all risks of a given type (such as cotton textile mills) that it insured.[39] Consequently, a firm seeking insurance could not get stock companies to compete for the firm's individual business on the basis of price (that is, the firm could not get a stock company to compete for the individual firm's business by offering a special lower price for that firm alone). Rather, competition among firms could only take place among whole categories of insureds. With few insurance firms offering policies, such competition was unlikely to be intense.[40]

Inspection and Safety Research

For many types of risks, close (and sometimes recurring) inspection of the insured is advantageous in assessing the risk, in discouraging moral hazard, and in suggesting to the insured further means of risk reduction. By these means, inspection can reduce the net cost of insurance. There are, however, disincentives to undertake inspections when the insurance company is organized as a stock company rather than as a mutual.

To begin with, inspection represents a transaction-specific investment by the insurance company. Since insurance contracts are short-term, this leaves open the possibility for the insured to act opportunistically, threatening to take its business elsewhere unless it is given unremuneratively low rates. Longer-term contracts might obviate this problem, but would presumably require excessive rigidity in rates or grant excessive discretion in rate setting to the insurer. And any effort to deal with the problem by having the insured pay separately for the inspections would simply put the shoe on the other foot, leaving the insurer in a position to act opportunistically.

Moreover, a stock insurance company has only a limited incentive to encourage its policyholders to undertake investments in cost-justified loss prevention measures as long as a large proportion of the benefit of such investments will be returned to the insured in the form of a reduction in premiums. And if loss-prevention measures taken by the insured are not so rewarded, there is insufficient incentive for the insured to undertake them when they are suggested.

The mutual form mitigates such conflicts of interest between the insurer and the insured. In fact, as noted above, the early mutual companies were distinguished by much more active inspection programs than were characteristic of the stock companies, and this difference in behavior presumably helped provide the mutuals with a competitive advantage.

The early mutuals also were distinguished by a more active program of research into loss prevention measures than were the stock companies. Since such research is a public good for the industry in which the insureds operate, a mutual obviously has much greater incentive than a stock company to undertake it. Such research would presumably afford a mutual a competitive advantage, however, only to the extent that its fruits were available to the firm's policyholders more quickly than to the insured industry at large.

Avoiding Moral Hazard

Some of the smaller mutuals also evidently serve the useful purpose of reducing losses due to moral hazard. In particular, this seems to be true of the local farm mutuals. These organizations had their heyday in the last quarter of the nineteenth century—there were over 1,400 at the century's end[41]—but continue to play an important role today. Though many are too small to diversify risk with optimum efficiency, this very smallness, which ensures that many of the policyholders will know one another well as neighbors, discourages moral hazard.[42]

Bearing Industrywide Risks

There are problems of risk sharing in property and liability insurance that parallel those discussed above with respect to life insurance.

To the extent that the average loss level of an industry cannot be accurately predicted, an insurance company writing property or liability insurance for that industry will bear risk that it cannot reduce by writing a larger number of policies. Such industrywide risk may be more efficiently borne by the firms in the industry than by an investor-owned insurance company. Although the potential variation in industrywide losses may be large as a proportion of expected earnings for a company insuring the industry, they are likely to be much smaller relative to the earnings of the industry itself. A mutual company has the advantage that it eliminates those risks that are idiosyncratic to individual firms within the industry, while it passes back, pro rata, to all firms in the industry the risk of variance in the overall loss experience of the industry as a whole. With a mutual company, consequently, the insured firms do not need to pay an insurance company the high premiums that would be necessary to induce the company to bear industrywide risks that would, in fact, be more easily borne by the firms themselves.[43]

This consideration will obviously be most important in those industries in which the loss experience of the industry as a whole is most difficult to predict. New industries, or old industries in new locations, are likely to be in this category. This may help explain why the mutual companies had such a strong competitive advantage over the stock companies in the mid-nineteenth century, when experience with industrial insurance was still quite limited, and why farm mutuals were so common in frontier farming communities.[44]

Overall industry loss levels also become more unpredictable when rules of liability become uncertain. This was the experience in the 1970s and 1980s, when American courts began expanding considerably the potential liability of manufacturers and service providers for injuries suffered by employees and by consumers of the firms' goods and services. The extent to which the courts would go in expanding the scope of liability and the amount of damages recoverable became highly uncertain. This was compounded by two factors that gave liability insurance a "tail" much longer than the nominal period of one or several years for which the policies were written. First, lawsuits were often not resolved until many years after the injury was caused—and hence after the policy covering the injury was written—leaving considerable time for legal standards to evolve in unforeseeable ways. Second, changes in technology and in legal standards made it increasingly possible for plaintiffs to bring suit for injuries whose cause could be traced to exposure to products or processes many years in the past.

As a consequence, the share of liability insurance written by mutual companies increased dramatically in the 1970s and 1980s. Over those two decades, premiums paid to mutual and "captive" (industry-owned) insurance companies increased from 1.5 percent to 32 percent of total liability insurance costs.[45] Most of this growth occurred in industries where legal standards had become most unpredictable; for example, new mutual insurance companies were formed to provide medical malpractice insurance in the 1970s, and to serve the drug, chemical, railroad, utility, banking, and nurse-midwife markets in the 1980s.[46]

One must ask, of course, why investor-owned insurance companies would be more averse to bearing the risk of overall fluctuations in average industry loss rates than would the firms or individuals in that industry. Mutual insurance firms are commonly confined to a single industry (such as malpractice insurance for pediatricians), evidently to assure homogeneity of interests among a firm's owners. As a result, the policyholders must bear all the risk associated with variance in average industrywide loss rates. The shareholders in an investor-owned firm writing insurance for that industry, however, should be able to eliminate some or all of that risk by diversifying their investments, holding shares in firms engaged in other types of business, and particularly noninsurance business.

Yet investor-owned property and liability insurers clearly act as if they are risk averse. An important reason for this, evidently, is that capital does not flow easily into and out of insurance firms as needed to make up for unexpectedly high average losses, both for tax reasons and because the firms have information about their past and future fortunes that cannot be costlessly conveyed to the capital market. Thus the investor-owned insurance companies have a relatively fixed supply of capital to deploy as reserves. If that capital is depleted owing to unusually large industrywide losses, their ability to write insurance in the future will be diminished. The investor-owned companies are therefore constrained to be risk averse.[47]

Moreover, investor-owned insurance firms may also be unable to gain much additional diversification by their greater flexibility, relative to mutuals, in writing insurance for more than one industry. For one thing, some of the important risks involved, such as the extent of judicial activism in expanding the scope of liability, may affect many different lines of insurance in the same way. Further, an insurance company writing insurance in widely disparate fields may face problems of internal capital allocation that parallel those that arise in the stock market: managers of a given division may have trouble conveying to central management their knowledge about their division's performance and prospects.[48]

Avoiding Regulation

Further encouragement for the mutual form has come from rate regulation. Although there have recently been substantial moves toward deregulation, property and liability insurance, unlike life insurance, has historically been subject to state regulation that establishes minimum rates for different types of policies. As applied to mutual insurance companies, such regulation commonly extends only to gross premiums—that is, to the nominal premiums that an insurance company charges its policyholders prior to determining any dividend that is owed them. The dividends paid by the mutuals are thus a means of undercutting rate regulation.[49]

Rate regulation was most rigid during the 1950s and 1960s, and there is evidence that this rigidity contributed to the growth of mutuals during that period. For example, the growth in mutual fire insurance from 14 percent of the market in 1951 to 20 percent of the market in 1970 has been attributed to the greater rate flexibility that dividends afforded the mutuals.[50] Rate regulation by the states did not begin until the twentieth century, however, while mutuals were already common in the eighteenth century and experienced their most spectacular growth in the nineteenth century. Mutuals have also continued to thrive in states without regulation. Thus avoidance of rate regulation cannot be anywhere near the whole story.

Cartelization

As early as 1840, property and liability insurance companies began conspiring to set rates through the formation of voluntary rate bureaus (which also served as means to share experience concerning loss rates). Such cartelization presumably contributed to the limited competition and high prices that provided the impetus for the mutual companies in this industry. It seems likely, however, that this factor has been more important in the twentieth century than it was during the formative stages of the industry in the nineteenth century. The success of price fixing was evidently limited throughout the nineteenth century owing to the repeated disintegration of the cartels and to hostile state action. It was only in the twentieth century that many states turned from fighting to aiding the rate bureaus. In addition, the property and liability insurance industry has been exempt from the federal antitrust laws throughout most of its history. Consequently, effective competition has generally been limited for most of the twentieth century even when there have not been state-established minimum prices.[51]

Homogeneity of Member Interests

In contrast to mutual life insurance companies, mutual property and liability insurance companies have often been subject to relatively effective member control. Indeed, as we have seen, policyholder control has been important in providing the property and liability mutuals with some of their advantages over investor-owned firms, such as avoidance of moral hazard and adverse selection.

At the same time, effective member control accentuates the importance of homogeneity of interest among the members of a mutual company, and this, too, is evident in the property and liability mutuals. As opposed to the investor-owned property and liability insurers, the mutuals often do not insure firms in more than one line of business, even though such diversification would have the advantage of spreading risk. This evidently explains why the structure of the mutuals in the property and liability insurance industry is so different from that in the life insurance industry. In the latter industry, proprietary firms far outnumber mutuals, but the mutuals are generally much larger and do a disproportionate amount of the total business. In property and liability insurance, the situation is just the reverse: mutuals outnumber the proprietary firms,[52] but the proprietary firms are commonly larger and do roughly three-quarters of the industry's business.[53] The evident reason for the disparity is that life insurance is a far more homogeneous commodity than is property and liability insurance.[54]

The Continuing Survival of Mutuals

With the important exception of the impetus created by the liability insurance crisis of the 1970s and 1980s, over the course of the twentieth century the balance of organizational costs and benefits seems to have moved increasingly in favor of investor-owned over mutual property and liability insurance companies. Transportation and communication costs have declined significantly since the nineteenth century, with the result that most insurance markets are now national in scope. At the same time, as experience has accumulated and as insurance companies have come to share their loss experiences, it has presumably become far easier to assess the risk presented by any given applicant for insurance. As a consequence, the environment for effective competition in property and liability insurance markets is now far better than it was in the nineteenth century, and the special protection afforded policyholders by the mutual form may no longer be a particularly significant advantage in most forms of property and liability insurance.

Some evidence to support this conclusion comes from the fact that mutual property and liability companies have come increasingly to look like their investor-owned counterparts. Effective policyholder control has long since disappeared in many mutuals. Many individual mutuals have extended their operations beyond the industry they were initially formed to serve, and now insure risks in a variety of different industries.[55] Such mutuals presumably survive partly out of institutional inertia (capital lock-in), partly as a result of the impetus given them by state rate regulation, and partly because, unlike mutual life insurance companies, mutual property and liability insurance companies have had the advantage of a system of federal corporate income taxation that has been intentionally designed to favor them vis-à-vis investor-owned insurers.[56]

Experience in Other Countries

In those countries for which data are readily available, the pattern of ownership in insurance seems to parallel the United States experience relatively closely.

The best-studied example is the Australian life insurance industry, which evolved very much as life insurance did in the United States. A number of investor-owned companies tried to sell life insurance in Australia in the 1830s and 1840s, but all had left the business by 1849. The first mutual life insurance company was formed in 1848, and was highly successful; from then until the 1880s, mutual companies dominated the business. State parliaments began introducing life insurance company regulation in the 1870s, and in the 1880s investor-owned companies first began having some significant success in the market. As of 1989, mutual companies continued to compete well with regulated investor-owned firms, selling 60 percent of new whole life policies.[57]

Conclusion

Although mutual companies are common both in life insurance and in property and liability insurance, they evidently play rather different roles in these two industries.

In property and liability insurance, the role of the mutual companies has often been similar to that which is commonly performed elsewhere by consumer cooperatives: they have provided a measure of protection against noncompetitive pricing. In life insurance, mutual companies seem to have been important historically, not in protecting consumers from simple price exploitation, but rather in avoiding opportunistic behavior on the part of sellers in a situation in which adequate contractual safeguards could not be established. This latter role has more in common with that commonly played by nonprofit firms than with that played by other types of consumer cooperatives.

This view of mutual life insurance companies is in keeping with the fact that their structure and behavior are in important respects closer to those of nonprofit firms than to those that characterize other consumer cooperatives. For example, the board of directors of the mutual life insurance companies is essentially self-appointing; the members have no effective right to distribute to themselves the accumulated surplus of the organization; and the companies, like many nonprofit educational and religious organizations, accumulate large surpluses (endowments) with which they insulate themselves from the pressures of the market. Like the patrons of a typical nonprofit, the policyholders in a mutual company derive protection, not from the exercise of control over the firm, but from the fact that the management of the mutual, unlike the management of a stock company, does not have a strong pecuniary incentive to exploit its policyholders. Indeed, some large life insurance companies are formally organized as nonprofit firms; TIAA, whose principal business is the administration of pension plans for university professors, is a prominent example. Here again, then, we see a blurring of the lines between owned and unowned enterprise.

Conclusion

As a general matter, one cannot say that one form of ownership is superior to another. Ownership by any group of a firm's patrons—whether investors, consumers, workers, or other suppliers—can be efficient in the appropriate context, and the same is true of nonprofit firms. Each type of ownership has its appropriate niche in the economy.

The relative efficiency of alternative forms of ownership in any given industry is determined by the costs of market contracting and the costs of ownership that confront the industry's consumers and suppliers. The preceding chapters suggest or reinforce a number of general conclusions about these costs.

The Firm as a Political Institution

One theme that has emerged with particular force is the importance of viewing the firm as a political institution. In large firms, ownership is commonly shared among a substantial number of persons. There are two important reasons for this. One is that the owners must collectively have sufficient assets or cash flow to absorb fluctuations in the firm's earnings. The second is that ownership mitigates the costs of contracting, and it is therefore advantageous to spread ownership as widely as possible among persons who transact with the firm, at least as long as the costs of ownership do not grow disproportionately as a result. If ownership is widely shared, however, some form of voting mechanism must be used for decision making. And voting has significant limitations—limitations that evidently play a decisive role in determining the patterns of ownership that we observe.

The Costs of Politics

Most fundamentally, political representation evidently performs poorly, relative to markets, where there is any significant conflict of interest among the participants. Or at least this seems to be the obvious conclusion to be drawn from the fact that, although there are hundreds of thousands of firms in the economy, and although these firms exhibit a diverse variety of ownership structures, including a surprisingly large number of firms in which ownership is not in the hands of investors, in virtually all cases the group of individuals to whom ownership is given is extremely homogeneous in its interests. It is extraordinarily rare to find a firm in which control is shared among individuals who have stakes in the enterprise that are at all dissimilar.

Consequently, in determining whether the costs of ownership are manageable for a given class of patrons, homogeneity of interest appears to be an especially important consideration. In particular, it is evidently a significant factor in the widespread success of the modern investor-owned business corporation, and it also appears to be an important reason for the relative paucity of worker-owned firms, which otherwise have some significant efficiency advantages.

The Value of Voting

To conclude that collective choice mechanisms work poorly where the participants have diverse interests is, of course, to conclude that they do not work very well at all. For there is little need for a collective choice mechanism where everybody has the same interests.

Indeed, the basic function served by giving voting control over a firm to a group of the firm's patrons is not to provide a means for conveying the patrons' preferences to the firm's management, but rather to make it more difficult for the firm to exploit those patrons as a class—that is, to prevent the firm from taking actions that will strongly disadvantage a substantial majority of those patrons. This is why, in most firms, voting control is given to a class of transacting parties who, if they were solely dependent on market contracting, would collectively be subject to exploitation by the firm, either because the firm has market power, because the firm has an informational advantage over them, or because the patrons must make transaction-specific investments that will compromise their exit option once they begin dealing with the firm.

In short, the principal role of voting in firms is much as it is in most democratic governments: not to aggregate and communicate preferences, but simply to give the electorate some crude protection from gross opportunism on the part of those in power.

There is clearly a need for good communication between patrons and the firm, just as there is between citizens and their government. Indeed, a recurrent theme in the management literature has been the need for managers to find better means of listening to their customers, suppliers, investors, and workers. But giving patrons voting control over the firm is not necessarily a good means to this end, creating possibilities for costly conflict and skewed decision making.

On the contrary, where the owners of a firm are at all heterogeneous in their interests, it is common to encounter devices designed to attenuate rather than increase the refinement and force with which electoral mechanisms convey the interests of the individual owners. For example, as we have seen, worker-owned firms with a diverse labor force sometimes require that directors be elected at large rather than by smaller constituencies, that they serve terms of several years rather than just one year, or that they be outsiders rather than members of the work force they represent. An extreme version of this attenuation is the formation of a nonprofit firm whose directors are charged with operating the firm on behalf of a given class of patrons but who are not elected by those patrons.

The Costs of Contracting

The other side of the coin is that, where a firm *does* have a class of patrons with highly homogeneous interests, ownership is often an attractive alternative to market contracting for those patrons. Market contracting, like politics, has its costs, and ownership can reduce those costs by removing the conflict of interest between firm and patron that lies at their root.

In this there is nothing special about investors of capital. Often they are the only reasonably homogeneous class of patrons, and thus the natural owners by default. But where another substantial group of patrons has the requisite commonality of interest—whether they are workers, other suppliers, or customers—it is evidently efficient to give ownership to that group even when the potential reduction in their costs of contracting is relatively modest.

Monitoring Managers

The importance of having owners monitor managers has been a great focus of the literature on organizations. The preceding chapters suggest that this theme has been overstated. There do not seem to be dramatic differences among ownership forms in agency costs deriving from poor monitoring of managers, whether the comparison is between investor-owned firms and firms owned by patrons other than investors, or even between owned and unowned (that is, nonprofit) firms. The degree of product market competition facing a firm seems far more important than the firm's ownership structure in determining the efficiency with which the firm is managed. As a consequence, the agency costs from weak monitoring of managers are often worth incurring for the sake of reducing the costs of market contracting. In deciding whether a given class of patrons could efficiently own the firm, it seems less important to determine whether that class's agency costs will be high if it does own the firm than whether its contracting costs will be high if it does not. Indeed, if it were otherwise, there would presumably be far fewer investor-owned firms, since in large firms often workers, and sometimes even customers, are in a better position to exercise strong and informed control over management than are the firm's shareholders.

This is not to say that owner control of management is not important at all. Where non-investor-owned firms have succeeded even in the absence of substantial contract failure, such as contemporary farm marketing and supply cooperatives or retailer-owned wholesale and supply cooperatives, their patron-owners have commonly been well organized to exercise substantial influence over management. Moreover, as discussed further below, some degree of owner control seems important at least for preventing the gross inefficiencies involved in accumulating unnecessary capital within the firm.

Nevertheless, when there is a choice of assigning ownership either to a group of patrons who can exercise effective control but who face low costs of market contracting or, alternatively, to a group of patrons who cannot exercise much effective control but who face potentially high costs of contracting, it is commonly the members of the latter group that make the more efficient owners. The costs of managerial slack are apparently small compared with the costs of having management tightly constrained to exploit market failures in ways that are profitable to the firm's owners but socially wasteful. The success of the early mutual companies in banking and life insurance offers a clear illustration.

Similarly, as between giving ownership to, on the one hand, a group of patrons who can effectively impose their will on management but who are divided among themselves, and on the other, a group that is highly homogenous in its interests but cannot police management closely, the latter group seems commonly to be the more efficient owners (holding constant the costs of contracting). Otherwise, worker ownership would be far more common than it is.

Capital Allocation

When comparing alternative assignments of ownership, differences in the efficiency of capital accumulation are more apparent than differences in the minimization of costs given the capital employed. Broadly speaking, there are two different problems here. The first is undercapitalization, which arises when difficulties in accumulating capital prevent firms from forming or expanding rapidly to meet demand for their services. The second is overcapitalization, which arises when firms accumulate more capital than they can efficiently utilize. Although the first of these problems has most commonly been the focus of the literature on alternative forms of ownership, the evidence suggests that the second problem is more important.

Firms owned by their customers, workers, or suppliers of factors other than capital often have greater difficulty accumulating capital than do investor-owned firms. But the differences are not striking, and it is not clear that this is a major impediment to the formation of such firms where they would otherwise be efficient. One reason for this is that the amount of capital, per worker or per customer, employed even in relatively capital-intensive firms is not remarkably large. For a worker to invest heavily in the firm she works for, of course, results in poor diversification of risk. But the evidence suggests that risk aversion is not an extraordinarily important consideration in choice of ownership.

In comparison with proprietary firms, nonprofit firms are generally slow in accumulating capital to meet demand. But this is a question of the speed with which nonprofits reach a given share of an industry's capacity, and not of what that share will ultimately be. Over the long run, nonprofits are capable of accumulating substantial amounts of capital, as the higher education and hospital industries demonstrate.

In the long run, then, capital accumulation does not seem to be a major obstacle to the dominance within an industry of firms owned by patrons other than investors or even of nonprofit firms. In contrast, there do seem to be important differences among different forms of ownership in shedding capital when it can no longer be employed efficiently.

In nonprofit firms, and also in many consumer-owned firms in which the customers do not have meaningful control (such as life insurance and banking), capital can become locked in. These firms tend to accumulate capital beyond their needs and, conversely, fail to shed capital, or to exit the industry, when they are inefficiently large or simply inefficient.

In a sense, capital lock-in is an aspect of the agency costs of management. Why, then, is this a major difference between ownership forms, while agency costs of management in general do not seem to differ greatly? The answer, perhaps, is that managers are responsive in eliminating many inefficiencies—such as those associated with unnecessarily high costs of production, or with failure to conform production to demand—because, in the face of product market competition, their organization's ability to survive, much less grow, will otherwise be threatened. But the same drive for institutional survival—whether it derives from the managers' desire to maintain their own jobs or, less selfishly, from the excessively high salience that the virtues of their organization's services have achieved in the managers' eyes—will push managers to maintain and even accumulate capital within the firm even when it is earning an inefficiently low rate of return. And a nonprofit firm, or a proprietary firm that pays no dividends, can survive and even grow as long as it is earning any positive net return on its invested capital, even if that rate of return is far below what could be earned if the capital were employed elsewhere. As a consequence, product market discipline will not suffice to drive capital out of a nonprofit firm or out of a proprietary firm whose owners have no effective control.

It follows that nonprofit firms, and also consumer cooperatives, can survive in industries well beyond the time when other ownership forms, and particularly investor-owned firms, have become more efficient. There is a similar problem of excessive capital accumulation within investor-owned firms. Publicly held companies that are effectively controlled by their managers frequently not only survive but invest and grow even when they are earning less than a market rate of return on their invested capital. Indeed, large publicly traded business corporations are apparently much more subject to this problem than are many types of cooperatives, such as the large farmer-owned production and supply cooperatives, or the retailer-owned supply cooperatives. With investor-owned firms, however, there is ultimately both the incentive and the mechanism to withdraw capital from the firm through a takeover of its management, by means of either a hostile tender offer or a proxy fight. These latter mechanisms are crude. But even those crude mechanisms are lacking in some common types of non-investor-owned firms.

Entrepreneurship

Entrepreneurship—that is, the creation of new firms—is surprisingly unimportant as a constraint on the development of firms owned by patrons other than investors. Where such firms have a clear efficiency advantage over investor-owned enterprise, they seem to form quite rapidly. One reason for this is that entrepreneurs can serve as brokers in the formation of firms, organizing them with their own capital and initiative and then selling them to the patrons who are ultimately to serve as the firm's owners. This is the way that publicly traded investor-owned firms are often formed, and it is a method that has been employed with a variety of other ownership forms as well, from worker cooperatives (as in plywood manufacturing) to housing condominiums.

In addition, it is relatively easy to transfer ownership from one large class of patrons to another even in a well-established enterprise. Large insurance companies have been sold by their investors to their policyholders, industrial firms have been sold by their investors to their employees, and investor-owned apartment buildings have been sold to their tenants. Transactions of the reverse character, in which investors purchase firms from other classes of the firms' patrons, are also commonplace. If a different ownership form offers clear efficiency advantages over the current one, then both the incentive and the means to change exist.

Again, the situation is a bit different with nonprofit firms. It is possible to form an investor-owned firm and then convert it to a nonprofit corporation, and make money on the transaction. Many nonprofit hospitals in the United States were created in that way, having begun as doctor-owned clinics. But the factors that make the nonprofit form efficient often preclude even the temporary formation of the firm under ownership of a private entrepreneur. Nonprofit firms must therefore generally be formed by large parent organizations (for example, established churches), by altruistic citizens, or by entrepreneurs who seek no larger gain for themselves than a role as salaried administrator of the firm they create. And, though these sources are remarkably prolific, they do not provide quite the responsiveness that one finds in the formation of owned enterprise.

Regulation

Although it might seem paradoxical, governmental regulation often plays an important role in permitting investor-owned firms to flourish where cooperatives or nonprofits would otherwise be dominant. This is most conspicuous in those industries, such as savings banking and life insurance, that have been characterized by severe problems of asymmetric information. But even general antitrust law enforcement has this effect, as evidenced by the grain marketing cooperatives formed in the United States in the late nineteenth century, when antitrust enforcement was not deployed against buyers' cartels, and as also evidenced by Sweden, where tolerance of producer cartels helped foster widespread consumer ownership.

Culture and Ideology

The importance of culture and ideology on organizational forms is often overstated. Ownership patterns are remarkably similar across nations that exhibit a similar level of economic development: worker ownership is common in the service professions and in transportation firms; farm marketing cooperatives are widespread in staple grains; consumer cooperatives and nonprofits played a large role in savings banking and life insurance in the nineteenth century, but are less important today. The United States, which in the common mind is a much less collectivist society than the nations of Western Europe, is unusually rich in producer and consumer cooperatives.

Moreover, just as culture and ideology do not seem to play a conspicuous role in the organizational forms that appear across different societies, nor do they show great force within societies. In the United States, worker ownership is widespread, not among blue-collar workers but among lawyers, accountants, investment bankers, and management consultants—prosperous professionals largely in the service of corporate capital. Consumer cooperatives are formed primarily by small businesspersons, such as farmers and hardware store owners, who are conspicuous for their individualism and political conservatism. Cooperatively owned apartment buildings have commonly been the residences of the wealthy.

This is not to suggest that culture and ideology play no role in economic organization. But the differences among economies in this respect are most conspicuous when it comes to governmentally owned enterprise, which we have largely ignored here. In those portions of their economies that societies have left to private enterprise, the logic of the market has been surprisingly strong and uniform in choosing forms of ownership. To be sure, taxes, subsidies, regulation, and organizational law all differ from one society to another in various ways for various industries, and these clearly have some importance for the patterns of ownership that we observe. But they are generally not so strong as to swamp the basic costs of market contracting and of ownership that were examined in Chapters 2 and 3.

The Direction and Pace of Evolution

The forms of ownership that are efficient within any given industry frequently change as the industry evolves. Nonprofit and consumer-owned enterprise, in particular, often play an important role in new industries in which consumers have difficulty judging the qualities of different producers, or vice versa. Subsequently, as the industry matures, experience, reputation, standards, and regulation develop and create an environment in which investor-owned enterprise has the advantage. But other patterns also appear. For example, the live performing arts in the United States have shown a clear trend from proprietary to nonprofit firms throughout the twentieth century. Likewise, agriculture has shown a long-term trend toward cooperative farm ownership among both supply and marketing firms, not just in the United States but throughout the developed world.

The consistency and coherence in patterns of ownership both within and across societies suggests that the pace of market selection is relatively rapid. We have seen a number of examples in which new organizational forms have arisen and become widespread within an industry over a span of one to three decades—including, within the United States, mutual life insurance in 1840–1860, investor-owned savings banks in 1880–1910, farm marketing cooperatives in 1890–1910, and condominium housing in 1960–1980. The industries in which the hand of history lies most heavily upon contemporary ownership patterns are those in which at some point nonprofit firms—or, what is very similar, retail consumer cooperatives whose customers lack meaningful control, such as the financial mutuals—came to have a large role. The reason for the latter exception, as we have seen, is that transactions in control are difficult to arrange with such firms, and consequently they tend to perpetuate themselves beyond the time in which they have an efficiency advantage over investor-owned enterprise.

The Contingency of Investor Ownership

There are strong efficiency reasons for assigning ownership of a firm to one or another group of the firm's patrons. Precisely which patrons constitute the most efficient owners depends on the particular context, however. An important reason for the prevalence of investor-owned firms in market economies is that contracting costs for financial capital are often relatively high compared with contracting costs for other inputs—including labor—and for most products. A second reason is that, however poorly situated investors may be to exercise effective control, there are often no other patrons who are in a better position, either because they lack the requisite homogeneity of interest or because they are too transitory and dispersed. Where either of these conditions fails, other forms of ownership arise. When there are serious imperfections in product or factor markets, one commonly finds consumer-owned firms, supplier-owned firms, or nonprofits. Similarly, when a substantial group of customers, employees, or suppliers is well situated to exercise collective control, consumer-owned, employee-owned, or supplier-owned firms appear even when the patrons in question are faced with only modest problems of market failure.

Freedom of enterprise is a fundamental characteristic of the most advanced modern economies. Capitalism, in contrast, is contingent; it is simply the particular form of patron ownership that most often, but by no means always, proves efficient with the technologies presently at hand.

Notes

1. An Analytic Framework

1. The phrase was brought into common usage by Adolph Berle and Gardener Means in their 1932 classic, *The Modern Corporation and Private Property*. In strict terms, of course, one cannot really speak of the separation of ownership from control, since ownership *means* (formal) control. Rather, one can speak only of the separation of ownership from *effective* control.

2. See Sanford Grossman and Oliver Hart, "The Costs and Benefits of Ownership: A Theory of Vertical and Lateral Integration," 94 *Journal of Political Economy* 691 (1986).

3. G. Martin, "Numbers Drop, But Co-ops Still Significant in Dairy Industry," *Farmer Cooperatives* 4, 5 (April 1990). In 1964, the cooperatives' share was only 25 percent; it reached a peak of 47 percent in 1980. Id.; Richard Heflebower, *Cooperatives and Mutuals in the Market System* 41 (1980).

4. See Chapter 9.

5. See, for example, Wisconsin Cooperative Corporation Act, Wis. Stat. Ann. §185.41, which explicitly provides for long-term marketing agreements.

6. See the discussion of the early mutuals in Chapter 14.

7. Alexander Dreier, "Shareholder Voting Rules in 19th Century American Corporations: Law, Economics and Ideology" (unpublished, Yale Law School, 1995).

8. Oliver Hart and John Moore, in "Property Rights and the Nature of the Firm," 98 *Journal of Political Economy* 1119–59 (1990), argue that ownership of a firm can be equated with control over items of firm-specific capital, and particularly physical assets. This view, however, is both unreflective of actual institutions and unnecessary for the general analysis offered by Hart and Moore. That analysis—which is discussed in slightly more detail in note 5 in Chapter 2—argues that ownership of firm-specific assets creates important indirect incentives for the assets' owners to make *other* firm-specific investments, such as investments in human capital. Yet ownership as I define it here—namely, control over an assemblage of contractual rights, none of which need involve physical assets or other items that we customarily term property (such as intellectual property or financial claims)—can put the firm's owners

in the same position of strategic advantage vis-à-vis one of the firm's patrons that is the focus of the Hart and Moore analysis. (That is, the patron in question may need to decide whether to make investments that will be specific to that nexus of contracts, and if the patron controls the nexus—that is, owns the firm—she will have a stronger incentive to make those investments.)

9. See the example in note 16 infra.

10. Even where the firm has title to physical assets, the members could still avoid maintaining any net investment in the firm by continually adjusting the firm's debt level to keep it equal to the value of the firm's assets, hence cashing out all changes in net asset value as they occur.

11. To form an investor-owned firm under a general cooperative corporation statute, such as the Wisconsin statute cited in note 5, would require that lending funds to the corporation be deemed "patronage" as that term is used in the statute. Although the cooperative statutes generally authorize the issuance of capital "stock," which typically carries no votes and has a ceiling on its rate of return, such stock would not have to be issued in forming an investor-owned firm as a capital cooperative.

12. Although, in theory, the cooperative statutes are more general than the business corporation statutes, which nominally require a contribution of capital for participation in ownership and allocate voting rights proportionately to that capital contribution, in fact modern business corporation statutes are highly flexible, and in practice can be manipulated to create almost any assignment of votes and earnings that one could wish. In particular, it is now possible to organize nearly any type of cooperative under the business corporation statutes, and for convenience those statutes are frequently used instead of the cooperative corporation statutes to form various types of cooperatives, such as worker cooperatives.

13. Frank Knight, *Risk, Uncertainty, and Profit* (1971 [1921]). It might be contended, however, that Knight himself saw a somewhat more activist role for the entrepreneur. Arguably Knight's own discussion of the reasons for assigning ownership of the typical corporation to investors of capital, though a bit vague, is consistent with the theoretical considerations discussed below. See, for example, id. at 300–301.

14. Of course, simply exercising control—that is, acquiring the information and making the decisions necessary to manage the firm—involves the supply of a necessary factor of production. Consequently, anyone who exercises control is also, in a reductive sense, among the firm's patrons even if he or she does not otherwise transact with the firm. Viewed this way, all firms are necessarily patron-owned. The question of ownership then becomes: when should this decision-making function be combined with some other form of patronage? The analysis developed here applies in much the same fashion no matter which way we frame the issue.

15. The concept of the firm as a "nexus of contracts" was given broad currency in the economics literature by Michael Jensen and William Meckling, "Theory of the Firm: Managerial Behavior, Agency Costs and Ownership Structure," 3 *Journal of Financial Economics* 305 (1976), building on Armen Alchian and Harold Demsetz, "Production, Information Costs, and Economic Organization," 62 *American Economic Review* 777, 783 (1972).

16. For example, one can easily imagine a firm, in the form of a sports team, whose only assets are contracts giving it (a) an exclusive claim on the services, for the coming year, of a group of football players and a coach, (b) access to a stadium on specified weekends and a practice field on other days, and (c) the right to play, and divide the receipts from, a series of games against other similar teams on particular days over the coming year. Even though the firm has title to no real estate, equipment, or other assets, the assemblage of contractual rights it holds could well make it a valuable enterprise. To be sure, for the purposes at hand there is little point in trying to draw a strong distinction between contractual rights and property rights. A firm that has a ten-year lease on a sports stadium, for example, may well have far more practical control over the use of that stadium than does the stadium's nominal owner. I invoke the distinction here simply to reinforce the point that, contrary to the view sometimes expressed, ownership of a firm need have nothing to do with title to assets or with investment or ownership of capital.

17. See Ian McNeil, "The Many Futures of Contract," 47 *Southern California Law Review* 691–816 (1974); Oliver Williamson, *The Economic Institutions of Capitalism* 163–205 (1986).

18. Thus if there are N different classes of patrons who transact with the firm, ownership will be assigned most efficiently to that class j that minimizes the sum

$$C_j^O + \sum_{i \neq j} C_{ij}^K$$

where C_i^O is the cost of ownership for the group of patrons in class i and C_{ij}^K is the cost of market contracting for the group of patrons in class i when class j owns the firm. For simplicity, I am here including among the costs of ownership any costs of market contracting that are not eliminated by making the patrons the owners of the firm. For example, if the firm is a monopolist vis-à-vis the patrons who own the firm, and if to some extent the firm exploits those patrons monopolistically even though they are owners—say, because the patron-owners are able to exercise only very weak control over the firm's managers, who use the monopoly profits to pursue pet projects or to purchase expensive perquisities for themselves—any resulting efficiency costs would be included among the costs of ownership for the patrons in question. By definition, then, costs of market contracting are the costs of transactions between a firm and patrons who are not owners, while costs of ownership are the costs of transactions between the firm and patrons who are owners.

19. To take just one familiar example, it required nearly forty years for the multidivisional form of managerial organization to replace the older and evidently less efficient line-and-staff form throughout American industry. Alfred D. Chandler, Jr., *The Visible Hand: The Managerial Revolution in American Business* (1977).

20. For a general discussion, see Richard Nelson and Sidney Winter, *An Evolutionary Theory of Economic Change* (1982).

21. By "to a greater degree" I mean that, even if it were possible to arrange costless transactions whereby the gainers from the alternative arrangement could compensate the losers, the amount that would have to be paid the losers to induce them to accept the alternative voluntarily would exceed what the gainers would be willing to pay to have that alternative. In other words, I shall use the term "efficient," as economists conventionally do, to mean "Kaldor-Hicks optimal."

2. The Costs of Contracting

1. An excellent introduction—accessible yet sophisticated—to the economic theory relevant to the issues discussed in this and later chapters is offered by Paul Milgrom and John Roberts, *Economics, Organization and Management* (1992).

2. I shall also make reference here, in the notes, to only the most basic items in the general theoretical literature, and shall largely reserve to later chapters the discussion of literature that specifically seeks to relate the costs of contracting to problems of ownership.

3. This issue has been most strongly developed in the work of Oliver Williamson. See, for example, Oliver Williamson, *The Economic Institutions of Capitalism* ch. 2 (1986).

4. See Williamson, id., chs. 4–5 (1986); Benjamin Klein, R. A. Crawford, and Armen Alchian, "Vertical Integration, Appropriable Rents, and the Competitive Contracting Process," 21 *Journal of Law and Economics* 297 (1978).

5. The analysis of ownership offered in Oliver Hart and John Moore, "Property Rights and the Nature of the Firm," 98 *Journal of Political Economy* 1119–59 (1990), can be understood as focusing on the problem of lock-in discussed here. Hart and Moore address themselves to situations in which a patron of the firm has the opportunity to make a firm-specific investment ex ante, prior to settling the terms on which she will (re)contract with the firm. If the patron owns (or shares in ownership of) firm-specific assets (which, as discussed in note 8 in Chapter 1, Hart and Moore equate with ownership of the firm), the patron's bargaining power will be greater when she contracts

with the (other patrons of the) firm. The patron's anticipation of this larger share will give her an incentive to make a larger (and hence more efficient) ex ante firm-specific investment. Thus as a general rule, the Hart and Moore analysis calls for assigning ownership of firm-specific assets to those patrons whose potential ex ante firm-specific investments (which may be in such things as skills rather than physical capital) are most valuable to the firm.

6. See Chapter 14 for further discussion of these and other problems of insurance contracting.

7. The classic model of this phenomenon is offered in George Akerlof, "The Market for 'Lemons': Quality Uncertainty and the Market Mechanism," 84 *Quarterly Journal of Economics* 488 (1970).

8. For a survey of relevant bargaining theory and its application to labor contracting, see John Kennan and Robert Wilson, "Bargaining with Incomplete Information," 31 *Journal of Economic Literature* 45 (1993).

9. This issue was first clearly analyzed in A. Michael Spence, "Monopoly, Quality, and Regulation," 6 *Bell Journal of Economics* 417 (1975). For a discussion of this and related issues in the labor context, see R. B. Freeman, "Political Economy: Some Uses of the Exit-Voice Approach," 66 *American Economic Review Papers and Proceedings* 361 (1976).

3. The Costs of Ownership

1. It will be taken for granted here that a firm of any substantial size and complexity needs a hierarchical form of organization for decision making, which means that the firm must have a single locus of executive power with substantial discretion and authority. This means that, where ownership of the firm is shared among a large class of patrons, highly participatory forms of decision making will not be efficient. Rather, in such situations, control will generally be exercised by the firm's owners indirectly through election of the firm's directors; direct participation in decision making will be confined to approval of major structural changes such as merger and dissolution.

Oliver Williamson, in *The Economic Institutions of Capitalism* ch. 9 (1986), presents a convincing analysis of the advantages of hierarchical decision making in the context of a discussion of worker management. He there argues for the superiority, in efficiency terms, of the capitalist firm with a strong central management over a highly participatory ("communal") form of worker ownership. By itself, however, Williamson's analysis simply shows the virtues of centralized management; it does not tell us which class of patrons, workers or lenders of capital (or yet some other group of patrons), can most effectively exercise the right to elect that management—a point noted in Louis Putterman, "On Some Recent Explanations of Why Capital Hires Labor," 22 *Economic Inquiry* 171 (1984), and Raymond Russell, "Employee Ownership and Employee Governance," 6 *Journal of Economic Behavior and Organization* 217

(1985), and acknowledged in Williamson, supra, at 265–268 ("The Producer Cooperative Dilemma") and in Oliver Williamson, "Employee Ownership and Internal Governance: A Perspective," 6 *Journal of Economic Behavior and Organization* 243 (1985).

2. The concept of agency costs, and a useful subcategorization of those costs, were given broad currency in Michael Jensen and William Meckling, "Theory of the Firm: Managerial Behavior, Agency Costs, and Ownership Structure," 3 *Journal of Financial Economics* 305 (1976). As noted by Jensen and Meckling, a firm's managers have an incentive to "bond" themselves to the firm's owners by setting up mechanisms, such as independent audits, that will reduce the costs incurred by the owners in monitoring the managers. Jensen and Meckling break out such bonding costs as a separate category of agency costs. In contrast, bonding costs are here included within the first of our two categories of agency costs, the costs of monitoring.

3. The importance of the frequency of transacting in making "unified governance" (which essentially means ownership) an efficient form for transactional relationships has been given particular emphasis in Oliver Williamson, *The Economic Institutions of Capitalism* ch. 3 (1986).

4. Sometimes, especially where self-dealing is involved, the costs to the owners from managerial opportunism are matched by benefits received by the managers. The amounts involved are therefore merely transfers from the owners to the managers; they have no social cost. If they are foreseeable, owners may be able to adjust for them by reducing the managers' direct compensation accordingly. The more serious problem arises where, as seems common, the costs to the owners from managerial opportunism substantially exceed any private gains to the managers, thus resulting in a net efficiency loss to the patrons of the firm as a whole.

5. Incentive pay schemes, such as stock options, can also help align managers' interests with those of owners. But if the owners are not in direct control, they are presumably in a poor position to design the compensation mechanism. Indeed, there is widespread suspicion that so-called incentive pay schemes have frequently been designed more to divert profits opportunistically from owners to managers than to provide appropriate productivity incentives for the managers. Clearly this is the supposition behind the disclosure rules for executive compensation in publicly held companies adopted by the Securities and Exchange Commission (SEC) in 1992. For a more sanguine view of the potential, though not the practice, of incentive pay, see Michael Jensen and Kevin Murphy, "Performance Pay and Top Management Incentives," 98 *Journal of Political Economy* 225 (1990).

6. See also Michael Jensen and Eugene Fama, "Separation of Ownership and Control," 26 *Journal of Law and Economics* 301 (1983), which emphasizes that a board with outside directors may exercise a significant check on man-

agerial discretion even in nonprofit firms in which the directors are not in the service of owners.

7. See Henry Hansmann, "Why Do Universities Have Endowments?" 19 *Journal of Legal Studies* 3, 29–30 (1990).

8. Michael Jensen, "Agency Costs of Free Cash Flow, Corporate Finance, and Takeovers," 76 *American Economic Review* 323 (1986).

9. A significant exception is Michael Jensen and William Meckling, "Rights and Production Functions: An Application to Labor-Managed Firms and Co-determination," 52 *Journal of Business* 469 (1979), which refers to this issue as the "control problem." Jensen and Meckling do not analyze the issue in detail, observing simply that "no one today has a viable theory of . . . political processes," id. at 488–489, and suggesting that the problem of reconciling diverging interests may be an important obstacle to worker-managed firms. They also make the important observation, which will be reaffirmed below, that a significant source of the efficiency of investor-owned firms may be the limited opportunity those firms afford for giving an advantage to one group of owners at the expense of another. Id. at 494. Another important exception is Yoram Barzel and Tim Sass, "The Allocation of Resources by Voting," 105 *Quarterly Journal of Economics* 745 (1990). In contrast to this book and to the Jensen and Meckling article just cited, Barzel and Sass examine the costs of voting in private firms not principally with an eye to choice of the class of patrons to whom voting rights are given, but rather by focusing on the allocation of voting rights among patrons of a given class (condominium housing being the empirical application they develop).

10. See, for example, Kenneth Shepsle and Barry Weingast, "Political Solutions to Market Problems," 78 *American Political Science Review* 417 (1984).

11. In a voting cycle, the electorate's choices become intransitive and hence unstable. For example, in choosing among three alternative policies *a*, *b*, and *c*, there is a voting cycle if preferences among the voters are such as to lead them, in successive pairwise decisions, to adopt policy *b* over policy *a* and then policy *c* over policy *b*, but then to adopt policy *a* in preference to policy *c*, hence returning to where they began and finding themselves in an unending circle of choices.

12. See Charles Plott, "Axiomatic Social Choice Theory: An Overview and Interpretation," 20 *American Journal of Political Science* 532 (1976).

13. R. D. McKelvey, "Intransitivities in Multidimensional Voting Models and Some Implications for Agenda Control," 12 *Journal of Economic Theory* 472 (1976).

14. See, for example, Barry Weingast and William Marshall, "The Industrial Organization of Congress; or, Why Legislatures, Like Firms, Are Not Organized as Markets," 96 *Journal of Political Economy* 132 (1988).

15. That is, a decision criterion that is so conspicuous or conventional that,

though arbitrary, it serves as a natural point of agreement. See Thomas Schelling, *The Strategy of Conflict* (1961).

16. Rather surprisingly, the empirical literature on the difficulty of reaching decisions within heterogeneous groups is extremely thin. One well-documented example, however, is the extraordinary difficulty of organizing multiple owners of drilling rights in a common oil pool to manage the pool collectively even when the potential efficiency gains from collective operation are extremely large. Gary Libecap and Steven Wiggins, "Contractual Responses to the Common Pool," 74 *American Economic Review* 87 (1984). See also Ronald Johnson and Gary Libecap, "Contracting Problems and Regulation: The Case of the Fishery," 72 *American Economic Review* 1005 (1982), documenting the difficulty of reaching agreement on efficient regulation of a fishery when fishermen are heterogeneous with regard to fishing skill.

Elizabeth Hoffman and Matthew Spitzer, "Experimental Tests of the Coase Theorem with Large Bargaining Groups," 15 *Journal of Legal Studies* 149 (1986), report results in which even groups with as many as nineteen persons experienced little difficulty in agreeing collectively to contract on efficient terms with an opposing individual or group. In these experiments, however, all of the individuals within a given group faced essentially identical payoffs; consequently, the results do not provide much insight into situations in which interests differ significantly among the individuals involved.

17. See, for example, Robert Dahl, *A Preface to Economic Democracy* 153 (1985) ("self-government in work need not be justified entirely by its consequences, for, as in the state, it is justified as a matter of right"); Samuel Bowles and Herbert Gintis, *Democracy and Capitalism* 3–4 (1986) (stating that they "will not seek to justify" their "commitment" to democracy as a process).

18. See, for example, Gerald Frug, "The City as a Legal Concept," 93 *Harvard Law Review* 1059 (1980), which argues for a kind of urban socialism, in the form of city ownership of consumer enterprise such as insurance companies and banks, on the grounds that this will enhance "the ability of persons to participate actively in the basic societal decisions that structure their lives."

19. See P. Blumberg, "Alienation and Participation: Conclusions," in J. Vanek, ed., *Self-Management: Economic Liberation of Man* (1975).

20. For example, Carole Pateman, *Participation and Democratic Theory* (1970); M. Carnoy and D. Shearer, *Economic Democracy: The Challenge of the 1980s* 126–127 (1980); J. Rothschild and J. Whitt, *The Cooperative Workplace* 13 (1986); Dahl, supra, at 94–98.

21. Dahl, supra, at 134–135. See also Pateman, supra.

22. See, for example, Robert Dahl, "Power to the Workers?" *New York Review of Books*, November 19, 1970, at 20. Dahl himself prefers worker governance to such a system of "interest group management." Nevertheless, he argues that "interest group management would be an improvement over the present arrangements, and it may be what Americans will be content with, if

the corporation is to be reformed at all." Id. at 23. A more recent brief for stakeholder (especially worker) participation in corporate governance is Margaret Blair, *Ownership and Control* (1995). For a broad range of views, see the numerous articles in the "Special Issue on the Corporate Stakeholder Debate: The Classical Theory and Its Critics," 43 *University of Toronto Law Journal* 297–796 (1993).

23. In theory, there is no reason why the owners of a firm need bear any of the unavoidable risks associated with the enterprise, such as the risk of fluctuations in demand or in factor costs. Such risks could be passed on to insurers in return for fixed premiums, leaving the owners bearing only those fluctuations in earnings that are attributable to the owner's own decisions and efforts. But in fact it is often impossible to distinguish clearly between those variations in a firm's fortunes that are due to exogenous market factors and those that are due to the actions of the firm's owners, so that insurance would create an unacceptable degree of moral hazard. Consequently, it is generally practicable for the owners of a firm to purchase insurance against only very limited classes of risks, such as loss by fire.

24. In particular, the three considerations mentioned in the text here will be discussed in Chapter 5.

25. Albert Hirschman, *Exit, Voice, and Loyalty* (1970).

26. In effect, what is at stake here is a trade-off between high-powered and low-powered incentives. See Williamson, supra, passim; Bengt Holmstrom and Paul Milgrom, "Multitask Principal-Agent analyses: Incentive Contracts, Asset Ownership, and Job Design," 7 *Journal of Law, Economics, and Organization* (special issue) 24 (1991); Bengt Holmstrom and Paul Milgrom, "The Firm as an Incentive System," 84 *American Economic Review* 972 (1994). It may not be possible to give managers high-powered incentives to minimize costs without also giving them high-powered incentives to exploit patrons, and the latter incentives may lead to inefficiency where an important group of patrons can confront managers only with lower-powered countervailing incentives to serve those patrons' interests. In the latter circumstances, it may be better to give managers low-powered incentives for all their activities.

4. Investor-Owned Firms

1. This problem has long been recognized in the context of determining debt-equity ratios for investor-owned firms. See Michael Jensen and William Meckling, "Theory of the Firm: Managerial Behavior, Agency Costs, and Ownership Structure," 3 *Journal of Financial Economics* 305 (1976).

2. In a sense, such pledges of security in themselves make the owners investors in the firm. But it is not quite the same thing. Assets pledged as security, unlike assets actually invested in the firm, can be productively invested elsewhere.

3. This is not to say the device is not used. English corporation law, for example, makes provision for corporations limited by guarantee rather than by shares. In such corporations, the members' liability is limited by the amount of their guarantees, not by the amount they have invested (which might be nothing). See Geoffrey Morse, *Charlesworth & Cain's Company Law* 38–40 (12th ed. 1983). Similarly, in the early days of the American banking industry, state law sometimes made the shareholders of a bank liable to the bank's creditors for an amount equal to twice the shareholder's investment in the firm (that is, the shareholder would be personally liable for a sum equal to the amount he or she had invested in the firm, in addition to running the risk of losing that investment). Jonathan Macey and Geoffrey Miller, "Double Liability of Bank Shareholders: History and Implications," 27 *Wake Forest Law Review* 31 (1992).

4. See Frank Easterbrook and Daniel Fischel, *The Economic Structure of Corporate Law* ch. 2 (1991); Paul Halpern, Michael Trebilcock, and Stuart Trumbull, "An Economic Analysis of Limited Liability in Corporate Law," 30 *University of Toronto Law Journal* 117 (1980). This justification for limited liability toward contract creditors does not easily extend to tort creditors, for whom the doctrine of limited liability is today arguably inappropriate. See Henry Hansmann and Reinier Kraakman, "Toward Unlimited Shareholder Liability for Corporate Torts," 100 *Yale Law Journal* 1879 (1991).

5. See Clifford Smith and Jerold Warner, "On Financial Contracting: An Analysis of Bond Covenants," 7 *Journal of Financial Economics* 117 (1979).

6. Benjamin Klein, Robert Crawford, and Armen Alchian, "Vertical Integration, Appropriable Rents, and the Competitive Contracting Process," 21 *Journal of Law and Economics* 297, 321 (1978), seem to have been the first to have noted clearly that problems of opportunistic expropriation of firm-specific assets are an important reason "why the owners of the firm (the residual claimants) are generally also the major capitalists of the firm." Oliver Williamson, *The Economic Institutions of Capitalism* ch. 12 (1985), also focuses on this factor—and stresses it in a fashion that would seem to leave no room for any form of ownership other than the conventional investor-owned firm.

7. See Lucian Bebchuk and Howard Chang, "Bargaining and Division of Value in Corporate Reorganization," 8 *Journal of Law, Economics, and Organization* 253 (1992); Philippe Aghion, Oliver Hart, and John Moore, "The Economics of Bankruptcy Reform," 8 *Journal of Law, Economics, and Organization* 523 (1992).

8. Mark Roe, *Strong Managers, Weak Owners: The Political Roots of American Corporate Finance* 173 (1994).

9. For a survey of the evidence on the current passivity of shareholders, including large institutional investors, and the possibility that they might be brought to behave more actively in the future, see Bernard Black, "Agents

Notes to Pages 57–60

Watching Agents: The Promise of Institutional Investor Voice," 39 *UCLA Law Review* 811 (1992); Bernard Black, "The Value of Institutional Investor Monitoring: The Empirical Evidence," 39 *UCLA Law Review* 897 (1992).

10. The work of Mark Roe, supra, has been of signal importance in demonstrating this; see also Bernard Black, "Shareholder Passivity Reexamined," 89 *Michigan Law Review* 520 (1990).

11. The SEC's 1992 amendments to the proxy rules have, however, relaxed these constraints somewhat.

12. See Roe, supra, ch. 11.

13. For a survey of the agency problem in corporate governance and its potential solutions, with attention to cross-national comparisons, see Andrei Shleifer and Robert Vishny, "A Survey of Corporate Governance," National Bureau of Economic Research Working Paper no. 5554 (April 1996).

14. The classic statement of this view is Henry Manne, "Mergers and the Market for Corporate Control," 75 *Journal of Political Economy* 110 (1965). See also Michael Jensen, "Takeovers: Their Causes and Consequences," 2 *Journal of Economic Perspectives* 21 (1988).

15. See Sanjay Bhagat, Andrei Shleifer, and Robert Vishny, "Hostile Takeovers in the 1980s: The Return to Corporate Specialization," *Brookings Papers on Economic Activity: Microeconomics* (special issue) 1 (1990); Michael Jensen, "The Modern Industrial Revolution, Exit, and the Failure of Internal Control Systems," 48 *Journal of Finance* 831 (1993).

16. See Gregg Jarrell, James Brickley, and Jeffry Netter, "The Market for Corporate Control: The Empirical Evidence Since 1980," 2 *Journal of Economic Perspectives* 49 (1988).

17. See Bhagat, Shleifer, and Vishny, supra.

18. John Pound, "The Rise of the Political Model of Corporate Governance and Corporate Control," 68 *New York University Law Review* 1003 (1993). This is not to say that hostile acquisitions of control through share purchases did not occur before 1956, but only that a controlling block of stock had to be accumulated through individual trades. It is quite possible that acquisitions of this character long played a significant disciplining role for managers. Id.

19. See Joseph Grundfest, "Subordination of American Capital," 27 *Journal of Financial Economics* 89 (1990).

20. As dramatically illustrated by the diagram of cross-shareholdings in the Allianz group that is reproduced in Theodor Baums, "Corporate Governance in Germany—System and Recent Developments," in Mats Isaksson and Rolf Skog, *Aspects of Corporate Governance* (1994).

21. Steven Kaplan, "Top Executives, Turnover, and Firm Performance in Germany," 10 *Journal of Law, Economics, and Organization* 142 (1994).

22. See Randall Morck, Andrei Shleifer, and Robert Vishny, "Management

Ownership and Market Valuation: An Empirical Analysis," 20 *Journal of Financial Economics* 293 (1988); Karen Wruck, "Equity Ownership Concentration and Firm Value," 23 *Journal of Financial Economics* 3 (1989); John McConnell and Henri Servaes, "Additional Evidence on Equity Ownership and Corporate Value," 27 *Journal of Financial Economics* 595 (1990).

23. In investor-owned firms, the problem of managerial opportunism may also be mitigated by the fact that, when it comes to investment policy, there is good reason to believe that—contrary to the behavior to be expected of owners who are not investors—the managers will be too conservative rather than too speculative, since their own human capital is on the line if the firm goes bankrupt. See, for example, Yakov Amihud and Baruch Lev, "Risk Reduction as a Managerial Motive for Conglomerate Mergers," 12 *Bell Journal of Economics* 605 (1981).

24. See, for example, Fabrizio Barca, "On Corporate Governance in Italy: Issues, Facts, and Agenda" (Research Department, Bank of Italy, 1995).

25. The only firms that we see that have roughly the character of nonprofit firms operated for the benefit of their investors are business corporations that are wholly owned by nonprofit corporations and that are used by the nonprofits as a source of income. The most famous example of such a firm in the United States is the Mueller Macaroni Company, which for roughly thirty-five years was wholly owned by New York University. Such firms are subject to the corporate income tax just like any other business corporation; the tax exemption of their nonprofit parent corporation does not extend to them. Consequently, they have no special subsidies, and differ from their competitors in the market simply in the fact that they are controlled by nonprofit holding companies.

26. Cf. Harry DeAngelo, "Competition and Unanimity," 71 *American Economic Review* 18 (1981).

27. Sometimes business corporations are designed so that voting control will shift from one class of securityholders to another upon the occurrence of specified events. For example, voting control may be designed to pass automatically from holders of a company's common stock to holders of its preferred stock if the company fails to pay dividends on its preferred stock for a given number of years, and then to pass back to the common stockholders after a stated amount of dividends on the preferred stock have been paid. Still, at any one time there is typically only one class of securities that votes.

28. Other companies that have issued targeted stock are USX (1991), Ralston Purina (1993), and Pittston (1993).

29. *Proxy Statement*, USX Corporation, April 4, 1991; Aaron Pressman, "Targeted Stock: Still Wide of the Mark," *Investment Dealers' Digest*, June 29, 1992, at 16.

30. See Pressman, supra; Stephanie Strom, "It's Called Targeted Stock; Shun It, Some Experts Say," *New York Times*, July 12, 1994, at D1.

31. See Patrick Maio, "Executive Update," *Investor's Business Daily*, February 8, 1994.

32. Conspicuously Michael Jensen, "The Eclipse of the Public Corporation," *Harvard Business Review* 61 (September–October 1989).

33. Steven Kaplan, "The Staying Power of Leveraged Buyouts," 29 *Journal of Financial Economics* 217 (1991).

34. An analogous situation, discussed in Chapter 12, involved the absence of a market in the United States for long-term (greater than seven-year) home mortgages before the federal government insured them in the 1930s. The mortgage insurance encouraged banks to experiment, the experiments demonstrated that the mortgages were good investments, and ultimately banks were willing to offer long-term mortgages even without the insurance (which had proved profitable for the government).

35. Although the firm that played the most conspicuous role in this respect—Drexel, Burnham, Lambert—ultimately collapsed.

5. The Benefits and Costs of Employee Ownership

1. See generally K. Berman, *Worker-Owned Plywood Companies* (1967); Edward S. Greenberg, "Producer Cooperatives and Democratic Theory: The Case of the Plywood Cooperatives," in R. Jackall and H. Levin, eds., *Worker Cooperatives in America* 175 (1984).

2. Greenberg, supra, at 175.

3. See Jackall and Levin, "Historical Perspectives on Worker Cooperatives," in R. Jackall and H. Levin, eds., *Worker Cooperatives in America* 35 (1984); Derek C. Jones, "American Producer Cooperatives and Employee-Owned Firms: A Historical Perspective," in id. at 37.

4. "Taxi cooperatives are currently operating in virtually every large American city in which local authorities permit these organizations to be formed. They are absent only from cities in which cooperatives are illegal, because local governments have granted monopolies to competing ownership forms." R. Russell, *Sharing Ownership in the Workplace* 141 (1985).

5. Id., ch. 3.

6. Because a survivorship test can plausibly be employed only in free-enterprise market economies, the discussion below largely ignores the experience with employee control of enterprise in those countries—such as the (formerly) communist countries of Asia and Eastern Europe—in which the state has precluded meaningful choice among organizational forms. In particular, we shall devote little attention to Yugoslavia's extensive experience with

employee-managed enterprise. The analysis developed here nevertheless provides a useful perspective on the Yugoslavian experiment.

7. R. Oakeshott, *The Case for Workers' Co-ops* 145–146 (1978).

8. Mark Holmstrom, *Industrial Democracy in Italy: Workers Co-ops and the Self-Management Debate* 6 (1989); see Oakeshott, supra, at 123.

9. Holmstrom, supra, at 21; see also Oakeshott, supra, at 146.

10. See Holmstrom, supra, at 21; Oakeshott, supra, at 129, 146.

11. Oakeshott, supra, at 124, 146; Alberto Zevi, "The Performance of Italian Producer Cooperatives," in D. Jones and J. Svejnar, eds., *Participatory and Self-Managed Firms: Evaluative Economic Experience* 239, 241 (1982).

12. Oakeshott, supra, at 129, 150, 157.

13. See id. at 130, 160.

14. Zevi, supra, at 243.

15. See, for example, Oakeshott, supra, at 108–120.

16. W. Whyte and K. Whyte, *Making Mondragon: The Growth and Dynamics of the Worker Cooperative Complex* 3 (1988).

17. Commission on the Swedish Cooperative Movement and Its Role in Society, *The Co-operative Movement in Society* (1979).

18. Indeed, there is only one Swedish manufacturing industry, fur and leather goods, in which more than 5 percent of the firms are worker cooperatives, and even there they account for only 6.5 percent of all firms. B. Lee, *Productivity and Employee Ownership: The Case of Sweden* 10 (1988).

19. Moreover, this has been the case in the territory that is now the state of Israel since the 1920s. Over the intervening decades, the various separate bus transport cooperatives have gradually merged into a single monopoly. Egged A. Daniel, *Labor Enterprises in Israel* 235–254 (1976).

20. Id. at 220.

21. Id. at 219–220.

22. See Adam Bryant, "After Seven Years, Employees Win United Airlines," *New York Times*, July 13, 1994, at 1. Originally, United's pilots sought to purchase the airline by themselves. See, for example, "United's Pilots Are Inching Closer to a Coup," *Business Week*, August 31, 1987, at 32; "Pilots Renew Bid to Buy Out Parent Company of United," *Aviation Week and Space Technology*, May 9, 1988, at 95.

23. Armen Alchian and Harold Demsetz, "Production, Information Costs, and Economic Organization," 62 *American Economic Review* 777 (1972). See also, for example, Michael Jensen and William Meckling, "Rights and Production Functions: An Application to Labor-Managed Firms and Codetermination," 52 *Journal of Business* 469 (1979); Raymond Russell, "Employee Ownership and Employee Governance," 6 *Journal of Economic Behavior and Organization* 217 (1985).

24. Alchian amd Demsetz (1972), supra, at 786.

25. Id. at 790.

26. Fred S. McChesney, "Team Production, Monitoring, and Profit Sharing in Law Firms: An Alternative Hypothesis," 11 *Journal of Legal Studies* 379 (1982), makes a similar argument regarding the Alchian and Demsetz monitoring theory. McChesney offers the alternative theory that lawyer ownership of law firms provides a necessary incentive for senior lawyers to undertake the promotional efforts necessary to attract business to the firm. "Profit sharing in law firms might be explained as akin to a salesman's commission in rewarding promotional factors in professional firms." Id. at 390. In essence, however, this is just a special case of the high-cost-of-monitoring theory. Undoubtedly employee ownership improves incentives for promotional efforts. Yet this factor seems inadequate in itself to explain the prevalence of employee ownership among law firms as opposed to other types of firms. It is not difficult to determine which clients were brought to the firm by which lawyers and thus to reward the lawyers simply by salary for their promotional efforts. Indeed, the productivity formulas by which many law firms set partner incomes, discussed further in Chapter 6, often do this explicitly. Moreover, not all partners play an important role in attracting business. Finally, there are many other industries in which attracting new clients is a major part of the job, but in which the employees responsible for this are not made owners.

27. There is some anecdotal evidence—for example, from the plywood industry—that employee ownership improves productivity. See, for example, Greenberg, supra, at 175–176. Efforts to obtain explicit empirical measures of the effect of employee ownership on employee productivity have so far been inconclusive, however. The evidence available to date, taken as a whole, suggests that profit-sharing alone has a weak positive effect on productivity. Martin Weitzman and Douglas Kruse, "Profit Sharing and Productivity," in Alan Blinder, ed., *Paying for Productivity: A Look at the Evidence* 95 (1990). Some studies suggest further that employee control has a positive effect on productivity beyond that which can be obtained simply with profit sharing, although the results are ambiguous and are clouded by the absence of a straightforward comparison between employee-controlled and investor-controlled firms. See, for example, D. Jones and J. Svejnar, "Participation, Profit Sharing, Worker Ownership and Efficiency in Italian Producer Cooperatives," 52 *Economica* 449 (1985); D. Jones, "British Producer Cooperatives, 1948–1968: Productivity and Organizational Structure," in Jones and Svejnar, supra, at 175.

28. This does not necessarily mean that the employees become much more productive and thus much harder for their employer to replace. It could equally well result if, over time, employees simply lose some of the general skills and the flexibility for retraining that they had at the beginning of their

work careers. Sometimes, of course, it is the employer who has a transaction-specific investment in the employee—for example, where the employer has invested in training that makes the employee more valuable to the firm than a new employee would be. In that case, the problem is the reverse: the employee is in a position to act opportunistically toward the firm. And, if both the employer and the employee have made transaction-specific investments, there remains the possibility that bargaining will be costly, since the parties stand in a situation of bilateral monopoly.

Pointing specifically to the need to protect employees' investments in firm-specific human capital, Margaret Blair, *Ownership and Control* (1995), argues for a policy of giving employees increased ownership rights in the corporations they work for, via larger employee shareholdings and employee representation on the board of directors. Her proposal is for only partial worker ownership, with investor shareholders retaining an important role. She does not directly address the question, discussed in the following chapter, of how, and how well, shared governance between investors and employees might work in practice.

29. Taxicab drivers may, however, experience some degree of lock-in. In many towns taxicab companies have substantial monopoly power. Thus a taxi driver may be forced to move to another town if he wishes to seek alternative employment. Such a move will not only cost him whatever investment he and his family have made in personal relationships in the community, but will also cost him his accumulated experience with the community's streets and traffic patterns.

30. Gilson and Mnookin note that lawyers who are insufficiently prominent to achieve substantial individual reputations outside their firms may experience a degree of lock-in owing to the fact that their present firm has much better information about their productivity than does any prospective new employer. Ronald Gilson and Robert Mnookin, "Coming of Age in a Corporate Law Firm: The Economics of Associate Career Patterns," 41 *Stanford Law Review* 567, 576–578 (1989). But even if this is true, it would seem much easier for a lawyer to demonstrate her competence to a prospective new employer than it would be for a manager in a large industrial firm.

31. For a survey of theoretical models and their fit with empirical data, see John Kennan and Robert Wilson, "Strategic Bargaining Models and Interpretation of Strike Data," 4 *Journal of Applied Econometrics* (supplement) S87 (1989).

32. It is apparently for reasons such as those stated here and in Chapter 4 that Gregory Dow, "Why Capital Hires Labor: A Bargaining Perspective," 83 *American Economic Review* 118 (1993), assumes without extensive discussion that an employee-owned firm is incapable of raising capital with which to purchase firm-specific assets—an assumption that is key to his conclusion that

an investor-owned firm can survive even when a labor-owned firm would (if feasible) produce a larger social surplus.

33. Personal correspondence from Terence Martin, March 1995.

34. Empirical studies seeking to link various indices of worker ownership or control to capital intensity have been largely inconclusive; they are judiciously surveyed in John Bonin, Derek Jones, and Louis Putterman, "Theoretical and Empirical Studies of Producer Cooperatives: Will Ever the Twain Meet," 31 *Journal of Economic Literature* 1290 (1993).

35. To be sure, if all of a firm's equity securities are held by its employees, they may no longer be evaluated and priced by the securities markets. Consequently, the firm will be subject to less monitoring by those markets than would be the case for a publicly held firm, and the market for corporate control may be less effective in policing the firm than if it were a publicly held investor-owned firm.

36. Greenberg, supra, at 175.

37. This is not, however, universally true. For example, some of the advertising and investment banking firms that have converted from partnership form to investor ownership in recent decades are now publicly traded firms.

38. Berman, supra, at 33–38.

39. Indeed, "adjustment through layoffs is substantially greater in unionized firms than in comparable nonunionized firms." James Medoff, "Layoffs and Alternatives under Trade Unions in U.S. Manufacturing," 69 *American Economic Review* 380 (1979).

40. In particular, collective bargaining may contribute importantly to the low level of job security in American industry. The prevailing seniority systems of job tenure give the elder half of a firm's employees an incentive to support a union bargaining stance that exchanges high wages for low job security, and thereby join with the firm's investor-owners in putting onto the firm's younger employees much of the risk of the enterprise. And, where the same union negotiates on behalf of the employees in all firms in an industry, competition among those firms cannot be relied on to eliminate even highly inefficient contractual arrangements of this sort. See Medoff, supra.

41. Low productivity could result from the reduced incentive for effort on the part of employees who have substantial job security or, perhaps more important, from the reduction in efficient reallocation of employees among firms.

42. Eirik Furubotn, "The Long-Run Analysis of the Labor-Managed Firm: An Alternative Interpretation," 66 *American Economic Review* 104 (1976); Jensen and Meckling (1979), supra.

43. Indeed, holders of the shares need not be currently employed at the firm. But since dividends are rarely paid on the shares, they are of little value to anyone who is not an employee. Berman, supra, at 148, 150.

44. This assumes that employees generally stay with the same firm for life. If we exclude a trial period of a few years at the beginning (during which an employee need not be made a voting member of an employee-owned firm), this may have been a roughly accurate assumption in many industries for much of the twentieth century (however much the situation may be different at present).

45. A prominent example is the Vermont Asbestos Group, a failing subsidiary of GAF that was sold to its employees in lieu of closing in 1975 and then, because of a dramatic improvement in its product market, became highly profitable. In 1978, the employees sold enough of their stock to a local businessman to enable him to assume control of the firm. M. Carnoy and D. Shearer, *Economic Democracy: The Challenge of the 1980s* 152–157 (1980).

46. A typical example from the literature advocating employee ownership is J. Rothschild and J. Whitt, *The Cooperative Workplace* 179–181 (1986). The most general analytic discussions of the issue are Avner Ben-Ner, "On the Stability of the Cooperative Type of Organization," 8 *Journal of Comparative Economics* 247 (1984); Hajime Miyazaki, "On Success and Dissolution of the Labor-Managed Firm in the Capitalist Economy," 92 *Journal of Political Economy* 909 (1984).

47. The argument is offered by Ben-Ner, supra, and by Miyazaki, supra.

48. If a new employee is brought into an established firm as an owner with a share in future profits equal to that of the already-existing members, and if the new employee is not required to make a capital contribution to the firm upon joining, there will be a redistribution of value from the existing members to the new one (or at least this will be the case if the firm has accumulated value in such forms as capital or goodwill). If these were the only terms on which a new member could be added to the firm, then there would of course be a strong incentive either to add new employees only as salaried employees or not to expand employment at all, even if employees were more productive as owners than as mere employees. The solution is either to give new members a smaller share in earnings than their counterparts who joined the firm earlier, or to require that new members make a capital contribution through which they effectively purchase a share in the firm's accumulated value from the already-existing members.

Since the former solution—which may lead to different profit shares for employees who have similar roles in the firm—may accentuate the governance problems discussed in Chapter 6, it is not surprising that, instead, established employee-owned firms commonly require capital contributions from new members. In some cases these contributions may be disguised a bit. For example, the much larger shares in profits given older partners in law firms, and the granting of a substantial share in a law firm's profits to semi-retired older partners, may be a means by which the younger partners effectively compensate the older partners for the firm's accumulated goodwill.

49. See K. Bradley and A. Gelb, *Worker Capitalism: The New Industrial Relations* 35–36 (1983).

50. Benjamin Ward, "The Firm in Illyria: Market Syndicalism," 48 *American Economic Review* 566 (1958).

51. For a concise and thoughtful survey of Ward's model, the literature it has spawned, and the efforts to test it empirically, see Bonin, Jones, and Putterman, supra.

52. American Bar Association, Model Rules of Professional Conduct Rule 5.4, reprinted in T. Morgan and R. Rotunda, *1988 Selected Standards on Professional Responsibility* 82, 159–160 (1988); American Bar Association, Model Code of Professional Responsibility DR 3–102(A), DR3–103(A), DR5–107(C) (1981), reprinted in Morgan and Rotunda, supra, at 1, 29, 30, 42 (1988); American Bar Association, Canons of Professional Ethics Canons 33, 34, 35 (1908), reprinted in Morgan and Rotunda, supra, at 379, 388–389.

53. The Rules, like the Code that preceded them, are typically adopted by the states through judicial rather than legislative action. See C. Wolfram, *Modern Legal Ethics* 56–57, 62–63 (1986). Most states have adopted some form of the Model Rules, and of these nearly all have followed Rule 5.4 without significant variation. ABA/BNA Lawyer's Manual on Professional Conduct Par. 01:3, 91:401 (1990).

54. When the Model Rules were adopted in 1983, the original draft called for eliminating this restriction. Ultimately, however, the ABA rejected the reform. G. Hazard and W. Hodes, *The Law of Lawyering* 469 (1989).

55. For example, the Wisconsin cooperative corporation statute, in providing that net earnings are to be paid to the corporation's "patrons," seems to impose no limitations that would prevent the organization's employees from being classified as its "patrons." Wis. Stat. Ann. §185.45 (West 1957).

56. David Ellerman and Peter Pitegoff, "The Democratic Corporation: The New Employee Cooperative Corporation Statute in Massachusetts," 11 *New York University Review of Law and Social Change* 441 (1983). Firms of service professionals are generally required to be formed as partnerships or under special professional corporation statutes in order to preserve personal liability for professional torts.

57. For example, of the four cooperatives involved in the tax cases cited in the following notes, two were incorporated under cooperative corporation statutes (one in Oregon and one in Washington) and two were incorporated under business corporation statutes (one in Oregon and one in Washington).

58. *Olympia Veneer Co., Inc., v. Commissioner,* 22 B.T.A. 892 (1931) (worker cooperative can deduct patronage dividend as wages even if, with the dividend, the effective hourly wage received by the members substantially exceeds that

prevailing in the industry, since members of cooperatives are more productive than hired employees).

59. *Linnton Plywood Assoc. v. U.S.*, 410 F. Supp. 1100 (D. Ore. 1976); *Linnton Plywood Assoc. v. U.S.*, 236 F. Supp. 227 (D. Ore. 1964); *Puget Sound Plywood, Inc., v. Commissioner*, 44 T.C. 305 (1965). More precisely, Subchapter T permits the exclusion from gross income, for purposes of the corporate income tax, of all net earnings that derive from work performed by members (as opposed to hired workers) in a worker cooperative and that are "allocated" to members, whether or not actually paid out.

60. See Chapter 6.

61. For example, Carnoy and Shearer, supra, at 144, 188.

6. Governing Employee-Owned Firms

1. See Robert Dahl, *A Preface to Economic Democracy* 94–98 (1985). The sad experience of Yugoslavia, which, after having a form of worker management imposed throughout its economy for three decades, quickly collapsed into viciously warring ethnic groups when communist rule ended, also throws some doubt on the effectiveness of worker control of enterprise as training for political democracy.

2. See Mayer G. Freed, Daniel D. Polsby, and Matthew L. Spitzer, "Unions, Fairness, and the Conundrums of Collective Choice," 56 *Southern California Law Review* 461 (1983).

3. Edward S. Greenberg, "Producer Cooperatives and Democratic Theory: The Case of the Plywood Cooperatives," in R. Jackall and H. Levin, eds., *Worker Cooperatives in America* 175, 206 (1984).

4. The discussion in the text emphasizes the importance of homogeneity in the roles played by the employee-owners within the firm. But similarity in culture and personal values among the employee-owners is evidently also important in making employee self-governance viable. See J. Rothschild and J. Whitt, *The Cooperative Workplace* 95–100 (1986). As observed below, the shared Basque culture may have been important in aiding the success of the Mondragon cooperatives.

5. For example, internal dissension seems to have been an important reason why the employees at the Vermont Asbestos Group ultimately sold control of their firm to an outside investor: "[T]he experience of bickering and inconclusive meetings convinced many of them that a system with '180 bosses' cannot work." M. Carnoy and D. Shearer, *Economic Democracy: The Challenge of the 1980s* 157 (1980). See also John Simmons and William Mares, *Working Together* 119–123 (1983). Raymond Russell, *Sharing Ownership in the Workplace* (1985), provides substantial anecdotal evidence of serious conflicts among employee owners, particularly over division of earnings, in three different

types of firms: scavenger (garbage collection) companies, id. at 81–83; taxi cooperatives, id. at 107, 111–114; and professional group practices in law and medicine, id. at 156–157, 184. Indeed, Russell generalizes: "The politics of sharing income appears to be the most volatile issue across all three sets of firms. In some cases, income sharing is equal, in others it is unequal, but in all cases a consensus is required that the existing compensation system is fair. When that consensus is lost, members are quick to express their sense of injustice either by storming out of the organization in a huff, or by fomenting revolution in their firms." Id. at 181. The conversion of the investment banking partnership of Lehman Brothers to investor ownership, discussed below, provides another example.

6. K. Berman, *Worker-Owned Plywood Companies* 151–156 (1967); Greenberg, supra, at 178.

7. R. Gilson and R. Mnookin, "Sharing among the Human Capitalists: An Economic Inquiry into the Corporate Law Firm and How Partners Split Profits," 37 *Stanford Law Review* 313 (1985).

8. This conclusion is reinforced by the tendency of lawyers to gather in firms in which they share the same specialty and have similar clients—as in firms of patent lawyers, labor lawyers, and so on. If lawyers were highly risk averse, one would expect to see a much stronger tendency toward firms that are highly diversified in terms of both specialties and clients.

9. Members of university faculties, which are employee-governed enterprises of a sort, are familiar with similar phenomena. For example, there is a strong tendency to equalize teaching loads within a given faculty, with respect to both number and nature of courses, regardless of the relative productivities of different individuals as teachers and scholars. Individuals, such as clinical faculty at professional schools, who must for curricular reasons be assigned a different mix of teaching responsibilities, may be given tenure but are commonly denied full voting rights. See Geoffrey Hazard, "Curriculum Structure and Faculty Structure," 35 *Journal of Legal Education* 326, 331–332 (1985).

10. This is true, moreover, of some of the firms that hold themselves out as being among the most progressive in their flexibility in permitting associates to work part time. See, for example, testimony of Antonia Grumbach of New York's Patterson, Belknap, Webb & Tyler before the A.B.A. Commission on Women in the Profession (Feb. 6–7, 1988).

11. Laurel Sorenson, "Life beyond the Law Office," 70 *A.B.A.J.* 68 (July 1984).

12. How does a firm determine, for example, how much and what kind of work is required to earn 60 percent of the amount a full-time partner would receive? Simply billing 60 percent as many hours to clients as the average full-time partner might be thought insufficient. For example, the firm may incur fixed costs, such as health insurance or office space and equipment, that

do not vary with a partner's billable hours. Or perhaps for most partners the first 60 percent of the hours worked in a given week are the easy ones to give up, while it is the other 40 percent, which often require working evenings and weekends and adjusting one's personal life, that are most begrudged and thus should be compensated at the highest marginal rate. So perhaps, to receive a 60 percent draw, one should be required to bill 75 percent—or 65 percent, or 85 percent—of the hours that a full-time partner bills. Objective criteria for making such a decision are likely to be lacking, and any choice therefore threatens to be contentious.

13. Robert Frank, "Are Workers Paid Their Marginal Products?" 74 *American Economic Review* 549, 549 (1984).

14. The same tendency to judge one's wages in relation to one's co-workers' can also lead to an inefficient rat race as each worker seeks to advance relative to the others, with the result that all work harder while their relative status in the firm remains unchanged. See Robert Frank, *Choosing the Right Pond: Human Behavior and the Quest for Status* (1985). Where all workers are paid the same, however, there is no incentive for such a rat race. Consequently, if sharing ownership significantly increases the tendency to judge one's welfare in relation to that of one's fellow workers, then rules of equal pay should be more common among employee-owned firms than among investor-owned firms.

15. See Peter Bart, "Advertising: Debate Rages on 'Going Public,'" *New York Times*, May 11, 1962, at 40, col. 2; Lawrence, "On Going Public," *New York Times*, Oct. 4, 1970, §III, at 13, col. 1; Lipman, "Young & Rubicam Operations in U.S. to Be Partnership," *Wall Street Journal*, Nov. 22, 1988, at B6, col. 4; Rothenberg, "Public Shop or Private, What's Best?" *New York Times*, May 9, 1989.

16. For example, even by 1979 only twelve of the forty largest investment banking firms (in terms of capital) were organized as partnerships. (Figures compiled from Securities Industry Association, *Securities Industry Yearbook* (1980).)

17. Although early HMOs were predominantly nonprofit, the recent trend has been strongly toward the for-profit form. As of March 1988, 47.6 percent of HMOs were for-profit rather than nonprofit, and 82.6 percent of plans less than two years old were for-profit. Interstudy, *The Interstudy Edge: Quarterly Report of HMO Growth and Enrollment as of March 31, 1988* 1 (1988). There appear to be no accurate data on the percentage of for-profit HMOs that are investor-owned rather than doctor-owned. Investor-owned HMOs are, however, common. For example, Prudential Insurance Company operates a chain of more than one hundred HMOs nationwide, many of which are directly owned by Prudential. Telephone interview with Kathy Nelson, Prudential Insurance plan reviewer (March 22, 1989).

18. *See* K. Auletta, *Greed and Glory on Wall Street* (1986).

19. *See* "Brains versus Brawn," *Institutional Investor* 156–158, 161–162 (May 1988).

20. Id. at 162.

21. See Gerald Kramer, "On a Class of Equilibrium Conditions for Majority Rule," 41 *Econometrica* 285 (1973).

22. The search for procedural mechanisms that can yield stable voting equilibria has, in fact, become a major focus of theoretical work in political science at least since Kenneth Shepsle's "Institutional Arrangements and Equilibrium in Multidimensional Voting Models," 23 *American Journal of Political Science* 27–59 (1979).

23. H. Thomas and C. Logan, *Mondragon: An Economic Analysis* 96–130 (1982).

24. R. Oakeshott, *The Case for Workers' Co-ops* 188 (1978); Thomas and Logan, supra, at 25–29; W. Whyte and K. Whyte, *Making Mondragon: The Growth and Dynamics of the Worker Cooperative Complex* 35–38 (1988).

25. W. Whyte and K. Whyte, supra, at 40.

26. Id. at 71. In light of the observations above about the tendency of employee-owned firms to adopt equal sharing rules, it is interesting to note that although the Mondragon cooperatives have not adopted equal wages as the norm, they have until recently deliberately kept the spread between the highest and lowest wages in the firm compressed to a 3-to-1 ratio. Employees toward the bottom of the wage scale receive wages roughly equal to those prevailing in the local economy; it is therefore on skilled employees, and particularly managers, that the compressed wage binds. To retain managers, the wage spread has recently been increased to 4.5 to 1, with consequences that are not yet clear. Id. at 45. These constraints on the wage spread apply only to employees who are members of the cooperative, however. Firms are free to employ up to 10 percent of their workers simply as hired employees who are not members, and this authority is used to hire skilled employees who must be paid a wage higher than that which can be paid members. Id. at 203.

27. This is in fact a requirement that Spanish law imposes on all cooperatives and did not originate within Mondragon. Id. at 42.

28. Id. at 69–71; Thomas and Logan, supra, at 149–158.

29. Personal correspondence from Terence Martin, April 1995.

30. W. Whyte and K. Whyte, supra, at 69.

31. Id. at 75. During 1983, for example, the bank intervened in the affairs of the constituent cooperatives on thirty-four occasions. In the process, it replaced two chief executive officers, the chairpersons of three boards of directors, and six department managers. Id. at 172.

32. This is reflected, for example, in the experience surrounding the 1974 strike at Ulgor, the largest of the Mondragon cooperatives. The changes in

firm policies that precipitated the strike, the (quite severe) response of the firm to the strikers, and the reforms in the social council undertaken after the strike all seem to have been undertaken by the firm's management acting largely on its own and not under the direct influence of the firm's rank and file. *See* W. Whyte and K. Whyte, supra, at 91–107; see also id. at 113–127 (describing the introduction of more participative forms of shop-floor work organization as being initiated by management).

33. Id. at 68–69. An important test of the Mondragon system will be whether leadership can be passed on successfully from its founders to the next generation.

34. Oakeshott, supra, at 205; Thomas and Logan, supra, at 35, 92.

35. Personal correspondence from Terence Martin, April 1995.

36. Id.

37. See W. Whyte and K. Whyte, supra, at 9–12, 255–256.

38. There is, however, a similar organization in Valencia, modeled explicitly on Mondragon. Formed in 1988, by the end of 1993 it encompassed nine firms with a total of over 2,500 workers. Martin, supra.

39. Oakeshott, supra, at 146.

40. Id. at 146, 154, 160, 162.

41. Id. at 124, 126, 150; Mark Holmstrom, *Industrial Democracy in Italy: Workers Co-ops and the Self-Management Debate* 25 (1989).

42. See generally Holmstrom, supra.

43. Oakeshott, supra, at 162–163; see Holmstrom, supra, at 57.

44. Id. at 141, 154; Alberto Zevi, "The Performance of Italian Producer Cooperatives," in D. Jones and J. Svejnar, eds., *Participatory and Self-Managed Firms: Evaluative Economic Experience* 242 (1982).

45. Holmstrom, supra, at 28, 92, 138.

46. Oakeshott, supra, at 52–73.

47. Id. at 74–107.

48. Id. at 74.

49. The 1980s brought many management buyouts of firms whose stock had previously been publicly traded. In these transactions, the firm is converted to private ownership through the repurchase of all of its stock by a group including the firm's senior management. The resulting firms might appear to be instances of a reductive form of employee ownership in which the employee-owners are confined to the firm's managers. As it is, however, these firms do not provide much evidence concerning the viability of employee ownership. Typically only a very small number of managers participate in the ownership of these firms, and these managers come from a fairly narrow stratum of the firm's employees. Further, the managers' share in ownership is often modest. In one sample of fifty-eight management buyouts, for example, the officers of the median firm already owned 11.5 percent of the firm's equity

before the transaction and increased this only to 16.7 percent afterward; other investors continued to hold the great bulk of the firm's stock. A. Smith, "Corporate Ownership Structure and Performance: The Case of Management Buyouts," 27 *Journal of Financial Economics* 143 (1990).

50. U.S. General Accounting Office, *Employee Stock Ownership Plans: Benefits and Costs of ESOP Tax Incentives for Broadening Stock Ownership* 18, 39 (1986).

51. "ESOPs: Are They Good for You?" *Business Week*, May 15, 1989, at 166, 118.

52. *See* J. Blasi, *Employee Ownership: Revolution or Ripoff?* 4 (1988) (estimating that as of his writing there were approximately 1,000 to 1,500 companies, with total of one million workers, in which an ESOP holds at least 51 percent of the company's stock).

53. See L. Kelso and M. Adler, *The Capitalist Manifesto* (1958); Granadas, "Employee Stock Ownership Plans: An Analysis of Current Reform Proposals," 14 *Journal of Law Reform* 15 (1980).

54. For a review of the tax and corporate finance advantages of ESOPs prior to the Tax Reform Act of 1986, see Richard Doernberg and Jonathan Macey, *ESOPs and Economic Distortion*, 23 *Harvard Journal of Legislation* 103 (Winter 1986). With the exception of the Tax Credit ESOPs, which were already slated for extinction after 1986, the 1986 act reaffirmed and extended somewhat the preexisting tax subsidies to ESOPs (the most important of which was the exclusion from taxable income of 50 percent of the interest income from loans to ESOPs, I.R.C. § 133) and added some new subsidies (including, prominently, a 50 percent exclusion from estate tax for the proceeds from the sale of stock to an ESOP or "eligible worker-owned cooperative," I.R.C. § 2057).

55. See, for example, *Shamrock Holdings, Inc., v. Polaroid, Fed. Sec. L. Rep. (CCH)* ¶ 94,176 (Del. Ch. Jan. 6, 1989, as amended Mar. 20, 1989) (permitting creation of ESOP as takeover defense under particular circumstances).

56. For a review of the literature, see Blasi, supra, ch. 8 and app. D.

57. Although the median ESOP holds 10 percent of the total stock of the sponsoring company, it holds only 5 percent of the voting rights. U.S. General Accounting Office, supra, at 39–40.

58. More precisely, this is the case for voting on the election of directors and other routine matters. The tax code requires that, even in closely held corporations, the votes be passed through to employees on major corporate restructurings such as merger or liquidation. I.R.C. § 409(e)(3). Even these voting rights, it should be noted, can be evaded by management through such measures as elimination or conversion of the plan itself.

59. I.R.C. § 4975(e)(7).

60. Blasi, supra, at 90–93, 103. A 1987 survey reported one publicly traded company in which an ESOP held more than 50 percent of the company's

stock. Employee Benefit Research Institute, Issue Brief 11 (No. 74, Jan. 1988). Note, moreover, that ESOPs in publicly held companies are commonly so-called leveraged ESOPs in which a substantial fraction of the stock held by the plan has been purchased with funds borrowed by the plan. In such ESOPs, the tax law permits the trustee rather than the employees to vote that portion of the stock that has been financed with debt, thus diluting the employees' voice.

61. U.S. General Accounting Office, supra, at 39, reports that only 25 percent of nonleveraged ESOPs (the type most commonly found in privately held firms) pass through full voting rights to plan participants.

62. Id. at 40. These figures may understate the degree of effective employee representation achieved through ESOPs. It has been suggested to me in correspondence that, among firms with ESOPs, "there are several hundred in which the employees elect the board of directors," but in which the employee representatives are evidently principally drawn from management. Letter from Corey Rosen (April 11, 1990).

63. In 1982 the Weirton Steel Company was purchased on behalf of its employees through an ESOP, which acquired 100 percent of the company's stock. The employees were not, however, given the right to vote the stock. Rather, all voting rights involving the board of directors were given to the ESOP trustee, who was in turn to vote as directed by a special committee of the board. The employees were given only the minimum voting rights required by law, namely the right to vote on all matters requiring a more-than-majority vote, such as amendments to the corporate charter or liquidation of the corporation.

Weirton's board of directors originally had 13 members: 7 "independent" directors, elected by the shareholders; 3 "inside" directors, consisting of Weirton's CEO and two other managers selected by the CEO; and 3 "union" directors, consisting of the union's president and two other individuals chosen by the union's executive committee. No present or past employee of the company may serve as an independent director. Owing to various voting restrictions, none of the independent directors—and hence none of the directors at all—was subject to election by the shareholders (including the employee-owners) until 1991, and only in 1992 were all independent directors made subject to shareholder election.

Sales of large blocks of Weirton stock to the public in 1989 and 1994 reduced the employees' share of total votes in the company to about 53 percent by the latter date. In response to employee complaints that their power was being diluted by these transactions, a fourteenth director, elected only by Weirton's ESOPs, was added to the board in 1994.

64. Typically, adoption of an ESOP not only fails to bring an increase in employees' formal participation in control but also fails to bring an increase in

informal participation by employees in firm decision making. See Employee Benefit Research Institute, supra.

65. In firms in which the ESOP does not own 100 percent of the firm's stock, passing control to the employees might also increase the costs associated with that portion of the firm's capital that is provided by nonemployee shareholders (for example, by creating the risk that the employees will opportunistically exploit them). This is not a problem in firms in which the ESOP already owns 100 percent of the firm's equity.

66. At People Express, a U.S. air carrier that flourished between 1980 and 1986, the employees at one point collectively held roughly one-third of the stock. Stock ownership was extended to all employees, not just pilots. Despite substantial employee participation in decision making at lower levels, however, control of the board of directors and of overall company policy remained in the hands of top management and outside investors. The board evidently never had members who were nonmanagerial employees, and the employees seem never to have participated actively in selecting representatives to the board. Telephone interview with Melrose Dawsey, former managing officer, People Express (June 21 and July 26, 1989).

67. For example, Dahl, supra, at 140–152; David Ellerman, "Workers' Cooperatives: The Question of Legal Structure," in R. Jackall and H. Levin, eds., *Worker Cooperatives in America* 270–273 (1984); Vanek, *Introduction*, in J. Vanek, ed., *Self-Management: Economic Liberation of Man* 24 (1975).

68. For analyses of the operation of codetermination in practice, see Alfred Thimm, *The False Promise of Codetermination* (1980); Wolfgang Streeck, *Industrial Relations in West Germany* (1984); James Furlong, *Labor in the Boardroom* (1977).

69. German workers' pensions, like those of American workers, are generally provided by their employers. Unlike American firms, however, German firms do not accumulate a dedicated reserve fund with which to pay the company's future pension obligations. As a consequence, German workers have a stake in the future welfare of their firm that to some extent helps to align their interests with those of the firm's stockholders. This does not quite make the workers residual claimants, however, but just substantial creditors.

70. A theoretical argument for adopting a structure of this general character has been offered by Aoki, reasoning that, since inefficiency is likely to result if either investors or employees alone have control over decision making concerning variables that cannot be explicitly governed by contract between them, greater efficiency might be achieved if some mechanism for shared decision making between employees and investors can be arranged. M. Aoki, *The Cooperative Game Theory of the Firm* (1984); M. Aoki, "A Model of the Firm as a Stockholder-Employee Cooperative Game," 70 *American Economic Review* 600 (1980). This analysis assumes, however, that workers have essen-

tially similar interests. Indeed, most of the theoretical work done on codetermination has assumed that workers are a homogeneous group who have clearly defined interests vis-à-vis shareholders. See, for example, the essays collected in H. Nutzinger and J. Backhaus, *Codetermination: A Discussion of Different Approaches* (1989). In his own contribution to that volume, Backhaus explicitly acknowledges this limitation, offering the qualification that his analysis is based "on the somewhat counterfactual assumption that labour and capital representatives each form homogeneous groups." Jürgen Backhaus, "Workers' Participation Stimulated by the Economic Failure of Traditional Organization: An Analysis of Some Recent Institutional Developments," id. at 229, 250.

71. Union members constituted 29 percent of the work force in 1975 but only 17 percent in 1987. U.S. Department of Commerce, *Statistical Abstract of the United States* 415, 416 (1989) (table nos. 683, 684).

72. In this vein, it is interesting to note that Aoki has suggested that a "preference for a relatively homogeneous labor force" on the part of management may be among the most important reasons why leading Japanese firms such as Toyota have chosen a low level of vertical integration with their suppliers. Aoki, "Aspects of the Japanese Firm," in M. Aoki, ed., *The Economic Analysis of the Japanese Firm* 28 (1984).

73. Under Section 8(a)(5) of the National Labor Relations Act, only "wages, hours, and other terms and conditions of employment" are mandatory subjects of bargaining between the employer and the union. 29 U.S.C. §158(a)(5). This provision does not prevent negotiation between the union and the employer concerning other issues, such as investment decisions, but instead simply makes bargaining over such issues optional (or "permissive") rather than mandatory. For a discussion of the current interpretation of the scope of the duty to bargain under Section 8(a)(5) see Katherine Van Wezel Stone, "Labor and the Corporate Structure: Changing Conceptions and Emerging Possibilities," 55 *University of Chicago Law Review* 73, 86–96 (1988).

74. See Aoki, *The Cooperative Game Theory of the Firm* 151–171 (1984).

75. There is some evidence, however, that unions are beginning to aspire to a broader role in corporate decision making. *See* Stone, supra.

76. For example, S. Lipset, M. Trow, and J. Coleman, *Union Democracy: The Internal Politics of the International Typographical Union* 3–13 (1956).

77. R. Michels, *Political Parties* (1962).

78. For example, P. Bernstein, *Workplace Democratization: Its Internal Dynamics* 91–107 (1976); Carnoy and Shearer, supra, at 183; Rothschild and Whitt, supra, at 66.

79. United's new twelve-member board is constituted as follows. First, there are three "employee directors," consisting of two "union directors"— one chosen by the leadership of the pilots' union and one by the machinists'

union—and one director chosen by a committee of the company's salaried and management employees. Second, there are four "independent directors" who must be otherwise unaffiliated with the company and who are appointed by a committee consisting of the incumbent employee directors and independent directors, with the concurrence of at least a majority of the independent directors and one of the union directors. Third, there are five "public directors," comprising three "outside public directors" who have never been employees of the company and two "management public directors" consisting of the CEO and another senior executive acceptable to the CEO. The five public directors are elected by the company's public (nonemployee) shareholders. The outside public directors are nominated by the incumbent outside public directors, while the management public directors are nominated by a majority of the entire board.

7. Agricultural and Other Producer Cooperatives

1. U.S. Department of Agriculture, "Farmer Cooperative Statistics, 1991," ACS Report No. 33, at 2–6 (1992).

2. Charles Kraenzle, "Co-Ops Increase Share of 1991 Farm Marketings and Production Supplies," *Farmer Cooperatives* 14 (May 1993).

3. Richard Heflebower, *Cooperatives and Mutuals in the Market System* 32–36 (1980). The overall market share of agricultural cooperatives decreased suddenly from 30 percent to 24 percent between 1982 and 1987. This decline may have been only a temporary fluctuation in the overall trend; after 1987 the cooperatives' market share again increased steadily, returning to 28 percent by 1991. Roger Wissman and David Cummins, "Co-op Share of Supply Sales Up, Marketings Slip during 1980s," *Farmer Cooperatives* 4 (February 1989); Kraenzle, supra.

4. Heflebower, supra, at 40–49; John Hetherington, *Mutual and Cooperative Enterprises: An Analysis of Customer-Owned Firms in the United States* 141–142 (1991).

5. See generally Heflebower, supra, at 49–54.

6. "The Leading 50," *Prepared Foods* 38 (July 1992).

7. "The Fortune 500 Largest U.S. Industrial Corporations," *Fortune*, April 19, 1993, at 182.

8. Ocean Spray was, for example, the first American firm to employ the popular "paper bottle," the cooperative's name for the single-serving flexible aseptic container originally invented in Europe. Ryck Lent, "Ocean Spray Cranberries Inc.: A Study of a Brand-Name Marketing Cooperative" (manuscript, 1990).

9. "Directory of the 500 Largest Industrial Corporations," *Fortune*, July 1963, at 177.

10. "The Fortune 500 Largest U.S. Industrial Corporations," *Fortune,* April 19, 1993, at 182. The figures for both years contain not just farm marketing cooperatives but also cooperatives that are partly or wholly engaged in the supply business—a group of firms that we shall examine more closely in the next chapter.

11. Tracey Kennedy and Arvin Bunker, "Exports by Ag Cooperatives Exceed $3.39 Billion in 1985," 52 *Farmer Cooperatives* 4 (1987).

12. Maurice Konopnicki, "Agricultural Production and the State," 46 *Annals of Public and Co-Operative Economy* 167 (1975); M. J. Sargent, "Agricultural Marketing Co-operatives and 1992: Joint Ventures a Way Ahead?" in Elise Bayley, Edgar Parnel, and Nicky Colley, eds., *Yearbook of Co-operative Enterprise: 1991* 20 (Oxford: Plunkett Foundation for Co-operative Studies, 1990); Gunther Aschhoff and Eckart Henningsen, *The German Cooperative System: Its History, Structure, and Strength* 76–78 (Frankfurt: Fritz Knapp Verlag, 1986).

13. See, for example, Asian Productivity Organization, *Agricultural Cooperatives in Asia and the Pacific* (1989); Pradit Machima, *Growth and Development of Agricultural Cooperatives in Thailand* (1976).

14. This point has long been familiar. See, for example, John Kenneth Galbraith, *American Capitalism: The Concept of Countervailing Power,* ch. 11 (1952).

15. Oscar Refsell, "The Farmers' Elevator Movement," 22 *Journal of Political Economy* 872–895, 969–991 (1914).

16. Prior to the 1890s, any potential market power held by local elevator operators was effectively countered by the presence of independent buyers who did not own elevators but simply purchased grain from individual farmers and loaded it directly onto rented railroad cars. This competition ended only after the elevator owners combined and drove the independent buyers out of business—something the elevator owners accomplished by employing cross-ownership or the threat of collective boycott to pressure the railroads, the Chicago receiving warehouses, and the Chicago grain brokers not to deal with independent buyers.

17. Refsell, supra, at 874–877.

18. See Heflebower, supra, at 42, 46. For evidence that Irish dairy cooperatives were formed at the end of the nineteenth century in a self-conscious effort to eliminate exploitation by natural monopsonies under proprietary ownership, see Louis P. F. Smith, *The Evolution of Agricultural Cooperation* 5–6 (1961).

19. Hetherington, supra, ch. 9.

20. This is most obvious when the business taken over by the cooperative is a local monopsony that resells its own output in a larger market that is competitive. In this case, the monopsonist is achieving all its gains by driving down local crop prices and hence keeping local production below the efficient

level. Displacement of the proprietary processor by a cooperative will increase local farm prices and production, and perhaps even put downward pressure on the market price of the processed product.

21. See *National Broiler Marketing Association v. United States*, 436 U.S. 816, 842 (1978) (White, J., dissenting).

22. For a basic exposition of the issues see F. M. Scherer, *Industrial Market Structure and Economic Performance*, ch. 14 (3d ed., 1990).

23. The Justice Department and the Federal Trade Commission have apparently never attacked a merger between agricultural cooperatives. Moreover, the government has brought relatively few cases in general asserting antitrust violations by agricultural cooperatives. See Comment, "Antitrust Implications of Agricultural Cooperatives," 73 *Kentucky Law Journal* 1033, 1037 n. 14 (1984). Indeed, until 1929, Congress explicitly forbade the Justice Department from using government appropriations to prosecute farmer cooperatives for activities relating to their establishment or to the marketing of their products. See, for example, Act of February 24, 1927, ch. 189, 44 Stat. 1194.

24. *Fairdale Farms, Inc. v. Yankee Milk, Inc.*, 635 F.2d 1037 (1980).

25. Richard Ippolito and Robert Masson, "The Social Cost of Government Regulation of Milk," 21 *Journal of Law and Economics* 33, 50–54 (1978).

26. David Baumer, Robert Masson, and Robin Abrahamson Masson, "Curdling the Competition: An Economic and Legal Analysis of the Antitrust Exemption for Agriculture," 31 *Villanova Law Review* 183, 226 (1986).

27. Ippolito and Masson, supra, at 40; Charles French, John Moore, Charles Kraenzle, and Kenneth Harling, *Survival Strategies for Agricultural Cooperatives* 165–173 (1980). Governmental price regulation schemes have had a role in promoting cooperatives in other products besides milk. For example, a major function of many fruit and vegetable cooperatives is to participate in establishing federal or state marketing orders. Heflebower, supra, at 61. And the federal regulation of the market for beet sugar played a significant role in encouraging the development of beet-sugar processing plants organized as growers' cooperatives. Lee Schrader and Robert Goldberg, *Farmers' Cooperatives and Federal Income Taxes* 93 (1975).

28. These cooperatives were strongly influenced by the pro-cartel theories of Aaron Shapiro. Heflebower, supra, at 63–64, 66.

29. See Galbraith, supra.

30. James Youde and Peter Helmberger, "Marketing Cooperatives in the U.S.: Membership Policies, Market Power, and Antitrust Policy," 48 *Journal of Farm Economics* 23 (1966). The authors gathered data, for the year 1964, on the 31 cooperatives they judged most likely to exercise significant market power. They grouped these cooperatives into four classes according to the degree of market power the cooperatives were deemed to possess based on

their market share, the degree of concentration in the overall market, product differentiation (measured largely by advertising expenditures), and other barriers to entry. Class I had the highest degree of market power and Class IV the lowest. Only cooperatives in Classes I and II had closed membership policies, lending strong support to the conclusion that such a policy is necessary to exploit market power. Moreover, the cooperatives in Class II that restricted membership claimed credibly that they did so either for reasons of plant capacity or in response to federal milk marketing regulation. Apparently only the four cooperatives in Class I with closed membership policies were likely to be using those policies to create and exploit market power. These results were reinforced, moreover, when the authors expanded their study to include a total of 150 regional marketing cooperatives. Of this larger group (including the 31 just mentioned), only 12 percent restricted membership at all and only 4 percent (6 of the firms) appeared to do so to exploit market power unrelated to federal milk regulation.

31. Hetherington, supra, at 145.

32. Id. at 271.

33. See Youde and Helberger, supra.

34. Hetherington, supra, at 145.

35. Why are the contracts so short? Perhaps because, given that the cooperatives cannot establish effective market power in any case, there is little incentive for longer contracts. Moreover, farmers may be concerned about putting their fate in the hands of a cooperative for a longer period, during which nonmembers might run away with the market.

36. Lent, supra, at 8–9.

37. See K. Oustapassidis, "Structural Characteristics of Agricultural Co-Operatives in Britain," 39 *Journal of Agricultural Economics* 231 (May 1988).

38. Refsell, supra, at 880–881.

39. See, for example, J. W. Ames, *Cooperative Sweden Today* 107 (1952): "Co-operation means to the Swedish farmer that the amount of time and study he needs to devote to the sale of his produce, to the position of the market, to price quotations, and to negotiation and transport questions is reduced to a minimum. He can deliver his eggs, milk, cereals, potatoes, and animals for slaughter to the county society of the appropriate association with the knowledge that he will be paid, after an impartial estimate of the quality of his produce has been made, at the highest current market price." See also Hetherington, supra, at 143 (discussing information economies in tomato bargaining cooperatives).

40. For example, this is offered as a justification for antitrust exemption for farm marketing cooperatives by the dissent in *National Broiler Marketing Association v. U.S.*, 436 U.S. 816 (1978), at 846, 849.

41. Heflebower, supra, at 63.

42. Roughly one-third of all farm cooperatives operate on a nonexempt basis. U.S. Department of Agriculture, *Legal Phases of Farmer Cooperatives* 381–384 (1976). This figure includes both marketing and supply cooperatives, and probably includes a disproportionate share of the latter since the burdens of Section 521 status are more onerous for them. See Schrader and Goldberg, supra, at 101. Nevertheless, it is clear that some marketing cooperatives also elect nonexempt status; see, for example, id. at 96 (discussing American Crystal Sugar).

43. Heflebower, supra, at 149–156; Martin Abrahamson, *Cooperative Business Enterprise* 321–332 (1976).

44. As of 1976, the Banks for Cooperatives provided 57 percent of the debt issued by farmer cooperatives, while commercial banks provided 10 percent, debt securities 23 percent, and other sources 10 percent. French et al., supra, at 199.

45. French et al., supra, at 199–206; Schrader and Goldberg, supra, at 56.

46. For example, Philip Porter and Gerald Scully, "Economic Efficiency in Cooperatives," 30 *Journal of Law and Economics* 489 (1987).

47. Porter and Scully, supra, present data showing greater average efficiency for milk processing plants that are proprietary than for those organized as farmer cooperatives. They conclude from this that the cooperative form in general is inherently less efficient than investor ownership, and they argue that tax exemption is responsible for keeping the cooperatives in business. Their data, however, show great variance in efficiency among both proprietary and cooperative firms. This results in low measures of significance for their efficiency findings. It also indicates that there are other factors that govern efficiency for both cooperative and proprietary firms that are not included in their data, and leaves open the possibility that some of these factors may be correlated with the choice of organizational form. (For example, the cooperatives in their sample may be a response to, or an effort to establish, monopoly power, and thus typically operate in different market settings—perhaps with less competition and less opportunity to exploit economies of scale—than the investor-owned firms in their sample.) Moreover, as we have noted, milk processing is an intensely regulated industry, and that system of regulation creates special opportunities for cooperatives. Consequently, milk processing is arguably a sector that is not well suited for a test of the underlying efficiency of the cooperative form. Schrader and Goldberg, supra, at 55, examining a sample involving other types of agricultural processing and marketing firms, did not find markedly different performance between cooperatives and investor-owned firms.

48. Both logic and numerical simulations reveal that the tax advantages afforded by Subchapter T are smallest in those situations where the cooperative is retaining substantial amounts of earnings for expansion and has mem-

bers whose personal income tax rates are higher than the corporate tax rate—in which case Subchapter T and ordinary corporate tax treatment tend to converge. See Schrader and Goldberg, supra, at 50.

49. Heflebower, supra, at 51. On the development of dairy cooperatives before World War I, see id. at 42–43.

50. Id. at 58.

51. Hetherington, supra, at 109–111.

52. For general discussion as well as particularly detailed descriptions of the California bargaining and processing cooperatives, see id. at 109–111, 154–163, 170–179. See also Lent, supra, at 10.

53. Lent, supra, at 10.

54. Heflebower, supra, at 65, 72.

55. Id. at 44.

56. Id. at 52.

57. Id. at 64, 65. See also id. at 73: "concentration of output of a product . . . in a small geographical area . . . facilitates organizing the cooperative."

58. Hetherington, supra, at 202.

59. Id. at 353.

60. See id. at 174–178. Even so, in the multiple-crop cooperatives, conflicts among members over the allocation of capital to promote one crop rather than another can also be an obstacle to growth, and particularly to growth through diversification. French et al., supra, at 138.

61. French et al., supra, at 100.

62. Lent, supra, at 7, 12.

63. Id. at 19, quoting Robert St. Jacques, chairman of the board, Ocean Spray, May 1990.

64. Hetherington, supra, at 152, 205.

65. Id. at 195.

66. Id. at 196.

67. On the modest role of cooperatives in vegetables and livestock, see Heflebower, supra, at 58, 68–70.

68. Id. at 65.

69. Peter Helmberger and Sidney Hoos, *Cooperative Bargaining in Agriculture* 185 (1965).

70. See Heflebower, supra, at 67–68, 73.

71. There are, to be sure, other potential sources of equity capital. For example, some cooperatives have put part of their operations in subsidiaries in which they have sold equity shares to the public. "Why Farm Co-Ops Need Extra Seed Money," *Business Week*, March 21, 1988, p. 96. Others have formed joint ventures with investor-owned firms. Bruce W. Marion, *The Organization and Performance of the U.S. Food System* 87–88 (1986) (discussing a number of joint ventures initiated by cooperatives); "Pepsi and Ocean Spray Testing

New Products," *New York Times*, April 23, 1993, p. D4 (joint venture for development and marketing of cranberry-flavored soft drinks).

72. As of 1976, the sources of capital for the hundred largest agricultural cooperatives (including both supply and marketing cooperatives) were 34 percent equity capital, 40 percent borrowed, and 26 percent other liabilities. French et al., supra, at 197. Whether marketing cooperatives consistently tend to carry more debt than comparable investor-owned firms is unclear. A comparison of twenty-three farm marketing cooperatives with twenty-one investor-owned food processing corporations for 1983–84 showed a ratio of long-term debt to equity of .66 for the former and .41 for the latter. Hetherington, supra, at 209. One wonders, however, whether the debt-equity ratio in the investor-owned firms would still be lower if computed after the corporate mergers and acquisitions movement of the 1980s. Debt-equity ratios for the largest dairy cooperatives, for example, have gone down over recent decades, and as of 1989 were low relative to investor-owned firms in that industry. Claudia Parliament, Joan Fulton, and Zvi Lerman, "Cooperatives and Investor Owned Firms: Do They March to the Same Drummer?" (Department of Agricultural and Applied Economics, University of Minnesota, Staff Paper 89–22, June 1989).

73. National Grape Co-Operative Association, Inc., and Welch Foods, Inc., 1992 Annual Report; see also Schrader and Goldberg, supra, at 90. The National Grape Cooperative is organized with closed membership, and a farmer has the right to transfer his membership in the cooperative to a purchaser of his vineyard acreage. Consequently, the value of the membership is capitalized into land values. As of the early 1970s, when the investment per acre in the cooperative was about $1,400, vineyard land sold for a premium of as much as $1,000 per acre when it was associated with membership in the cooperative. Schrader and Goldberg, supra, at 90. This capitalization presumably mitigates the intergenerational conflicts of interest over capital investments that are discussed below.

Most other farm marketing cooperatives have open membership, and thus cannot so easily make their memberships transferable at a price that reflects the cooperative's net worth. Although one might take this as an indication that other cooperatives will generally be more handicapped in raising capital than is the National Grape Cooperative, one can as easily take it as an indication that most cooperatives find that the other devices for capital accounting discussed below are adequate to handle potential conflicts of interest, and thus closed membership is not necessary to remedy the situation.

74. Lent, supra, at 17.

75. Hetherington, supra, at 207.

76. French et al., supra, at 76, 89–90.

77. The unavoidable seasonality of most agricultural crops is presumably an

important reason for the absence of economies of scale. At any given time of the year, there is one particular operation that must be performed—planting in the spring, for example, and harvesting in the fall. As a consequence, the opportunities for division of labor are limited. If some workers were to specialize just in planting and others just in harvesting, workers of both types would be unoccupied during part of the year. Workers on farms, therefore, must to an important degree be generalists who have competence in all phases of production. The consequence is that the opportunities for increasing the division of labor by increasing the scale of production are much more limited in farming than they are in products that can be produced by continuous processes that permit all phases of production to take place simultaneously.

78. Alva Benton, "Large Land Holdings in North Dakota," *Journal of Land and Public Utility Economics* 405 (October 1925); John Brewster, "The Machine Process in Agriculture and Industry," 32 *Journal of Farm Economics* 69 (1950).

79. Benjamin Klein, Robert Crawford, and Armen Alchian, "Vertical Integration, Appropriable Rents, and the Competitive Contracting Process," 21 *Journal of Law and Economics* 297, 310–311 (1978).

80. Steven Wiggins and Gary Libecap, "Oil Field Unitization: Contractual Failure in the Presence of Imperfect Information," 75 *American Economic Review* 368 (1985).

8. Retail, Wholesale, and Supply Firms

1. U.S. Department of Agriculture, Agricultural Cooperative Service, *Farmer Cooperative Statistics 1983* 10, 26 (1983); U.S. Department of Agriculture, Agricultural Cooperative Service, *Farmer Cooperative Statistics 1990* 4 (1990); Charles Kraenzle, "Co-ops Increase Share of 1991 Farm Marketings and Production Supplies," 60 *Farmer Cooperatives* 14 (1993).

2. The six firms were Gold Kist (a combined marketing/supply cooperative), Farmland Industries, Agway, CENEX, CF Industries, and National Cooperative Refinery Association. "Fortune 500 Largest U.S. Industrial Corporations," *Fortune*, April 19, 1993, at 182.

3. Richard Heflebower, *Cooperatives and Mutuals in the Market System* 81 (1980).

4. Id., ch. 8.

5. Id. at 78–79, 81.

6. Telephone interview with Terry Nagle, director of communications, Land O'Lakes, July 17, 1986.

7. Heflebower, supra, ch. 7 (figures from 1969).

8. These shares are distinct from the memberships themselves, although membership can be made conditional upon purchasing such stock. Although

a cooperative could just sell its memberships for a price rather than requiring an initial purchase of stock, this approach seems to be rare.

9. As of 1970, retained earnings and per-unit retains accounted for 85 percent of the equity capital of the hundred largest farmer cooperatives, including both supply and marketing cooperatives. Lee Schrader and Robert Goldberg, *Farmers' Cooperatives and Federal Income Taxes* 60 (1975). Marketing cooperatives evidently rely on sale of capital stock much less than do supply cooperatives, so this 85 percent figure presumably overestimates the percentage that would be found in supply cooperatives alone. John Hetherington, *Mutual and Cooperative Enterprises: An Analysis of Customer-Owned Firms in the United States* 112 (1991).

At least one canning cooperative, rather than relying exclusively upon the three methods described here, finances capital improvements by forming voluntary limited partnerships among members and then renting the facilities from the partnership. This method allows differential investment by members while avoiding the agency problems associated with investment by nonmembers. See id. at 349.

10. See Comptroller General of the United States, "Family Farmers Need Cooperatives—But Some Issues Need to Be Resolved," U.S. General Accounting Office, Report to the Congress CED-79-106 (1979), at 39; U.S. Dept. of Agriculture, *Equity Redemption Issues and Alternatives for Farmer Cooperatives* 11 (Agricultural Cooperative Service Research Report No. 23, 1982); Hetherington, supra, at 211–219.

11. There is no reason in principle why memberships in cooperatives could not be made redeemable at a fair value; presumably they are not largely because doing so would create difficult problems of valuation. The result, however, is that increments in the cooperative's aggregate value, as in the form of goodwill, may be passed on to the continuing members, creating a shift of wealth among generations of members. One way of controlling this shift is to maintain a reasonably high debt-equity ratio, as farmer cooperatives do.

12. See generally Phillip F. Brown and David Volkin, *Equity Redemption Practices of Agricultural Cooperatives* (U.S.D.A. Farmer Cooperative Service Research Report No. 4, 1977).

13. Hetherington, supra, at 215.

14. In 1985 farmers spent $9.5 billion on farm machinery. In comparison, during the same year they spent $24 billion for feed and seed, $13.6 billion for petroleum products and machine maintenance (separate figures are not available), and $8.9 billion for fertilizer and lime—all supplies in which cooperatives have a large market share. U.S. Department of Agriculture, *1986 Fact Book of U.S. Agriculture* 4 (1985).

15. In addition, Ford had 8 percent of the market and White had 6 percent,

giving the top four firms a total of 96 percent. Gale Research, *Market Share Reporter* (1st ed., 1991).

16. W. G. Phillips, "The Farm Machinery Industry," in John R. Moore and Richard G. Walsh, eds., *Market Structure of the Agricultural Industries* 325, 348 (1966); Gale Research, supra.

17. Sunkist, the citrus growers' cooperative, develops and leases packing-house equipment. *1992 Annual Report of Sunkist Growers, Inc.* Since many of the citrus packinghouses are cooperatively owned by Sunkist growers, and since the type of equipment required is presumably similar in all citrus pack-inghouses, this type of machinery may present unusually little opportunity for divergence of interest among members of the cooperative.

18. "Hardware Age Verified Directory of Hardlines Distributors," *Hardware Age* RU-15 (December 1990).

19. Progressive Grocer, *Progressive Grocer's Marketing Guidebook: 1989* 11 (1989).

20. Heflebower, supra, at 101, 111–112.

21. Id. at 114–115.

22. See id. at 118–121.

23. As of 1992, True Value had 8,098 member retailers, Ace had 5,200 members, and Servistar had 4,396 members. Hardware Wholesalers, which does not license a nationally recognized brand name, had 3,066 members. Since some member retailers own more than one hardware store, the number of hardware stores involved is somewhat greater than the numbers given here. "Hammering Out New Strategies: Old-Style Hardware Stores Mix Service, Buying Power," 9 *Business First—Columbus*, sec. 2, at 1 (November 2, 1992).

24. Heflebower, supra, at 114–115.

25. See Gillian Hadfield, "Problematic Relations: Franchising and the Law of Incomplete Contracts," 42 *Stanford Law Review* 927, 952 (1990).

26. Id. at 972–978.

27. For example, to join the Ace Hardware cooperative a retailer must pay a nonrefundable $400 application fee and then, if accepted, purchase $5,000 worth of stock in the cooperative. To join the Servistar cooperative, a hard-ware retailer must purchase $800 worth of common stock and pay an entrance fee of $1,300. In addition, each of these cooperatives pays a portion of its patronage dividends in stock and notes. Telephone interviews with John Cam-eron, manager of public relations, Ace Hardware, August 2, 1993; Deborah Tishey, securities and licensing agent, Servistar, August 11, 1993. Spartan Stores, a midwestern grocery wholesale cooperative whose members have a minimum turnover of $50,000 per week, requires member retail stores to make an $8,800 application fee, purchase $10,000 in stock, and make a capital contribution equal to 1.5 times the store's weekly purchases up to a maximum of $125,000. Members are given up to five years to purchase the stock and

make their initial capital contribution. Telephone interview with Francis Lin-
gren, new business development, Spartan Stores, August 12, 1993.

28. *Progressive Grocer's Marketing Guidebook: 1989* 11 (1988).

29. Consumer cooperatives made an early and promising entry into prepaid
primary health care. This may have been occasioned in part by the prevailing
legal restrictions on investor-owned prepaid health care. The spread of the
cooperatives was then itself frustrated, however, by the American Medical
Association's successful lobbying, between 1939 and 1949, for legislation—
ultimately enacted in twenty-six states—that effectively barred consumer
cooperative health plans. Although federal legislation swept away most state-
level restrictions on both investor-owned and cooperative prepaid health plans
in 1973, there seems to have been no further important entry by cooperatives
since that date, suggesting that consumer cooperatives do not have a strong
efficiency advantage in this field. Group Health Cooperative of Puget Sound,
with about 200,000 members, is the largest of the health-care cooperatives
that have survived. See generally Paul Starr, *The Social Transformation of American Medicine* 306, 321, 439 (1982).

30. Heflebower, supra, at 124.

31. International Cooperative Alliance, *Cooperation in European Market
Economies*, Statistical Annex, at 12 (1967). This figure, which is dated, may
overstate the current market share owing to the subsequent demise of two
large German cooperatives. See Commission of the European Communities,
Panorama of EC Industry 93 20–22 (1993).

32. Co-Operative Union Limited, *Co-Operative Statistics 1990–91* 6 (1991).

33. Commission on the Swedish Cooperative Movement and Its Role in
Society, *The Co-operative Movement in Society* 8 (1979). (Figure for 1970.)

34. Commission of the European Communities, *Panorama of EC Industry
93* 100 (1993).

35. For example, in the United States, 40 percent of the population changed
residences in the period 1980–1985, while only 10 percent of the French
population changed residences within the longer period 1975–1982. Germany
and Italy, though employing a measure of mobility not strictly comparable
with that used in the United States, appear to have even lower mobility rates
than France. Charles Nam, William Serow, and David Sly, eds., *International
Handbook on Internal Migration* 129, 147, 242, 394 (1990).

36. For a concise but dated survey of Swedish antitrust law, see Ulf Bernitz,
Swedish Anti-Trust Law and Resale Price Maintenance (1964).

37. E. Ernest Goldstein, *American Enterprise and Scandinavian Antitrust Law*
222–226 (1963).

38. Id. at 196–200.

39. For example, Heflebower, supra, at 18.

40. For example, Heflebower, supra, begins his book with a discussion of

economic theory that emphasizes the average-cost theory described here, but then makes no direct use of this theory in his subsequent chapters discussing different types of cooperatives.

41. Schrader and Goldberg, supra, at 60.

9. Utilities

1. Joseph Fuhr, Jr., "Should the U.S. Subsidize Rural Telephone Companies?" 12 *Journal of Policy Analysis and Management* 582 (1993).

2. Richard Heflebower, *Cooperatives and Mutuals in the Market System* 131 (1980).

3. Energy Information Administration, *Electric Power Annual 1989* 5 (1991); telephone interview with Frank W. Bennett, director, Southeast Area-Electric, Rural Electrification Administration, February 19, 1987.

4. National Rural Electric Cooperative Association, *People—Their Power: The Rural Electric Fact Book* 152 (1980).

5. Paul Joskow and Richard Schmalensee, *Markets for Power* 12, 19 (1983); Rural Electrification Administration, *A Brief History of the Rural Electric and Telephone Programs* 51 (1985).

6. Telephone interview with David J. Hedberg, director of regulations and rate design, National Rural Utilities Cooperative Finance Corporation, March 24, 1987.

7. "Our Vital Statistics," *Rural Electrification* (November 1986).

8. Heflebower, supra, at 132.

9. Id. at 136.

10. Rural Electrification Administration, *REA Loans and Loan Guarantees for Rural Electric and Telephone Service* 8 (1983).

11. See *Tri-State Generation and Transmission Association v. Shoshone River Power, Inc.*, 805 F.2d 351, 353 (10th Cir. 1986).

12. Rural Electrification Administration, supra, at 31.

13. National Rural Electric Cooperative Association, supra, at 26.

14. Since the government charged no risk premium even when providing loans for 100 percent of a utility's capital needs, it arguably offered an interest rate that was effectively subsidized. But since, as noted above, the default rate on the loans turned out to be negligible, the extent of this subsidy, calculated ex post, was nearly zero.

15. National Rural Electric Cooperative Association, supra, at 26–27.

16. An exception is the interest in "competitive rules joint ventures" that developed in the Antitrust Division of the U.S. Department of Justice in the mid-1970s and began to receive some attention among economists a decade later. See Dan Alger, Susan Braman, and Russ Porter, "Using Competitive Rules Joint Ventures to Regulate Natural Monopolies" (December 1989); Frederick Warren-Boulton and John Woodbury, "The Design and Evalua-

tion of Competitive Rules Joint Ventures for Mergers and Natural Monopolies" (December 1989).

17. See, for example, W. Kip Viscusi, John Vernon, and Joseph Harrington, *Economics of Regulation and Antitrust* chaps. 10–18 (1992).

18. There is now broad consensus that franchise bidding could not be made superior to conventional rate regulation for utilities, such as electricity and telephone service, that involve substantial fixed costs, for reasons first clearly discussed in Oliver Williamson, "Franchise Bidding for Natural Monopolies—In General and with Respect to CATV," 7 *Bell Journal of Economics* 73 (1976). In fact, franchising was widely employed in the generation and distribution of electricity in the late nineteenth century, when the industry was first forming, and was subsequently abandoned for many of the same reasons suggested by its more recent critics. David Schap, *Municipal Ownership in the Electric Utility Industry* 21–22 (1986).

19. This observation is supported by interviews with the staff of utility regulatory commissions in three states: Michigan, Texas, and Florida. Denise McMillan-Leftow, "Rural Electric Cooperatives: An Empirical Study" (1987).

20. Of the 496 municipal utilities that responded to a 1986 survey, 80 percent served fewer than 15,000 customers. American Public Power Association, *Survey of Administrative and Policy-Making Organization of Publicly Owned Electric Utilities* (1987).

21. Telephone interview with Scott Choate, American Public Power Association, March 25, 1993.

22. Id.

23. Of the 496 municipal utilities (out of a total of roughly 1,500) that responded to a 1986 survey, 46 percent were controlled by a city governing board while 54 percent were controlled by an independent utility board. Among the independent boards, 32 percent were elected and 68 percent were appointed. American Public Power Association, supra.

24. For example, about a third of municipal utilities with independent governing boards require city council approval to issue long-term bonds, and 8 percent have their rates directly set by the city council. Id. at 5.

25. National Association of Regulatory Utility Commissioners, *Utility Regulatory Policy in the United States and Canada, Compilation 1991–1992* 52–57 (Karen Bauer, ed., 1992).

26. A thoughtful survey and critique of the literature is offered in William Hausman and John Neufeld, "Public versus Private: A Summary of the Empirical Literature on the Comparative Performance of U.S. Electric Utilities" (American Public Power Association, 1990).

27. The historical evolution of municipal utilities in the United States is surveyed in David Schap, *Municipal Ownership in the Electric Utility Industry* (1986).

28. Commission of the European Community, *Panorama of EC Industry* (1990).

29. C. Chullakesa, "Local Participation in Rural Electrification," in *Power Systems in Asia and the Pacific, with Emphasis on Rural Electrification* 397, 399 (1990).

30. Commission of the European Community, supra.

31. Z. A. Santos, "Managing Rural Electric Co-operatives in the Philippines," in *Power Systems in Asia and the Pacific, with Emphasis on Rural Electrification* 402, 403 (1990).

10. Clubs and Other Associative Organizations

1. Benjamin Klein, Robert Crawford, and Armen Alchian, "Vertical Integration, Appropriable Rents, and the Competitive Contracting Process," 21 *Journal of Law and Economics* 297, 322–323 (1978).

2. National Golf Foundation, "Research Summary: The Growth of U.S. Golf" (May 1992).

3. On the social exclusivity of private golf clubs, see the two-part series by Marcia Chambers in *Golf Digest*, "A Revolution in Private Clubs," May 1990, and "Knocking on the Clubhouse Door," June 1990.

4. See Zecharia Chafee, "The Internal Affairs of Associations Not for Profit," 43 *Harvard Law Review* 993 (1930).

5. For a more formal mathematical exposition, see Henry Hansmann, "A Theory of Status Organizations," 2 *Journal of Law, Economics, and Organization* 119 (1986).

6. See id.

7. See Henry Hansmann and Alvin Klevorick, "Competition and Coordination in Markets for Higher Education and Other Associative Goods" (November 1995).

11. Housing

1. U.S. Department of Commerce and U.S. Department of Housing and Urban Development, *American Housing Survey for the United States in 1991*, Part A, Table 1 (Current Housing Report series H-150-91, 1993).

2. As discussed below, however, in a cooperative the board of directors sometimes retains a veto right over sales.

3. *New York Times*, Jan. 27, 1929, sec. 12, at 1, col. 8. At least thirty more cooperative apartment buildings appear to have been constructed in New York City before the First World War. Id.; *New York Times*, Feb. 10, 1907, at 16, col. 5; *New York Times*, Apr. 25, 1909, sec. 7, at 2.

4. Twentieth Century Fund, *American Housing: Problems and Prospects* 233

(1944); *New York Times*, Jan. 25, 1929, sec. 12, at 1, col. 6. By the 1920s there were also some lower- and middle-income cooperative apartment buildings, a number of which were sponsored by unions. Burr Henly, "Financing Housing Cooperatives" 71–84 (unpublished master's thesis, University of Washington, 1982). Low-income cooperatives still exist; their principal role, however, is to ensure that housing subsidies are passed through to tenants; absent subsidies they would probably be rare.

5. Otis H. Castle, "Legal Phases of Cooperative Buildings," 2 *Southern California Law Review* 1 (1928); Twentieth Century Fund, supra, at 233.

6. Chester C. McCullough, "Cooperative Apartments in Illinois," 26 *Chicago-Kent Law Review* 303, 305 (1948).

7. Foundation for Cooperative Housing, "Cooperative Development with Federal Assistance," in Jerome Liblit, ed., *Housing—The Cooperative Way* 226 (1964); International Labor Office (Geneva), *Housing Cooperatives* 108 (1964). There were 13.8 million multifamily housing units in 1960. U.S. Dept. of Commerce, *Statistical Abstract of the United States, 1988*, at 688, Table 1221 (1987).

8. U.S. Dept. of Housing and Urban Development, *The Conversion of Rental Housing to Condominiums and Cooperatives*, App. 1, Part III, at 7, Table IV-2 App. (1980).

9. Alberto Ferrer and Karl Stecher, *Law of Condominium* 129–133 (1967).

10. J. Lewis Gausch and Robert C. Marshall, "A Theoretical and Empirical Analysis of the Length of Residency Discount in the Rental Housing Market," 22 *Journal of Urban Economics* 291 (1987). Earlier studies, whose methodology is criticized by Gausch and Marshall, had found evidence of discounts for renewing tenants. Allen C. Goodman and Masahiro Kawa, "Length-of-Residence Discounts and Rental Housing Demand: Theory and Evidence," 61 *Land Economics* 93 (1985); William A. Clark and Allan D. Heskin, "The Impact of Rent Control on Tenure Discounts and Residential Mobility," 58 *Land Economics* 109 (1982). If length-of-residence discounts are in fact given, they might be interpreted not as reflecting the direct costs to a landlord of finding a new tenant but rather as an inducement that landlords give to tenants who have revealed themselves during the initial lease term to be good tenants. See Gausch and Marshall.

11. J. Henderson and Y. Ioannides, "A Model of Housing Tenure Choice," 73 *American Economic Review* 98 (1983), offer a countervailing theory, arguing that, ceteris paribus, an increase in an individual's wealth will decrease the likelihood that he will be an owner-occupant. As they note, this result is at odds with observed patterns of tenure choice. One reason, perhaps, is that these authors' conclusion depends entirely on their definition of an "increase in wealth," which involves an increase in exogenous income in each future period that is of equal present value, hence increasing demand for consump-

tion without increasing the need for saving. But increases in wealth taking this form are rare.

12. The ability to choose one's fellow tenants was commonly mentioned in ads and articles concerning cooperatives during this period. See, for example, "Cooperative Homes Old to Manhattan," *New York Times*, Jan. 27, 1929, sec. 12, at 1, col. 8; *New York Times*, Jan. 3, 1926, sec. 10, at 4, col. 7 ("In many instances the [cooperator's] controlling motive is the desire to escape from undesirable neighborhood conditions and to associate and identify himself with conservative surroundings and with people of his own class.").

13. It is widely thought, particularly in New York City, that an important reason for choosing the cooperative over the condominium form is that the former provides the occupants of a building with the opportunity to be discriminating when screening new applicants for membership. The usual arrangement in a cooperative is that, subject to the requirements of fair housing legislation, the board of directors may reject any applicant without having to state a reason, thus barring a tenant from assigning his lease until a tenant acceptable to the board is found. In a condominium, in contrast, the board is typically empowered to prevent a sale only by buying the unit itself at the contract price, and condominium boards seldom screen tenants on social criteria. See Michael de Courcy Hinds, "When a Co-op Board Rejects a Buyer," *New York Times*, Nov. 2, 1986, sec. 8, at 1, col. 2. There are no legal obstacles to giving a condominium board screening powers equivalent to those generally exercised by cooperative boards. The reason that the cooperative form is more commonly used for purposes of personal discrimination perhaps stems from the fact that the members of a cooperative have a strong incentive to screen prospective members to ensure that they will carry their share of the collective mortgage on the building—something that condominiums, with their smaller degree of joint financial commitment, have less need for. This financial screening provides a convenient opportunity and cover for engaging in non-financial screening as well.

14. Henderson and Ioannides, supra, suggest that, absent problems of risk bearing, this "fundamental rental externality" (as the authors term it) makes ownership more efficient than rental for all households. The authors suggest that risk bearing considerations are the principal countervailing factor that induces individuals to rent rather than own. They do not deal with the problems of collective ownership, or with the tax subsidies, that are the principal focus of the analysis offered here.

15. U.S. Bureau of the Census, *Annual Housing Survey: 1985*, Series H-150, Table 2-1.

16. See Richard Lyons, "More Co-op Owners Battling Their Boards," *New York Times*, April 24, 1988 (emphasizing the problem of lack of expertise among co-op board members). On the other hand, for some building occu-

pants—particularly retirees—participation in governance may itself be a consumption good and on balance a source of benefits rather than costs.

17. See, for example, Iver Peterson, "Budget Battles in Co-ops and Condos," *New York Times*, Jan. 15, 1989, sec. 10, p. 1, col. 4; Ira Robbins, "Methods of Holding Residential Property," 190 *Annals of the American Academy of Political and Social Science* 109, 111 (1937); *Thiess v. Island House Assoc.*, 311 S.2d 142 (1975); *Kaye v. Mount La Jolla Homeowners Assoc.*, 252 Cal. Rptr. 67 (1988).

18. See, for example, testimony of Drayton Bryant, Hearings before the Committee on Banking and Currency, U.S. House of Representatives, 81st Cong., 2d Sess., on H.R. 6618 and H.R. 6742 (Superseded by H.R. 7402), January 30–February 14, 1950, p. 119: "very definitely . . . the most successful cooperatives have been either in a socially homogeneous group like a union or veteran group or even a church group."

19. For the period 1970–1986 median household income, measured in constant 1986 dollars, reached its highest value ($25,936) in 1973, and declined to its lowest value ($22,913) in 1982; in 1979 it was $24,866. U.S. Bureau of the Census, *Statistical Abstract of the United States: 1988*, Table 691 (1987).

20. See P. Hendershott and J. D. Shilling, "The Economics of Tenure Choice, 1955–79," in C. F. Sirmans, ed., *Research in Real Estate* 105 (1982).

21. Special factors might, however, have led to increased liquidity among apartment occupants as opposed to the general population. For example, it seems likely that in the late 1960s and 1970s there was a substantial increase in the general liquidity of the elderly owing to the combined accumulated influence of pension funds and social security, and this may have led to an increase in the demand for condominiums among that subset of the population. It is also sometimes said that the 1970s saw the advent of a large new class of highly liquid apartment dwellers consisting of the relatively affluent childless young households resulting from the increasing tendencies for marriage and childbearing to be postponed and for women to enter the work force. Although it is difficult to locate sufficient demographic data on occupants of apartments to assess this latter argument, it is questionable whether any such demographic shift could have been so pronounced as to correlate well with the rapid expansion of cooperative and condominium housing in the 1970s.

22. Another factor affecting the liquidity of occupants of apartment buildings has been the advent of federal mortgage insurance. Federal Housing Administration (FHA) mortgage insurance, which was first made available for single-family dwellings in the 1930s, was extended to the construction and purchase of cooperative apartments in 1950 and to condominiums in 1961. The result may have been to increase the availability of debt financing for cooperatives and condominiums, and thus to increase liquidity for occupants of apartment buildings. There is good reason to believe, however, that federal mortgage insurance contributed little to the spread of cooperatives and con-

dominiums in the U.S. housing market. Federal mortgage insurance has always been sold at a rate that is remunerative for the government, and thus has not provided a subsidy for owner-occupancy as opposed to rental. Further, the numbers of cooperative and condominium units insured have been only a small fraction of the total constructed or converted. Finally, federal mortgage insurance became available for cooperatives and condominiums long before the marked expansion in their popularity. See Henry Hansmann, "Condominium and Cooperative Housing: Transactional Efficiency, Tax Subsidies, and Tenure Choice," 20 *Journal of Legal Studies* 25, 58–59 (1991).

23. Leyser, "Ownership of Flats—A Comparative Study of Flats," *International and Comparative Law Quarterly* 31, 32 (1958); Terence Burke et al., *Condominium: Housing for Tomorrow* 7 (1964).

24. U.S. Dept. of Housing and Urban Development, *The Conversion of Rental Housing to Condominiums and Cooperatives* ii (1980).

25. For example, Chicago, which does not have rent control, had a far higher rate of conversion over the period 1970–1979 (5.44 percent of the rental housing stock) than did New York (.58 percent), which does. The reason for this pattern may be that jurisdictions with rent control have sought to protect those controls by adopting stricter regulation of conversions than have jurisdictions without rent control. Id. at App. 1, 10–11.

26. Charles Baird, *Rent Control: The Perennial Folly* (1980); National Multi Unit Housing Council, *The Spread of Rent Control* (1982).

27. I.R.C. secs. 163, 164 (1986). These deductions were well established by 1936, the earliest year covered by the data below. I.R.C. sec. 23 (1936).

28. To see clearly the nature of the subsidy, imagine a situation in which two identical taxpayers occupy identical houses. Then consider two different ways in which these individuals might structure ownership of their houses: in the first, each occupant simply owns his own house; in the second, each individual owns the house occupied by the other, and rents the house to the other for a fair market rental (which is identical for the two houses). In the absence of taxes, and setting aside transaction cost and incentive issues of the type discussed above, the two different ownership structures are financially equivalent, and the individuals should be indifferent between them. Their invested capital and annual net income flows are the same in each. Under the tax laws, however, the second approach is far less attractive, since the amount each individual receives as rent on the house he owns is taxable income, while the (equivalent) amount he pays as rent on the house he occupies is not deductible. The reason for the distinction is that in general the tax code only taxes transactions between two distinct persons. When an individual is his own landlord, there is no such transaction.

There are several ways to eliminate the disparity in the taxation of rented and owner-occupied housing. One is to tax the imputed rental income of owner-occupants. Another is to permit tenants a deduction for rental payments. A third is to permit landlords to exclude from income the rental payments they receive from tenants. If everyone were in the same marginal tax bracket, and if the expense deductions permitted landlords and owner-occupants were also equalized (for example, by extending depreciation deductions to owner-occupants as well as landlords), then these three approaches would all be equivalent, except that the second and third would maintain a subsidy for housing in general (whether rented or owner-occupied) as opposed to investments in other income-producing assets, while the first would create a less favorable tax regime for housing than for other consumer durables such as automobiles and appliances, which are also subject to a tax bias in favor of ownership rather than leasing.

29. It is also the case that owner-occupants, in contrast to landlords, are not permitted to take deductions for current expenses such as maintenance and utilities. Unlike the denial of depreciation deductions, however, this does not create a bias in favor of rental. The reason is that an owner is also permitted to exclude from income the imputed amount he would have to pay himself as landlord to cover these costs, and this exclusion just balances the absence of the deduction. Or, viewing it the other way, the landlord must include as income the amounts charged tenants for maintenance and utilities, and then gets a deduction in equivalent amount for these expenses, thus making the net tax effect zero, just as it is for an owner.

30. Several European countries have at various times taxed imputed rental income from housing—including England, France, Germany, Italy, Sweden, and Switzerland—though there is reason to doubt the efficacy of these efforts. See R. Goode, *The Individual Income Tax* 121 (1964) (England); Harvard International Tax Program, *World Tax Series: Taxation in France* 532–537 (1966), and comparable volumes in the same series for the other countries mentioned.

31. I.R.C. sec. 216 (1986), originally enacted as sec. 128 of the Revenue Act of 1942. A cooperative housing corporation, like a condominium association, is not itself exempt from taxes. *Commissioner v. Lake Forest, Inc.*, 305 F.2d 814 (4th Cir. 1962). They rarely pay taxes, however, since they generally assess their members for an amount no greater than their expenses, and thus have no taxable income. See 2 P. Rohan and M. Reskin, *Cooperative Housing: Law and Practice* sec. 15.01 (1986).

32. See Rohan and Reskin, supra, at sec. 13.01.

33. This is most easily seen by comparing (a) the situation in which a homeowner purchases a $100,000 home outright, with no mortgage, with (b) that in which the same home is purchased entirely with borrowed money, while the owner's $100,000 is instead invested and the returns from that investment used to help pay the interest on the mortgage. If the homeowner's

interest rates for borrowing and lending were the same, then for tax purposes the two transactions would be identical if mortgage interest were a deductible expense. But if mortgage interest were not deductible, then only transaction (a) would have the advantage of the tax subsidy described in the preceding note.

34. Rev. Rul. 64–31, 1964–1 C.B. 300, 302.

35. See D. Clurman and E. Hebard, *Condominiums and Cooperatives* 140 (1970).

36. I.R.C. sec. 167 (1986). For the years before and after this, straight line depreciation was the method generally called for. I.R.C. sec. 23(1) (1936), (1946); I.R.C. sec. 167 (1988).

37. The value of the excess depreciation deductions has, however, been limited in some years by two devices. The first is a "recapture" rule under which, at the time a building is sold, taxes must be paid at ordinary income rates on some or all of that portion of the capital gain accounted for by accelerated depreciation deductions. The recapture rules first came into effect in 1963, and were subsequently stiffened in 1970 and 1976. The second device is a "minimum" tax rate applied to certain tax preference items if they exceed a given total. Accelerated depreciation and capital gains are among the tax preference items affected. The minimum tax first took effect in 1970, with a rate of 10 percent. In 1976 the rate was increased to 15 percent, and the tax was otherwise tightened then as well. In 1983 the rate for the minimum tax was raised to 20 percent.

38. In particular, taxpayers were prohibited from offsetting ordinary earned income with "passive" losses from investments in real estate, and an "at-risk rule" was adopted to prevent investors from using nonrecourse debt as leverage to increase the value of depreciation deductions they could claim per dollar invested.

39. These costs were computed over the period of years that an average individual would be likely to own a home. Because of the nature of the tax rules applicable to owner-occupied housing, the calculation is in most cases invariant to the number of years assumed.

40. The term "landlord" is used here to refer collectively to the owners of a building, which will often include a number of investors acting as limited partners. The relevant tax bracket is the tax bracket of the investors.

41. It is possible that, at least for buildings below a certain scale, landlords are often of a socioeconomic status not far removed from that of their tenants. This is likely to be the case, for example, where there are substantial economies from having the owner reside in or near the building. As a result, the marginal tax bracket for landlords of such buildings might be lower than that for landlords of large or luxury buildings.

42. The marginal bracket for landlords may, however, nevertheless be lower

than the top bracket, or even that of the ninety-ninth percentile of the household income distribution. For example, the tax rate at which the after-tax interest on municipal bonds equals that on comparable taxable bonds has generally been well below the maximum bracket, indicating that the marginal investor in such bonds is not in the top bracket.

43. The calculations of tax savings from owner-occupancy presented here are reasonably robust. Computations of the sensitivity of the results to differing assumptions concerning a variety of variables, including interest rates and expected inflation, show that the net tax savings from owner-occupancy in any given year is not much affected by these assumptions, with the exception of expectations concerning housing price increases, which are discussed in the following note.

44. The computation of tax savings offered here, it should be noted, is probably conservative for recent decades. In particular, the calculations have been made on the assumption that potential purchasers of housing foresaw none of the unusually rapid increase in housing prices that occurred in the 1970s, but rather assumed that housing prices would just keep pace with the overall inflation rate. The expected savings from owner-occupancy shown here would be considerably larger for the 1970s if consumers were assumed to have correctly anticipated that housing prices would increase substantially in the future.

45. That is, unless we assume that the marginal landlord was then in the top tax bracket. But that seems highly implausible. Although Table 11.3 shows a net subsidy to ownership over rental for occupants in all income classes when the landlord is in the top tax bracket, this is a consequence of the higher taxes paid by a landlord in that bracket rather than a subsidy to ownership; consequently, there would be no incentive for individuals in the top tax bracket to serve as landlords, and the right-hand column in Table 11.3 can be ignored for 1936.

46. This constraint has been relaxed recently as banks have begun to make personal loans secured by an individual tenant's shares of stock in a cooperative apartment building.

47. For example, in France, where condominiums had been known since the Middle Ages and recognized to some degree by statute since the Code Napoleon of 1804, it was not until 1938 that legislation was enacted that specified in any detail the rights and obligations of the unit owners. The first modern condominium statute was adopted in Belgium in 1924; Italy and Spain, like France, adopted their modern condominium legislation in the 1930s; Germany and the Netherlands did not do so until the 1950s. L. Neville Brown, "French Co-Property Apartments: A Model for English Law?" 110 *Solicitors Journal* 591 (1966); Leyser, supra, at 35; Ferrer and Stecher, supra, at 14–40.

48. A condominium-enabling act had been adopted in Puerto Rico as early as 1901, and revised in 1951; it was not until 1958, however, that a truly workable statute was fashioned. P.R. Civ. Code sec. 403 (1902); P.R. Laws Ann. tit. 31, sec. 1275 (1954); P.R. Laws Ann. tit. 31, sec. 1291 et seq. (1958). The Puerto Rican statutes were patterned after those adopted in various Latin American countries, which in turn were influenced by the European, and particularly the Spanish, condominium statutes. See Ferrer and Stecher, supra, at 51. (The 1958 statute, in particular, was modeled after an earlier Cuban act. W. Robert Folkes, "Legal and Practical Aspects of Condominiums," 19 *Business Lawyer* 233 (1963).) Then, evidently influenced by lobbying from Puerto Rican banking and real estate interests, who were seeking to improve financing for the condominium housing that was already being developed in Puerto Rico, Congress in 1961 approved FHA-insured mortgages for condominiums; to implement this, the FHA promulgated a model condominium act that essentially followed the Puerto Rican statute. See Hearings on General Housing Legislation before the Subcommittee on Housing of the House Committee on Banking and Currency, 86th Cong., 2d Sess. 246–274 (1960); Aaron Schreiber, "The Lateral Housing Development: Condominium or Home Owners Association?" 117 *University of Pennsylvania Law Review* 1104, 1110 (1969). Within a few years most states adopted a condominium statute based on the FHA model, though perhaps in considerable part only because this was a costless measure that might make state residents eligible for additional federal mortgage insurance and thus gave the appearance of addressing housing problems. Federal mortgage insurance involves no subsidy, and, although its advent evidently stimulated the enactment of condominium-enabling statutes, it probably was not an important stimulus to the actual formation of condominium housing.

49. See Edwin Mansfield, *Industrial Research and Technological Innovation* (1968); L. Nasbeth and G. F. Ray, *The Diffusion of New Industrial Processes* (1974); Stephen Davies, *The Diffusion of Process Innovations* (1979).

50. As of 1986 there were 57,000 condominium units in New York City (28,000 from conversion and 29,000 from new construction) and 246,000 cooperative units (227,000 from conversion and 19,000 from new construction). The latter figures exclude an additional 83,000 cooperative units that receive public subsidies under various programs. New York State Dept. of Public Service, Office of Energy Conservation and Environmental Planning, *New York City Housing Market* (April 1986).

51. In 1987 there were a total of 35,619 cooperative units created (34,450 through conversion and 1,169 through new construction) in contrast to 9,479 condominium units (2,188 through conversion and 7,291 through new construction). Id. There are evidently no special regulatory restrictions in New York on the conversion of rental units to the condominium rather than the

cooperative form that would in themselves account for the disproportionately large number of cooperative units formed there through conversion. Interview with Gary Glatter, associate general counsel, M. J. Raines Company, May 15, 1989.

52. Rohan and Reskin, supra, at 3.

53. It was estimated in 1981 that there were then only 400–600 commercial condominiums in the United States. "Outlook for Commercial Industrial Condominiums," *Mortgage and Real Estate Executives Reporter*, April 1, 1981, at 5, cited in Note, "Commercial Condominiums: Statutory Roadblocks to Development," 34 *University of Florida Law Review* 432, 433 n. 8 (1982). (Despite the title of the latter article, there seem to be no significant statutory obstacles to the formation of office condominiums in most states.)

54. Housman, "Office Condominiums and Cooperatives: Manhattan's Underground Success Story," 15 *Real Estate Review* 71 (Fall 1985).

55. See, for example, Rohan and Reskin, supra, at 3.

56. In the 1920s there was a similar and apparently successful development involving cooperatives under which, to maintain competent management and avoid tenant disagreements, control of many cooperative buildings was placed in the hands of a self-perpetuating board of trustees. Twentieth Century Fund, supra, at 234–235.

12. Nonprofit Firms

1. Henry Hansmann, "The Changing Roles of Public, Private, and Nonprofit Enterprise in Education, Health Care, and Other Human Services," in Victor Fuchs, ed., *Individual and Social Responsibility: Child Care, Education, Medical Care, and Long-Term Care in America* (1995).

2. Bureau of Economic Analysis, *National Income and Product Accounts of the United States, 1929–88*, vol. 1 at 9, vol. 2 at 8 (1993).

3. As of 1986, public universities accounted for 24 percent of college students in Japan, with the other 76 percent being enrolled in private institutions. *Japan Statistical Yearbook* 660, table 19-17 (1987). The private institutions are less visible to foreigners, since the elite institutions in Japan are public.

4. See generally Henry Hansmann, "The Role of Nonprofit Enterprise," 89 *Yale Law Journal* 835 (1980), from which the following discussion draws.

5. See Henry Hansmann, "Nonprofit Enterprise in the Performing Arts," 12 *Bell Journal of Economics* 341 (1981).

6. Between 1976 and 1989, total enrollment in proprietary institutions of higher education in the United States increased from 44,000 to 225,000, or over 400 percent, while total enrollment in nonprofit institutions increased only 17 percent, from 2,314,000 to 2,718,000. National Center for Education Statistics, *Digest of Education Statistics 1991* 167 (Table 161) (1991).

7. Hansmann (1995), supra.

8. This is not to deny that doctors, who may have staff privileges only at particular hospitals, can have a conflict of interest in choosing a hospital for a patient or in monitoring that hospital's performance.

9. See Bradford Gray, *For-Profit Enterprise in Health Care* (1986).

10. For reviews of the literature, see Bradford Gray, *The Profit Motive and Patient Care: The Changing Accountability of Doctors and Hospitals* ch. 5 (1991); Mark Pauly, "Nonprofit Firms in Medical Markets," 77 *American Economic Review* 257 (1987).

11. American Hospital Association, *Hospital Statistics* (1971, 1993–94).

12. See Henry Hansmann, "The Effect of Tax Exemption and Other Factors on the Market Share of Nonprofit versus For-Profit Firms," 15 *National Tax Journal* 71 (1987); Bruce Steinwald and Duncan Neuhauser, "The Role of the Proprietary Hospital," 35 *Law and Contemporary Problems* 817 (1970).

13. National Center for Health Statistics, *Nursing Homes: A County and Metropolitan Area Data Book* (1974); National Center for Health Statistics, *The National Nursing Home Survey: 1985 Summary for the United States* (1989). See also Burton Weisbrod, *The Nonprofit Economy* 142–159 (1988), for empirical observations suggesting that for-profit nursing homes provide lower quality care than do nonprofit homes, even after controlling for revenue per patient (which tends to be higher in nonprofit homes).

14. Empirical studies, however, have failed to demonstrate a clear effect of tax exemption on the market share of nonprofit versus for-profit firms. Hansmann (1987), supra; Cyril Chang and Howard Tuckman, "Do Higher Property Tax Rates Increase the Market Share of Nonprofit Hospitals?" 43 *National Tax Journal* 175 (1990).

15. Property tax exemption is the single important privilege that extends back earlier.

16. For a survey of the historical pattern, see Henry Hansmann, "The Evolving Law of Nonprofit Organizations: Do Current Trends Make Good Policy?" *Case Western Reserve Law Review* 807 (1988–89).

13. Banks

1. I neglect here the substantial system of farm credit institutions established by the federal government beginning in 1916. Although these institutions commonly have the nominal form of a cooperative, they have in fact been under the more or less direct administrative control of the federal government for most of their history. These banks served as conduits for substantial federal farm credit subsidies at least until the late 1940s. They were apparently established as nominal cooperatives at least in part to ensure that these subsidies

would all go to the benefit of the farmers for whom they were intended, similar to the nominally "cooperative" multi-unit housing projects that have been created as channels for governmental and private subsidies to tenants. The history and structure of farm credit institutions are summarized in Richard Heflebower, *Cooperatives and Mutuals in the Market System* 149–157 (1980).

2. This chapter draws upon Henry Hansmann, "The Economic Role of Commercial Nonprofits: The Evolution of the U.S. Savings Bank Industry," in Helmut Anheier and Wolfgang Seibel, eds., *The Third Sector: Comparative Studies of Nonprofit Organizations* (De Gruyter, 1989). When that article was still in draft, I discovered, also then in draft, the article by Eric Rasmussen, "Mutual Banks and Stock Banks," 31 *Journal of Law and Economics* (1988), which develops similar themes. In the exposition here I have (as noted below) sometimes drawn upon the evidence presented by Rasmussen, as well as upon research undertaken after both of these articles appeared.

3. Alan Teck, *Mutual Savings Banks and Savings and Loan Associations: Aspects of Growth*, 13 (1968). In addition, depositors in mutual savings banks arguably have the right, upon dissolution of the organization, to share among themselves the organization's accumulated surplus, although this is a bit unclear. See Teck at 13–14; *In re Dissolution of Cleveland Savings Society*, Ohio Ct. Com. Pls. (1961); *Morristown Institute for Savings v. Roberts*, 42 N.J. Eq. 496, 8 A. 315 (1887).

4. On the early history of the mutual savings banks, see Teck, supra; Weldon Welfling, *Mutual Savings Banks* (1968).

5. Murray E. Polakoff, *Financial Institutions and Markets* 68 (1970).

6. Benton E. Gup, *Financial Intermediaries: An Introduction* 137 (1980).

7. Polakaoff, supra, at 17.

8. Frank P. Bennett, *The Story of Mutual Savings Banks* 20–21 (1924).

9. William D. Scoggs, *A Century of Banking Progress* (1924).

10. Paul B. Trescott, *Financing American Enterprise: The Story of Commercial Banking* 19 (1963).

11. Elvira and Vladimir Clain-Steffanelli, *Chartered for Progress: Two Centuries of American Banking* 51 (1975).

12. Welfling, supra, at 5.

13. Teck, supra, at 13.

14. Welfling, supra, at 31–32, 281–282.

15. See Teck, supra, at 18–28.

16. See Teck, supra, at 28–42.

17. Over the period 1935–1980, moreover, interest rates on deposits were fixed by law, thus depriving the MSLAs of the one mechanism available to them, short of dissolution, to distribute their net earnings to their members. During that period, MSLAs were in form as well as in practice effectively nonprofit rather than consumer-owned firms, with members who not only had

no meaningful participation in control but who also lacked even a formal claim on residual earnings.

18. M. Manfred Fabritius and William Borges, *Saving the Savings and Loan: The U.S. Thrift Industry and the Texas Experience, 1950–1988* 17, Table 2.2 (1989).

19. Lawrence J. White, *The S & L Debacle: Public Policy Lessons for Bank and Thrift Regulation* 21, 58 (1991).

20. John Lintner, *Mutual Savings Banks in the Savings and Mortgage Markets* 473 (1948), as reported in Rasmussen, supra, at 416.

21. For surveys of banking regulation in the late nineteenth and early twentieth centuries, see Eugene Nelson White, *The Regulation and Reform of the American Banking System, 1900–1929* (1983); Robert Craig West, *Banking Reform and the Federal Reserve, 1863–1923*.

22. Jonathan Macey and Geoffrey Miller, "Double Liability of Bank Shareholders: History and Implications," 27 *Wake Forest Law Review* 31 (1992).

23. These figures may include some savings and loan associations organized on a stock (investor-owned) basis, which some states began chartering in the 1920s.

24. Rasmussen, supra, at 395, 414.

25. Although the failure rates for investor-owned banks reported here are high, it must be remembered that the failure of an investor-owned bank did not necessarily mean that depositors lost most, or even any, of their funds. In fact, payoffs to depositors were relatively high in investor-owned bank failures—presumably owing, in good part, to the double liability of bank shareholders—and the expected loss for depositors from investor-owned bank failures was quite low in the late nineteenth and early twentieth centuries. Macey and Miller, supra.

26. Benjamin Hermalin and Nancy Wallace, "The Determinants of Efficiency and Solvency in Savings and Loans," 25 *Rand Journal of Economics* 361 (1994). Efforts to obtain direct evidence of managerial inefficiency by seeking to establish that the managers of mutual banks indulge themselves with larger salaries and other perquisites of office than do the managers of stock banks have yielded ambiguous results. See Loretta Mester, "Testing for Expense Preference Behavior: Mutual versus Stock Savings and Loans," 20 *Rand Journal of Economics* 483–498 (1989); Richard B. Carter and Roger D. Stover, "The Effects of Mutual to Stock Conversions of Thrift Institutions on Managerial Behavior," 4 *Journal of Financial Services Research* (1990).

27. Rasmussen, supra, at 409.

28. On the history of the U.S. credit union movement and its antecedents, see Mark J. Flannery, *An Economic Evaluation of Credit Unions in the United States* (1974); Roy F. Bergengren, *Credit Unionism: A Cooperative Banking Book* (1931); Roy F. Bergengren, *Credit Union North America* (1940).

29. Board of Governors of the Federal Reserve System, *Federal Reserve*

Bulletin (1972, 1976); Surandra Kaushik and Raymond Lopez, "The Structure and Growth of the Credit Union Industry in the United States: Meeting Challenges of the Market," 53 *American Journal of Economics and Sociology* 219, 220–227 (1994).

30. See Heflebower, supra, at 159; Flannery, supra, at 70–76.

31. Investor-owned bankers have argued that the continuing growth of credit unions, even after the elimination of federal interest rate limitations on investor-owned banks in 1982, is to be blamed on the unfair advantage given them by tax exemption. See James Cook, "Level Playing Field?" *Forbes*, June 25, 1990, at 69–70.

32. See Joseph H. Sommer, "The American Origin of the Separation of Banking and Commerce" (Federal Reserve Bank of New York, 1993).

33. See Clifford Geertz, "The Rotating Credit Association: A 'Middle Rung' in Development," 10 *Institutional Development and Social Change* 249–263 (1962).

34. James Brooke, "Informal Capitalism Grows in Cameroon," *New York Times*, November 30, 1987, at D8.

35. For a survey of the costs of market contracting to which rotating credit associations respond, see Karla Hoff and Joseph Stiglitz, "Introduction: Imperfect Information and Rural Credit Markets—Puzzles and Policy Perspectives," 4 *World Bank Economic Review* 235–250 (1990).

36. See David Fairlamb and Jenny Ireland, *Savings and Co-operative Banking* (1981); Gino Cardinali, *Appunti sulle Casse di Risparmio: Origine e Sviluppo, l'Ordinamento Amministrativo-contabile* (1953); Alfio Titta, *Le Casse di Risparmio nel Mondo: Origini e Sviluppo* (1955). As these sources observe, European nonprofit savings banks in fact trace their roots to experimentation at least as early as the late eighteenth century in Germany, England, and elsewhere, and nonprofit credit institutions can be found in Italy as early as the fifteenth century.

37. As one recognition of this, Italy, which seminationalized its nonprofit savings banks in the late nineteenth century, in 1990 adopted a statute aimed toward converting them into investor-owned firms in two steps: first, converting each bank into a joint stock company with its stock held by the nonprofit foundation that formerly managed it, and second, encouraging the foundations to sell their bank stock on the capital market—although at this writing the second step is not at all assured. See Adamo Acciaro, "Le Casse di Risparmio nella Forma di Società per Azioni," 48 *Bancaria* 99 (January 1992).

14. Insurance Companies

1. "The Fortune Directory of the Largest U.S. Industrial Corporations," *Fortune*, May 2, 1983, at 226, 228; *Fortune*, June 13, 1983, at 152, 166.

2. This chapter draws on Henry Hansmann, "The Organization of Insur-

ance Companies: Mutual versus Stock," 1 *Journal of Law, Economics, and Organization* 125 (1985).

3. J. Owen Stalson, *Marketing Life Insurance: Its History in America* 83–99, 110, 227–228 (1969 [1942]).

4. Id. at 103–125; Charles Knight, "The History of Life Insurance in the United States to 1870" 105 (Ph.D. dissertation, University of Pennsylvania, 1920).

5. Stalson, supra, at 750.

6. Stalson, supra, at 83–99, 118; Knight, supra, at 101, 118.

7. Stalson, supra, at 225–226; Knight, supra, at 102.

8. J. M. Belth, *The Retail Price Structure in American Life Insurance* (1966); J. M. Belth, "Author's Reply," 36 *Journal of Risk and Insurance* 495–496 (1969); Randall Geehan, "Returns to Scale in the Life Insurance Industry," 8 *Bell Journal of Economics* 497 (1977).

9. Dan M. McGill, *Life Insurance* 61 (1967).

10. Stalson, supra, at 315–325.

11. Eugene Fama and Michael Jensen, "Agency Problems and Residual Claims," 26 *Journal of Law and Economics* 327, 336–341 (1983), assume that customers can easiy withdraw their patronage from financial mutuals, and conclude that this is important in understanding the viability of such firms. Their argument is that the small amounts of organization-specific assets required by firms in those industries in which mutuals are common make it relatively easy to permit consumer/members to exit from the firm by withdrawing their patronage and their capital contribution. The partial liquidation involved in such a withdrawal is, Fama and Jensen suggest, a means of sanctioning the managers of the firm, and thus makes up to some extent for the fact that such firms are not subject to the discipline afforded by the market for corporate control that characterizes investor-owned corporations. Indeed, Fama and Jensen state (338) that "the unique characteristic of the residual claims of mutuals, which is important in understanding their survival value, is that the residual claims are redeemable on demand," and they focus their entire discussion of financial mutuals on this presumed characteristic. Full redeemability of claims has not, however, been a characteristic of mutuals in the life insurance industry, which is the industry in which financial mutuals play the largest role by far. Indeed, in the early years of the life insurance industry, when mutuals were at their historical high in terms of market share (namely, 1843–1859), policyholders had no right at all to redeem their life insurance policies for cash or even to borrow against them; rather, a policyholder had only the options of paying premiums at the contracted rate throughout the term of his policy (that is, until his death in the case of a whole life policy) or of forfeiting to the company the full accumulated value of his policy. Stalson, supra, at 315–325. Furthermore, as noted above, even today

life insurance policies generally have cash surrender values substantially smaller than the accumulated value of the premium payments that have been made on them. McGill, supra, at 61.

12. David Mayers and Clifford Smith, "Contractual Provisions, Organizational Structure, and Conflict Control in Insurance Markets," 54 *Journal of Business* 407, 425–428 (1981), were apparently the first to offer this explanation for the formation of mutual insurance companies. In their brief initial discussion of the issue, however, they do not distinguish between life insurance and property/liability insurance. As suggested in Hansmann (1985), supra, however, and as discussed in the text here and below, this explanation is far more persuasive for the former type of insurance than it is for the latter.

Mayers and Smith subsequently pursued the argument of their 1981 article further in "Ownership Structure and Control: The Mutualization of Stock Life Insurance Companies," 16 *Journal of Financial Economics* 73 (1986); "Ownership Structures across Lines of Property-Liability Insurance," 31 *Journal of Law and Economics* 351 (1988); "Executive Compensation in the Life Insurance Industry," 65 *Journal of Business* 51 (1992). In each of these articles, Mayers and Smith argue that mutual insurance companies have the advantage of avoiding the stock companies' incentive to appropriate the policyholders' premiums through speculation or excessive dividends, thus opportunistically creating the risk that the company will not be able to pay off on its claims, while the stock companies have the advantage of avoiding, owing to the market for corporate control, some of the agency costs that mutuals suffer from as a result of the excessive discretion that managers of mutuals have owing to the poor ability of the policyholder-owners to police the managers. There is surely some important truth to this. In focusing only on these two competing considerations, however, Mayers and Smith leave out other seemingly important sources of costly contracting (such as market power, excessive risk creation, and poor risk sharing) and of ownership (such as conflicts of interest among the policyholder-owners in a mutual). Moreover, these authors perhaps accept too quickly the effectiveness of the market for corporate control in policing managers of stock companies, and the ineffectiveness of policyholders in policing the managers of many types of mutual companies. As a consequence, there is sometimes reason to differ with Mayers and Smith in their predictions and in their interpretations of the data, as suggested by the further discussion of their work in subsequent notes.

13. Mayers and Smith (1988), supra, at 360, state: "Our analysis suggests that if the cost of controlling management in mutual insurance companies is higher than in stock firms, then mutuals should be more prevalent in lines of insurance where management exercises little discretion in setting rates (for example, in lines of insurance for which there are 'good' actuarial tables and where claims can be adjudicated within a relatively stable legal environment)."

For the reasons suggested in the text here and in the preceding section, however, it seems that instead one should expect to find that mutual companies have a stronger comparative advantage over stock firms where the actuarial tables are *least* reliable. Similarly, as discussed below, one would expect that mutuals would have a stronger comparative advantage over stock firms where the legal enviroment is *most* uncertain, and this is in fact clearly what one observes in liability insurance.

14. Stalson, supra, at 323–324. Another indication that investors in life insurance companies were sensitive to the amount of nondiversifiable risk they bore can be found in the evidence that the widespread bankruptcies in the fire insurance business after the great New York fire of 1835 discouraged investors from all forms of insurance, including life insurance. (Stalson at 109.)

15. Life insurance companies today engage in substantial product differentiation: policies offered by different companies differ in terms of the scheduling of premiums, cash surrender values, loan values, rights to purchase additional insurance, convertability into other forms of insurance, and so on. As a consequence, it is difficult to compare the prices offered by different companies, and the effectiveness of market competition is blunted. Some consumers, faced with this problem, perhaps choose to patronize mutual rather than stock companies to obtain additional assurance that they are not paying an excessive price for their policy.

Whatever the validity of this theory as applied to today's market, it does not seem persuasive in explaining the historical emergence of the mutuals. In the 1840s and 1850s, when the mutuals first arose and came to dominate the market, the terms of policies were remarkably uniform. Companies issued level premium, whole life policies with no cash surrender values or other complications, based the premiums solely on age, and published the premium schedules in their advertisements. There was no difficulty in comparing the terms of policies across companies, and competition in fact caused prices to be quite uniform across companies. Stalson, supra, at 126–155, 323–324.

16. Stalson, supra, at 292–315.

17. Id., Table A, at 743.

18. In the study of the Australian life insurance industry discussed below, it was found that the only stock companies that were able to succeed alongside the mutuals before the end of the nineteenth century were those that offered participating policies. Mark Blair, "Choice of Ownership Structure in the Australian Life Insurance Industry" (Ph.D. dissertation, Department of Accounting, University of Sydney, 1991).

19. Stalson, supra, at 94–97.

20. Knight, supra, at 103, 106; see also Stalson, supra, at 110–112.

21. Although some early studies purported to find higher expenses among mutual firms, the most recent and thorough econometric studies of the cost

structure of the life insurance industry find no significant difference between mutual companies and stock companies in average costs. Among the latter studies, see Mary Ann Boose, "Agency Theory and Alternative Predictions for Life Insurers: An Empirical Test," 57 *Journal of Risk and Insurance* 499–518 (1990); Randall Geehan, "Returns to Scale in the Life Insurance Industry," 8 *Bell Journal of Economics* 497–514 (1977); David Houston and Richard Simon, "Economies of Scale in Financial Institutions: A Study in Life Insurance," 38 *Econometrica* 856–864 (1970).

22. Mayers and Smith (1992), supra, find that, controlling for firm size, managers of stock life insurance companies are more highly compensated than are managers of mutual companies. They interpret this as consistent with their prediction that agency costs in mutuals are higher, all other things equal, owing to the lower ability of the owners to police the managers in mutuals. This may be the correct interpretation. But the opposite interpretation may instead be true: the higher pay received by the managers of the stock companies may simply be a direct indication that managers of stock companies are freer to pay themselves unjustifiably high salaries than are the managers of mutuals.

23. Evidence of a binding limitation on mutuals' access to capital can be found in the fact that, by the 1980s, mutuals had begun transferring large numbers of policies to stock companies via coinsurance agreements (although this phenomenon may also reflect tax incentives), and had also begun to charter stock company subsidiaries, commonly for the purpose of writing specialty lines of insurance. *Best's Insurance Reports, Life-Health* x (Oldwick, N.J.: A. M. Best Company, 1983). Further, the need to obtain capital and to diversify were commonly cited as the major reasons why, in the 1980s, a number of the largest mutuals began seriously considering conversion into investor-owned firms. Frederic Dannen, "Is Time Running Out for the Big Mutuals?" *Institutional Investor* 159 (June 1984).

24. Mayers and Smith (1986), supra, find that, in a sample of thirty companies that converted from stock to mutual over the period 1879 to 1968, the average rate of growth of premium income increased after mutualization, and they interpret this to mean that policyholders were not disadvantaged by the mutualization. But for the reasons mentioned in the text, fast growth in a mutual is not necessarily to the advantage of existing policyholders. The faster rate of growth in the companies after mutualization may simply indicate that the managers were freer to indulge in empire building, devoting the net earnings that formerly went to shareholder dividends to finance rapid growth that may or may not have been efficient.

Somewhat counterintuitively, Mayers and Smith also infer that those stock insurance companies that had concentrated stock ownership prior to mutualization, and particularly those where the management controlled a majority of the stock, were less likely to be efficiently managed than those companies with dispersed stock ownership, the argument being that management would find it easier to resist a takeover in the former. They find support for their inference in the fact that, upon mutualization, the growth rate of premium income increased substantially for the companies with concentrated ownership structures but not for those with dispersed stock ownership. But again, one might quite reasonably conclude the reverse: the firms with dispersed stock ownership were essentially controlled by their managers, who indulged themselves by retaining earnings excessively to finance a rapid rate of growth; thus, upon mutualization, there was little room for further increase in the growth rate in those firms. This interpretation is supported by the fact that the growth rate prior to mutualization was much higher for the firms with dispersed stock ownership than for those that were manager-owned.

Mayers and Smith (1992), supra, find that compensation to managers of stock life insurance companies, but not mutual life insurance companies, is correlated with the growth rate of the firm's premium income, and interpret this as consistent with their managerial discretion hypothesis, which states that "mutuals have a comparative advantage over stocks in business activities requiring less managerial discretion." Id. at 51. One problem with this conclusion is that growth in premium income is not necessarily a good index of growth in net earnings per share, which is what owners of a stock company should desire; indeed, the two figures may be negatively correlated. But a more obvious problem is that, as noted in the text here, the current policyholder-owners of a mutual life insurance company are generally hurt by a rapid rate of growth, and thus a link between executive compensation and the rate of growth would create perverse incentives for the mutuals' managers.

25. John A. C. Hetherington, "Fact v. Fiction: Who Owns Mutual Insurance Companies?" 1969 *Wisconsin Law Review* 1068 (1969).

26. Hetherington, supra, argues that, since the policyholders in a mutual life insurance company in fact do not enjoy the usual attributes of ownership—namely effective participation in net earnings and control—there is no reason to place obstacles in the path of managers of mutuals who wish to convert the firm to the stock form, even if the result of the transaction will be, as it apparently often has been, that the management will capture for themselves a substantial share of the firm's accumulated net surplus. The policyholders, he suggests, cannot be hurt by losing what they never had.

This reasoning is not, however, valid if the mutual companies continue to play a fiduciary role vis-à-vis their policyholders of the same sort that nonprofits play toward their patrons, or if the mutuals avoid risks of long-term contracting that investor-owned firms cannot.

27. Stalson, supra, at 430, 562.

28. Id. at 759.

29. R. Carlyle Buley, *The American Life Convention, 1905-1952* 199-205 (1953); H. Roger Grant, *Insurance Reform: Consumer Action in the Progressive Era* 37-46 (1979); Humbert Nelli and Robert Marshall, "The Private Insurance Business in the United States Economy" 27-32 (Research Paper No. 48, Bureau of Business and Economic Research, School of Business Administration, Georgia State College, 1969); Stalson, supra, at 558-559.

30. Stalson, supra, at 558-559.

31. Grant, supra, at 36.

32. Halsey Josephson, *Life Insurance and the Public Interest* 99-100, 102 (1971).

33. Hetherington, supra.

34. Nelli and Marshall, supra, at 35 note 5; *Best's Insurance Reports, Life-Health*.

35. American Council of Life Insurers, *1992 Life Insurance Fact Book*, 109 (1992).

36. Robert C. Clark, "The Federal Income Taxation of Financial Intermediaries," 84 *Yale Law Journal* 1603, 1637-64 (1975).

37. John Bainbridge, *Biography of an Idea: The Story of Mutual Fire and Casualty Insurance* (1952); Manufacturers Mutual Fire Insurance Company, *Factory Mutuals, 1835-1935* (1935).

38. See Joseph Stiglitz and Andrew Weiss, "Credit Rationing in Markets with Incomplete Information," 71 *American Economic Review* 393 (1981).

39. Manufacturers Mutual Fire Insurance Co., supra, at 33.

40. Moreover, where individual insurance companies charge the same rate to all firms they insure, customers will tend to stratify across companies according to the level of risk the customers present. The result is to create market power for the companies of the type described for social clubs and other associative organizations in Chapter 10. The available evidence does not make it clear whether in fact such stratification of policyholders among insurance companies was evident in the nineteenth century.

41. Bainbridge, supra, at 171.

42. S. S. Huebner and Kenneth Black, *Property Insurance* 507 (1957).

43. A simple model illustrating the point is offered in Neil Doherty and Georges Dionne, "Insurance with Undiversifiable Risk: Contract Structure and Organizational Form of Insurance Firms," 6 *Journal of Risk and Uncertainty* 187 (1993).

44. Bainbridge, supra, at 162.

45. George Priest, "The Modern Expansion of Tort Liability: Its Sources, Its Effects, and Its Reform," 5 *Journal of Economic Perspectives* 31, 45 (1991).

46. Ralph A. Winter, "The Liability Insurance Market," 5 *Journal of Economic Perspectives* 115, 119 (1991).

47. Id.; Ralph A. Winter, "Solvency Regulation and the Property-Liability 'Insurance Cycle,' " 29 *Economic Inquiry* 458 (1991).

Bruce Smith and Michael Stutzer, "Adverse Selection, Aggregate Uncertainty, and the Role for Mutual Insurance Contracts," 63 *Journal of Business* 493 (1990), offer a different explanation for the presence of mutual insurance companies in industries in which there is aggregate risk that cannot be eliminated by diversification within the industry. They argue that, even if stock insurance firms were risk neutral, in environments where stock companies cannot distinguish high-risk from low-risk customers, mutual companies might be formed by the low-risk purchasers of insurance as a form of participating policy that only the low-risk insureds would be willing to purchase, leaving the high-risk insureds to deal with stock insurers. Since the mutual form causes the policyholders to bear only undiversifiable risk, this signaling/ screening role for mutuals can exist only where there is undiversifiable risk.

This theory would seem to predict that mutuals would be unusually common in providing insurance for industries that faced unusual amounts of undiversifiable risk, but that they would insure the low-risk members of that industry and leave the high-risk policyholders to the stock companies. As the following note indicates, however, other factors discussed here might lead to the same pattern, making this theory difficult to confirm empirically.

48. Joan Lamm-Tennant and Laura Starks, "Stock versus Mutual Ownership Structures: The Risk Implications," 66 *Journal of Business* 29 (1993), compare the variance in loss ratios (losses/premiums) for stock and mutual insurers in a large sample of insurance firms. They find that, by this measure, stock firms are on average significantly riskier than mutual firms. They also find that stock firms tend to have a larger market share, relative to that of mutuals, in those lines of insurance that are unusually risky. They suggest that this result is consistent with the monitoring theory of Jensen and Meckling, the managerial discretion theory of Mayers and Smith, and the self-selection theory of Smith and Stutzer, but inconsistent with the risk-bearing theory of Doherty and Dionne, which is similar to that offered here.

But the degree of consistency or inconsistency between theory and empirical results here is problematic. One difficulty is that the results obtained by Lamm-Tennant and Starks do not control for the other, seemingly more important factors that influence the balance between mutual and stock insurance firms in any line of insurance, such as the homogeneity of the firms purchasing insurance in that line or the degree of past or present market power exercised by the insurance companies writing that line of insurance. Further, Lamm-Tennant and Starks are constrained to aggregate their results according to the twenty-six broad lines of insurance employed in standard insurance accounting, which clouds interpretation.

A mutual writing insurance for any given industry—say, nurse-midwives, or

Rhode Island textile manufacturers—might be expected to have as its policy-holders the lower-risk members of that industry, for two reasons that are largely unrelated to the particular agency-cost-of-management theories offered by Jensen and Meckling and by Mayers and Smith. First, the incentive to have members with relatively homogeneous interests will create an incentive to exclude customers presenting high risks, since they would require a more differentiated rate structure and are likely to be idiosyncratic in other dimensions as well, such as the nature of their business. Second, to the extent that mutuals serve to reduce moral hazard and adverse selection among their policyholders, they should have lower-risk customers than their stock counterparts.

Perhaps a more exacting test of the theory, offered here, that mutuals have an advantage over stock firms in dealing with undiversifiable risk, holding other factors constant, would be to examine longitudinal data to see if, when the variance in the loss ratio within a given line of insurance increases over time, the ratio of insurance written by mutual versus stock firms increases.

49. *General Ins. Co. of America v. Earle*, 65 P.2d 1414, 1416–17 (Oregon, 1937); Kimball and Denenberg, supra, at 226 note 38.

50. Richard Heflebower, *Cooperatives and Mutuals in the Market System* 167 (1980).

51. Id. at 165–171; Nathan Weber, "Introduction: Reversals and Continuities," in N. Weber, ed., *Insurance Deregulation: Issues and Perspectives* (1982).

52. Paul MacAvoy, *Federal-State Regulation of the Pricing and Marketing of Insurance* 8 (1977).

53. One recent text suggests that this difference is a product of history: the older (and thus larger) life insurers are mutual, while the older (and thus larger) property and liability insurers are stock companies. Robert Mehr and Emerson Cammack, *Principles of Insurance* 90 (1976). This logic is, however, quite unconvincing. It places a great deal of faith in the ability of companies to maintain their market share over periods of more than a century. Moreover, it ignores the fact that the very earliest life insurance companies in the United States were all proprietary, while the very earliest property and liability companies were all mutuals. See Bainbridge, supra, at 45; Manufacturers Mutual Fire Insurance Co., supra, at 15–25.

54. Mayers and Smith (1981), supra, state: "If it is less expensive to concentrate voting/control rights in small than large corporations, then the potential for stockholders to expropriate policyholder wealth is greater in small stock insurance firms. This implies that in a given line of insurance, the smallest firms (e.g., measured by total assets) should be mutuals." (Footnote omitted.) As with the same authors' conclusions concerning the influence of actuarial risk (discussed in note 13 above), this reasoning seems to take too strong and too simple a view of the differences between mutual and stock

companies in avoiding agency costs of management, and to neglect other factors, discussed in the text here and elsewhere, that seem far more important in determining the relative size of mutual and stock firms.

Mayers and Smith (1988), supra, seek to test the authors' "managerial discretion hypothesis" using data on property and liability insurance firms. Contrary to their predictions, they do not find that mutual firms are on average either smaller or confined to fewer different lines of insurance than are stock firms. The finding on size, however, is presumably biased by the fact that their sample includes only the larger and more geographically dispersed of the mutuals. Moreover, their data on lines of insurance, which is largely based on the types of risks covered, arguably does a poor job of capturing the type of homogeneity that is important to mutuals, which presumably involves the number of different types of industries that their policyholders come from rather than the number of different types of risks that the policyholders are insured for. By the measure employed by Mayers and Smith (a measure to which they are confined by readily available data), a mutual insurance firm that wrote insurance only for textile mills in Rhode Island, but that insured those firms for fire, theft, earthquake, workmen's compensation, employee health, and products liability, would be far more "diverse" than a firm that wrote only product liability insurance, but provided such insurance for firms in three hundred different industries ranging from steel manufacturing to day care.

55. Heflebower, supra, at 162–176; Bainbridge, supra.

56. Clark, supra, at 1650, 1664–75.

57. Mark Blair, "Choice of Ownership Structure in the Australian Life Insurance Industry" (Ph.D. dissertation, Department of Accounting, University of Sydney, 1991). Blair's study was undertaken explicitly to test the theories of Mayers and Smith (1981, 1986), supra, and Hansmann (1985), supra, against the Australian experience.

Sources

Some of the ideas in this book were developed in earlier articles. Most portions that appear here have been substantially revised; any passages that are reprinted appear by permission of the publisher.

"Condominium and Cooperative Housing: Transactional Efficiency, Tax Subsidies, and Tenure Choice," 20 *Journal of Legal Studies* 25–71 (1991).

"The Economic Role of Commercial Nonprofits: The Evolution of the Savings Bank Industry," in H. Anheier and W. Seibel, eds., *The Nonprofit Sector: International and Comparative Perspectives* 65–77 (Berlin: Walter de Gruyter & Co., 1990).

"The Organization of Insurance Companies: Mutual versus Stock," 1 *Journal of Law, Economics, and Organization* 125–153 (1985).

"Ownership of the Firm," 4 *Journal of Law, Economics, and Organization* 267–403 (1988), reprinted in Lucian Bebchuk, ed., *Corporate Law and Economic Analysis* (Cambridge: Cambridge University Press, 1990).

"The Role of Nonprofit Enterprise," 89 *Yale Law Journal* 835–901 (1980), reprinted in part in Susan Rose-Ackerman, ed., *The Economics of Nonprofit Institutions* (Oxford University Press, 1986).

"A Theory of Status Organizations," 2 *Journal of Law, Economics, and Organization* 119–130 (1986).

"When Does Worker Ownership Work? ESOPs, Law Firms, Codetermination, and Economic Democracy," 99 *Yale Law Journal* 1749–1816 (1990).

Index

Harvard University Press is a member of Green Press Initiative
(greenpressinitiative.org), a nonprofit organization working to
help publishers and printers increase their use of recycled paper
and decrease their use of fiber derived from endangered forests.
This book was printed on 100% recycled paper containing
50% post-consumer waste and processed chlorine free.